The Southern Hospitality Myth

SERIES EDITOR

Riché Richardson, Cornell University

FOUNDING EDITOR

Jon Smith, Simon Fraser University

ADVISORY BOARD

Houston A. Baker Jr., Vanderbilt University

Leigh Anne Duck, The University of Mississippi

Jennifer Greeson, The University of Virginia

Trudier Harris, The University of Alabama

John T. Matthews, Boston University

Tara McPherson, The University of Southern California

Claudia Milian, Duke University

The Southern Hospitality Myth

ETHICS, POLITICS, RACE,
AND AMERICAN MEMORY

Anthony Szczesiul

The University of
Georgia Press
ATHENS

This publication is made possible in part through a grant from the Bradley Hale Fund for Southern Studies.

Paperback edition, 2019
© 2017 by the University of Georgia Press
Athens, Georgia 30602
www.ugapress.org
All rights reserved
Set in 10/13 Kepler by Graphic Composition, Inc.

Most University of Georgia Press titles are
available from popular e-book vendors.

Printed digitally

The Library of Congress has cataloged the hardcover edition of this book as follows:

Names: Szczesiul, Anthony, author.
Title: The Southern hospitality myth : ethics, politics, race, and American memory / Anthony Szczesiul.
Description: Athens : The University of Georgia Press, 2017. | Series: The new Southern studies series | Includes bibliographical references and index.
Identifiers: LCCN 2016049005| ISBN 9780820332765 (hard bound : alkaline paper) | ISBN 9780820350738 (e-book)
Subjects: LCSH: Southern States—Social life and customs—1775–1865. | Hospitality—Southern States—History. | Hospitality—Moral and ethical aspects—Southern States—History. | Southern States—Moral conditions. | Racism—Southern States—History. | Southern States—Public opinion—History. | Regionalism—United States—History. | Memory—Political aspects—United States—History. | Memory—Moral and ethical aspects—United States—History. | Public opinion—United States—History.
Classification: LCC F213 .S96 2017 | DDC 305.800975—DC23
LC record available at https://lccn.loc.gov/2016049005

Paperback ISBN 978-0-8203-5551-1

For Stacy

CONTENTS

ACKNOWLEDGMENTS ix

INTRODUCTION   What Can One Mean by Southern Hospitality? 1

CHAPTER ONE   A Virginian Praises "Yankee Hospitality":
                Rethinking the Historicity of Antebellum
                Southern Hospitality 28

CHAPTER TWO   The Amphytrion and St. Paul; the Planter and
                the Reformer: Discourses of Hospitality in
                Antebellum America 48

CHAPTER THREE   Making Hospitality a Crime:
                The Fugitive Slave Law of 1850 77

CHAPTER FOUR   Southern Hospitality in a Transnational Context:
                The Geopolitical Logic of the South's
                Sovereign Hospitality 104

CHAPTER FIVE   Reconstructing Southern Hospitality in
                the Postbellum World: Reconciliation, Commemoration,
                and Commodification 130

CHAPTER SIX   The Modern Proliferation of the Southern Hospitality
                Myth: Repetition, Revision, and Reappropriation 168

EPILOGUE   New Strangers of the Contemporary South 211

NOTES 219

BIBLIOGRAPHY 263

INDEX 281

ACKNOWLEDGMENTS

This book has taken far too long to complete, and given the length of time devoted to the research and writing process (well over a decade), I have incurred a very long list of debts. The origins of this project lie in some lively class discussions that took place in one of my southern literature courses over a decade ago, so my first debt of gratitude goes to my past and present students at the University of Massachusetts Lowell, who not only inspired this project, but who also inspire me every day with their earnest curiosity and general goodwill. I feel lucky to go to my job every day. As I initially explored this subject before the archival research began, Michael Pierson of the UMass Lowell History Department was an important resource of information. At this early stage, I also benefitted from several long, meandering conversations about the project with my colleagues Julie Nash and Todd Avery and my good friends Gavin Sturges and Jake Bridge. Their thoughtful and generous interactions gave me the confidence to move forward and proved invaluable over the years of my research and writing. Early research was conducted at the South Caroliniana Library at the University of South Carolina, and my friends Keen and Nancy Butterworth put me up for a good part of a summer in their home in Columbia.

This project simply would not have been possible had I not lived in close proximity to one of America's great archives: the American Antiquarian Society in Worcester, Massachusetts. What originally began as a more traditional literary studies project evolved into this current form largely through my time spent at the AAS, and through the many forms of collegial assistance I received there. In addition to many (generally happy) days spent in the reading room at AAS, I took advantage of two of their Summer Seminars in the History of the Book (first with Phil Gura and later with Lloyd Pratt and Jeannine DeLombard), and I also received a Kate B. and Hall J. Peterson Fellowship in the summer of 2005. Each of these experiences provided amazing opportunities for collegial interaction with fellows, seminar participants, and the incredible librarians and support staff at AAS. I would list every seminar participant and fellow and librarian if I could, but the list would be too long, and I would surely miss somebody. Special mention does go, however, to Camille Dungy and Kathryn Koo, both of whom were on concurrent fellowships with me in the summer of 2005. Our daily conversations over lunch certainly influenced the direction this project took in the years that followed.

The Society for the Study of Southern Literature has provided one of the main forums through which I have received feedback and developed my thinking on this subject over the years, particularly at the society's biennial conferences. I am grateful for the collegial community that SSSL provides, and the responses I received at the conferences always rejuvenated my interest in this project when it was flagging or even failing. Special thanks to Cole Hutchinson, Michael Bibler, Leigh Anne Duck, Jennifer Greeson, Julia Eichelberger, Daniel Cross Turner, Tom Haddox, Michael Kreyling, Jack Matthews, and Lisa Hinrichsen, all of whom offered meaningful encouragement or particularly thoughtful responses to my work at key moments. Thanks also to Kathleen Diffley, who provided significant feedback on a section of chapter 5 that first appeared in her edited essay collection, *Witness to Reconstruction: Constance Fenimore Woolson and the Postbellum South, 1873–1894* (University Press of Mississippi, 2011). Portions of chapter 1 and chapter 6 were first published in an earlier form in a special issue of the *European Journal of American Culture* in 2007. Thanks to the press and to the journal for permission to reprint this earlier work. Sincere thanks also go to the many artists who provided permission to include their works in my study: Pierre Bellocq, Fran DiGiacomo, Karen Dupre, Larry Dyke, Britt Ehringer, Kevin Liang, and Frank Tarpley.

The University of Georgia Press has been both encouraging and patient in its support of this project. Thanks to Nancy Grayson for expressing an early interest in my work and to Walter Biggins for seeing the manuscript across the finish line. Thanks also to the series editors, Jon Smith and Riché Richardson, for having the faith that this would be a worthwhile addition to the series, and to Jon and Scott Romine, who served as the (formerly) anonymous reviewers of the manuscript. Their meticulous and thoughtful feedback truly helped me to find my way when I was still quite lost. Thanks also to John Joerschke and Thomas Roche of the press, who served as project editors, and to Barbara Wojhoski, who copyedited the manuscript.

I have received many forms of support at the University of Massachusetts Lowell, including a semester sabbatical and research and travel funding to support my work. Deborah Friedman and Rose Paton of University Libraries have always been especially helpful to me during this long process. As a faculty member and department chair, I have been fortunate to work under two outstanding deans: the late Nina Coppens and Luis Falcón. Luis has been especially supportive and encouraging as I have neared the completion of this project. This book was especially difficult to complete while I have been serving as the English department chair, and I am forever thankful to my colleague and friend Bridget Marshall, who, with the support of Luis, agreed to step in as interim chair for a semester so that I could complete the manuscript (what Bridget got out of this in exchange was the prescient knowledge that she will never again agree to be chair). Many thanks also to Jacky Ledoux, whose remarkable efficiency and contagious laugh make my work as chair more manageable. I am very lucky to work in a vibrant and collegial department, and I appreciate the way that so many of my colleagues have provided encouragement as I have worked to complete this book. Special thanks go to Mike Millner, who generously read and discussed draft chapters with me and who always had an uncanny knack for asking just the right question to keep me moving forward, and to Sue Kim, who carefully read the manuscript prior to my initial submission to the press. Many thanks also to my dear friends and colleagues Julie Nash and Paula Haines, who have always been invaluable sources of emotional support along the way.

Finally, and most importantly, I would like to thank my family for their constant faith that this would get done. I am blessed with parents who have provided nothing but constant love and support throughout my life, and brothers and sisters who have always offered their encouragement. My sister Karen deserves special mention for providing much-needed moral support and for serving as a trusted reader at various stages of the writing process. My greatest debt of all is owed to Stacy, who, unlike me, never doubted that this would be completed, and to our wonderful daughters, Adelaide, Zoe, and Emma, who always manage to put things in proper perspective for me. I am lucky to go home to them every day (but even more so now that this is done).

The Southern
Hospitality Myth

INTRODUCTION

What Can One Mean by Southern Hospitality?

> The southerner is indeed hospitable to this day, loving nothing more than to entertain family and friends with the best food and drink he can afford. The automobile and the telephone make visiting far simpler than in the early times; normally only guests who have traveled great distances stay overnight, and the length of such visits is limited by the construction of the modern home. But if the circumstances of southern hospitality have changed, the spirit remains the same.
>
> — *Encyclopedia of Southern Culture*, Charles Reagan Wilson and William Ferris, eds.
>
> We do not yet know what hospitality is.
>
> —Jacques Derrida, "Hostipitality"

How important is "southern hospitality" to "your definition of today's South?" So asked question 82 of the spring 1995 edition of the Southern Focus Poll conducted by John Shelton Reed and the Howard W. Odum Institute for Research in Social Science at the University of North Carolina, Chapel Hill. Reed and the Odum Institute ran the Southern Focus Poll from 1992 to 2001, interviewing by phone thousands of southerners and nonsoutherners, seeking their responses on a wide range of political, economic, social, and cultural issues, as well as their sense of regional identity and cultural characteristics. Question 82 was one of a series of eight questions from the spring 1995 poll that were described as being "about the South in general," and the overall response to it was unique both for the high degree of importance respondents placed on southern hospitality and for the remarkable similarity in the responses from southerners and nonsoutherners. Of the 917 southerners polled, 73.7 percent rated southern hospitality "very important" to their "definition of today's South," and another 17.8 percent rated it "somewhat important." Of the 506 nonsoutherners polled, 67.9 percent rated it "very important," and 21.6 percent rated it "somewhat important." Overall, 91.5 percent of southerners and 89.5 percent of nonsoutherners placed some degree of importance on southern hospitality in their "definition of today's South." But what, exactly, does this poll reveal about the definition of the South, about the behavior of southerners, about southern culture? Does it confirm that hospitality is a traditional and integral element of southern cultural heritage, or does it simply tell us that the phrase "southern hospitality" has a high rate of recognition among Americans, whether they are southern or not? Hospitality has indeed been associated with the South for well over two centuries, but how did we get from the origins of southern hospitality—what historically were a limited set of antebellum planters' social practices in a slave economy—to what was, at the close of the twentieth century, an apparently surveyable regional trait? Moreover, how and why have we taken something as particular as the social habit of hospitality—which is exercised among individuals and inevitably must be infinitely varied in its particular practices—and so generalized it as to assign it to an entire region of the country? Why have we chosen to remember and valorize this particular aspect of the South? And what of the fundamental ethical questions that underlie the concept of hospitality—how do these figure into our estimations of hospitality as a cultural trait of the American South, particularly in light of the South's historical legacy of slavery and segregation? These are some of the questions that initially motivated this study, and I set out to answer them in the chapters that follow.

Historians have offered a variety of explanations of the origins and cultural practices of hospitality in the antebellum South. Economic historians have at times portrayed southern hospitality as evidence of conspicuous consumption and competition among wealthy planters. Cultural historians have treated it peripherally as symptomatic of the southern code of honor and have pointed to circumstances such as the large distances between plantations, the dearth of public inns, and the relative lack of public welfare, all of which resulted in more pressure on the plantation home. Though historians differ on the origins and early practices of hospitality in the antebellum South, they generally agree that the mythic dimensions of southern hospitality eventually outran its practices. In *The Transformation of Virginia*, for example, Rhys Isaac goes so far as to claim that the social reality on which the myth was based went out of fashion as early as 1800.[1] Still, the myth of southern hospitality persisted even as social and political conditions underwent the drastic transformations of slavery, sectionalism, the Civil War, Reconstruction, Jim Crow segregation, and the long struggle for civil rights. Indeed, this myth of southern hospitality has been an essential, foundational narrative within the larger national project of southern exceptionalism—the persistent belief that the South is a distinct, unique, and separate culture within the larger United

States. This notion of an exceptional South has been a basic belief in American culture for well over two centuries, and it has served as the very assumption that motivated the scholarly fields of southern literary, historical, and cultural studies from their inceptions through most of the twentieth century.

Since roughly the turn of the twenty-first century, however, scholars have increasingly questioned or abandoned the assumption of southern exceptionalism, seeing it as a historically constructed concept rather than a natural essence. Instead of trying to understand and define what the South and southern culture supposedly are, they have asked questions such as What are the motivations behind this constructed belief in the exceptional South? How was this idea of the South created, and how has it evolved and been deployed over time? What sorts of "ideological functionings" or cultural work has it performed, both within the region and the nation? And with what consequences? For example, in the field of literary studies Michael Kreyling has deftly exposed the conservative politics that motivated the modern invention of the southern literary canon and its corresponding discipline of southern literary studies. Considering the South in broader national contexts, Tara McPherson, Leigh Anne Duck, and Jennifer Greeson have all demonstrated ways in which the concept of the South has been central to the national imaginary, and they have argued that southern exceptionalism and American exceptionalism have been mutually constituted since the nation's founding. McPherson, Duck, and Greeson have respectively described the South as "a fiction," "the nation's region," and an "internal other," a site for repressed fears as well as for "projective fantasies" within the national imaginary. Alternatively, historian Grace Elizabeth Hale has shown how the South's emerging cultural logic of segregation became the model for the simultaneous construction of a national white identity in the modern consumer marketplace. Recent essay collections have taken interdisciplinary approaches to the imagined South and its very real consequences and have attempted to explode this myth of southern exceptionalism altogether. In his introduction to *Creating and Consuming the American South*, for example, Martyn Bone explains that the collection's goal is to "reorient our attention to the ways in which ideas and stories about 'the South' and 'southerners' have social and material effects that register on various local, regional, national, and transnational scales." A few years earlier, the title of another essay collection, *The Myth of Southern Exceptionalism*, clearly announced an intention to tackle head-on the belief in southern exceptionalism; editors Matthew D. Lassiter and Joseph Crespino bluntly explain in their introduction that "the notion of the exceptional South has served as a myth, one that has persistently distorted our understanding of American history." The essays in this groundbreaking volume repeatedly show that these distortions have been greatest and most consequential in how we view America's complex racial history. Regarding that history, Lassiter and

Crespino explain that their goal in dismantling southern exceptionalism "is not to absolve the South but to implicate the nation." They rightly conclude that "discarding the framework of southern exceptionalism is a necessary step in overcoming the mythology of American exceptionalism, transforming the American Dilemma [of racial injustice] into a truly national ordeal, and traversing regional boundaries to rewrite the American past on its own terms and in full historical perspective."[2] In this same spirit I set out in this study to deconstruct what is perhaps the most persistent and ubiquitous myth of southern exceptionalism (southern hospitality), to show how this discursive formation of southern hospitality first emerged and how it has historically functioned within our national imaginary, and to push the topic of national cultural memory regarding the American South beyond the more transitory realm of politics and toward an abiding realm of ethical consideration.

While historians have provided various explanations of the antebellum practices that gave rise to the southern hospitality myth, no one has yet addressed the persistent appeal and evolving meanings of the myth itself. Instead, for the past two centuries southern hospitality more often than not has been unquestioningly accepted as an essential and natural cultural attribute of the South. The first epigraph, drawn from the *Encyclopedia of Southern Culture*, provides a concise example of this tendency as well as some of the problems that go along with it. While the editors of the *Encyclopedia*—a serious academic work published by the University of North Carolina Press—rightly include the discussion of southern hospitality in a section of the *Encyclopedia* devoted to the "Mythic South," the tone of the entry suggests more interest in justifying the reality of southern hospitality than in exploring or explaining its status as a cultural myth. Indeed, the passage reflects the way that many academics devoted to the study of the South have been invested in maintaining and justifying a sense of regional distinctiveness and exceptionalism. The author of the entry emphasizes the historical origins and "intensely real" quality of southern hospitality, and he concludes that "if the circumstances of southern hospitality have changed" from the antebellum period to the present, "the spirit remains the same."[3] He creates a narrative of continuous development, rhetorically linking the antebellum South with the contemporary South, the historical origins of southern hospitality with the contemporary "spirit" of southern hospitality. Southern hospitality becomes a common denominator of both the past and the present, an unchanging cultural attribute that has somehow survived the social, political, economic, and cultural upheavals that have occurred in the South over the past two centuries.

This way of portraying southern culture as an unchanging essence is precisely the sort of rhetorical turn that interests Immanuel Wallerstein in his essay "What Can One Mean by Southern Culture?" Wallerstein, a sociologist and leading figure of World Systems Theory, makes an important and revealing disclaimer early in the essay, noting that he is concerned "not ... with what this culture [of the South] is supposed to be, but [with] whether and in what sense it is meaningful to suggest that it exists." Wallerstein is particularly interested in the ways in which scholars who have written about the South have used the concept of "culture" in their work; the most prevalent habit is to see (southern) "culture as a description of a set of traits, culture as 'tradition.' By culture in this sense is meant some summum of institutions and ideas/values that is thought to be long-existing and highly-resistant to change." Other prominent tendencies include seeing southern culture as a binary counterpoint to the North or as a virtue to be defended against threats such as change and modernization. After considering several examples from cultural historians whose approaches illustrate these various tendencies, Wallerstein concludes that "for all these writers, culture ... turns out to be less an analytic concept or analytic construct than a rhetorical flag around which one rallies, a weapon in the larger political battles."[4] As for the tendency to see the South and its culture as "solid" or "unchanging," Wallerstein rightly reminds us of the diversity, constant change, and fluidity of historical reality, particularly when we shift our attention to smaller, more local scales of affiliation:

> As soon as we allot "cultures" to entities within entities, there is no logical end. The West has a culture, the United States has a culture, the South has a culture, Georgia has a culture, and I suppose Atlanta has a culture. In addition, blacks and whites in Georgia/the South/the United States have distinct cultures. And so on. Why not each community, each kin network, each household? And why not each generation of each group? The answer is there is no reason why not, and people do speak of culture at these levels. Can we then assume each of these cultures represents some kind of enduring set of behaviors and values that is resistant to change? We can if we want to, but where does that get us?
> As soon as we look closely at the smaller-scale entities, we become very conscious of how constantly changing are the sets of practices and values of small groups—within an individual's lifetime, not to speak of over longer periods.... Furthermore, we know that even if group values remain constant over any period of time, we can never assume that all individuals in that group either affirm those values or engage in behavior consonant with them. At most, the statement of group values is a statistical mean of specific ways of behaving and professed beliefs with a presumable low standard deviation. As to this presumption, we have in practice virtually zero hard evidence. Perhaps the standard deviation varies from group to group, from time to time. Perhaps? All too probably.[5]

Given this diversity of human experience at the local level, Wallerstein asserts that it is probably "far more defensible intellectually to assume that variability is the norm and that continuities" are exceptional.[6] If we consider all the change that occurs on this micro-level as Wallerstein describes it, how is it possible to speak of the constancy of the South as a culture? More particularly for this study, how is it possible to think of hospitality as a cultural trait of the entire South, if we consider the diversity of these individual practices, habits, and conceptions that occur at any given moment, let alone over time? According to Wallerstein,

> It has been possible because groups, in seeking to pursue their interests, will be able to do so insofar as they can persuade their "members" to act in some unified fashion. And a crucial mode of persuading these individuals, who in fact hold multiple group memberships (and hence, . . . are individuals of divergent interests), is to persuade these individuals that the desired behavior is normal, "traditional," hallowed by time and therefore expected in the present. The re-creation of an ever-varying tradition requires the spread of the belief that no change has in fact occurred.[7]

It should be noted that Wallerstein's description of the power of persuasion involved in creating group identities begins a shift away from a simple consideration of the social practices that supposedly constitute group identities and toward the various discursive methods—narratives, images, rhetorics, fictions—used to persuade individuals that they are participating in such a supposedly unchanging tradition. The "belief that no change has in fact occurred" is the implicit assumption of the *Encyclopedia of Southern Culture*'s entry on southern hospitality and of most utterances of the phrase "southern hospitality." To speak of southern hospitality is always to gesture to the past, to link the present to the past in an ongoing, seemingly unchanging tradition. In this way the discourse of southern hospitality forms a pervasive habit of cultural memory and serves as part of a broader persuasive appeal that "the South" exists as a distinct region and meaningful cultural category.[8]

Like Wallerstein in "What Can One Mean by Southern Culture?" I am not especially concerned in this study with what southern hospitality "is supposed to be"; rather my interest is "whether and in what sense it is meaningful to suggest that it exists." In other words, I am interested not in defining the practices that supposedly constitute southern hospitality but rather in how southern hospitality has functioned in the national imaginary, both as a form of persuasion and as a meaning-making story that has been told about the South for more than two centuries.[9] More specifically, I approach southern hospitality as a discourse, a system of representations and narratives through which southerners and nonsoutherners alike have defined, understood, interpreted, and collectively remembered the South. This discourse includes language, narratives, and images, in addition to social practices. Indeed, even when we think we are speaking about southern hospitality as actual social practices (whether of antebellum planters or of contemporary readers of *Southern Living* magazine), these practices achieve their meaning—their *rec-*

ognition as "southern hospitality"—only in relation to this broader discursive system of southern hospitality and its long history of repetition and citation, for nothing can have meaning outside discourse.[10]

The Southern Hospitality Myth explores the cultural work that this discourse has performed in the national imaginary for the past two centuries. More specifically, I argue that this myth has served as a master discourse about race in America, consistently encoding American racial ideologies in a regressive manner. Rather than promoting an ethics of universal welcome, the discourse of southern hospitality has expressed a retrograde politics of exclusion. First against the backdrop of sectional strife and later in the wake of the fratricidal Civil War, the southern hospitality myth has been used to create and promote a sense of transregional white community, solidarity, and privilege. It has done so by naturalizing and extending the racial hierarchies of slavery and segregation and by consistently portraying black Americans as either an invisible or an alien population, incapable of being assimilated into mainstream American culture. Historically considered, then, southern hospitality has functioned primarily as a white mythology, produced by whites, directed to a white audience, and invested in the project of maintaining white status and privilege. Only in the wake of the civil rights movement and the subsequent return of many African Americans to the South has this myth slowly, fitfully begun to be renovated in potentially more inclusive ways. The exclusionary patterns of the past, however, still persist.[11]

Foregrounding the historical gap between the ethical ideal of hospitality and the restrictive politics of southern hospitality, I examine a range of texts and forms (travel writing, fiction, conduct and etiquette books, sermons, political discourse, travel and tourism literature, advertisements, film, cookbooks, and lifestyle magazines, among others) to show that while the discourse of southern hospitality has been constantly adapted to suit changing conditions and needs, its underlying racial meaning remained constant. While the southern hospitality myth has been an important vehicle for self-definition among southerners over the past two centuries, it has simultaneously provided one of the main tropes through which nonsoutherners have imagined their relationship with the region.[12] Faced with a series of real, national conflicts and traumas associated with the South—slavery, sectionalism, secession, the Civil War, Reconstruction, and the long struggle for civil rights—Americans have consistently relied on the discourse of southern hospitality to help them connect, in their imaginations at least, the region to the nation, and the South of the past to the South of the present.[13] As a system of representation, the discourse of southern hospitality forms an axis around which numerous perceptions of nineteenth- and twentieth-century southern culture have revolved: ideas of home and community; relations with outsiders and strangers; the sense of a distinct regional identity and regional pride; the image of an agrarian lifestyle of leisure; the rise of travel, tourism, and hospitality industries in the postbellum and modern South; and social hierarchies of class, gender, and—most subtly and yet most ubiquitously—race. Southern hospitality has functioned as a free-floating nostalgic image, an effective commercial concept, and a consumer commodity. To northerners faced with the pressures of industrialization and modernization both before and after the Civil War, it provided a nostalgic image of a simpler, better time and a regional ideal upon which to hang the hopes of regional reconciliation in spite of sectional political tension and fratricidal war. To southerners, it has consistently stood as an image of regional pride, exceptionalism, and superiority. To non-southerners and southerners alike, the discourse of southern hospitality has provided an adaptable means for imagining amicable political and social relations between the region and the nation, despite the injustices of slavery and segregation.[14] Slavery and segregation are absolutely antithetical to the ethics of hospitality, yet southern hospitality has generally been a basic assumption in the national imaginary for the past two centuries. The persistence and proliferation of the southern hospitality myth can be seen as a corollary of the nation's centuries-long failure to fulfill its original promise of an inclusive, democratic republic. Indeed, as a particularly subtle yet tenacious form of cultural memory, it has both enabled and ameliorated this failure.

To briefly introduce the racial politics underpinning the discourse of southern hospitality, I would like to consider a *Life* magazine cartoon from a special "Dixie" issue published in 1925 (figure 1). The title of the cartoon is "That Southern Hospitality," and it provides something of a paradigmatic image for this study, illustrating the fraught ethical and political dimensions within the discourse of southern hospitality, as well as the politics of collective memory. The focal point of the cartoon is the two figures standing in the foreground, both of whom are white: an older southern gentleman is speaking to a younger man, a guest who has apparently just arrived for an overnight visit. The two seem to be looking out a window, with the young man gazing over the older man's shoulder. In the caption, the older southerner tells the guest, "I've given you, sah, the guest chamber overlooking where the mint bed used to be." Perhaps in the past the mint juleps flowed freely but no more. The hospitality exchange taking place in this image is marked by nostalgia and a palpable sense of declension: the older generation is speaking to the younger generation, and the man's words carry a subtle reminder of how things used to be but unfortunately no longer are. The suggested exchange between the figures in the cartoon's foreground conveys a reverence and longing for the idealized image of the Old South, but the third figure in the cartoon—an African American servant standing behind the two men—both complicates and confirms this meaning. The black servant appears to be dropping off the

FIGURE 1. "That Southern Hospitality." Cartoon from January 15, 1925, issue of *Life* magazine.

guest's luggage and overhearing the conversation, seemingly unnoticed—or at least unacknowledged—by the two central figures. Despite the servant's background role, his presence truly confirms the picture's meaning. His position in this background service role—excluded and unacknowledged—confirms the identity of the main figures: their social standing, their superiority, their community of belonging, in short, their whiteness. In the social practices of antebellum southern hospitality, the slave was perpetually present and perpetually unacknowledged and excluded, both relied on for service and reviled for supposed racial inferiority. This racism cannot be separated from the antebellum social practices of southern hospitality; indeed, it was the labor of the slave that provided the master the leisure to be so hospitable. Consider, for example, Thomas Jefferson's architectural design at Monticello and particularly his creation of a complex system of dumbwaiters designed to entirely conceal the toiling of dozens of slaves as he and his guests dined on the fruits of their unseen labor.[15] Likewise, for much of the history of the discourse of southern hospitality, the black slave, servant, or citizen has been perpetually present and perpetually excluded. This constructed status as perpetual outsider has similarly been used to confirm the solidarity, superiority, and community of white American identity.

While southern hospitality—the hospitality of slavery and segregation—has generally been lauded and memorialized in American culture, many instances when the southern hospitality myth has been contested have been forgotten, as have the many voices of reformers, antislavery advocates, abolitionists, and African Americans who have proposed more progressive visions of hospitality as a possible model for a more inclusive republic. As a study devoted to interpreting the cultural significance of the southern hospitality myth in the national imaginary, this book attempts to recover some of these debates and alternative discourses and thereby provide a fuller historical perspective. By considering both the political and the ethical dimensions surrounding this discourse of southern hospitality, we can better understand the persistence of its appeal in the past and also begin to imagine how it may be shaped in the future, for as an ethical question, hospitality is as relevant today as it was in the past.

To counter the common practice of viewing southern hospitality as a natural and essential cultural attribute of the South, I would like to consider Richard Gray's comments on regional identification and southern self-fashioning, for his comments provide a useful starting point for the consideration of southern hospitality *as discourse*. As Gray writes in the foreword to *South to a New Place: Region, Literature, Culture*, "The South has customarily defined itself against a kind of photographic negative, a reverse image of itself with which it has existed in a mutually determining, reciprocally defining relationship. The South *is* what the North *is not*, just as the *North* is what the

South is not." Gray goes on to explain that while such acts of southern self-fashioning are not "fake," they are "fictive" in the sense of being imaginatively created and sustained. First, they are fictive because "they involve a reading of existence as essence" and "form a notion of a cultural 'type' based on a real specificity but divorced from history." Second, they are fictive in that they deny the real diversity of southern cultures by positing one South that is "stamped with an inalienable, nonevolutive character." But as Gray reminds us, "readings of the South are just that, readings—of its past, present, and possible futures, the plurality of its cultures; for better or worse, [these readings] . . . involve a figuring and, in the purest sense of the word, a *simplifying* of history."[16]

Gray's comments, like Wallerstein's cited earlier, provide a useful framework for rethinking southern hospitality more broadly as a set of discursive practices rather than just as social practices. Clearly any utterance of the phrase "southern hospitality" implicitly signifies its opposite: northern reserve, aloofness, or haughtiness—a general lack of hospitality. Moreover, while southern hospitality may have first existed *in* history as social habits of the antebellum planter classes, it also exists as discourse "divorced from" this specific history, as a meaning-making story told about the South and southerners. Such discursive practices are essential to southern self-fashioning, which Gray concisely describes as the interplay of speech acts and communal ritual: "Southern self-fashioning . . . has surely not altered since the invention of the South. It is a matter of language and communal ritual, the human habit of positioning the self with the help of the word and others, giving a local habitation and a name to things to secure their and our identity, and establishing a connection or kinship with other people that is also an anchorage, a validation of oneself."[17] But a long view of southern hospitality shows that in the give-and-take between speech acts and social rituals described here by Gray, language can eventually trump practice. Perhaps "southern hospitality" initially came into being as a reflection of actual social practices associated with the antebellum planter classes, but over its long history of iterations the phrase became unmoored and increasingly removed from these restricted antebellum origins—so much so that the utterance of "southern hospitality" is like a performative speech act: it is the *expression* of "southern hospitality" that *creates* southern hospitality.

New research tools available through digitized databases allow us to begin to quantify and consequently visualize these historical trends in the usage of the phrase "southern hospitality." Consider the graph in figure 2, which shows the frequency of the use of "southern hospitality" between 1700 and 2000 in over 5,195,769 digitized books available on Google Books.[18] While this data is hardly definitive, it is nonetheless highly suggestive. Notice that the first usages of "southern hospitality" occur in the second and third decades of the

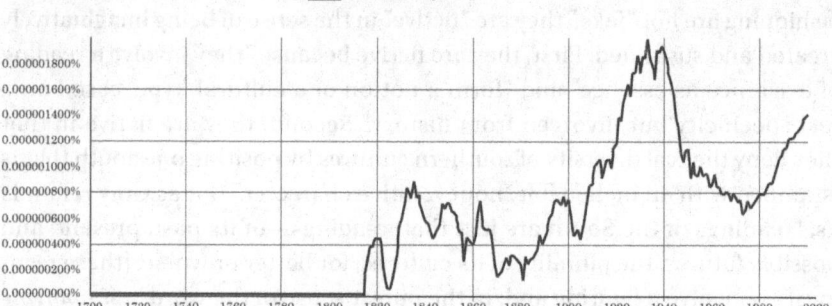

FIGURE 2. Google Ngram Viewer graph illustrating the frequency of the use of "southern hospitality" between 1700 and 2000 in over five million digitized books available on Google Books.

nineteenth century; I should add that nearly all of these are from a passage in Sir Walter Scott's novel *Rob Roy* and do not refer to the American South at all. While cultural historians often locate the origins of the social practices that came to be identified as southern hospitality in the 1700s and the colonial era, writers of that period were more likely to refer more specifically to the hospitality of Virginians, Carolinians, Georgians, and the like.[19] In contrast, this graph shows that the earliest uses of "southern hospitality" in American culture actually occurred in the mid-1820s, and it only seemed to become a common expression between the 1830s and the 1860s. This does not mean that southerners were exceptionally hospitable during these decades; rather, this was a period of increasing political tension and animosity between the South and the North over slavery. In other words, the discourse of southern hospitality was not simply an emergent linguistic reflection of pleasant social practices; instead, it emerged as a mode of persuasion in the sectional crisis over slavery. As political tension increased between the North and the South, residents of southern states increasingly imagined and defined themselves as "the South," as members of a distinct, separate, and superior culture in opposition to the North. As a phrase repeated again and again, "southern hospitality" became a form of shorthand in the national imaginary for a host of attributes and associations identified with "southern culture," foundational among these being the South's racialized cultural hierarchy. My claim here that southern hospitality emerged and proliferated as a discourse during this period of sectional crisis is very much in line with Trish Loughran's thesis in *The Republic in Print: Print Culture in the Age of U.S. Nation Building, 1770–1870*. As Loughran shows, only in the 1830s and 1840s did a "'national' print culture" emerge in America. But rather than enhancing national identity, this development led to "profound cultural fragmentation" as Americans recognized their deep regional divisions, particularly over slavery. According to Loughran, the "more connected regions appeared to be (in print), the more regionalized (rather than nationalized) their identities became."[20] The discourse of southern hospitality is unique in that it both embodied *and* alleviated this paradox of regional and national identity, emphasizing regional distinctiveness while simultaneously promising (to white Americans, at least) an imagined sense of welcome and connection to the South.

To return to figure 2, also notice that the frequency of usage of "southern hospitality" drops off sharply during the Civil War (1861–65) and Reconstruction (1865–77), but that it increases quite steadily as the Civil War recedes in the distance and a nostalgia industry surrounding the Old South emerges in the late nineteenth and early twentieth centuries, reaching a peak in the Depression era of the 1930s, when a novel and film like *Gone with the Wind* (1936, adapted to film in 1939) could capture the American imagination with its romantic depiction of the patriarchal and agrarian Old South.[21] Another sharp drop in usage coincides roughly with the civil rights movement of the 1950s and 1960s (perhaps no surprise here). In the last two decades of the twentieth century, these struggles over racial equality receded in the distance, and like a century earlier, we see another steady increase in usage. It's worth noting that this latter rise seems to occur even as the definition of the South and of southerners has become increasingly fluid and elusive in an era of globalization, the incessant cultural reproduction of late capitalism, and ever-shifting population demographics, as Martyn Bone and Scott Romine, among others, have described.[22]

Today we recognize southern hospitality not from having experienced it so much as from having heard about it repeatedly in this long history of repetition and citation, and in most instances, this discourse today seems entirely emptied of any real meaning or higher ethical or moral significance. To illustrate, I would like to briefly consider a series of contemporary paintings, all of which share the same title: "Southern Hospitality." The fact that there are numerous contemporary paintings with this title (more than I discuss here) might seem at first to confirm the sense of southern hospitality's naturalness: it is just one of those things that goes without saying when people think of the South. But what, if anything, do these images really convey about southern culture? Do they help us define the South any better than, say, the Southern Focus Poll that I cited earlier? In turning to these paintings I want to emphasize that I am not in any way criticizing the individual artists for the possible meanings of their works; rather, I approach their work simply as visual reflections of the way American culture has memorialized southern hospitality.

Several of these paintings are still lifes. Fran DiGiacomo's richly detailed and traditional still life "Southern Hospitality" (figure 3), for example, conveys a sense of formal elegance, featuring magnolia blooms pouring out of a low-set

FIGURE 3. Fran DiGiacomo, "Southern Hospitality," 1998, oil, 24 × 36 in. Courtesy of the artist.

vase onto a marble tabletop that is partially covered in a richly textured crimson fabric. Other still-life paintings of southern hospitality convey a similar sense of elegance and refinement. For example, Eddie Glass's "Southern Hospitality" chooses as its subject the proverbial pineapple—longtime symbol of hospitality—presiding in this instance over an elegant centerpiece of a formal dining table with two wineglasses.[23] Cherrie Nute's version of southern hospitality lacks a pineapple, but it has grapes, apples, peaches, and pears set amid fine china, rich fabrics, and flowers. In contrast to these more lavish depictions, Frank Tarpley's "Southern Hospitality" (figure 4) focuses on a simpler-looking table setting: peaches and grapes surround a silver teapot sitting on a more modest table linen. Alternatively, artist Kevin Liang's depiction of "Southern Hospitality" (figure 5) broadens the perspective beyond the narrow parameters of still-life painting; instead it features a welcoming sunroom or living room well lit by a bank of windows. The room's eclectic style conveys a sense of casual elegance: a formal fireplace, gilt-framed landscape painting, and Queen Anne end table contrast with other, more casual furnishings such as soft throw pillows and a wicker chair. On the end table in the foreground lie freshly cut flowers, a plate of fruit, and two glasses filled with red wine, ready to be enjoyed. Given their shared titles, each of these paintings purports to be conveying something about southern culture, but what, specifically, makes

FIGURE 4. Frank H. Tarpley, "Southern Hospitality," 1999, oil, 16 × 20 in. Courtesy of the artist (www.georgiasunrise.com).

FIGURE 5. Kevin Liang, "Southern Hospitality," 1995, oil, 30 × 50 in. Courtesy of the artist.

FIGURE 6. Karen Dupre, "Southern Hospitality," 2002, giclée print on paper, 24 × 30 in. Courtesy of Phoenix Art Group.

them "southern" other than the shared proclamations of their titles? Pineapples have long been symbolic of hospitality beyond the South, magnolias and peaches grow in other regions of the country, and the painting by Kevin Liang could be just about anywhere, so long as the income level of the homeowners could support such a lifestyle. Still, prints of these paintings are available for purchase at several online sites, so there is a market for them under their regional titles.[24] For some consumers, then, these images might provide a means for what Richard Gray describes as "southern self-fashioning," providing "an anchorage," "a connection or kinship," or a "validation of oneself."

Further broadening the perspective, both Karen Dupre's and Larry Dyke's paintings titled "Southern Hospitality" shift to the more obviously iconic southern image of the plantation home. Dupre's representation of southern hospitality (figure 6) focuses on the plantation home from a distance; the perspective is that of a visitor approaching the gateposts that mark the entrance to the plantation grounds. The home features iconic white pillars, and two empty chairs sit on the lawn just to the right of the portico. While this image may be more recognizably southern than the previously discussed paintings, print versions of this painting available online include a title banner running across the bottom that may create a moment of cognitive dissonance in

FIGURE 7. Larry Dyke, "Southern Hospitality," 2005, oil, 20 × 40 in. Courtesy of Somerset Fine Art (www.somersetfineart.com).

the viewer. The banner includes the artist's name and the title in elaborately scrolled lettering that seems to fit the subject well, but in the center of the title banner and in a modern typeface that offsets the elaborate scrolls appear the words "Phoenix Art Group," referring to a studio and gallery in Arizona. Apparently southern hospitality has spread further into the West, or perhaps this is more evidence of the "southernization" of America discussed by John Egerton and others.

Larry Dyke's "Southern Hospitality" (figure 7) presents what most would agree is a quintessentially southern scene: live oaks and blooming azaleas abound in the foreground, and the white-pillared edifice of the plantation mansion sits off in the distance. In contrast to Dupre's painting, however, the perspective is somewhat askance. We see the home not as a typical visitor might, approaching up the drive leading to it, but from the side of the mansion, peering at it from a distance through the trees and azaleas. Perhaps the perspective is that of a welcome guest out for a stroll on the plantation grounds, but given the slightly voyeuristic quality of the perspective, it could just as well be that of an uninvited visitor lurking among the azaleas. Or shifting perspectives more dramatically, what happens if we imagine the viewpoint as that of a slave approaching the "big house" from the more mundane slave quarters that would have surrounded the plantation home? After all, the historical time frame for this image of the iconic plantation home is ambiguous. When we view this painting, we might, on the one hand, imagine that we are looking at an antebellum mansion as it existed before the Civil War, or we might, on the other hand, imagine that the painting represents a southern mansion in the contemporary moment that has apparently survived the vicissitudes of history. In other words, associating southern hospitality with this image of the plantation home raises important though neglected questions regarding southern hospitality's work as a form of cultural memory. In memorializing southern hospitality through such an image, what is it that we are actually choosing to remember, and what are we choosing to forget? Looking to the past, can we imagine ourselves as guests of a hospitality based on slave labor? For that matter, can an owner of slaves ever be said to be hospitable at all? As I will discuss later, just as an ethics is involved in hospitality, so too is an ethics involved in how we choose to remember the past.

Overall, these contemporary pictorial iterations of "southern hospitality" seem disconnected from both the historically real and the ethically ideal. Pineapples, magnolias, white-pillared plantation homes: these are jaded repetitions, empty echoes, gestures toward an incomplete vision of the past. And yet "southern hospitality" in the present moment is still open to the possibility of resignification, to the construction of new meanings. As an example, take yet another contemporary painting titled "Southern Hospitality," this by California artist Britt Ehringer (figure 8). In contrast to the straightforward representational nature of the other paintings, this oil challenges viewers through a collage-like construction, as a range of competing images are both juxtaposed with and superimposed on one another. While the initial impression is chaotic and confusing, the underlying formal structure of the painting—a large central section framed by two narrower fields on the sides—subtly calls to mind a triptych, a form traditionally used for religious iconography. Given what can sometimes seem like a religious reverence for the past in the South—the United Daughters of the Confederacy, the Sons of Confederate Veterans, the cult of the Lost Cause, and so on—the use of such a formal structure for this subject would be appropriate. Indeed, in the central field of the painting, in the background, is a Civil War battle scene, with Confederate cavalry engaging Union forces and wounded Confederates lying in the foreground. Though this image takes up the largest section of the painting, it is indistinct at first glance, for it is upside down, and another image is superimposed over it: a yellow-throated warbler in a mason jar. The captive bird—whose summer breeding range extends across the states of the former Confederacy—literally dwarfs the soldiers who are engaged in their life-or-death struggles of the historical past. Alongside this central frame, the narrower fields on the left and right depict contrasting views of women. The figure on the left presents the woman as sexual object: she wears black lingerie and strikes a provocative pose, returning the gaze of the viewer. A ribbon of color that flows across the entire painting covers her mouth. Just above her appears another, smaller female figure who is nude and seems to be standing on a stage before a curtain, effectively underscoring this idea of the objectified female form. In contrast to these sexualized figures, the woman who appears on the opposite side of the painting represents a re-

FIGURE 8. Britt Ehringer, "Southern Hospitality," 2005, oil on canvas, 76 × 58.5 in. Courtesy of the artist.

strictive, traditional feminine propriety: at first glance she looks like a 1950s housewife, but closer scrutiny reveals Japanese ideograms on her dress. A voice bubble appears above her, but there are no words in the bubble, only a labyrinthine pattern in two shades of pink. In contrast to the "Southern Hospitality" paintings considered heretofore, Ehringer's painting disrupts our assumptions and expectations, creating space for us to momentarily question and possibly reconsider such received cultural myths. History in this version of "Southern Hospitality" literally is turned on its head, while nature in turn is constrained by suffocating human constructions. Ehringer's painting deconstructs the myth of southern hospitality with an ethical edge that questions the negative effects of such myths, particularly, in this case, on women. According to Ehringer's version, women performing the myth of southern hospitality are on stage and on display; they are either silenced or reduced to speaking in little more than meaningless pink patterns, a critical reading of southern hospitality that parallels Tara McPherson's comments on the performative quality of southern hospitality in *Reconstructing Dixie: Race, Gender and Nostalgia in the Imagined South*.[25]

Ehringer's portrayal of southern hospitality offers a stunning contrast to the other contemporary paintings that I have discussed. It almost seems a direct response to them. Perhaps the most telling point of contrast is that

Ehringer's "Southern Hospitality" is the only one to include human figures. In the other paintings we see objects, empty rooms, and vacant landscapes—lawn chairs and sofas with no one to sit on them, food and wine with no one to partake of them. If we think of hospitality as an exchange between a host and a guest or a host and a stranger, this consistent lack of human figures in these paintings celebrating southern hospitality seems particularly curious: it is as if we cannot even begin to imagine what southern hospitality might actually look like; perhaps even more so, we cannot begin to imagine what ethical obligations it might entail. These empty images seem a subtle confirmation of Jacques Derrida's statement: "We do not yet know what hospitality is." Derrida's point is that true hospitality is an ethical ideal that we can only strive *toward* but never fully realize. My own approach to the discourse of southern hospitality is deeply indebted to Derrida's philosophical meditations on hospitality, a subject that took up much of his critical attention as he increasingly saw it as the most fundamental of ethical questions. In particular, I use the distinction Derrida draws between the ethics and the politics of hospitality as a heuristic, a way of framing and comparing a variety of historical moments in the long arc of the myth's history.

Today, whether we are speaking of the South or not, we have largely lost sight of hospitality as either a moral imperative or an ethical question, a fact that belies its rich heritage in Western culture.[26] Derrida, in contrast, came to see the question of hospitality as the most fundamental category of ethics: "Hospitality is not merely one ethics among others, but the ethics par excellence."[27] Philosophically considered, hospitality is central to questions of identity, for the site of hospitality is always the threshold between difference, the site at which boundaries are *both* crossed *and* maintained. Hospitality, in other words, can both confirm and challenge identity. As Derrida describes it, hospitality is a "paradoxical law" that defines the "sometimes ungraspable differences between the foreigner and the absolute other," between those who can be welcomed, even conditionally, and those who, for whatever reason, never can be.[28] Hospitality, then, can never be completely separated from its opposite, hostility; in fact, the two words share an etymological origin in the Latin word *hostis*, which can variously mean stranger, foreigner, alien, guest, or enemy.[29] As Derrida explains, "hospitality" is "a word which carries its own contradiction incorporated into it, a Latin word which allows itself to be parasitized by its opposite, 'hostility,' the undesirable guest... which it harbors as the self-contradiction in its own body."[30] This etymological self-contradiction is emblematic of the aporia Derrida outlines in the concept of hospitality itself. In outlining this paradox, he draws on a philosophical tradition going back through Emmanuel Levinas to Immanuel Kant. Drawing from Kant in particular, Derrida emphasizes that hospitality is a universal right, but by this he means the right *to* hospitality: the right of the stranger not to be treated with hostility when entering the lands of another.[31] Derrida privileges this right of the guest, raising the guest to equal status with the host; in this regard, it is worth noting that the French language uses the same term to designate both "guest" and "host": *hôte*. With this idea of hospitality as universal right in place, Derrida goes on to distinguish between the infinite "ethics of hospitality," which dictate the welcoming of all equally, and the "politics of hospitality," which involve the way we define the threshold and negotiate borders between ourselves and those we deem foreign or strange.[32] In short, the politics of hospitality is about determining who belongs and, perhaps more importantly, who does not. Such exclusionary acts are transgressions against the universal right to hospitality; while seeming welcoming, they are simultaneously acts of mastery, power, and even violence. For in order for hospitality to exist between a host and a guest, the host must maintain the sense of authority and mastery in his or her own place. The gift of hospitality, then, is never absolute but always limited. Says Derrida,

> There is almost an axiom of self-limitation or self-contradiction in the law of hospitality. As a reaffirmation of mastery and being oneself in one's own home, from the outset hospitality limits itself at its very beginning, it remains forever on the threshold of itself.... It governs the threshold—and hence it forbids in some way even what it seems to allow to cross the threshold.... It becomes the threshold....
>
> To take up the figure of the door, for there to be hospitality, there must be a door. But if there is a door, there is no longer hospitality.... As soon as there are a door and windows, it means someone has the key to them and consequently controls the conditions of hospitality.... Hospitality thus becomes the threshold or the door.[33]

I must emphasize that the point of Derrida's deconstruction of hospitality is not to simply and cynically argue that hospitality is impossible; rather, it is a call to *do* the seemingly impossible. Derrida goes on to draw an important distinction between "the hospitality of invitation" and "the hospitality of visitation." The hospitality of invitation, synonymous with the politics of hospitality, is exclusive and confirms our comfortable self-identity, our sovereignty, our mastery of our own space. In contrast, the hospitality of visitation, synonymous with the absolute ethic of welcoming all equally, carries an inherent sense of risk that can challenge this sense of sovereignty and self-possession. To move from one to the other we must be willing to give up control of the threshold, to allow the stranger—whoever or whatever that may be—to have access to it. Obviously, this carries great risk, threatening our own sense of mastery and possibly our self-identity, even our safety, but this is precisely Derrida's point: "Pure, unconditional or infinite hospitality cannot and must not be anything else but an acceptance of risk. If I am sure that the newcomer that I welcome is perfectly harmless, innocent, that (s)he will be beneficial to me... it is not hospitality. When I open my door, I must be ready to take the greatest of risks."[34] Such an unconditional ethic of welcome has never animated the southern hospitality myth, but the inherent risk involved in such true, unconditional hospitality was poignantly and tragically illustrated in the South on June 17, 2015, when members of the historically black "Mother Emanuel" AME church in Charleston, South Carolina, opened their doors to a young white supremacist. Given the long history of this black church in the South, given the fraught history of racial discrimination and violence in the nation, and given the church members' probable own life experiences (some were elderly and had lived under Jim Crow segregation), self-interest may have dictated caution when facing an unknown white man, but in accordance with the "hospitality of visitation" described above, they unconditionally welcomed this stranger in and invited him to participate in their scheduled Bible study, which he did for nearly an hour before pulling a gun and shooting to death nine church members: Cynthia Marie Graham Hurd, Susie Jackson, Ethel Lee Lance, Depayne Middleton-Doctor, Tywanza Sanders, Daniel Simmons, Sharonda Coleman-Singleton, Myra Thompson, and the Reverend Clementa C. Pinkney, the church's pastor who also served as a South Carolina state senator.

How many of us are willing to open ourselves up and accept such risk? With such an unconditional ethical standard in mind, it is no wonder that Derrida repeatedly says, "We do not yet know what hospitality is."[35] Derrida's analysis invites us to move beyond the limitations he describes as the politics of hospitality and to think more expansively about hospitality as an ethical ideal, as *the* ethical ideal. From this perspective, true hospitality is not about confirming our comfortable assumptions and reaffirming our self-identity; it is about opening ourselves to difference. It is also about opening ourselves to both the challenges and the possibilities of the future, for Derrida's vision of pure hospitality is oriented toward the future and *not* the past. Indeed, when the church members at Mother Emanuel opened their doors, they were accepting the possibilities of the future over the traumas of the past, which might have dictated suspicion or fear. As Derrida explains, "Hospitality can only take place beyond hospitality, in deciding to let it come, overcoming the hospitality that paralyzes itself on the threshold which it is.... In this sense, hospitality is always to come..., but a 'to come' that does not and will never present itself as such, in the present and a future... that does not have a horizon, a futurity—a future without horizon."[36]

Given this progressive and future-oriented concept of the ethics of hospitality as outlined by Derrida, what can we say about the discourse of southern hospitality, a narrative form of cultural memory that is so oriented toward and invested in the past and in maintaining a sense of "tradition"? This question provides a second ethical dimension to consider when we reflect on the discourse of southern hospitality, for just as there is an ethics of hospitality, so too is there an ethics of memory. As the philosopher Paul Ricoeur argues, memory, whether individual or collective, is not simply a passive form of knowledge or experience; rather, it is an action, a way of "*doing* things." Consequently, we can speak of the ethics of memory, of both the "use" and the "abuses of memory."[37] As Ricoeur explains, we use narratives to create an identity, whether individual or collective, that seems stable and continuous amid the flux of time. The construction of such narratives necessarily involves "eliminating" or "dropping" some details and events as others are foregrounded "according to the kind of plot we intend to build." Narratives of collective identity, then, are simultaneously acts of remembering *and* forgetting. While this process is necessary for the creation of collective identities, it is also open to abuses, particularly when the past in question includes collective traumas and humiliations. These wounds of the past can have a profound effect, resulting in abuses of collective memory; in the face of past traumas, many groups and cultures block or manipulate memory as they construct a shared cultural identity, selectively remembering some events or details of the historical past while repressing others, allowing them to be forgotten.[38]

The American South certainly has more than its fair share of traumas and humiliations in its collective memory, many of which are linked to the region's fraught racial history: the trauma of slavery, the humiliation of defeat in the Civil War, a legacy of sectional animosity and suspicion, the failures of Reconstruction, the daily humiliations suffered under Jim Crow segregation, the often violent struggles of the long civil rights movement, and countless episodes of racial violence that have taken place since the first Africans arrived in Jamestown in 1619. Obviously, these wounds of the past are experienced in very different ways by different populations, black and white: what was victory for one group was bitter loss for the other, what was a moment of hope for one group was a moment of humiliation for the other, what brought pride to one group brought shame to the other.[39] It is in just such a situation of competing, conflicting historical experiences that collective memory is perhaps most open to abuses, to the privileging and valorizing of some details of the past and the repression of others. This is certainly the case when we take a historical view of the discourse of southern hospitality, a form of cultural production and collective memory that is about both remembering and forgetting, a form that has been both used and abused. Since the Civil War and through segregation, the discourse of southern hospitality has largely been used to connect the postbellum South with the antebellum South in a way that reveres the patriarchal power structure and aristocratic sensibilities of the Old South, while forgetting that the historical origins of southern hospitality (its founding events) lie in an economy of slave labor. Indeed, the legendary hospitality of antebellum planters—the "origins" of the myth—was only possible through slaves, whose labors provided their masters both the wealth and the leisure to entertain their guests so freely. Since the Civil War, Americans have largely chosen to forget this basic historical fact. The empty repetitions of "southern hospitality" in the paintings discussed earlier—particularly the uninhabited plantation scenes—are perhaps symptomatic of this forgetfulness, a result of repression and the consequent compulsion to repeat.[40]

But keeping in mind the appropriate work of memory, Paul Ricoeur notes that narratives of the past can also be sites of healing "because it is always possible to tell in another way. This exercise of memory is here an exercise in *telling otherwise*. . . . It is very important to remember that what is considered a founding event in our collective memory may be a wound in the memory of the other." This observation takes us to what Ricoeur defines as the "ethico-political level" of collective memory and the "duty to remember." For Ricoeur, the duty to remember "consists not only in having a deep concern for the past, but in transmitting the meaning of past events to the next generation. The duty, therefore, is one which concerns the future; it is an imperative directed towards the future, which is exactly the opposite side of the traumatic character of the humiliations and wounds of history. It is a duty, thus, to tell."[41] Tracing the discourse of southern hospitality through its evolving contexts from the beginnings of the sectional crisis up to the present, *The Southern Hospitality Myth* is an attempt at "telling otherwise," an effort to reconnect traces of the past that have largely been forgotten in American collective memory.

The chapters of this study are arranged chronologically and begin with the period of American history when the discourse of "southern hospitality" was being invented: in the 1820s and 1830s and against the backdrop of the rising sectional crisis that continued to the Civil War. In the first two chapters, I engage the historiography of the social practices that gave rise to the discourse of southern hospitality, but in contrast to the prevailing historiography, I complicate our regionalist understanding of hospitality by placing southern hospitality in a national context, by linking southern hospitality more directly to slavery, and by raising fundamental ethical questions about what actually constitutes hospitality. Hospitality was in fact a national concern, and there were widely diverse opinions among antebellum Americans regarding the moral, social, economic, and political dimensions of hospitality. Relying on a variety of texts (travel literature, etiquette books, sermons, religious texts, reform literature, fiction, poetry, and essays), I show that the discourse of southern hospitality emerged as Americans were already debating competing ideas of hospitality in the domestic sphere and amid a changing economy and culture. While most texts of the period point to the Christian spirit as the basis for true politeness in manners, they nonetheless reveal different views of what constitutes "true" hospitality. Many texts articulate an elitist, class-conscious sense of hospitality that emphasizes taste, refinement, and display, while others advocate a more "republican" approach that emphasizes simplicity, equality, and openness. In these early chapters I also rely on controversial literature on slavery to show that the discourse of southern hospitality emerged in conjunction with "abolition hospitality," a self-conscious counterdiscourse espoused by abolitionists and progressive reformers of the period, a historical fact that has been lost to our collective memory as Americans and which I attempt to restore for our consideration. These reform-minded Americans developed radical ideas of hospitality, viewing it less as a pleasant social ritual and more as a moral imperative and a catalyst to social change. To understand the regressive racial appeal of the discourse of southern hospitality during the antebellum period and in debates on slavery, it is important to understand these alternative discourses as well.

Chapters 3 and 4 also focus on the period of antebellum sectional crisis, with an emphasis on the 1850s, but here I go beyond the local and domestic considerations of the first two chapters to consider legal, political, and ethical dimensions of hospitality in both national and global contexts. In particular, the chapters focus on contentious national debates surrounding, first, the Fugitive Slave Law of 1850, which made it a federal crime to extend hospitality to runaway slaves; second, the antebellum Negro Seamen Acts, by which free foreign sailors of color were routinely imprisoned upon entering southern ports; and third, the nation's 1851 reception of Louis Kossuth, the exiled Hungarian revolutionary who was initially welcomed as the "guest of the nation" but who eventually received a hostile reception from both the South and northern abolitionists. Historians have examined all three of these episodes, to varying degrees, yet they have not fully considered how these conflicts raised important ethical questions around hospitality, which I argue was a particularly important frame of reference for antebellum Americans, both North and South. All three of these national debates remind us that hospitality entails much more than mere sociability carried out within the domestic sphere of individuals or the ethical and moral obligations between individuals and strangers; the question of hospitality also extends into the realms of international law and universal human rights. As Seyla Benhabib concisely explains, hospitality encompasses "all human rights claims which are cross-border in scope."[42] Drawing on sources such as antislavery almanacs, tracts, newspapers, sermons, newspaper editorials, poems, fiction, and the Congressional Record, these chapters show that the discourse of hospitality was used in competing ways by southerners and antislavery northerners to navigate boundaries within and between the region and the nation, and between the region and the international world, but it was also an important discourse for defining "foreignness" more generally, both within the South (in the form of the slave) and without.

Chapters 5 and 6 shift to the post–Civil War era, focusing on how the discourse of southern hospitality continued to evolve, even though the Civil War had made defunct the entire social order that supposedly embodied southern hospitality. Chapter 5 considers how the discourse of southern hospitality assumed new meanings, met new needs, and expressed new desires and anxieties in the postbellum era of Reconstruction and early segregation culture. While the myth of southern hospitality was vigorously contested in the antebellum period, it was now increasingly and uncritically accepted throughout the nation. In the postwar context of reconciliation and national unity, earlier national debates over the nature, obligations, and limitations of hospitality yielded to a growing national assumption that the South was the home of hospitality. In the emerging consumer culture, southern hospitality evolved into a free-floating nostalgic image, an effective commercial concept, and a consumer commodity. In all these areas, the ethical dimensions of hospitality were lost as the discourse of southern hospitality increasingly functioned (implicitly or explicitly) as an exclusionary white myth that appealed to and was sustained by northerners as much as southerners. I draw here on Lost Cause literature, plantation fiction, Civil War commemoration, the literature of a burgeoning travel and tourism industry, and texts promoting northern and foreign emigration to the South. These texts reinforce the myth of southern hospitality while simultaneously reminding readers of the "foreignness" of the African American population. There were, however, alternative views to this trend—though few and far between. I begin the chapter by considering works of fiction by women writers who counter this trend by tentatively reimagining hospitality during Reconstruction as a potential step toward a racially inclusive democracy, and I conclude it by turning to critiques of southern hospitality by African American writers at the turn of the twentieth century, with a specific emphasis on Charles W. Chesnutt.

In the twentieth century, popular culture and mass marketing allowed for the dramatic proliferation of the myth of southern hospitality, allowing the myth to reach a greater audience than ever before. I begin chapter 6 with a contextualized reading of the 1964 film and pop culture classic *Two Thousand Maniacs!* From there, I examine how southern hospitality has been used in the overall "branding" of the South and its economic endeavors, focusing first on the development of the South's hospitality and tourism industries in the early and middle decades of the twentieth century and then on the more recent emergence of lifestyle industries around the South, most particularly with the example of *Southern Living* magazine. The history of the southern hospitality myth in the twentieth century could easily be the subject of a book, whether concentrating on pop culture, literature, or African American reappropriations of the myth post–civil rights. I conclude my study by focusing on these particular areas—tourism and lifestyle—because they have been major generators of economic wealth for the South and for some southerners in the twentieth and twenty-first centuries. The tensions between the ethics and the politics of hospitality in the South continue even after the civil rights movement, and I use the ethical lens of hospitality to examine more recent controversies such as the NAACP boycott of the South Carolina hospitality and tourism industries over the flying of the Confederate flag atop the statehouse and the dramatic fall of celebrity chef Paula Deen. Finally, in the epilogue, I consider the contentious debate over Alabama's anti-immigration law, HB56. I ask whether southern hospitality remains an adaptable discourse, one that can potentially be renovated to provide a meaningful ethical lens with which to approach such challenges that go hand in hand with globalization.

Although the chapters of this study are arranged chronologically, my goal is not to provide a comprehensive historical survey of the discourse of southern hospitality; in light of its pervasiveness in American cultural history, that would be impossible. Instead, I am most interested in turning to the past as a way of recovering competing discourses on southern hospitality that, taken together, foreground the ethical dilemmas and paradoxes that surround this discourse at particular historical moments. This recovery effort is driven by the conviction that the ethical dilemmas surrounding the question of hospitality are not confined to the past. As the contemporary South and the nation as a whole are faced with the economic, political, social, and regional effects of globalization, the question of the South's or the nation's hospitality is potentially more urgent than ever before.[43] In the context of globalization, philosophers such as Seyla Benhabib and Kwame Anthony Appiah have called for a new cosmopolitan ethics to guide us into the future, and the concept of hospitality is central to these efforts.[44] As we transition toward a global society and face calls for cosmopolitan human rights, Benhabib describes how states are "caught between *sovereignty* and *hospitality*, between the prerogative to choose to be a party to cosmopolitan norms and human rights treaties, and the obligation to extend recognition of these human rights to all."[45] The question I pose in my epilogue is, can the regional ideal of southern hospitality serve as a meaningful frame of reference for a South and for southerners faced with the demands and pressures of globalization? In other words, can southern hospitality develop from a discursive practice that gestures toward an incomplete vision of the past into a discursive practice oriented toward the challenges of the future, one that calls for an ethical response to the foreigner, the stranger, and the risk of the unknown?

CHAPTER ONE

A Virginian Praises "Yankee Hospitality"

Rethinking the Historicity of Antebellum Southern Hospitality

In the early years of the sectional crisis between the northern and southern states, a southerner could still praise the hospitality of northerners and even suggest that "Yankee hospitality," though admittedly different, was possibly more sincere and meaningful than the hospitality of the South. Lucian Minor's "Letters from New England" were published in the first volume of the *Southern Literary Messenger*, appearing in five installments between November 1834 and April 1835. His second letter opens with the following extended comparison between "Yankee hospitality" and "good old Virginia hospitality":

Of *Yankee hospitality* (curl not your lip sardonically—you, or any other Buckskin,)—of *Yankee hospitality* there is a great deal, *in their way*—i.e. according to the condition and circumstances of society. Not a little more can be said of Virginia hospitality. Set one of our large farmowners down upon a hundred, instead of a thousand, acres; let him, and his sons, cultivate it themselves; feed the cattle; rub down and feed the horses; milk the cows; cut wood and make fires; let his wife and daughters alone tend the garden; wash, iron, cook, make clothes, make the beds, and clean up the house; let him have but ten acres of wood land, in a climate where snow lies three, and frost comes for seven, months a year; surround him with a dense population—80, instead of 19, to the square mile; bring strangers, constantly, in flocks to his neighborhood; place a cheap and comfortable inn but a mile or two off; give him a ready and near market for his garden stuffs, as well as for his grain and tobacco—and ask yourself, if he could, or would, practice our "good old Virginia hospitality?" To us, who enjoy the credit and the pleasure of entertaining a guest, while the drudgery devolves upon our slaves; the larger scale (wastefully large) of our daily *rations*, too, making the presence of one or more additional mouths absolutely unfelt;—hospitality is a cheap, easy, and delightful virtue. But put us in place of the yankees, in the foregoing respects, and any man of sense and candor must perceive that we could not excel them.[1]

While I am attracted to the sheer anecdotal novelty provided by an antebellum southerner praising the hospitality of the North, I begin this chapter with Lucian Minor for more substantive reasons. On the one hand, Minor's comments on the unique material and social circumstances of southern hospitality confirm many of the main assertions that cultural historians have made about the origins of the social practices that came to be identified as "southern hospitality," so his portrayal of southern hospitality provides a convenient opportunity to review what historians have had to say about the material circumstances, complex motivations, and cultural meanings of these practices.² On the other hand, Minor's comparative comments on northern and southern hospitality can also complicate our understanding of southern hospitality in important ways. First, the opening lines of his essay, in which he anticipates his readers' incredulous response to the mere suggestion of northern hospitality, suggest the already-legendary status of the hospitality of southerners, its importance as a defining trait of "the South." Indeed, he later refers to hospitality as "our most prominent virtue" and admits that allowing northerners to be compared with southerners in this regard amounts to "audacious heresy."³ But considering Minor's comments on hospitality in light of the overall context to "Letters from New England" also shows that southern hospitality was an adaptable discourse, a well-recognized story that allowed northerners and southerners to imagine an amicable interregional social union in spite of, or instead of, sectional political animosity. As I discuss later, this discourse of southern hospitality was both a symptom of and, often, a proposed remedy to sectional suspicion and animosity. Second, Minor unsettles our regionalist understanding of hospitality by placing southern hospitality in a national context, reminding us that hospitality was an important subject throughout antebellum America and not just in the South. Antebellum discourses of hospitality were multiple, wide-ranging, and mobile, sliding along shifting boundaries that defined the stranger or foreigner and along lines of region, race, and class. Discourse on *southern* hospitality was only one strand of discourse among many. To understand how antebellum Americans imagined and understood southern hospitality, it is essential to consider it amid these broader, more disparate discourses on hospitality, a topic I take up in chapter 2. Finally, by linking southern hospitality directly to slavery, Minor implicitly—though no doubt, unintentionally—raises fundamental ethical questions about what actually constitutes hospitality. For if antebellum southern hospitality is—in Minor's words—an "easy virtue," one that is contingent on slave labor, is it a virtue at all?

Lucian Minor was a graduate of the College of William and Mary, a Virginia commonwealth attorney, and a public southern intellectual from the 1830s until his death in 1858. In 1833 he had been Thomas Willis White's first choice for the editor's position at the fledgling *Southern Literary Messenger*, a magazine whose expressed hope was to establish for the South its "just rights" and "proper representation in the republic of letters."[4] When Minor refused White's offer to head the *Messenger* for eight hundred dollars a year—a decent salary at the time—White offered the position to the struggling Edgar Allan Poe at a much lower rate of ten dollars per week. Still, Minor maintained close ties with White and the *Southern Literary Messenger*, and he would be one of its "best and most frequent contributors" in the years that followed.[5] As can be gleaned from his five "Letters from New England," Minor could in many ways be classified as a progressive southern intellectual of the period, and his often-approving observations of New England range through topics such as public education, local government, architecture, the judicial system, agriculture, public lyceums and lectures, and the treatment of women, among other things. He states that his goal in writing the letters is to "draw ... [southern] attention to some traits of Yankee life which we may advantageously copy," and to "disabuse" southerners "of a few of the prejudices, which ignorance and misrepresentation have fostered against our northern brethren."[6] In his other writings, Minor was known to advocate public education reform, prison reform, and temperance. Though he certainly opposed the abolition of slavery (in his first letter he rails against "Garrison, and his will-o'-the-wisp, the *Liberator*"), he did write approvingly of the colonization of Liberia by former American slaves in an 1836 essay written for the *Southern Literary Messenger*.[7]

By the time Minor wrote his "Letters from New England," the hospitality of southerners had already achieved legendary status in American culture, having been celebrated by travelers to and citizens of the South for well over a century. As early as 1705, for example, Robert Beverly in his *History of Virginia* offered this description: "A stranger has no more to do, but to inquire upon the road, where any Gentlemen or good House-keeper Lives, and there he may depend upon being received with Hospitality. This good Nature is so general ... that the Gentry when they go abroad, order their Principal Servant to entertain all Visitors. ... And the Poor planters, who have but one bed will very often sit up, or lie upon a Form or Couch all Night, to make room for a weary Traveller."[8] According to Rhys Isaac in *The Transformation of Virginia*, many of the early social practices on which the legends of southern hospitality were based—particularly the "open-house customs" that conjured up legends of planters actively seeking out strangers to entertain—went out of fashion as early as 1800. Even so, hospitality was consistently identified by southerners and nonsoutherners alike as a distinguishing social characteristic of the wealthier planter classes and, increasingly in the 1800s, as a defining trait of the South more generally.[9]

Still, by portraying "Virginia hospitality" as a circumstance of the unique environmental and social circumstances of the South, Minor attempts to dispel some of the legendary aura surrounding southern hospitality, as well as the reciprocal stereotype that northerners are inhospitable. In doing so, he perhaps hoped to create a common ground of benevolence and goodwill between northerners and southerners. At the same time, his analysis also confirms many of the assertions that cultural historians of the antebellum South have made about the origins and social practices of southern hospitality—as well as their complex cultural meanings. For example, Minor cites the denser population patterns in the North as well as the common availability of inns for travelers as reasons why hospitality is not so readily associated with the North. Historians have similarly argued that the southern practices of hospitality were in part the consequence of the distances between and general isolation of plantations. If one made the effort to travel a great distance to visit, it seems logical that one was more likely to stay for a while. The South also had far fewer public inns than the North, so some instances of southern hospitality were the result of necessity; in these cases, strangers were often expected to pay for services rendered. At the same time, having strangers visit could provide a personal benefit to slave owners living in relative isolation, alleviating what some of them described in diaries and letters as the numbing boredom of a life without work. Entertaining strangers and learning news from travelers could alleviate the ennui of plantation life. Hence we have the accounts of planters sending their slaves to nearby inns to invite any guests to dine at their plantation, as well as the apocryphal anecdotes of planters forcing their hospitality on strangers at gunpoint.[10]

Hospitality between Men of Honor

According to Bertram Wyatt-Brown, many of the social practices of hospitality in the antebellum South were primarily "family-centered," and this can be tied to the unique social conditions of the South, relative to the North (notice how Wyatt-Brown's reference to "Yankeefied" traits in the following quote relies on the very sort of regional stereotypes that Minor's essay attempts to dispel):

> The planter of means was obliged to share the good fortune with less well-fixed kinfolk or be severely criticized for Yankeefied tightfistedness. When no other agency existed to care for the weak, the family was the first and often sole resort. Northerners likewise felt obliged to lend the helping hand, and did so with no less and no more willingness than Southerners. However, there was, one may speculate, a sense of deeper obligation in the South, if only because the slave holding states were slow to find public means to house the dependent and indigent—asylums, hospitals, poorhouses, or rooming houses. Moreover, it was much more dignified for a widowed distant cousin ... to accept an invitation for a visit that lasted over a year than to request a handout.[11]

But benevolence surely was not the primary impulse behind the polymorphous social practices that gave rise to the legendary southern hospitality of the antebellum South. Steven M. Stowe argues, for example, that many of the rituals of planter society in the Old South were an important way of establishing "legitimacy and dominance[,] ... the knot that the planters had to keep tight if they were to survive, and, as they steadily came to understand by the 1830s, if their survival was to have the strength of tradition." With the intensifying political climate and the changing economic and social conditions that emerged during the sectional crisis, such rituals became more and more attractive to "an increasingly embattled elite." As Stowe concisely explains, "There were ... advantages in a slave society to one's appearing larger-than-life and smoothly in charge." In other words, it was important to the elite planters that they had the opportunity to exhibit their power, privilege, and mastery, for mastery was, "after all, the final measure of things" in this particular social order.[12] Inviting guests and strangers into one's home provided just such opportunities to display one's self.

These practices of hospitality among antebellum southern planters were also deeply embedded within the complex social codes and rituals of southern honor. Many social exchanges of hospitality in the antebellum South—ranging from buying drinks and extending and accepting invitations to meals and entertainments to offering assistance to gentlemen in need—took place among men of honor seeking to establish their place in a hierarchical social order; consequently these exchanges could be fraught with a deep sense of competition, coercion, and potentially insulting meanings. As Wyatt-Brown explains, "Hospitality could not be divorced from honor, nor honor separated from the coercions of public opinion.... In all the coercions and obligations that surrounded the custom of hospitality there ran an undercurrent of deep mistrust, anxiety, and personal competition."[13] Kenneth Greenburg similarly approaches southern hospitality through the cultural lens of southern honor, arguing that the rites of hospitality provided an essential form of gift exchange among men of honor. According to Greenburg, gift exchanges—rather than, say, market transactions—were the most meaningful interactions among members of the wealthy planter class, helping to create a sense of community and belonging. This explanation is very much in line with Marcel Mauss's seminal work *The Gift: The Form and Function for Exchange in Archaic Societies*. According to Mauss's comparative analysis, the most important social aspect of a gift is the sense of indebtedness and obligation it creates in the recipient, an important means of creating a sense of solidarity and community. While gifts such as hospitality may seem "voluntary, in reality they are given and reciprocated obligatorily."[14]

According to Greenburg, in the patriarchal world of southern honor, even the relationship between a master and his slaves was imagined in these terms, with the "benevolent" master providing the slave the "gifts" of security, a home, and all the necessities of life; in fact, to be a master in the cultural economy of slavery was to be a giver of gifts: "Gifts flowed in only one direction in the master-slave relationship. Men of honor, on the other hand, both gave and received gifts. To be immersed in a system of reciprocal gift giving was to be part of a community of free men. In fact, gift exchange was one of the defining features of that community."[15] While a community of gift givers may sound pleasant on the surface, southerners often viewed gifts with suspicion. Certainly there is a coercive aspect in the giving of any gift because the recipient of the gift feels obliged to reciprocate. And among men of honor in the antebellum South, one had to have the means to reciprocate in style if one wanted to maintain one's status. In light of the insights of both Wyatt-Brown and Greenburg, it is no wonder, perhaps, that some economic historians have described the practices of hospitality among wealthy planters in terms of conspicuous consumption.[16] Whatever terms we use to describe the phenomena, without doubt the public display of personal wealth—whether through a home and its furnishings or the ritualized practices that occurred within—played an important role in defining one's place in the social order of wealthy southern planters. Or, as Rhys Isaac explains, "the stress on hospitality arose from and contributed to the sacred importance attached to the house. A man's homeplace—his plantation and house—were special extensions of the self."[17]

A fascinating and particularly disturbing example of this logic may be found in the diaries of James Henry Hammond, the South Carolina politician, virulent supporter of states' rights, and uncompromising defender of slavery based on white supremacy. In a long diary entry dated December 9, 1846, Hammond momentarily enters into a diatribe against his brother-in-law (Wade Hampton) and his political enemies, and his invective reveals the deep sense of competition that could often be the primary impulse behind hospitality: "The truth is he [Hampton] felt, and so did all his set, Manning, Preston, etc., my great superiority over them, and they could not ordinarily brook it. He threw away $30,000 to make his house . . . finer than mine. And he was galled, all of them were, that, besides every thing else, I beat them in *their own line*, furniture, balls, and dinner parties. All were exceedingly jealous of me. . . . Manning could not conceal it. He built his fine house in Clarendon to beat me."[18] The passage indicates the potentially competitive undercurrent of hospitality among wealthy southerners, but the entire context of this particular diary entry makes the solace Hammond takes in his hospitable displays of wealth especially disturbing. For the majority of Hammond's diary entry on December 9 is devoted to the circumstances surrounding his serial molestations of his four nieces (Wade Hampton's daughters), and the fact that his transgressions have recently become known to the Hampton family. As Hammond ponders the appropriate course of action, it becomes apparent that he can live quite comfortably with his guilty conscience—indeed, he often seems to feel justified in his appalling behavior; what he cannot abide is losing his place in the social order:

> Notwithstanding my letter to Hampton and my announcement of my intention to leave Columbia their low and cowardly malignity led them to seek a most pitiful revenge. Their desire was to black ball me and to mortify me and mine by keeping us out of Society and all respectable persons from coming to our House.... I was careful in selecting guests at my dinner parties and they were well attended. Our Ball [went] brilliantly, tho' I knew they endeavoured to keep many from attending.[19]

Though Hammond obviously represents an extreme example, his diary entries show that appearances were what mattered most to men of honor. Or as Kenneth Greenburg concisely puts it, "Southern men of honor were 'superficial.' They were concerned, to a degree we would consider unusual, with the surface of things—with the world of appearances."[20]

Lucian Minor, in contrasting northern and southern hospitality, laments just this sort of superficial, profligate, and self-aggrandizing display of hospitality suggested by the example of Hammond. His second letter from New England goes on to relate several anecdotal personal experiences from his travels as evidence of New England hospitality, and he draws the following comparative conclusions:

> The result of all my observation is, that the New Englanders have in their hearts as much of the *original material* of hospitality as we have; that, considering the sacrifices it costs them, and the circumstances which modify its application, they *actually use* as much of that material as we do; and that, although their mode of using it is less *amiable* than ours, it is more *rational*, more *salutary*—better for the guest, better for the host, better for society. And most gladly would I see my countrymen and countrywomen exchange the ruinous profusion; which, to earn, or preserve, a vainglorious name, pampers and stupefies themselves and impoverishes their country, for the discriminating and judicious hospitality of New England: retaining only those freer and more captivating traits of their own, which are warranted by our sparser settlements, our ampler fields, and our different social organization.[21]

As both Minor's comments and the historiography I have been reviewing suggest, the social practices of hospitality—in all their complexities and contradictions—formed an important element in both the daily lives of individuals in the antebellum South and their self-perception. At the same time, though, we should remember that the social practices I have been discussing were confined to a very small part of the southern population as a whole, namely, the wealthiest slaveholding population. Still, by the time of Minor's writing, there was an increasing tendency to identify hospitality as a defining characteristic of the entire region of the South and southerners more generally. This tendency was perhaps as much a result of increasing sectional tensions between the regions as it was a reflection of the social practices themselves. As political tension grew between the North and the South, southerners increasingly defined themselves as members of a distinct culture in opposition to the North; in this regard, it is worth noting that the term "southern hospitality" became common parlance only in the 1820s and 1830s, decades in which sectional tensions between the North and South were on the rise. Prior to this period, writers were more likely to refer more specifically—as Lucian Minor still did—to the hospitality of Virginians, Carolinians, Georgians, and the like.[22]

Hospitality among Sovereign Regions

Among the earliest uses of "southern hospitality" that I have found in print occurs in an 1826 travel sketch by A. Foster initially printed in the *Repository & Observer*, a New Hampshire newspaper, and reprinted in the *Western Recorder* magazine. The early publication of the sketch provides a convenient instance for reflecting on the important relationship that developed between the circumscribed hospitality exchanges carried out by the antebellum planter class and the emerging discursive practices that these exchanges generated in the national imaginary. In the short sketch, titled "Visit to a Southern Plantation," Foster recounts his few days' visit with "one of the wealthiest of the wealthy southern planters" residing along the Savannah River in South Carolina. He describes the plantation mansion as having an air of "aristocratical independence," surrounded as it is by nearly a thousand acres of corn and cotton, and the humbler cabins that house at least a hundred "servants" (Foster never uses the word "slave").[23] Following his description of the plantation itself, he offers the following assessment of southern hospitality (notice that the opening line implies a comparison with the hospitality of New England):

> The hospitality of South Carolina is proverbial in New-England, and it is not overrated. A *visit*, in the language of the country, is a stay of two or three days, or a month if you choose. Neither the gentleman nor the lady of the house feel themselves under any *obligation* to entertain a visitor with conversation, or with invitations to partake of the hospitality of the house. Every thing is at your command. The wine is upon the sideboard, the povisions [sic] upon the table at the regular hour, the servants are on hand to supply you with whatever you wish, and there is your chamber for retirement. Every member of the family attend to their regular duties, as though you had not been there. These, however, are

not so numerous, as not to allow you sufficient time for conversation. Thus relieved from all ceremony and all restraint, the host and guest are placed on equal terms; under equal obligation to entertain each other with conversation; under equal obligations to perform the common civilities of the dining table. This is the secret of southern hospitality and politeness, and certainly it is altogether the most genteel and agreeable mode of entertaining company.[24]

In the sketch certain qualities emerge that have been noted and will continue to be repeated about southern hospitality: that it is generous, elegant, and aristocratic, while also seeming less formal and more spontaneous than the social practices of the North. One can imagine that many northerners would find a depiction such as Foster's appealing. It is, in short, an aristocratic fantasy come true: "Every thing is at your command." Every "thing" in this case of course includes the human chattel belonging to the master of the house, here put at the disposal of the guest. During the visit, the guest becomes like a slave owner. One can imagine that southern hospitality held a certain seductive power for some visitors, creating a bond of equality between guest and host as privileged members of the white race. Of course, as noted earlier, this gift of hospitality also carries a sense of reciprocal obligation for the guest, and we can sense this obligation in Foster's refusal to use the term "slave," perhaps out of respect to his southern host. After all, one would not want to come across as an ungrateful guest. Moreover, even his decision to write of and publicize his amiable encounter with a southern slave owner is a sort of reciprocal gift. The overall result of this hospitality exchange is seen in Foster's conclusion: "On taking our leave in the afternoon, there were many expressions of good will on either side, and a warm invitation on the part of the family to repeat the visit."[25]

Considered through the lens of Pierre Bourdieu's theories on the forms of capital (economic, social, cultural), the rituals of hospitality exercised by the antebellum planter class can be seen as an embodied form of social and cultural capital, a reproductive and legitimating strategy that enhanced and extended its own power and influence. In short, the plantation owner who hosted A. Foster in 1826 was investing in his own social capital, and by extension, the social and cultural capital of the entire slaveholding elite. As Bourdieu explains, social capital is the result of a production process:

> The existence of a network of connections is not a natural given, or even a social given.... It is ... the product of investment strategies, individual or collective, consciously or unconsciously aimed at establishing or reproducing social relationships that are directly usable in the short or long term.... This is done through the alchemy of *consecration*, the symbolic constitution produced by social institution (institution as a relative—brother, sister, cousin, etc.—or as a knight, an heir, an elder, etc.) and endlessly reproduced in and through the

exchange (of gifts, words, women, etc.) which it encourages and which presupposes and produces mutual knowledge and recognition.... The reproduction of social capital presupposes an unceasing effort of sociability, a continuous series of exchanges in which recognition is endlessly affirmed and reaffirmed.[26]

This sense of recognition here extends to the visitor or guest from the North who experiences the ritual practices of southern hospitality. The goodwill and mutual recognition, however, are not limited in this case to A. Foster himself; as was increasingly the case, the hospitable exchange has been recorded and shared with thousands of northern readers, who in turn can imagine their own visit to an aristocratic plantation and the warm hospitality and leisure that such a visit would presumably entail. The amount of social capital an individual possesses depends, according to Bourdieu, "on the size of the network of connections he can effectively mobilize and on the volume of the capital (economic, cultural or symbolic) possessed in his own right by each of those to whom he is connected." This is an important thing to keep in mind when we consider the relationship between the limited social practices of the antebellum planters and the extensive cultural myth that these circumscribed practices generated in print and by word of mouth. The myth of southern hospitality exerted a "multiplier effect"—to borrow Bourdieu's term—on these limited social exchanges, essentially creating a larger field or connection network for interpreting them, while simultaneously imbuing "southern hospitality" with deeper symbolic value in the national imaginary.[27] Indeed, these original social practices were an investment that paid off *for generations* of white southerners, as the following chapters will show.

So even if the emergence of the discourse of southern hospitality was in some ways a result of increasing sectional division, it could nonetheless palliate these same divisions.[28] As an adaptable discourse about the South, southern hospitality provided southerners *and* northerners alike with a way of reimagining interregional social and political relationships in the face of growing sectional tension. Many northerners who traveled south and visited planters recorded very favorable impressions of the hospitality of benevolent southerners, and their stories of gracious southern hospitality would have appealed to many northern readers. Arousing such benevolent feelings between northerners and southerners could also prove useful in this time of heightened sectional political tensions. Lucian Minor's essay again provides a case in point. In the years immediately preceding Minor's "Letters from New England," sectional suspicions and animosities had been intensifying. In 1833 the country emerged unscathed from the nullification crisis that pitted the state of South Carolina against the Union, and in 1831 and 1832, William Lloyd Garrison established *The Liberator* and founded the New England Anti-Slavery Society, respectively. Also Nat Turner's bloody but ultimately unsuccessful slave rebellion, which many southerners believed was precipitated by abolitionist influence on the slave population, occurred in 1831. Evidence of such sectional suspicions emerges near the end of Lucian Minor's first letter from New England, when he pointedly attacks Garrisonian abolitionism. He begins by assuring his readers that "*abolition*, if not dead here, is too desperately feeble to give us an hour's uneasiness." Still, the amount of print he devotes to the subject at the end of this letter—not to mention the shift in tone accompanying it—indicates that he may have felt more uneasy than he let on. Whatever the case, he informs his readers that most "intelligent men" in the North view Garrison as a "miserable fanatic" and a "contemptible poor creature."[29] After relating a few anecdotes illustrative of abolitionism's lack of popular support, he offers the following summation of New England attitudes on slavery:

> I find almost every New Englander readily assenting to the positions,—That two millions of slaves could never be turned loose amongst us and live, while *we* lived: that the existence of the two *castes* in the same country, in a state of freedom and equality, is morally impossible: that emancipation, without removal, therefore, is utterly chimerical; that, unjustifiable as slavery is in the abstract, rights of property in slaves have been acquired, which, sanctioned as they are by the constitution, cannot be violated without an outrage, destructive at once of our social compact: that, let slavery be ever so wrong, abolition ever so just and easy, it is a matter which concerns *us alone*; and as to which, we are so sensitively jealous of extraneous interposition, that every agitation of the subject in other states is calculated to weaken our attachment to them, and bind faster the chains of slavery.[30]

This passage from the conclusion of Minor's first letter is the most overtly political moment in all five of his letters, and considering the more strident, even hectoring, tone he assumes here, it is perhaps understandable that he begins his second letter on more amicable, salutary terms, praising his northern hosts for the hospitable reception he has experienced in his travels. Moreover, his comments on slavery intersect with the concept of hospitality in two important ways. First, we should remember that the politics of hospitality is concerned with how we define the stranger or foreigner—and how we consequently treat them. Minor here portrays slaves as a foreign population living in our midst, a population of strangers who can never be welcomed into society as equals. When he says that "*we*" could not live with freed slaves as equals, he includes white northerners as well. Similarly, his conclusions regarding southern and northern hospitality in his second letter remind northern readers that they have more in common with southern slave owners than with southern slaves. Second, the discourse of southern hospitality also asserts regional boundaries by maintaining the sovereignty of the southern master. Hospitality and sovereignty are inextricably linked concepts, and both were important terms in the self-definition of antebellum southerners. To have hospitality, you must have a host, and to be a host implies a sense of mastery of your space. Accordingly, even as Minor reminds his readers of the South's famed hospitality, he also declares that slavery is "a matter which concerns *us alone.*" Minor's letters show how the discourse of southern hospitality provided a way of extending a hand of friendship to sympathetic northerners while subtly affirming southern sovereignty, exceptionalism, and superiority. Minor praises his northern brethren for their hospitality as a way of dispelling sectional prejudices and creating a common ground of benevolence and goodwill in their place. This, indeed, seems the overall goal of his series of letters. "The perpetuity of our union," according to Minor, depends on "more frequent intercourse" between the sections and the consequent "expurgation" of "long cherished prejudices"; or, as he concisely puts it in the conclusion of his fifth and final letter, "*The North and South need only know each other better to love each other more.*"[31]

Complicity, Slavery, and Southern Hospitality

Not all Americans, however, were sympathetic to such characterizations of southern hospitality; many in fact argued passionately that southern social practices simply could not even be called "hospitality." If antebellum southern hospitality is—in Minor's words—a "cheap" and "easy virtue," one that is contingent on slave labor, is it a virtue at all? This is just the sort of question abolitionists routinely asked in the decades leading up to the Civil War. For example, the same year that Minor's "Letters from New England" were published in the *Southern Literary Messenger,* George Bourne offered this assessment of southern hospitality in his *Picture of Slavery in the United States of America*:

> We frequently hear of liberality and kindness developed by slave-holders, but it is toward their own associates; and obviously more for show or fame, or from the force of example, than from principle; because they are not manifested in the proper form, and in favour of the legitimate objects.
>
> Slave-holders are often eulogized for their hospitality; and the fact implied is true, if by hospitality is intended a willingness to feast with those who are of similar character, habits, and principles. "They make dinners and suppers, and call their friends, their brethren, their kinsmen, and their rich neighbors, who bid them again, and make recompense to them,"—but who ever heard of a slave-driver's obedience to the Lord's admonition, Luke 14:12–14, to "make a feast, and call the poor, the maimed, the lame, and the blind" enslaved descendants of the

kidnapped Africans, who till his lands, and honestly can claim the reward of their unintermitting fatigue and toil? It is manifestly impossible, that genuine religious, moral, or even merely human sensibility can exist in the same heart where the arrogance of slavery reigns.[32]

Bourne reminds readers of the biblical injunction of hospitality and, with this in mind, argues that the sociable habits of southern planters do not really constitute hospitality.

Also in the same year and in a fashion parallel to Minor's "Letters from New England," an anonymous writer (going by "X Y Z") wrote a series of "Letters from the Southwest" (from Mississippi) that were published in the *American Anti-Slavery Reporter*. At the end of his third letter, from March 1834, the writer gives a lengthy account of and reflection on the hospitality he received when recently dining at a plantation home; his initial description of the dinner accords with similar reports in many travel narratives of the day:

> On the next day I was invited to a dinner party. And as it was rather late when I arrived, the dinner was already upon the table. So sumptuously was the table spread that I cannot stop to give any particular description, in short half the world seemed to have been plundered and heaped up before us. Various kinds of soup began the feast. Then came a dozen kinds of meats, and from the turkey down to the pigeon. After we had wandered over these numerous dainties—then appeared the dessert of sweetmeats, nuts, and almost every variety of West India fruits. After all came the Champaigne with many other species of wines. Such is the hospitality that turns the heads and hearts of so many grateful strangers. Few I believe have in the term of four years experienced more of southern hospitality than I have. And I truly appreciate the kindness of these generous men.[33]

Had the narrative ended here, it would have read much like scores of other travel accounts of the South, such as that cited earlier by A. Foster, in which visitors are amazed at the lavish abundance and generous spirit of the hospitality of the southern planter. But it does not end with this reflection on the generous planter class. Instead, like George Bourne, the writer cannot help but reflect on the role of the slave in the festivities:

> But my gratitude [to these planters] ought never to be weighed against truth and justice. I never sit down to these tables, without reflecting, that all these good things have been purchased at the expense of the groans and blood of human beings. While we eat and drink, the slave bleeds. While we are fanned by cool breezes in the pleasant galleries; the slave is wasting his life under an intense sun, or writhing under the merciless lash. While our eyes are delighted with elegant furniture and rich clothing, the slave is in rags, exposed to fevers,

and raising his weary eyes to the slowly moving sun,—longing for the night, that he may lose in the forgetfulness of sleep, the remembrance of wrongs that will soon end his days. O give me rough and barren New-England and poverty with it, rather than wealth and luxury at such a price.[34]

In contrast to the account written by A. Foster, which ends with a sense of equality and bonds of goodwill and sympathy between the guest and the slave-owner host, this passage attempts to redirect the reader's attention away from the slave owner's lavish hospitality and toward the toiling of the slave that makes such hospitable exchanges possible. The passage returns us to the idea that southern hospitality is a form of social and cultural capital that is fungible, or exchangeable in economic terms. While such pleasant social exchanges may seem on the surface like gratuitous wastage lavished on the guest, someone ultimately has to pay. Bourdieu describes the conversions that take place among economic, social, and cultural capital as acting in accordance with "the principle of the conservation of energy":

> Profits in one area [social, cultural, economic] are necessarily paid for by costs in another (so that a concept like wastage has no meaning in a general science of the economy of practices). The universal equivalent, the measure of all equivalences, is nothing other than labor-time (in the widest sense); and the conservation of social energy through all its conversions is verified if, in each case, one takes into account both the labor-time accumulated in the form of capital and the labor-time needed to transform it from one type into another.[35]

In their critiques of southern hospitality, antislavery advocates often tried to remind readers of the forced and unpaid "labor-time" that was required to produce this peculiar form of social capital. For example, consider figure 9, an illustration from *The American Anti-Slavery Almanac for 1839*, which almost seems like a pictorial representation of the passage just cited from "Letters from the Southwest." The image depicts two elegantly dressed couples dining at a well-appointed table. As one young slave girl approaches from the left with a serving dish, another stands near the window and fans the diners. Outside the window and behind this scene of domestic elegance we can see the horrors of slavery unfolding: an overseer whips a naked black figure tied to a tree as other slaves toil in the fields. Under the headline, "SOUTHERN ARGUMENTS TO STOP THE MOUTHS OF NORTHERN GUESTS," the caption reads, "A northern man goes south, sits at a table loaded from the slave's unpaid toil,—who eats his corn bread in the sun,—marries a slaveholder, and then—finds out that slavery is a divine institution, and defends it in southern and *northern* pulpits, religious newspapers, &c. For examples,—consult memory or observation."[36] From this perspective, the social practices of southern hospitality

FIGURE 9. "SOUTHERN ARGUMENTS TO STOP THE MOUTHS OF NORTHERN GUESTS," *The American Anti-Slavery Almanac for 1839* (New York: S. W. Benedict; Boston: Isaac Knapp, 1838), 23. Courtesy of American Antiquarian Society.

are nothing more than performative propaganda designed to enlist northerners in the cause of slavery. This charge was made repeatedly by abolitionists from the 1830s up until the Civil War.

For example, an 1840 article in the *Liberator* (excerpted from a longer article in the *New York Evangelist*) opens with the assertion that "there are multitudes of families in New England, who have sons and daughters, brothers or sisters, cousins, &c. at the South, whom Southern hospitality, avarice, or lust of power has won over to the system; and these, either writing home, or spending their summers among their friends, persuade them that the slaves are well treated, and that slavery is not so bad a thing, after all."[37] To abolitionists and others opposed to slavery on moral grounds, this seductive power of southern hospitality—its ability to transform one into a supporter of the system of slavery—could literally cloud moral judgment and imperil the soul. In a report prepared by the "Committee on Slavery" and adopted by the Methodist Anti-Slavery Convention in 1837, the committee, after noting how many northerners become slaveholders after settling in the South, admits, "We fear that even ourselves would be unable to retain our convictions of the claims of moral justice in the midst of southern hospitality."[38] And if individuals could be swayed from their moral convictions by the social practices of southern hospitality, could the proliferating discourse on southern hospitality in the world of print be just as damaging?

Rather than being accepted, then, as a natural and essential cultural attribute of the South, the South's claim of hospitality was openly debated and contested on ethical grounds during these decades of intensifying sectional crisis. Narrative accounts and images of southern hospitality routinely appeared in travel narratives, almanacs, pamphlets, and fiction. While southerners and sympathetic northerners typically portrayed southern hospitality as evidence of southerners' gracious civility and natural refinement, abolitionists and opponents of slavery vigorously questioned if southern social practices could be called "hospitality" at all. Indeed, arguments evolved emphasizing the complicity of the guest who is the recipient of southern hospitality. An example is seen in Louisa Jane Whiting Barker's "Influence of Slavery upon the White Population, by a Former Resident of Slave States," an American Anti-Slavery Society tract of 1855. Acknowledging that "the south is proverbial for its hospitality, kindness, and generosity," Barker reminds her readers that in the case of slave owners,

> it must be remembered that hospitality *costs* nothing. Guests ... are feasted on the proceeds of the labor of the slave, ... and why should not stolen wealth be lavishly bestowed? But one cannot infer, from the master's generosity toward the guest a similar one toward the slave. It were as wise to infer that the highway robber would show the same "honor" towards the traveller who chanced to fall in his power, as to his companions in crime, with whom he shares the spoils. I have attended a Christmas party where the table groaned under the weight of luxuries, and piles of wood blazed high on the hearth (for the day was bitter cold,) and the little boy who opened the gate to admit our carriage was bareheaded, barefooted, and had nothing but the remains of a cotton shirt to cover him. This was on the estate of one of the wealthiest men in South Carolina.[39]

As in the illustration from the *Anti-Slavery Almanac*, Barker implicates the recipients of southern hospitality, making them equal partners in the crime of slavery. While some readers—both of Barker's time and of today—may be inclined to dismiss such abolitionist responses to southern social practices as propaganda, doing so would deny both the important ethical questions these texts raise and the very historicity of antebellum discourses on hospitality, southern and otherwise. It is important to note that in these debates over southern hospitality, both sides basically agree on the reality of the social practices being described. The passages from George Bourne and Louisa Barker, along with the almanac illustration, all acknowledge that southerners are sociable and their habits of entertaining are elegant and luxurious. On the other side, Lucian Minor admits that southerners are able to enjoy hospitality so much because "the drudgery devolves upon [their] slaves" and also complains that some southerners are too fond of show, points underscored in the antislavery texts. Unlike the debates that took place in print over the reality of scenes of torture and cruelty on plantations (consider, for example, the response to *Uncle Tom's Cabin* from Stowe's contemporaries), the debate over southern hospitality was not about whether these social practices existed as reported; instead it hinged on whether these practices could be called hospitality at all. If we acknowledge hospitality as an ethical ideal, can a slave owner *ever* claim to be hospitable? And what of guests of that hospitality—are they implicated in the system of slavery by partaking of the master's generosity? And what if, like Louisa Barker, they partake of that hospitality only to write negatively of it after the fact—does their greater sympathy for the black slave make them bad or ungrateful guests? Southerners certainly felt so. In fact, a common criticism of antislavery northerners was that they abused the hospitality of southerners, a charge made so frequently that the abolitionist James Redpath, in his travels throughout the South to interview slaves, determined that he would not take any outright gift from a slave owner: "I had so often seen anti-slavery travellers accused of abusing hospitality, that, when I went South, I resolved to partake of none. I never even took a cigar from a slaveholder without seizing the earliest opportunity of returning it, or giving him its equivalent in some form."[40] Redpath's comments here suggest the degree of importance that both northerners and southerners and pro- and antislavery advocates placed on the concept of hospitality as it related to the South and the obligations it might entail.

Historiographies of Southern Hospitality

Despite the importance that many antebellum Americans placed on debates over the ethics of southern hospitality, these ethical questions surrounding southern hospitality have largely been lost to us over time as southern hospitality has passed into the realm of regional or, more accurately, national mythology. Cultural historians have gone a long way in explaining the origins of these practices of hospitality, what they meant to southerners, and how they figured within the complex code of southern honor, but they have not adequately considered the ethical questions raised in antislavery texts. These texts ask legitimate ethical questions that are relevant today since southern hospitality is still widely accepted as a unique quality of the region, and a thriving nostalgia industry still valorizes the culture of the Old South. As is often the case, certain historical narratives are privileged and become the norm, while other, alternative narratives are relegated to footnotes or forgotten entirely.

An instructive example of this is seen in Eugene Genovese and Elizabeth Fox-Genovese's *The Mind of the Master Class*, a massive study of the intellectual and religious world of the aristocratic planter class. More specifically, in the chapter titled "The Bonds of Slavery," the Genoveses spend numerous pages outlining "southern distinctiveness" and defining the main cultural differences between antebellum southerners and northerners. Throughout, they quote heavily from historical sources to illustrate their claims, and not surprisingly, they laud the hospitality of southerners on several occasions. Interestingly, rather than directly addressing abolitionist and antislavery critiques of southerners, the Genoveses spend several paragraphs citing examples of antislavery northerners praising the character of these aristocratic southern planters, including the example of abolitionist James Redpath, whom I just cited. The Genoveses introduce Redpath as "a South-hating abolitionist" who "admitted to being surprised by the slaveholders of Savannah: 'I saw so much that was noble, generous, and admirable in their characters.'"[41] From both the narrative arc of their chapter on southern character and their use of Redpath in this quote, the Genoveses make it seem as though southerners were so noble, hospitable, generous, and friendly that even their critics were swayed to their side. But they take this quote from James Redpath in particular out of context. Redpath's point is not that his hatred of southerners is transformed into admiration; rather, it is transformed into pity. The question of the rights of the slave always remains front and center in his consideration of the southern elite. Here is the quote cited by the Genoveses in a broader context:

> My opinion of the slaveholders, and my feelings toward them, were greatly modified during my residence in Savannah. I saw so much that was noble, generous and admirable in their characters; I saw so many demoralizing pro-slavery influences—various, attractive, resistless—brought to bear on their intellects from cradle to tomb, that from hating I began to pity them. It is not at all surprising that the people of the South are so indifferent to the rights of the African race. For, as far as the negro is concerned, the press, the pulpit, the bench, the bar, and the stump, conspire with a unity of purpose and pertinacity of zeal, which is no less lamentable than extraordinary, to eradicate every sentiment of justice and brotherhood from their hearts. They sincerely believe Wrong to be Right, and act on that unhappy conviction.[42]

If there is no sense of justice and brotherhood, can there indeed be hospitality among the southern elite? Not from Redpath's perspective. Interestingly, his analysis of the various forces that shape southern ideology anticipates Louis Althusser's formulation of Repressive and Ideological State Apparatuses.

Importantly, Redpath elsewhere pointedly contrasts "White and Negro Hospitality" in the South, and the slaves and free blacks come out on top in Redpath's accounting:

> Travelling afoot, and looking rather seedy, I did not see any of that celebrated hospitality for which the Southerners are perpetually praising themselves. They are very hospitable to strangers who come to them well introduced—who don't

need hospitality, in fact; but they are very much the reverse when a stranger presents himself under other and unfavorable circumstances. The richer class of planters are especially inhospitable. The negroes are the hospitable class of the South.[43]

Redpath here draws contrasts not only between white masters and black slaves but also between entirely different concepts of hospitality itself: between an elitist, aristocratic hospitality, which from Redpath's point of view is no hospitality, and a more democratic, universal hospitality. In drawing this contrast, he places southern hospitality amid broader discourses of hospitality that were coursing through American culture in the antebellum period, a subject I take up in chapter 2. To illustrate his claim regarding the hospitality of the slaves and the inhospitality of the masters, Redpath goes on to recount being lost at night and desperately seeking shelter as a storm approached. He was turned away from a planter's home, only to be taken in at a small "negro hut" that slept six in its one room.[44]

The picture of the "master class" drawn by Redpath is quite unlike the picture created by the Genoveses in *The Mind of the Master Class*.[45] In addition to taking Redpath's comments out of context in the example I just cited, they also fail to question southern hospitality in their depiction of the planter classes of the antebellum South. Certainly there are few scholars with the Genoveses' accumulated knowledge regarding the antebellum South, but their depiction of southern hospitality in *The Mind of the Master Class* is remarkably one-sided and overly celebratory, eliding the important ethical questions raised by antebellum critics of slavery such as James Redpath. If anything, their depiction naturalizes the myth of southern hospitality, making it something unquestioned, something that goes without saying when we talk about the South. What is especially interesting in this regard is that early in his career, Eugene Genovese's Marxist approach to the culture of slavery led him to interpret southern hospitality as an irrational form of conspicuous consumption among the elite planters, but as he shifted later in his career to a conservative and traditionalist perspective, he came to celebrate the antebellum southern elite, and the supposed continuity of "the southern tradition."[46] The Genoveses write in their prologue to *The Mind of the Master Class*, "We do not disguise . . . our respect for the slaveholders who constituted the hegemonic master class of the Old South. Nor do we disguise our admiration for much in their character and achievements."[47]

As Paul Ricoeur argues, the creation of historical narratives requires a certain amount of forgetting. The Genoveses' goal is to present the mind of the master class that they admire, believing that these historical figures of the past have much to teach us today. In doing so, they privilege some narratives and neglect or forget others, and in the case of their depiction of southern hospitality, it is the mind of the master class that has prevailed. Such a depiction of antebellum southern culture would seem to confirm the origins of what many today see as an unchanging southern tradition. But in this study, I hope to offer a more complete picture of the history of southern hospitality, one that is open to the ethical dimensions and debates that have surrounded this story about the South for nearly two centuries. For when it comes to southern hospitality, as many of these sources I have cited in this chapter suggest, there are other forgotten histories and voices, and these too have much to teach us today.

CHAPTER TWO

The Amphytrion and St. Paul; the Planter and the Reformer

Discourses of Hospitality in Antebellum America

While the Virginian Lucian Minor could praise "Yankee hospitality" during the early years of the sectional crisis in the 1830s, by the 1850s sectional tensions had caused regional prejudices, stereotypes, and suspicions to harden to such an extent that such praise would have seemed impossible. The language of "southern hospitality" emerged in the 1830s amid the growing sectional crisis that began to consume American culture, and it would only proliferate as the crisis intensified in the decades leading up to the Civil War. As Americans became preoccupied by the political and moral questions of slavery, they also defined, discussed, and debated what they had increasingly come to see as the unique attributes of distinctly different northern and southern civilizations. Southern hospitality emerged as a persuasive pro-southern and pro-slavery story in these debates. The role slavery played in the emergence of "southern hospitality" cannot be underestimated. In a material sense, slave labor made possible the social habits that came to be known in the 1830s as "southern hospitality," but in a broader cultural sense, the growing crisis over slavery likewise caused this emergent discourse on the South to proliferate through American culture from the 1830s to the Civil War. Against abolitionist attacks, the discourse of southern hospitality provided an affirmation and a defense of southern exceptionalism, as well as a subtle way of persuading nonsoutherners to both admire and identify with southerners and their cause. To understand the basis of this persuasive appeal, we should recognize the various and complex ways in which Americans thought about hospitality in this period. Theories of hospitality evolved dramatically over the course of the nineteenth century amid changing economic and social landscapes, and Americans consequently were forced to navigate competing and even contradictory discourses of hospitality. These discourses on hospitality permeated American culture at the time when the notion of "southern hospitality" was emerging. In this chapter, I will review a range of materials—essays, etiquette books, sermons, and fiction—to map out some different strands of antebellum discourse on hospitality, to place the discourse of southern hospitality on this map, and to show how a strong counterdiscourse to southern hospitality, namely, "abolition hospitality," also emerged during this period.

First, though, I would like to consider a short story published in *Godey's Magazine and Lady's Book* in 1853 because it provides a telling comparison of prevailing stereotypes of northern and southern hospitality that had hardened by midcentury. The story focuses on what happens to a family of aristocratic and hospitable southerners who are suddenly forced to seek out the miserly hospitality of their Ohio relations. Sardonically titled "Modern Hospitality," the story portrays southern hospitality as a noble virtue that is sadly vanishing in "modern" America. Little is known regarding Mrs. P. W. B. Carothers, the author of this chauvinistically pro-southern story, other than the fact that she was a resident of northern Illinois, where she briefly served as assistant editor of the Lockport, Illinois, newspaper.[1] Perhaps she was a transplanted southerner, or perhaps she was a northerner who held pro-southern, pro-slavery political beliefs. Whatever the case, she was one of the thousands of women who subscribed to and contributed to *Godey's*, and her story laments the changing practices of hospitality in America, particularly by providing a scathing critique of the hospitality of northerners, relative to southerners. "Modern Hospitality" details the changing fortunes of the Beverlys, a declining aristocratic family of Maryland planters, whose patriarch, "Colonel Beverly[,] was one of a remnant fast fading from [the] land . . . an 'old-school aristocrat.'"[2] Importantly, it is the colonel's aristocratic, openhanded hospitality, combined with his wife's failure to understand that their fortunes are diminishing, that ultimately drives the family to financial ruin. Colonel Beverly repeatedly warns his wife of their dwindling resources, but she fails to heed these warnings. Carothers's description of Mrs. Beverly's hospitality bridges two competing discourses of hospitality that were most prevalent in American culture at the time: one emphasizing conspicuous consumption and another privileging Christian benevolence: "She was exceedingly fond of show, and no representations or persuasion could induce her to relinquish or alter her luxurious style of living. Accustomed to believe hospitality a virtue, she rarely went abroad, but took special pride in entertaining company at home. And to her credit be it remembered, that the poor and wayfaring man were treated as kindly as he whose rank was known, and all his wants as beneficently supplied" (121). Without the last sentence, a reader might perhaps be inclined to dismiss Mrs. Beverly as a vain and selfish fool, but Carothers manages to shroud her ostentatious and prideful display in the mantle of Christian benevolence. Her habits are not so much the result of pride as they are the result of a Christian virtue taken to excess; hospitality to the poor traveler is a matter of noblesse oblige. The primarily female, bourgeois audience of *Godey's* is expected to empathize with the plight of Mrs. Beverly and her daughters, Gertrude and Cecilia, even though their excessive habits bring about the ruin of the family.

Upon the colonel's death, the Beverly women are forced to throw themselves at the feet of their cousin Hebe and her husband, Dr. Steele, residents of Ohio. The visit is not so much an encounter with extended family as it is a clash of two worlds—the modern and the archaic, the northern and the southern. The Beverly women are utterly flummoxed by the modern ways of Hebe: she keeps no servants, calling them "wasteful and troublesome," and extends no form of social hospitality to friends, calling it a "foolish" extravagance. Stunned by their frigid initial reception, Gertrude makes an allusion to "the kind, old-fashioned hospitality of her father, that placed all his guests at ease, and that . . . aided the wayfarer and entertained the traveller" (123). Hebe can only respond with ridicule. She calls it "ostentation in its worst form, because it spent on strangers what would minister to the comforts of a family"; she even "coarsely" suggests "that they were living illustrations of the truth of her assertion" (123). Hebe is the true villain in the story, as Carothers makes it clear that her stingy hospitality was "from will, not from want of means" (123). Hebe and Dr. Steele grudgingly allow the women to stay, but Hebe puts them to work cooking, cleaning, knitting, and caring for her baby. The Steeles become such tyrants that, in an interesting reversal, the Beverly women are reduced to a state not unlike their former slaves: "Their cousin's cottage had thus become their prison, from whence all society or amusement was banished, and where continual labor and confinement during the warm summer months was telling sadly on the health of these high-bred, delicate women" (125).

Luckily for the Beverly women, they are saved by the sudden appearance of two former suitors who had years earlier courted the daughters. Finally, in a just turn worthy of Grimms' fairy tales, the Steeles suffer a reversal of fortune and are forced to seek out the hospitality of Gertrude and her beau. Even so, we are told in the story's closing lines that "Hebe never learned, not even from Gertrude's graceful example, to practice the kindly rites of hospitality, that ancient virtue that yielded, even to foe, 'Rest and a guide, and food and fire'" (128).

The story's characters hail from Ohio, a free state, and Maryland, a slave state, and they embody easily recognizable and prevailing antebellum stereotypes of northern and southern social traits: Hebe is cold, aloof, miserly, and utilitarian; the Beverlys are warm, sociable, refined, and generous. Hebe's "modern hospitality" is no hospitality at all, presumably leaving readers nostalgic for the good old southern hospitality of legend. While it is easy today to recognize a certain nostalgia for the "Old South" in many contemporary iterations of southern hospitality, this short story shows that antebellum

Americans could already project their nostalgia onto the South while the "Old South" was still in existence.[3] This discourse of southern hospitality provided an appealing fantasy and a traditionalist alternative to the accelerating, increasingly modern, consumer culture Americans faced in their daily lives. What is particularly noteworthy in this story is the way the Christian ethos of hospitality is transferred to the aristocratic southerners, in direct contrast to the abolitionist texts cited in the previous chapter.

The fact that this story was published in *Godey's* in 1853 raises intriguing questions about audience and reception. *Godey's* was the most popular and influential women's magazine of the period, with a national readership of 150,000 by the time of the Civil War. The magazine emphasized gentility, refinement, and tasteful domesticity, and while this message was aimed primarily at women of leisure, it could also be enjoyed by members of the working classes who aspired to that lifestyle.[4] Importantly, the magazine avoided politics and conflict at all cost, instead viewing itself as a unifying force in the country. At the time "Modern Hospitality" was published, however, sectional animosities in the nation had reached a fever pitch following the passage of the Fugitive Slave Law of 1850. This law made hospitality to a runaway slave a federal crime and prompted Harriet Beecher Stowe to publish *Uncle Tom's Cabin* in 1852. The context of this story suggests the persuasive logic and political underpinnings of the discourse of southern hospitality in the antebellum period, but how would *Godey's* national readership have responded to such a comparative portrait of southern hospitality and its antithetical counterpart, northern hospitality?

Sacred and Secular Models of Hospitality in Antebellum America

Today we generally give little thought to hospitality as an ethical, moral, or religious question, let alone as a social practice with a long history of cultural meanings; instead, the term "hospitality" is generally considered a commodity or industry (as in the hospitality and tourism industry). As Tracy McNulty ruminates, "In some ways hospitality [today] seems to have barely survived its separation from the religious sphere, as seen by the disproportion between the enormous significance of hospitality in ancient times and up through the Enlightenment, and its present archaic, or even quaint, signification."[5] In contrast to today, Americans of the nineteenth century thought about hospitality obsessively and in ways that may seem foreign and perhaps excessive to us today. The question of hospitality was, for them, foregrounded in daily social rituals while also occupying a central place in their moral and religious worldviews. At the same time, their culture was changing in ways that produced often-competing claims on their sense of appropriate habits and attitudes of hospitality. On the one hand, they had inherited both the classical and the biblical traditions of hospitality, and they were not so far removed from Continental customs and manners. On the other hand, they believed in their status as a new, democratic republic and a hospitable asylum for immigrants, and they often self-consciously sought to define themselves against the customs of the Old World. Against the backdrop of accelerating consumerism and increasing class fluidity, both of which put unique pressures on traditional conceptions of hospitality, nineteenth-century Americans negotiated a variety of competing impulses concerning questions of hospitality. They were living through the very changes that Tracy McNulty describes: the slow separation of hospitality from its religious sphere in the context of rising economic interests and consumer impulses.[6] The discourse of southern hospitality that emerged amid this changing cultural landscape was particularly well suited to the emerging, consumer-oriented, cultural demands.

A brief survey of topics covered in chapter 11 of Julia McNair Wright's *The Complete Home*, published late in the century just after Reconstruction, suggests the contradictory quality of these obsessions over hospitality as a moral obligation, an important daily social ritual, and a growing form of consumerism. Titled "Hospitality in the Home," the chapter refers to hospitality as "the queen of social virtues" and lists *more than thirty* subheadings. From this list of topics, we can sense that Americans in the latter part of the century still saw hospitality as an important yet increasingly fraught subject:

> HOSPITALITY IN THE HOME—A garden of roses—The queen of social virtues—Varieties of hospitality—Ostentatious hospitality—Spasmodic—Nervous—Mrs. Smalley's hospitality—Common-sense hospitality—Hospitality without apology—Biblical hospitality—Selfish hospitality—Excessive hospitality—Elegant hospitality—The right kind of hospitality—A sewing society discussion—What our minister said—Bible instances—Plainness in hospitality—Manners of guests—As good as a sermon—A home view of hospitality—A guest-room—The mother's room—Abuse of hospitality—Good Samaritan deeds—The poor—A remarkable instance—Valuable thoughts—Decrease of hospitality—Old-time manners—A singular incident—Choicest form of rural hospitality.[7]

This rangy list of topics shows that Americans of the period saw hospitality as a practical concern involving daily social circumstances and choices, but they also considered these day-to-day rituals and interactions against the backdrop of broader ethical ideals (particularly through the Christian tradition): how does one guard against "selfish" motivations and "ostentatious" display in order to preserve the Christian spirit of hospitality? Even so, they sensed that hospitality's traditional role was diminishing in an increasingly secular and consumer-oriented culture. They lamented the "Decrease of hospitality" and the loss of "Old-time manners." Etiquette books from the period in particular reveal that in the contexts of rising consumerism, growing class fluidity, and the gradual cultural shift from a religious to a secular worldview, Americans espoused competing notions of manners and hospitality, what I would term aristocratic and republican. The former, more secular view, to which southern hospitality was aligned, emphasized refinement, display, and consumption and was essentially antidemocratic; exclusivity is in fact the essence of its appeal. The latter, republican model drew more on Christianity as its basis to offer a more democratic, inclusive, and potentially progressive alternative. In other words, the tension described by Derrida between the politics and the ethics of hospitality was a keenly felt, lived experience for antebellum Americans.

Two essays published within a year of the appearance of Lucian Minor's comparative discussion of northern and southern hospitality in "Letters from New England" provide a useful starting point for thinking about these aristocratic and republican models of hospitality because they offer what in many ways are two extreme, antithetical poles of the discourse: the secular and the sacred, the politics and the ethics, the sensibility of the amphytrion and the morality of St. Paul. The first of these essays, titled "The Science of Hospitality," was published in 1833 under the pseudonym "Hermes" in the *New-York Mirror*, a popular weekly newspaper "Devoted to Literature and the Fine Arts." The exact identity of this essay's author is not known, but Hermes also published in the same year several romantic historical fictions and sketches in the *New-York Mirror* and the *Philadelphia Album and Ladies' Literary Portfolio*.[8] In "The Science of Hospitality," the author draws on the classical and Old World traditions of hospitality to emphasize consumption, taste, refinement, and aristocratic exclusivity. He claims that he was inspired to write about hospitality by his "perusal" of a recently published French work titled *Devoirs de l'Amphytrion*, which he translates as the "Science of Hospitality." Citing Molière's play *Amphytrion* for the "fashionable title of the host," the essay traces a concise history of the "science of hospitality" from antiquity through contemporary genteel society. Hermes emphasizes hospitality as both a classical tradition and an Old World, aristocratic privilege, but never as a moral imperative or ethical ideal. Instead, the essential principles of the science put forth are luxury, indulgence, refinement, and display. The author contends that it was the ancients who truly understood the science of hospitality, for they were concerned with the entire sensual experience of entertaining, developing over time an increasingly complex code of manners: "Manner, elegance, and taste in arrangement had for them an engrossing charm, and every thing that could delight the ear or eye, was joined to the gratification of the palate.... As luxury increased, new and indispensable ceremonial rules were introduced for the conduct of the guest and host." Those who failed in the proper exercise of the rules "lost caste." Such elaborate, extravagant, and exclusive practices represent the pinnacle of hospitality for Hermes; contemporary fashionable society pales in comparison with the extravagance of this past. In turning to the present, the author turns his attention to the proper conduct of the amphytrion, or host, in contemporary society. The ultimate goal of the host is to "secure the greatest amount of personal comfort to all, and render a man as much at ease and as well served in a party of a hundred, as though he were sitting alone at the table." Rather than treat all guests equally, however, the amphytrion must draw proper distinctions among his guests. Hermes laments the "abominable fashion" of certain hosts who merely pass plates around the table "indiscriminately," an act that will inevitably "destroy all convivial delight" at the table, breeding resentment in its place. In contrast, the properly discriminating host ranks his guests according to both their social standing and their appetites. For Hermes, hospitality is not an ethical ideal so much as an idealized form of consumption that also reinforces social hierarchies. While he concedes that the complete code of table manners contained in the French text he perused "may appear ridiculous to the uninitiated, and those who imagine the operation of eating the sole object of dinner," they are nonetheless essential to "the finished gentleman." Of those who would question the importance of such manners, he concludes, "Such incorrigibles we leave to be the Hectors of boarding-houses and steamboats, and to bring our national habits into disrepute with . . . discerning travellers."[9] Overall, the vision of hospitality promoted by Hermes is secular, Continental, aristocratic, and—as indicated in this final quote—ultimately suspicious of the social fluidity of American democracy in the nineteenth century. One can imagine that readers who agreed with the author of this essay would likewise be inclined to look favorably on legends of southern planters' elegant and aristocratic hospitality.

How different is the vision of hospitality put forth in the essay "On Hospitality," published in the Quaker magazine the *Friend* in January 1834. Despite Hermes's secular emphases, many Americans in the antebellum period thought of hospitality first and foremost as a biblical injunction, and this second essay portrays hospitality as a Christian ideal with profound and potentially far-reaching social consequences. The exact identity of the author, who published under the initials C.C.O., is not known, but he or she also published a handful of devotional poems and essays in the *Friend* between August 1833 and February 1834, including an essay advocating for female preaching and ministry. C.C.O.'s essay "On Hospitality" shows that the ideal of Christian hospitality, in its purest form, stood as a powerful counterdiscourse to conspicuous consumption and the sort of writings on hospitality that emphasize luxury and refinement. The epigraph for the essay, for example, implies nothing less than an alternative definition of "luxury," urging the reader, "Press thou the bashful stranger to his food, / And learn the *luxury* of *doing good*."[10] Readers are challenged to resist the physical temptations of a consumer society, for these, according to the author, are nothing but false luxuries when compared to the true luxury that arises from exercising the Christian spirit of hospitality. C.C.O. cites the apostle Paul's attention to the "social duties of life," claiming that Paul understood "that they might be used as instruments of great power in the advancement of Christianity." This "rich repast" of Christian hospitality—which is "pure and blameless"—is "totally unknown to those who court the false joys of folly and sensuality."[11]

An open attitude toward the stranger is central to this pure Christian ethic of hospitality, and as is often the case in such Christian discourse on hospitality, the author cites Paul's injunction, "Be not forgetful to entertain strangers—for thereby some have entertained angels unawares." As an example, C.C.O. cites the story of Lot's hospitality to the angels sent to destroy Sodom. As a reward for his hospitality to these strangers, Lot was spared from the destruction of the city. Opening oneself to the stranger and treating the stranger as an equal member in the body of Christian fellowship heighten mutual feelings of benevolence and love, which in turn can advance God's work in the world. The author in the conclusion again cautions readers to be wary of the worldly distractions that are commonly mistaken for hospitality. Unlike the "Science of Hospitality" and its emphasis on elegant display and the drawing of social distinctions, the ideal Christian ethic of hospitality is about simplicity, justice, equality, and, ultimately, the very erasure of such social distinctions:

> Its demands upon us are in all cases limited by the strictest laws of justice. It does not ask robbery for its promotion—and sickens at the thought of being supported by the dues that belong to others. It aims to be associated with prudence—and there is no mansion which it loves to inhabit more than that wherein moderation and temperance reside. It consists more in feeling than in the display of equipage, and sideboards loaded with gold and silver. Cordiality is the welcome which it most desires—and the hand held out with this sentiment, is always esteemed and reciprocated, whether it be the rough one of humble labour, or the more delicate one of titled distinction.[12]

The social rites of hospitality, when carried out lavishly, are not praiseworthy, particularly when they are supported by "robbery" or the "dues that belong to others," as in the case of the slave labor that made southern practices of hospitality possible. The author here extends the philosophical exchange of hospitality beyond that of a simple guest-host relationship to larger questions of power. The concern of hospitality, in other words, shifts from a concern with *rites* to one with *rights*.[13] In contrast to "The Science of Hospitality"'s description of the way the rites of hospitality assert class boundaries and social hierarchies—what Derrida would call the politics of hospitality—this essay instead proposes hospitality as an ethical ideal that erases those very boundaries: the common laborer is placed on equal footing with the titled gentleman. In these two essays, then, we see two opposite poles in the antebellum discourses of hospitality: put simply, one expresses an exclusionary politics of hospitality, and the other strives toward an infinite ethics of hospitality.[14]

Philosophically considered, though, this progressive and infinite ethical ideal is never attained; instead, hospitality in this form is a horizon that is always opening before us and challenging us, always presenting strangers in new forms—and with new rights claims. Even in the Quaker essay "On Hospitality," the distinction between politics and ethics, between rites and rights, becomes blurred to a certain extent, particularly if we recall the full details of the story of Lot entertaining the strangers, who were in fact angels sent to destroy Sodom. More specifically, the author here does not mention one particularly troubling detail from the story: that when a mob of Sodomites threatened the strangers who were Lot's "sacred guests," he offered his virgin daughters to the mob in their stead. Reflecting on this aspect of the story, Mireille Rosello finds it problematic "that hospitality should be presented as a law that can be in contradiction with another law (a woman's honor) or that a woman's honor cannot be included in a definition of hospitality." As Rosello asks, "Is the ultimate lesson, then, that women can never be guests, that they can never be hosts?"[15] Even this oft-cited biblical example illustrates a politics of hospitality in which the rights of the stranger outweigh the rights of certain individuals within the household; Lot's choice makes all women strangers in a patriarchal world. It is not too difficult to make the leap from the exclusionary gender politics of this biblical scene to the exclusionary racial (and gender) politics in the southern plantation home, with white southerners and their guests being served by slaves who could never be considered guests. Overall, the story of Lot again shows the ways that hospitality defines the boundaries between the stranger who can be welcomed as a "sacred guest" and the absolute other or alien who has no rights, even as an inhabitant of the household.[16]

Hospitality as Etiquette

Etiquette books were essential to codifying domestic habits during the antebellum period when southern hospitality was developing as a recognized discourse in the national imaginary, and these texts provide useful reminders that hospitality was an essential social ritual of the day-to-day life of many Americans. They also reveal the pressures Americans faced as they tried to determine the obligations and demands of hospitality in an altering cultural landscape. The etiquette books and domestic manuals I now turn to were directed toward a national rather than a specifically regional readership, and they generally sought to efface regional distinctiveness in favor of promoting national identity. Generally speaking, etiquette rules for the middle and upper classes in the North were likewise the etiquette rules for the middle and upper classes of the South. In fact, it was primarily women from the North who promoted and disseminated an understanding of etiquette in the South.[17]

Hospitality is a central principle in these etiquette books, both the broad moral concept of hospitality and the minute particulars of being both a guest and a host. For example, Florence Hartley's *The Ladies Book of Etiquette and Manual of Politeness* devotes ten of the book's twenty-six chapters to the etiquette guidelines for being either a "hostess" or a "guest." Visiting, entertaining, and dining were essential to ideas of social order, so in most social interactions among the middle and upper classes, one was usually obliged to assume one of the two roles and play it by the rules. At the same time, however, Hartley claims that the basis for these etiquette rules can be traced to Christian principles. In the introduction, she asserts,

> In preparing a book of etiquette for ladies, I would lay down as the first rule, "Do unto others as you would others should do to you." You can never be rude if you bear the rule always in mind, for what lady likes to be treated rudely? True Christian politeness will always be the result of an unselfish regard for the feelings of others, and though you may err in the ceremonious points of etiquette, you will never be impolite. Politeness, founded upon such a rule, becomes the expression, in graceful manner, of social virtues. The spirit of politeness consists in a certain attention to forms and ceremonies, which are meant both to please others and ourselves, and to make others pleased with us.[18]

Hartley's explanation seems to have it both ways: on the one hand, politeness is a transcendent Christian principle, and on the other hand, politeness is attention to historically and culturally situated "forms and ceremonies," such as leaving an appropriate card when calling on acquaintances or using the correct utensil at the appropriate moment when dining. Like many texts of the period, Hartley navigates the inherent tension between the ethics and the politics of hospitality.

Many etiquette books of the period contrast the old, aristocratic customs of the Old World and the unique needs of the young American nation.[19] *The Art of Good Behavior*, for example, claims to be fulfilling the need to teach manners to all the upwardly mobile Americans who were inevitably finding themselves entering into higher social realms. The book's subtitle claims it to be "A complete guide for Ladies and Gentlemen, particularly those who have not enjoyed the advantages of fashionable life." This more democratic book of manners boldly proclaims, "In this free land, there are no political distinctions, and the only social ones depend upon character and manners. We have no privileged classes, no titled nobility, and every man has the right, and should have the ambition to be a gentleman—certainly every woman should have the manners of a lady."[20] Notice the contradiction here: in this democratic country manners should be for all, and in this same democratic country the only "social" distinctions are based on these very manners.

Even though some texts profess to be filling this democratic need, they can at times reveal anxiety about perhaps too much democracy, showing the same sensitivity to the perception that Americans are rude and unrefined and calling to mind the "Hectors of the boarding houses" lamented by the author of "The Science of Hospitality."[21] Americans prided themselves on democratic principles, but in an emerging consumer culture, status and lifestyle could potentially be purchased. An example of this contradiction may be found in *The Art of Pleasing; or the American Lady and Gentleman's Book of Etiquette*. Again, the discussion of manners and etiquette is placed in a uniquely American context. America is a new land that cannot rely on the jaded forms of the Old World: "The want of a book adapted to the requirements of THE PEOPLE has been one great obstacle to the study of THE ART OF PLEASING; as almost, if not all the works offered have been republications of foreign books adapted to the atmosphere of courts and palaces, and filled with forms and ceremonies useless and ridiculous as applied to this land of liberty and equality." The author boldly promises that this book "will prove equally acceptable to the laborer, the mechanic, the clerk, the merchant, and the man of wealth, leisure, and refinement."[22] Interestingly enough, despite the author's claim that too many etiquette books are simply republications of foreign titles not suited to American democracy, when discussing hospitality in the home, sections of the text are plagiarized from Baroness de Calabrella's *The Ladies' Science of Etiquette, by an English Lady of Rank*, first published in 1844, and republished in a variety of forms over the next two decades. The baroness's text emphasizes genteel refinement and the importance of appearances, and *The Art of Pleasing*'s discussion of hospitality lifts entire passages from her earlier work, including a discussion of hospitality that privileges elegance, refinement, and the material accoutrements of entertaining over any notion that hospitality has an ethical dimension. Indeed, the hierarchy of hospitable behavior expressed in the text is contingent on material wealth.[23]

Still, *The Art of Pleasing* in the end puts forth a much simpler, more democratic approach to hospitality than the baroness does. In a chapter titled "Etiquette of the Dinner Table," for example, the author warns against ostentatious display: "Too great a display of plate, or too dazzling a show of crystal, unless upon some particular occasion, is in bad taste. Simplicity is the soul of good breeding, . . . and to put your visitor on a footing with yourself, is the best compliment you can pay him . . . let the table be set out tastefully, but not ostentatiously; in a manner suitable to your station, but not, as it were, to exhibit your pride and wealth, more than your hospitality and social feeling." In contrast to Baroness de Calabrella, the emphasis here is on the benevolent spirit and feeling that lie behind hospitality rather than the material contexts in which its rituals are enacted. To further emphasize the point, the author concludes by claiming, "The greatest hospitality is generally to be found among persons of small income; who are content to live according to their means, and never give any great dinners; for nothing can be further from true hospitality, than the spirit in which such entertainments are usually given."[24] An 1846 essay in *Godey's* titled "A Chapter on Hospitality," by Mrs. C. M. Kirkland, makes similar points, warning against "ostentatious hospitality" and claiming that "the poor—and children—understand hospitality after the pure model of Christ and his apostles." Kirkland laments the growing commodification of hospitality as well as the increasing emphasis on social display, which she sees as a false, Old World influence: "We have attempted to dignify our simple republicanism by far-away, melancholy imitations of the Old World; but the incongruity between these forms and the true spirit of our institutions is such, that all we gain is a bald emptiness, gilded over with vulgar show.... When shall we look at the spirit rather than the semblance of things—when give up the shadow for the substance?"[25]

Catharine Beecher's *Treatise on Domestic Economy*, published first in 1841 (and later expanded with Harriet Beecher Stowe as *The American Woman's Home*), provides a unique interpretation of hospitality as a Christian imperative with an important role in America's uniquely democratic social order. She first cites hospitality as a Christian obligation: "There is no social duty which the Supreme Law-giver more strenuously urges than hospitality and kindness to strangers, who are classed with the widow and the fatherless as the special objects of Divine tenderness."[26] She immediately clarifies, however, that this Christian principle is especially important in America in light of its migratory populations and fluid economic order. But while the other texts I've discussed talk of the need for manners for upwardly mobile citizens, Beecher focuses on the *downwardly* mobile members of the population, those who find themselves strangers to American prosperity:

> There are some reasons, why this duty [of hospitality] peculiarly demands attention from the American people.
>
> Reverses of fortune, in this land, are so frequent and unexpected, and the habits of the people are so migratory, that there are very many in every part of the Country, who, having seen all their temporal plans and hopes crushed, are now pining among strangers, bereft of wonted comforts, without friends, and without the sympathy and society, so needful to wounded spirits. Such, too frequently, sojourn long and lonely, with no comforter but Him who "knoweth the heart of a stranger."[27]

Beecher consequently encourages her readers to pay special and immediate attention to "new-comers" who enter their communities, and she also extends this principle of hospitality to the stranger to social gatherings, saying that in these instances "the claims of the stranger are too apt to be forgotten; especially, in cases where there are no peculiar attractions of personal appearance, or talents, or high standing." Instead of being overlooked, such an individual "should be treated with attention, *because he is a stranger*; and when communities learn to act more from principle, and less from selfish impulse, on this subject, the sacred claims of the stranger will be less frequently forgotten."[28] Such a sentiment brings us back to the ethical ideal of hospitality espoused in the Quaker essay "On Hospitality."

Overall, these etiquette books and essays on hospitality show Americans negotiating among competing traditions and discourses of hospitality. In the accelerating consumer marketplace, the subject of hospitality would only grow increasingly complicated over the course of the nineteenth century. Still, while general discourses on hospitality became more disparate and dissimilar, the discourse of southern hospitality became both more clearly defined and diffusive, helping to codify the sense of regional difference and distinctiveness between the North and the South. The aristocratic image of southern hospitality had the capacity to appeal to both southerners and nonsoutherners, but this image of southern hospitality was also the most difficult to reconcile with other prevailing discourses on hospitality of the antebellum period, namely, the Christian and the "republican" views outlined above.

Making a Case for Southern Hospitality: C. H. Wiley's *Roanoke*

Antebellum southerners probably felt no contradiction when defining themselves as Christian in their morality, republican in their political philosophy, and aristocratic in their manners, yet the irony could be noticeable to outsiders. When the English novelist William Makepeace Thackeray toured the United States in the 1850s, he noted the paradox of having an aristocratic Virginia hostess lecture him on "republican simplicity." He "threw himself back in his chair, gazed at the beautiful artistic frescoes on the ceiling, worthy of a royal palace, and with arms extended exclaimed, 'Oh! Mrs. Stanard, I do admire this republican simplicity.'"[29] As an outsider, Thackeray could see the incongruity of the situation, but Mrs. Stanard of Richmond probably really believed in the ideals of republican simplicity, just as she probably believed that the Bible mandated the existence of slavery, and that entertaining an illustrious English author was a chance to show him the truth behind southerners' legendary hospitality.

As Michael O'Brien has meticulously argued in *Conjectures of Order: Intellectual Life and the American South, 1810–1860*, southerners lived amid contradictions in a fluid world where "little settled into coherence"; as O'Brien explains it, "in the early nineteenth century, Southerners were national, postcolonial, and imperial, all at once, and partly invented their culture in the tense encounters among these conditions." They were national in that they had helped to create the United States through revolution and had provided a significant amount of its early political leadership. They were postcolonial in that, more so than in the North, their intellectual traditions were still conditioned by the Old World, even though they had thrown off the political authority of that world. They were imperial in that they ambitiously pursued an expansionist plan to "make an empire of liberty and slavery." It was largely through these efforts that the disparate southern states came to be known collectively as "the South." According to O'Brien, these three conditions of the South "mingled unstably," producing, on the one hand, "doubt" and "cultural anxiety," and on the other hand, a sense of "mastery, "moral sanction," and "certainty."[30] These lived conflicts and contradictions in antebellum southern identity can be seen in the way they imagined what, alongside the concept of honor, was perhaps their most boasted regional characteristic: their hospitality. As was the case with all Americans, southerners inherited a variety of traditions and discourses of hospitality. They, like other Americans, saw hospitality as both a Christian moral imperative and a pleasing social ritual; more than other Americans, they also saw it as a manifestation of an inherently aristocratic, hierarchical social order. To some outsiders, this aristocratic tradition of southern hospitality might seem to conflict with both republican idealism and Christian morality, but southerners did not necessarily recognize such conflict.

Calvin Henderson Wiley's 1849 historical romance, *Roanoke, or, Where Is Utopia?*, provides an instructive example of the contortions necessary to reconcile southern aristocratic ideals of hospitality with, on the one hand, a Christian ethic of hospitality and, on the other, republican principles of equality. *Roanoke* is a hyperbolic celebration of southern cultural exceptionalism, or, as Wiley terms it, the region's "ancestral virtues" (12). Wiley's novel was republished several times and under different titles between 1849 and 1866.[31] A native of North Carolina, Wiley was a lawyer, editor, and author who also served as superintendent of common schools for the state of North Carolina from 1853 to 1865. Over the course of his career in education, he earned a reputation as one of the most important advocates for educational reform in the South, described variously as "the missionary of popular education in North Carolina" and the "Horace Mann of the South."[32]

Set in coastal North Carolina in the days leading up to the American Revolution, *Roanoke* attempts to construct an origin myth of regional identity that is both deeply patriotic and chauvinistically southern.[33] Not surprisingly, then, the question of hospitality figures prominently in the book, but Wiley's portrayal of it as it pertains to southern identity is often conflicted and at times contradictory. The text shifts from first asserting that hospitality is a moral obligation to the stranger, to then railing against the exclusionary practices and politics of an aristocratic hospitality, to finally reasserting the seeming naturalness of such aristocratic hierarchies and practices.

The "Utopia" of Wiley's title refers both to the novel's idealized heroine and the setting of its opening chapters: a primitive coastal community along the Outer Banks, whose citizens engage in the commercial servicing—and occasional plundering—of shipwrecks, as well as in a ritualized form of wife swapping that, in a scene that oddly echoes auction scenes in antislavery literature, threatens to separate the young white heroine, Utopia, from her mother. Set in the days leading up to the American Revolution, the novel's early chapters detail how the hero, Walter Tucker, a proud young woodsman from the interior, arrives in the settlement of Utopia with his father, Dan Tucker, a rustic known for his prowess as a fiddler. Dan has brought Walter to Utopia to seek employment, but Walter, feeling himself to be above the primitive Utopians, sullenly resists the prospect of living among them. Despite the Utopians' apparent backwardness and simplicity, however, we are told that they "were profusely generous and hospitable" to strangers and particularly to anyone unlucky enough to suffer a shipwreck off the Outer Banks. The early chapters of the novel foreground and celebrate the simple hospitality of these Utopians, most notably in the chapter titled "Utopian Hospitality," where they willingly open their hearts to strangers in need, in this case the English victims of a shipwreck that suddenly appears off the coast: "The passengers . . . found, to their surprise, that they were among a kind and considerate people, who ministered to their wants with a tact and delicacy not to be expected in a race so rude. . . . All seemed to feel for and sympathize with the forlorn and suffering strangers" (27–28). The "utopian" hospitality that Wiley initially celebrates is not the aristocratic hospitality of the planter classes, whose social practices generated the legends of the South's hospitality; rather, it is the simple hospitality of these rustic Utopians. Though the legends of southern hospitality were initially generated by the practices of aristocratic planters, as it became a generally accepted and celebrated cultural trait of the South, all white southerners could be identified with it, including, in this case, the unrefined, wife-swapping, shipwreck-scavenging Utopians.

As the novel unfolds, Wiley draws a pointed contrast between this simple hospitality of the Utopians and the social practices of the elite, aristocratic society of New Bern, the capital of the colony, where much of the novel's action takes place. Most of the novel seems an outright attack on such aristocratic and exclusive social orders. The young hero, Walter Tucker, aspires to be accepted in these exclusive social circles, but due to his common origins, he seems to have little hope of achieving this goal, a fact made all the more painful by his developing love interest, Alice Bladen, a member of the English aristocracy and survivor of the shipwreck at Utopia. Walter Tucker pines away for Alice for much of the novel but finds himself lost between two worlds: the rustic, backwoods way of life of his father and the Utopians, and the aristocratic circles to which he aspires, particularly among the social elites of New Bern.

Possessing a strong sense of honor, courage, and pride, Walter feels he is above the Utopians and likewise is often ashamed of his own father, both for his father's uncouth manners and for the company he keeps. Dan Tucker is often accompanied by Zip Coon, a fiddling companion who hails from Virginia. Walter faces constant embarrassment because of the uncouth behavior of the two fiddlers. Conversely, he repeatedly feels slighted and shunned by his social betters, and he consequently rails against the arbitrary power of the caste system on several occasions. His diatribes against this aristocratic social order fit the democratic spirit of the novel's setting in the days leading up to the revolution, but they seem to run against the aristocratic sensibilities of elite southern culture (not to mention against the discourse and logic of slavery). For example, Walter lectures Utopia on the arbitrary power of the aristocratic classes of New Bern:

> Now I'll tell you my notions of the world. Some men, by fraud, and violence, and meanness, make fortunes and get into power; then they make laws, and make themselves titles, and are called the higher ranks. When they get into these ranks they become separated, in heart, and soul, and feeling, from those who are just like them, only in a lower rank; they think themselves a superior race, and they talk about their blood as if it were not all descended from Adam, and as if they did not rise from the common people.... They look on us as made for them; and when they condescend to speak kindly to us, they expect to make use of us just as we make use of horses and cattle, and feed them and use them kindly. (76)

Walter seems here to have learned the lesson that Thomas Sutpen learns when sent to the back door in Faulkner's *Absalom, Absalom!*: power is for whoever will take it, and once taken, it is to be maintained by whatever means necessary. Unlike Sutpen, who cynically and unscrupulously seeks to attain and hold power, however, Walter believes honor is real and not merely superficial; he still hopes to *earn* his place among the social elite. When he feels that he has been insulted by Alice Bladen, whom he loves from afar, he embarks on a series of heroic adventures against the backdrop of the impending revolution, determined to earn a place at the table of power and in the highest circles of society.

The novel's plot often hinges on a politics of hospitality, as Walter repeatedly feels snubbed by both the New Bern social elite and, later, the leaders of the revolutionary movement. A good example occurs after he saves the life of Frank Hooper, a frail, bookish young gentleman whom Walter finds wandering the depths of the Dismal Swamp. Walter and Frank quickly form an unusually intense, platonic bond, but when Walter manages to bring Frank to Rock Castle, home of Cornelius Harnett and unofficial headquarters of the rebellion leadership of Harnett and Colonel Ashe, Walter bristles at what he senses to be the unequal treatment offered to him and Frank Hooper. Frank, still recovering from his experiences in the swamp, is offered a bed, while Walter is not.

> His cheek flushed as he saw that he was not treated as the equal of Frank Hooper; and his proud heart swelled and throbbed against his bosom as if determined to force its way from its prison....
>
> "You might kneel and kiss my hand," thought Walter, "but not even this would be sufficient, as long as you treat another and my equal as if I were only his dog or his slave.... May I be cursed if I ever sleep upon the bed or break the bread of a house where I'm regarded as an inferior," said the young hero to himself as he noiselessly opened the door and walked out, for what purposes he hardly knew, except that of escaping from the roof of one of those aristocrats whom he so much disliked. (112)

Remarkably, after rejecting the hospitality of Harnett and Ashe because of this snub, Walter immediately accepts the hospitality of one of the slaves on the estate. This action can be interpreted, on the one hand, as his ultimate rejection of these aristocrats, or, on the other, as an unconscious projection of his own debased self-perception. Whatever the case, after spending the night in the slave quarters, he returns to Rock Castle and leaves a small sum of money for Colonel Ashe and Harnett to cover the previous evening's meal. Though his pride will not allow him to accept the charity of these aristocrats, he is willing to accept the hospitality of a slave. Still, Wiley's novel is in no way progressive in its racial politics.[34]

Walter's diatribes against the aristocracy and his apparent belief in the natural rights of man make him naturally sympathetic to the revolutionary fever sweeping the colonies, and he does, indeed, take part in the revolution and become a hero at the Battle of Moore's Creek. But he still hopes to enter elite society through his actions. His military heroics seem for a moment to earn him the respect he has been seeking throughout the novel, but once again he is embarrassed by the antics of his father and Zip Coon, who put on a rollicking performance following the military victory. Their behavior seems to resign Walter to his fate and his plebian caste; he is "mortified beyond expression" and "instantly ... [bids] Alice Bladen and aristocratic society a mental farewell for ever" (134).

The concluding chapters, however, veer away from this seeming critique of aristocratic society by providing a natural explanation for Walter's aristocratic desires: he is, in reality, an aristocrat. You might say he is the *original*

American aristocrat. Walter, it is revealed, is descended from the sole survivor of the "Lost Colony" of Roanoke. This survivor "was a natural son of Sir Walter Raleigh, . . . a brave and sprightly lad" who had been taken in by the Roanoke tribe and married Chief Manteo's daughter. Dan Tucker, then, is not Walter's real father; rather, Dan had been given the charge of raising Walter, the last surviving member of this royal bloodline, until the latter had "proved himself worthy of his name . . . WALTER ROANOKE, the descendant of Sir Walter Raleigh, and of Manteo, the Lord of Roanoke" (137). Further, it is revealed that Frank Hooper, whom Walter has loved in a platonic sense, is in fact Alice Bladen in disguise. She has been in love with Walter from the beginning, and only Walter's wounded ego has prevented him from seeing it, prompting her to take great risks in pursuing him on his exploits. Wife swapping, miscegenation, cross-dressing, a slave revolt, a revolution, a changeling prince, and a seemingly homoerotic attraction that turns into the heterosexual "natural" attraction between two aristocrats—this historical romance has it all. Following these contortions of plot, Walter and Alice, natural aristocrats of the Old and the New Worlds, are free to marry and propagate in the new nation founded by revolution. The novel's conclusion is unique in that it forces a synthesis of the conflicting strands of southern identity outlined by Michael O'Brien. Walter is an Old World (and New World) aristocrat, a patriot, and a revolutionary all in one; he has earned his place through his actions, yet in retrospect, his noble bloodline seems to be the first cause of those actions. He is simply acting according to the dictates of his white (and native), aristocratic bloodlines. Interestingly, the simple hospitality of the Utopians celebrated in the novel's opening pages disappears by the novel's conclusion, and Utopia herself, who has embodied Christian principles and whom "all met . . . as if she were the guest of all mankind," is brutally murdered by a dissipated and guilt-ridden Robert Bladen, Alice's brother.[35] Walter, to whom Utopia had displayed an attraction, is left with his rightful partner, the English aristocrat Alice.

Taken together, P. W. B. Carothers's short story "Modern Hospitality," with which I began this chapter, and Calvin Henderson Wiley's novel *Roanoke* both attempt to reconcile the well-known, aristocratic images of southern hospitality with the other prevailing discourses of hospitality in American culture at that time—namely, those that articulate Christian and "republican" ideals of hospitality. Many Americans, southerners and nonsoutherners, found images of refined, aristocratic southern planters lavishly entertaining strangers and friends alike both attractive and appealing. But not all readers of the period would have necessarily subscribed to the nostalgic valorization of aristocratic hospitality and social practices—southern or otherwise—seen in Carothers's short story or Wiley's novel. An anonymous poem published in *Godey's* in 1847 provides an alternative to such aristocratic characterizations of hospitality,

FIGURE 10. "Hospitality of the Olden Time," *Godey's Magazine and Lady's Book*, March 1847, 126. Courtesy of American Antiquarian Society.

calling instead for a more egalitarian ideal of hospitality. Titled "Hospitality of the Olden Time," the poem appears with an accompanying illustration on the facing page. The illustration (see figure 10) seems fitting for the pages of Sir Walter Scott's *Ivanhoe* or *Lady of the Lake* or any other medieval romance. It centers on a medieval noblewoman who has just returned from a hunt. Dogs repose in the foreground of the scene, as servants tend to the horses. Wearing a quiver of arrows on her back, the lady sits sidesaddle on her horse and is receiving a libation in a goblet from her cavalier, in celebration of a successful hunt. The text of the poem is a direct commentary on the illustration. The first stanza reinforces its romantic images, noting that the "fashions" and "hospitality" of the "olden time" seem to us "a precious wonder" now and describing how the "fairest lady" and "her cavalier" went "a-hunting and a-hawking" "through the merry wood."[36] Over the next two stanzas, however, the attitude toward this subject changes from the seeming praise of the first stanza to a tone of indictment that portrays the woman on a pedestal at the center of a violent social order. The romantic picture of the past is dismantled, and in the fourth and final stanza the author dismisses this so-called hospitality of old in favor of the possibility of "true hospitality" in the present and the future:

> Well let them laud those "olden times;" I frankly must avow
> I cannot join the strain; I think the better times are *now*;

> And that the best are still to come, and in the future see,
> What ne'er has been, the triumph of true hospitality—
> When "strangers" shall, like brothers, meet a welcome everywhere—
> But the theme requires a folio, and I've but a line to spare—
> So let your noblest fancies aid the falterings of my pen,
> And your dream of angels now will show what WOMAN will be then![37]

Though this anonymous poet could only "spare a line," other Americans in the antebellum period did indeed produce what would amount to much more than a folio dedicated to this theme of true hospitality—an ethical ideal here oriented toward the future instead of the past and in which all strangers are transformed into "brothers" and "sisters" or, as the last line suggests, "angels unawares." As these Americans pushed the ethical horizon of hospitality by expanding the definition of the stranger, hospitality was redefined as both a liberal state of mind—"mental hospitality"—and a means of progressive reform and social change.

"Mental Hospitality" and Progressive Social Change

Versions of the progressive idea of "mental hospitality" were disseminated through sermons preached from the pulpit by liberals and circulated by reformers in print. This particular discourse of hospitality was closely tied to the antislavery movement; indeed, as the sectional crisis deepened, it developed into a coherent and effective counterdiscourse to prevailing ideas of southern hospitality, particularly as it became linked to the plight of the fugitive slave. An 1833 sermon by William Fox titled "Mental Hospitality" provides an early example of the progressive potential of this discourse. Fox was a leading English Unitarian and advocate of radical reforms; his sermons were published and circulated in America as well as Britain, and he was a known proponent of abolition. This particular sermon was included in an 1833 Boston edition of his sermons titled *Christian Morality*; excerpts of the sermon were also published in the *Christian Register*, a Unitarian magazine, in 1834. Fox begins with a passage from Paul's Letter to the Hebrews 13:2 (King James Version): "Be not forgetful to entertain strangers; for thereby some have entertained angels unawares." He goes on to explain that even though the old, biblical ways of hospitality are obsolete in today's society, we must still be mindful of this biblical injunction. More specifically, if we believe in a world of continuing progress toward God's truth, then we must be hospitable *in mind*, for God's truth must always appear in the form of the stranger. Fox writes:

> Well would it have been for the Jewish nation, when Christ came to them... in a character which was, to their prejudices and hearts, *a stranger*, if they had entertained the consideration of his claims and doctrines, instead of at once rejecting

> him as an impostor.... The lesson is a warning against what we may term mental inhospitality. It admonishes us never hastily to refuse a tenet merely because it is a stranger to our previous notions. Had they received him, he would have been to them the angel of the covenant.... How much is the progress of truth delayed in the world, by this summary mode of shutting the door of conviction against doctrines, because they are thought strange? When creeds have become corrupt, truth must have become strange.[38]

The phrase "mental hospitality" subtly links thought to action and moral and ethical ideals to the social sphere. The sort of mental hospitality that Fox calls for has real social and political consequences, bringing strangers together for the common cause of justice: combining with "personal strangers" can ultimately lead to "that cooperation of knowledge, zeal, and benevolence, by which liberty is gained for slaves, and restrictions on human rights are obliterated, and unjust laws are repealed, or just ones enacted, or religious information diffused over the face of the country."[39] Mental hospitality, then, is an essential aspect of progressive social change, particularly extending human rights, as in the abolitionists' efforts to end slavery.[40]

A more expansive and eloquent case for mental hospitality is made in an 1859 sermon delivered by the Unitarian preacher Octavius Brooks Frothingham and published in the *Christian Inquirer*. Titled "Christian Hospitality," the sermon yet again begins by citing the same passage from Paul's Letter to the Hebrews. Frothingham laments the fact that thinking of hospitality merely as social ritual has caused us to "become reserved, exclusive, distant, slow in our sympathies, narrow in our prejudices, and niggardly in our ways." He goes on to explain that we cannot "revive the ancient virtue of hospitality" because "we cannot recall the state of society to which it belonged." Nonetheless, "hospitality itself cannot be obsolete." It is a timeless virtue and to truly exercise the spirit of hospitality we must "enlarge its sphere": "The duty of hospitality requires us not to open our houses to any belated wanderer who may chance to pass, but to open our *minds* to the thoughts that come to us with unfamiliar aspect, and ask admittance to our consideration." Without a "large and generous" mental hospitality, "it is impossible for a human intellect to live" in this world full of "*dead* truths that lie in men's understandings, like venerable rubbish in houses."[41] But opening one's self to new, living truths is difficult, for they will always seem to pose a threat to our comfort: "New ideas almost always look hungry and wild. We know not whence they come, we know not whither they go, nor what their intents may be. We think it safer to let them slide by. And yet, if angelic truths are ever to visit us, they must visit us as *strangers*; for certainly no one will be so insane as to imagine that he has them all as perpetual inmates of his house."[42] As Frothingham goes on to describe these potential strangers, he emphasizes the inherent risk that true hospitality poses to our comfortable self-satisfaction. Indeed, the manner in which he portrays hospitality as risk is remarkably similar to the way Jacques Derrida describes it. Consider how Frothingham challenges the comfort of his listeners, powerfully asserting that

> God's angels rarely look like angels when they accost us. They come in the awful shapes of duty, in the sad guise of renunciation. They come robed in the black drapery of mourning, and clad in the iron armor of law. They look like enemies; they look like errors, and misfortunes, and sorrows, and deaths. They look like faded hopes, and crippled beliefs; they look like gaunt infidelities and sly secrets. If they looked otherwise, where would be the merit in opening the door and taking them in?[43]

Who in his or her right mind would welcome such strangers? How far we have come from the pleasures of the amphytrion discussed earlier in the chapter. In contrast to the pleasant rituals and self-indulgence of the amphytrion, here we are faced with seemingly impossible social duties and moral obligations. But this is indeed the "impossible" that must be done if we are to have true hospitality. We must be willing to put ourselves at risk in the open encounter with the stranger. To illustrate this point, Frothingham immediately follows with his personal testimonial, and significantly, it involves his transformation on the issues of race and slavery. He describes how as a "conservative and dainty youth" he first encountered William Ellery Channing's writings on the Christian duty to oppose slavery. Frothingham describes how he initially did not want to accept this "stranger":

> I did not like its appearance. It looked vulgar, low and ridiculous; its robes were covered with the dirt heaped on it by respectable people; its aspect was lean and rapid, like that of a fanatic; its history was obscure; it was friendless and an outcast; I expected to hear from its lips nothing but vituperation and blasphemy. At length I went down and opened the door—rather it came in, as the door stood ajar, and seated itself in my parlor—and O what a gracious figure I found it then to be! How this stranger enriched my heart! How he enlarged my conscience! What insight he gave me into the meaning of the gospel! What knowledge of Christ![44]

Notice how Frothingham's imagery suggests surrendering control over the threshold. He does not exactly invite the stranger in; instead, the door, left open, allows the stranger to enter both uninvited and unannounced. Rather than guarding the door against ideas that may challenge our assumptions, we should be open to entertaining these ideas. This is similar to what Derrida describes as moving beyond the "hospitality of invitation" and toward "the hospitality of visitation" in which the host surrenders the threshold to the stranger, allowing the stranger to come as he or she will.[45] The hospitality of invitation, synonymous with the politics of hospitality, is exclusive and confirms our comfortable self-identity, our sovereignty, our mastery of our own space. In contrast, the hospitality of visitation, synonymous with the absolute ethic of welcoming all equally, carries a sense of risk that can challenge this sense of sovereignty and self-possession.

These liberal Christian reformers I have cited articulate a concept of hospitality very much in line with that outlined by Jacques Derrida, and they did so in an effort to effect progressive social change. So important is this idea of mental hospitality that Frothingham goes on to characterize it as the very essence of his progressive Christian faith: "If I were to characterize by one word the true genius of Liberal Christianity, that word would be *hospitality*."[46]

"Abolition Hospitality" and the Example of J. G. Whittier's Cosmopolitanism

For many Americans of the antebellum period, these lofty meditations on hospitality were not simply ethereal speculations; rather, they were ethical ideals with political contexts and consequences, and they formed a powerful counterdiscourse to the prevailing attitudes and discourse of southern hospitality, as succinctly illustrated in a short column published in William Lloyd Garrison's antislavery paper, the *Liberator*, in 1837. The column bears the bold headline "ABOLITION HOSPITALITY" and appeared the week before the Fourth Annual Meeting of the New England Anti-Slavery Convention, to be held in Boston that May. It urged Boston residents to open their doors to the many convention delegates who would be arriving from the numerous antislavery societies scattered around New England. Given the newspaper's oppositional stance toward slavery and all things southern, the title can be read as a self-conscious response to the slave owners' well-known boasts of southern hospitality. Given that Americans by this time were increasingly thinking of "North" and "South" and "abolition" and "slavery" as opposing cultural terms, the phrase "abolition hospitality" implicitly transforms its opposite, "southern hospitality," into "slavery hospitality." The column begins by citing the familiar passage of Paul's Letter to the Hebrews; here, however, the injunction takes on a decidedly political prospect:

> To be "given to hospitality" is an apostolic injunction, repeated on many occasions. "Be not forgetful to entertain strangers," says Paul; "for thereby some have entertained angels unawares." And in the very next verse he adds—"Remember them that are in bonds as bound with them; and them which suffer adversity, as being yourselves also in the body." It seems, therefore, that there is a close affinity between sympathy for the oppressed and a hospitable reception of those who plead their cause in the face of a gainsaying generation. If we obey the first

injunction, by entertaining abolition strangers, we shall be likely to fulfill the second, by a lively remembrance of the woes and sufferings of the slave.

Many delegates will doubtless attend the N.E. Anti-Slavery convention next week: some will come from a great distance, at considerable expense, and others will be embarrassed in their circumstances. It is very desirable, therefore, that as many of them should be as kindly entertained as possible, without charge. All who are able and willing to accommodate one or more of them, for a few days, are requested to leave their names and place of residence at 25, Cornhill, as early as convenient. The plainer the fare the better.[47]

This call for hospitality among Boston residents, based again on Scripture, broadens the act of hospitality in a revealing and important way. The crucial exchange here is not the material exchange of hospitality between the host and the guest; rather, it is what ultimately results from this exchange: the imagined, empathetic opening of the self to the ultimate strangers (slaves). By universal right, these slaves should have places at the table, but due to unjust laws, they are held in bondage. This exchange, then, is not about self-indulgence and pleasure ("The plainer the fare the better"); it is about altering one's mind and heart and instilling a greater sense of personal responsibility for the oppressed stranger.[48] While the particular exchanges of hospitality between Boston residents and these "abolition strangers" must still be carried out within and consequently limited by the material rites of hospitality, the imagined, expansive sense of mental hospitality that informs them strains toward the absolute ethical law of universal hospitality, which exists beyond the realm of fallible human laws. Perhaps the hosts and the guests involved in these exchanges imagined them as rehearsals for the future arrival of the oppressed strangers, those held in slavery who nonetheless could quite literally appear at the door in the forms of fugitive slaves, whom abolitionists recognized as fellow citizens, if not of the nation then of the world.

Indeed, under the banner of every issue of the *Liberator*, in which "Abolition Hospitality" appeared, ran the decidedly cosmopolitan motto, "Our Country Is the World—Our Countrymen Are All Mankind." This idea of being a citizen of the world calls to mind Immanuel Kant's cosmopolitan theories of world citizenship outlined in *Perpetual Peace: A Philosophical Sketch*, an essay that proposes the right of "universal hospitality." In *Perpetual Peace*, Kant outlines a series of six "preliminary" and three "definitive" articles necessary for the achievement of perpetual peace among the nations of the world. The third definitive article goes to the question of hospitality and marks a seminal moment in philosophical thinking about the ethics of hospitality. Kant's third definitive article reads, "The Law of World Citizenship Shall Be Limited to Conditions of Universal Hospitality." Significantly, Kant maintains that hospitality is not a matter of a host's "philanthropy" toward a guest; instead, it is the inherent "right" of the stranger: "Hospitality means the right of the stranger not to be treated as an enemy when he arrives in the land of another." Kant considers this a natural right that all humans have "by virtue of their common ownership of the surface of the earth, where, as a globe, they cannot infinitely disperse and hence must finally tolerate the presence of each other. Originally, no one had more right than another to a particular part of the earth."[49]

The Quaker poet, abolitionist, and reformer John Greenleaf Whittier's 1845 book, *The Stranger in Lowell*, provides an interesting example of the overarching ethics of mental hospitality and cosmopolitanism. This modest volume is composed of sketches and reflections on the industrial city of Lowell, Massachusetts, written during a "brief sojourn" in the city that brought the Industrial Revolution to America. In many ways, Whittier's text is the thematic and regional antithesis of Calvin Henderson Wiley's chauvinistically southern novel *Roanoke*, published a few years later.[50] The industrial laborers of Lowell and the slave laborers of southern plantations were inextricably linked through the raw material of cotton, grown and harvested by southern slaves and transformed into durable goods by northern factory workers, and the debate over slavery often focused on comparative discussions of the plight of northern factory operatives and southern slaves. As a progressive, reform-minded abolitionist, Whittier in *The Stranger in Lowell* celebrates a unique form of liberal hospitality, one far removed from the aristocratic myth of southern hospitality. The title itself suggests the overall theme of the stranger—and the intertwined theme of hospitality that always accompanies the boundaries through which the stranger is defined. While, on the one hand, Whittier is a stranger visiting Lowell, the city of Lowell itself becomes a broader metaphor of all that is new—and consequently foreign and strange—in this period of radical change in American culture. As Whittier writes in the opening chapter describing his first impressions of the city, "A stranger, in view of all this wonderful change, feels himself as it were thrust forward into a new century; he seems treading on the outer circle of the millennium of steam engines and cotton mills. Work is here the Patron Saint. Every thing bears his image and superscription. Here is no place for that respectable class of citizens called gentlemen, and their much vilified brethren, familiarly known as loafers"(9–10). In addition to seeing Lowell as a precursor to a new industrial millennium, Whittier also considers it a precursor to a new social millennium. Rather than focusing on the figures of "respectable" society cited above, Whittier devotes chapters throughout the book to the often-marginalized outsiders of society, writing in an open-minded and progressive manner on recent immigrants ("The Heart of a Stranger"), laboring women ("The Factory Girls"), former slaves ("The Black Man"), followers of unconventional religious sects ("A Mormon Conventicle," "Father Miller," and "Swedenborg"), and even Yankee vagrants ("The Yankee Zincali").[51]

For example, in the second chapter, titled "The Heart of the Stranger," Whittier describes the range of immigrants who make up Lowell's population (Scotch, German, Swiss, Irish, Polish, Jewish), and his thoughts on immigrants at several points allude to scriptural injunctions on hospitality. Reflecting on the city's many Irish immigrants, he exclaims, "It is no light thing to abandon one's own country and household gods. Touching and beautiful was the injunction of the prophet of the Hebrews: 'Ye shall not oppress the stranger, *for ye know the heart of the stranger*, seeing that ye were strangers in the land of Egypt'" (17). Whittier is writing in a moment of widespread suspicion and animosity toward foreign immigrants in America, especially toward the Irish and Catholics, but he rejects the growing nativist and xenophobic sentiments of the day, saying, "[I am] no friend of that narrow spirit of mingled national vanity and religious intolerance, which, under the specious pretext of preserving our institutions from foreign contamination, has made its appearance among us. I reverence man, as man. Be he Irish or Spanish, black or white, he is my brother man" (18).[52] Similarly, Whittier claims to have "no prejudices against other nations," and he dismisses the "blustering shampatriotism" he finds rampant in American society. Our common humanity, according to Whittier and like-minded progressives, must be placed before our national or even personal identity. According to them, our country is, indeed, the world.

In the chapter titled "The Yankee Zincali," Whittier's liberal theories of hospitality are put to the test in the form of a duplicitous beggar, and through this chapter, he engages a common theme in antebellum discourse on charity and benevolence.[53] In a democracy supposedly based on the doctrine of self-reliance, Americans struggled to define appropriate boundaries and practices of charity. How could one separate the worthy from the unworthy poor?[54] A fear of duplicity led many etiquette books to instruct their readers to never give alms to beggars, suggesting that it promotes more social ill than it relieves. Whittier suggests otherwise. The main action of the chapter details a potential moment of hospitality that doesn't quite come to fruition—or so it seems at first. Whittier recounts how on a dreary, rainy autumn afternoon he was aroused from a melancholy reverie on the weather by an unexpected knock at his door. Given the gloominess of his thoughts, he exclaims that he is inclined to "welcome any body, just now," but when he throws open the door, his eyes are met by a "shambling" and "ragged" stranger who puts on a "dumb show of misery quite touching" and hands Whittier an official-looking document that identifies the bearer as a "survivor of shipwreck and disaster" who is "sorely in want of the alms of all charitable Christian persons" (63). Whittier is immediately suspicious, and his reflections concisely convey the anxieties and contradictions in antebellum discourse on charity, benevolence, and self-reliance:

Here commences a struggle.... "Give," said Benevolence, as with some difficulty I fish up a small coin from the depths of my pocket. "Not a cent," says selfish Prudence, and I drop it from my fingers. "Think," says the good angel, "of the poor stranger in a strange land, ... thrown half-naked and helpless on our shores, ignorant of our language, and unable to find employment suited to his capacity." "A vile imposter!" replies the left hand sentinel. "His paper, purchased from one of those ready writers in New York, who manufacture beggar-credentials at the low price of one dollar per copy, with earthquakes, fires, or shipwrecks, to suit customers." (63–64)

The internal debate results in a "confusion of tongues," but Whittier is afforded a way out of the impasse when he realizes that the stranger is perhaps not a stranger after all. He has seen the face many times before in different guises: as a "travelling preacher" exhorting a crowd of young boys, as a "poor Penobscott Indian, who had lost the use of his hands," as a "forlorn father of six small children" who had been "crippled," and as a "down-east unfortunate ... whose hand shook so pitifully when held out to receive ... [his] poor gift" (64). Indeed, Whittier realizes that he knows this beggar by name as one "Stephen Leathers of Barrington." He decides to "conjure him into his own likeness" by addressing him by name. The game up, Leathers admits his identity, claiming that he thought he recognized Whittier as well. Following a brief exchange of pleasantries, he takes his leave, supposedly to find a more willing dupe.

Rather than taking this visit of the duplicitous beggar—this "ragged Proteus," as Whittier calls him—as evidence of the dangers of indiscriminate charity and hospitality, Whittier says he "cannot be angry with such a fellow": "He has gone; and knave as he is, I can hardly help exclaiming, 'Luck go with his!' He has broken in upon the sombre train of my thoughts, and called up before me pleasant and grateful recollections." The visitation of this protean stranger has blessed Whittier unawares, calling up memories of his boyhood home and the many such "wandering beggars" and "old stragglers" whose unannounced visits broke the "monotonous quietude of [his family's] farm-life" (66). Whittier recalls that his mother developed quite a reputation for her open hospitality among these "wandering tests of benevolence," although many were what respectable society no doubt would consider worthless drunks and lazy ne'er-do-wells. As Whittier relates, "It was not often that ... my mother's prudence got the better of her charity" (71). As he recalls, such was the case despite the sense of risk inherent in these encounters with strangers, for their farmhouse was isolated in a valley with no neighbor in sight.

His mother's reputation for generous and open-hearted hospitality notwithstanding, there was a "tribe of lazy strollers ... whose low vices had placed them beyond even the pale of her benevolence" (71). These shiftless wanderers hailed from Barrington, New Hampshire, and the stranger who showed up at Whittier's door was one of them. Whittier recalls, "They came to us in all shapes and with all appearances save their true one, with most miserable stories of mishap and sickness.... It was particularly vexatious to discover, when too late, that our sympathies and charities had been expended upon such graceless vagabonds as the 'Barrington Beggars'" (71–72). Rather than simply dismiss the likes of the Barrington Beggars, as period literature on charity was wont to do, Whittier inquires after them, believing that "no phase of our common humanity is altogether unworthy of investigation." He describes how a few summers before he had decided to return, "once for all, their numerous visits" and pay a visit to the gypsy-like community near Barrington. He finds the small settlement in the midst of a "desolate region": "Unfenced, unguarded, open to all comers and goers, stood the city of the beggars—no wall or paling between the ragged cabins, to remind one of the jealous distinctions of property. The great idea of its founders seemed visible in its unappropriated freedom. Was not the whole round world their own, and should they haggle about boundaries and title-deeds? ... That comfortable philosophy which modern Transcendentalism has but dimly shadowed forth ... —which gives all to each and each to all—is the real life of this city of Unwork" (73–74). The members of this community are the absolute strangers to all that Lowell, the city of work and the new era of industry, represents. Yet Whittier is even willing to entertain these ne'er-do-wells. Indeed, it was the duplicitous beggar, the protean stranger standing at Whittier's door, who inspired his reminiscences of his family's hospitality, and for this, he feels grateful: "When again the shadows of the outward world fall upon the spirit, may I not lack a good angel to remind me of its solace, even if he comes in the shape of a Barrington beggar" (74).

Through its protean manifestations of the stranger in antebellum culture—laboring women, liberated slaves, members of alternative religious sects, immigrants, and even con men and ne'er-do-wells who seem to exist outside of the American myth of progress—Whittier challenges his contemporary readers, prompting them to examine their prejudices and expand their sense of mental hospitality. He pushes them to question and rethink their categorical views on women, Christian faith, class, ethnicity, and race. As an abolitionist and activist, his expansive, cosmopolitan vision of hospitality stands in opposition to the discourse of southern hospitality that permeated American culture at the time. This counterdiscourse found in the documents of history—in poems, newspapers, sermons, essays, and antislavery publications—raises important questions about southern hospitality and the motivations behind American cultural memory. Why has the myth of southern hospitality been memorialized in American culture, while this alternative discourse of hospitality from the same period has been forgotten (even and especially among the work of historians of the South who have attempted to understand southern hospitality)? Why have we remembered a form of hospitality that is aristocratic, undemocratic, and that is sustained by slave labor, and generally forgotten those who imagined hospitality as nothing less than an extension of America's democratic principles of individual rights and justice? The answers to these questions revolve largely around the fraught and traumatic American history of slavery and segregation, as we will see in the chapters that follow.⁵⁵

CHAPTER THREE

Making Hospitality a Crime
The Fugitive Slave Law of 1850

In the early 1850s, Americans North and South entered into a bitter, protracted debate over the relationship between hospitality and slavery. This debate—carried out in the halls of Congress, in newspapers and magazines, in sermons and denominational papers, in poems and novels, and in the domestic space of American households—was sparked by the passage of the Fugitive Slave Law of 1850, the most controversial provision of the set of legislative acts known collectively as the Compromise of 1850. The compromise, ushered through Congress largely through the efforts of Senators Henry Clay of Kentucky, Stephen Douglass of Illinois, and Daniel Webster of Massachusetts, was designed to put an end to decades of sectional strife over slavery. Instead of ending sectional tension, however, the compromise's most controversial provision, the new Fugitive Slave Law, only added fuel to the fire, fundamentally transforming the landscape of antislavery politics in American culture. Southerners deemed the 1850 Fugitive Slave Law necessary because the Fugitive Slave Law of 1793 had become entirely ineffectual due to nonenforcement, the passage of personal liberty laws in northern states, and the efforts of the Underground Railroad.[1] The 1850 law contained several provisions that favored the slaveholders. It made it more difficult for alleged fugitives to prove possible claims of being free men and women, and it also seemed to provide financial incentives for officials to arrest and return fugitives (officials received ten dollars for every fugitive slave returned South and five dollars for cases where the alleged fugitive could prove he was indeed a free citizen). The law also required citizens to assist federal officers in capturing fugitives and, perhaps most galling to opponents of slavery, forbade Americans from offering any form of assistance to those fleeing from slavery. In other words, the act of extending hospitality to a runaway slave was now a federal crime, punishable with excessive fines and imprisonment.

Because it involved the obligations and limitations of hospitality, the debate over the Fugitive Slave Law was also, by necessity, a complex debate over differences of race, class, region, and the very nature of American identity. Religious arguments for and against the law, for example, were based largely on competing ideas of community. While all Christian Americans would have agreed with the scriptural injunction to "love thy neighbor as thyself," the new reality of the Fugitive Slave Law forced them to ask, "And who is my neighbor?"[2] Both the ambiguity and the implications of this question are seen in a scriptural passage that was repeatedly cited by both pro- and antislavery advocates to support their positions on the Fugitive Slave Law: Paul's Letter to Philemon. One of the shortest epistles in the New Testament, it was among the most often cited passages in debates over the Fugitive Slave Law.[3] In the epistle Paul writes to Philemon, a fellow Christian, from prison, where he has come to know Philemon's runaway slave, Onesimus, whose name translates as "useful." Though Onesimus is no longer useful to Philemon as a runaway, he has become useful to Paul as a convert to Christianity. In fact, Paul has grown exceedingly fond of Onesimus, referring to him as "my child Onesimus whom I have begotten in my imprisonment," a reference to his conversion to the faith under Paul's spiritual guidance. Though Paul would like to keep Onesimus with him, he sends him back to Philemon with this letter, advising Philemon to receive him "no longer as a slave, but more than a slave, a beloved brother, especially to [Paul], but how much more to [Philemon], both in the flesh and in the Lord" (1:16 New American Standard Bible). One can see why both sides of the debate cited this biblical passage. On the one hand, Paul instructs Philemon to receive Onesimus as more than a slave, as a brother in Christ. On the other hand, Paul's actions seem to uphold the legal and social status quo of slavery. Seeming to both acknowledge the institution of slavery and uphold the law of rendition, he has sent a fugitive back to his master. Paul even goes so far as to offer to compensate Philemon for any wrong committed by Onesimus before he ran away.

Here, then, lies the crux of the debate over the Fugitive Slave Law—who has the better claim of being a neighbor: Philemon or Onesimus, slave owner or slave, the white southerner or his human chattel? Those opposed to slavery viewed the runaway slave first and foremost as a Christian neighbor in need but also in many cases as a fellow citizen, discursively expanding the boundaries of American identity to include blacks, both slave and free. In contrast, supporters of slavery felt their allegiances must lie with the slave owners, with whom they shared a common racial, cultural, and national heritage. The two sides of the debate consequently articulated radically different theories of hospitality and consistently posed two fundamentally different questions to the American public. Opponents of slavery envisioned hospitality as an element of "higher law," an ethical imperative that superseded one's obligations to what they believed was a perverse and immoral human law. In contrast and in direct response, supporters of slavery articulated a restrictive and exclusionary politics of hospitality, portraying blacks as an alien presence unworthy of the hospitality of white Americans while emphasizing white cultural solidarity. While opponents of slavery repeatedly asked Americans, "Could you really turn a runaway slave from your door without providing any assistance?" supporters of slavery essentially shifted the question from the threshold of the home to the domestic social space itself, asking, "Could you really sit down at the table, as a social equal, with the African, whether slave or free?" Contrasting the two sides of this national debate over the Fugitive Slave Law exposes the stark logic and subtle cultural meanings behind antebellum southerners' claims of being a uniquely hospitable people. It also exposes why so many nonsoutherners in this period found the discourse of southern hospitality so appealing: as a form of persuasion, it allowed them to imagine amicable social and political relationships with white southerners in the face of sectional tensions over the Compromise of 1850, all at the expense of black claims of freedom and equality. While historians and literary scholars have written extensively on the compromise and the Fugitive Slave Law, it has not been considered through the ethical lens of hospitality, a perspective that was lived and felt by many antebellum Americans, as my previous chapter indicated.

Hospitality as "Higher Law": Antislavery Response to the Fugitive Slave Law

While Americans in the antebellum period negotiated among a variety of competing and often contradictory discourses of hospitality, the passage of the Fugitive Slave Law in 1850 suddenly cast the subject of hospitality in a new light, prodding them to fully confront, perhaps as never before, the implications of hospitality as both an ethical ideal and a subject of legal, political, and moral conflict.[4] In the debate over the Fugitive Slave Law, Americans were repeatedly confronted with arguments portraying hospitality as a higher law beyond social, institutional, or governmental law, a tendency that emerged early in the debate, before the Fugitive Slave Law was even passed. In his famous "Higher Law" speech delivered during the Senate debate over the compromise bill, New York senator William Seward, commenting on the pending provisions of the new Fugitive Slave Law, pointedly remarked, "Your constitution and laws convert hospitality to the refugee from the most degrading oppression on earth into a crime, but all mankind except you esteem that hospitality a virtue." According to Seward, the new rendition provisions were a violation of both the "law of nations" and "the law of nature, written on the hearts and consciences of freemen." He believed that the law would be doomed to fail, for it was such an affront to the "moral convictions" of citizens that they would find it impossible to obey. As he famously concluded later in his address, "There is a higher law than the Constitution."[5]

Despite Seward's objections, many Americans initially welcomed the 1850 compromise. They hoped that it would end once and for all decades of sectional agitation and conflict over slavery. Such hope proved utterly chimerical, as moral anxiety and agitation over the provisions of the new Fugitive Slave Law quickly reached a fever pitch, galvanizing the abolitionist movement. Historians have noted that this law provided abolitionists with a new avenue for propaganda against slavery. While this may be the case, it also allowed them to confront Americans with profound ethical questions regarding American democratic identity.[6] References to the Fugitive Slave Law—in articles, poems, letters, and editorials—pervaded the pages of the *Liberator* throughout 1850 and the years that immediately followed.[7] Throughout this anti–Fugitive Slave Law discourse, extending hospitality to the fugitive slave was portrayed foremost as the fulfillment of a basic Christian principle and, more subtly, as the fulfillment of a more democratic, inclusive republic; again and again, readers were essentially posed the question that concludes the poem, "The Fugitive Slave to the Christian":

> I seek a home where man is man,
> > If such there be upon this earth,
> To draw my kindred, if I can,
> > Around its free, though humble hearth.
> The hounds are baying on my track!
> > O Christian! will you send me back?[8]

The poem, published in the *Liberator*, trades on the Christian imperative of hospitality—directly appealing to the reader as a Christian—but it also subtly pushes the traditional boundaries of American identity: the "home where man is man" implies, on the one hand, the homes of individual readers who share this Christian belief and, on the other hand, the domestic space of a nation founded on the principle that "all men are created equal." As potential recipients of hospitality, runaway slaves become potential compatriots in the American domestic household.

Effects of the Fugitive Slave Law (figure 11), a political broadside by Theodor Kaufman printed in 1850, makes this connection between biblical imperative and American dream more explicit. In the illustration, four runaways in the foreground are being shot in the back as they emerge from a cornfield. Two are succumbing to bullet wounds, while the others recoil in horror. In the background stands a party of well-dressed men preparing to fire another round. At the bottom of the cartoon, on either side of the title, are two quotes, one from the Bible and one from the Declaration of Independence. The bibli-

FIGURE 11. *Effects of the Fugitive Slave Law*, political broadside by Theodor Kaufman, 1850. Courtesy of American Antiquarian Society.

cal quote is from Deuteronomy (23:15–16): "Thou shalt not deliver unto the master his servant which has escaped from his master unto thee. He shall dwell with thee. Even among you in that place which he shall choose in one of thy gates where it liketh him best. Thou shalt not oppress him." The second quote reads, "We hold that all men are created equal, that they are endowed by their Creator with certain unalienable rights, that among these are life, liberty and the pursuit of happiness." The juxtaposed quotes characterize the Fugitive Slave Law as a violation of both the Bible and the Declaration, but the use of the latter implies that African slaves should be assimilated into the American body politic as free and equal citizens.

The Fugitive Slave Law also prompted Americans to simultaneously think about the threshold of their own domestic spaces in legal, political, moral, and ethical terms. Particularly for many women involved in the abolitionist cause, the plight of the fugitive transformed their own feminine and domestic identities into an avenue of special authority: the domestic space of the household was suddenly a political space as a potential asylum for the oppressed.[9] Indeed, the family's domestic space and the individual's conviction that it would be open to any fugitive slave in need could be imagined as the only stay against the juggernaut of American slavery, as may be gleaned from the cover illustration of the *Liberty Almanac for 1852* (figure 12). The illustration, which the almanac advertised could also be purchased and proclaimed "should be hung up in every place of public resort, and be in the possession of every family in the country," is a damning allegory of the "iniquitous Fugitive Slave Law." The caption reads "NO HIGHER LAW," and the illustration is dominated by a figure who, according to the almanac's detailed interpretation, is "the personification of AMERICAN SLAVERY": a tyrant seated upon his throne, holding aloft a whip and shackle in his right hand, while before him a minister and a senator (the second figure from the right is clearly Daniel Webster) stand ready to do his bidding. Behind the senator "stands a figure representing Liberty... with a desponding expression," and further in the background, the Statue of Liberty falls from its pedestal. In the left foreground, a runaway slave struggles against a pack of slave catcher's dogs as his wife and children escape in the distance. The *only* countervailing element in this picture is in the upper left corner: before a modest-looking home, a woman extends her arms in a gesture of welcome to the mother and two children, providing "an asylum in her dwelling."[10] The image suggests that the only way to circumvent the perverse and destructive power of the Fugitive Slave Law is for individual households to act in accordance with the higher law of hospitality by providing a safe haven to fugitives. The allegorical illustration appeals to a range of ideals: patriotism, Christian principles, the sanctity of family and domestic space, and the higher moral imperative of hospitality. It also contends that actions that occur in individual, gendered, domestic spaces could in fact disrupt the unjust authoritative laws of the national domestic space.

If the crisis over the new law galvanized abolitionists, it also forced moderate Americans to reexamine their assumptions regarding slavery. Prior to the passage of the law, moderates on the slavery issue might be against the idea of slavery in an abstract sense or lament its existence from a safe distance without having to commit themselves to its abolition. Now, however, every American home was essentially touched by slavery, as the national law superseded the right of the host to govern the threshold of his or her domestic space. To many, it seemed that slavery had suddenly become the law of the North as well as the South. As Ralph Waldo Emerson reflected, "I have lived all my life without suffering any known inconvenience from American Slavery. I never saw it; I never heard the whip; I never felt the check on my free speech and action, until the other day, when Mr. Webster, by his personal influence, brought the Fugitive Slave Law on the country."[11]

Now Americans were faced with the very real question of whether they would obey a law that many found to be utterly repugnant to their moral and ethical sensibilities: could they turn someone in need away from their door? As Gregg D. Crane explains, the Fugitive Slave Law "created a searing moral crisis for Northerners imagining the moment when the shivering fugitive might appear at their door seeking comfort and aid.... That the barest

FIGURE 12. "No Higher Law," *Liberty Almanac for 1852* (published by the American & Foreign Anti-Slavery Society, 1851). Courtesy of American Antiquarian Society.

sketch of the decent citizen forbidden by law from aiding the shivering fugitive could so powerfully reveal the moral nullity of the Fugitive Slave Law, in effect, created a special role for the literary rendering of this jurisprudential crisis."[12] Such literary renderings of the plight of the fugitive slave appear well beyond the radical abolitionist press, surfacing in everything from poems to sermons to novels, and these representations created bonds of community and common purpose among the growing number of antislavery Americans. For example, Walt Whitman included the following brief, though pointed, vignette in his first edition of *Leaves of Grass* (1855) in the poem that came to be known as "Song of Myself":

> The runaway slave came to my house and stopped outside,
> I heard his motions crackling the twigs of the woodpile,
> Through the swung half-door of the kitchen I saw him limpsey and weak,
> And went where he sat on a log, and led him in and assured him,
> And brought water and filled a tub for his sweated body and bruised feet,
> And gave him a room that entered from my own, and gave him some coarse
>   clean clothes,
> And remember perfectly well his revolving eyes and his awkwardness,
> And remember putting plasters on the galls of his neck and ankles;
> He staid with me a week before he was recuperated and passed north,
> I had him sit next me at table . . . my firelock leaned in the corner.[13]

The passage suggests that the narrator holds a liberal position as an opponent of the Fugitive Slave Law. He is already a lawbreaker for taking in the runaway, and the rifle in the corner indicates his willingness to defend the runaway—with deadly force if necessary—against his pursuers. What is more striking, though, is Whitman's emphasis on the physical intimacy established between the white speaker and the black fugitive. Whitman highlights the bodily contact involved in bathing and dressing wounds, and the social intimacy of dining at the same table and sleeping in adjoining rooms, not for a night but for a week. Such a suggestion of intimacy would have pushed the boundaries of the imagination for many of Whitman's readers, but this is precisely the goal of much of the discourse protesting the Fugitive Slave Law: to provoke readers to consider that runaway slaves are worthy recipients of hospitality, both in their individual households and, by extension, in the broader domestic space of the nation.[14] With their recurring themes of simple, humble Christian hospitality offered to the slave, these antirendition narratives and images offered a meaningful counterdiscourse to prevailing images of southern hospitality, wherein slaves featured as mere accoutrements to hospitable exchanges among white Americans. In the antirendition literature, the case is made again and again that fugitive slaves are appropriate *subjects* of white

Americans' hospitality, prompting them to consider the possibility of a racially integrated national household.

Charles Beecher's 1851 sermon titled "The Duty of Disobedience to Wicked Laws: A Sermon on the Fugitive Slave Law," for example, figuratively places a fugitive slave at the door of every member of his congregation, creating a melodramatic scene designed to maximize the contradiction between the law of the land and the law of God. Beecher relies heavily on the power of sentiment as he attempts to conjure up the palpable image of a fugitive slave and place her before his audience and readers. He asks his congregants to imagine themselves in the comfort of their own warm homes during a driving, nighttime blizzard. Moreover, he asks them to imagine that it is "a Sabbath evening" and they "have just come from the communion table, with the taste of the bread and the touch of the wine upon [their] lips. The memory of Jesus thrills yet within [their] soul[s]." At this moment of comfort and moral certitude, Beecher asks his congregation to further imagine "a faint low cry," a "faint footstep," "a timid hand" knocking at the door, and this figure standing at the threshold: "Feeble with hunger, ragged, with naked feet, pressing to her bosom a pining infant, a mother totters before you, just sinking to the earth. 'For the love of Jesus,' she cries, 'grant me a hiding place from my pursuers! Grant me a morsel of food! Save me, save my child, from a fate worse than death!'"[15]

As is often the case in texts arguing against the Fugitive Slave Law, Beecher goes on to use a variety of descriptive and rhetorical strategies to diminish the distance between black slaves and free white citizens, pointing out that the runaway slave in this case is a fellow Christian who has likewise "tasted the sacred bread and wine" and is likewise an "heir of heaven." Moreover, she flees "from a master and from a system that would sink her to the depths of shame and licentious degradation." Having emotionally pulled his listeners in with this melodramatic scene, Beecher concisely reminds the congregation what obedience to the Fugitive Slave Law requires: "You must shut your door in her face, or you must take her captive, and shut her up until the hounds of officers can come up."[16] He employs repetition to rhetorically embody the relentless power of the Fugitive Slave Law as it undermines all aspects of Christian hospitality and charity:

> This is obedience; and if you do not do this you are a law-breaker. If you give her a crust of bread, you break the law. If you give her a shawl, a cloak; if you let her warm herself by your fire an hour, and depart, you break the law. If you give her a night's rest, and let her go, you break the law. If you show her any kindness, any mercy, if you treat her as Christ treated you, if you do to her as you would wish to be done by, you have broken the law.[17]

Given the demands of hospitality among fellow Christians, Beecher preaches no patience for gradual change through legislative means; instead, he urges his congregation to acts of civil disobedience, to break the law the first chance they get: "In conclusion, therefore, my application of the subject is—DISOBEY THIS LAW. If you have ever dreamed of obeying it, repent before God, and ask his forgiveness. I counsel no violence.... I speak as the minister of the Prince of Peace.... But if a fugitive claim your help on his journey, break the law and give it to him.... Feed him, clothe him, harbor him, by day and by night, and conceal him from his pursuers, and from the officers of the law."[18]

Kazlitt Arvine challenged his congregation in a more elaborate manner in his sermon titled "Our Duty to the Fugitive Slave." For example, instead of simply placing the fugitive slave at his audience's door, at one point he creates a complex scenario that places the members of his congregation in the position of the fugitive slaves themselves, as white settlers fleeing Indians who have taken them captive.[19] Like Beecher, Arvine reminds his audience that many slaves are "our Christian brethren." But he goes even further, asserting that the fugitive slave is more than just a fellow Christian; he is Christ himself: "It is Jesus Christ, in the person of that poor disciple, that appeals to you for aid. Though he be the 'least' of all Christ's 'brethren,' though ignorance degrades and want afflicts him, and though frightful scars may seam his coarse, dark visage, yet he is loved by God." Arvine appeals to his listeners to look at the crisis over the Fugitive Slave Law as a unique opportunity to show one's love for Jesus Christ, and to carry out the simple dictates of the Gospels. Conversely, he warns that shutting the door on the runaway slave would be shutting the door on the "Saviour himself."[20]

The most famous literary rendering of the fugitive slave's plight is, of course, Harriet Beecher Stowe's *Uncle Tom's Cabin*, published in 1852. Even as Congress was preparing to pass the law in August 1850, Stowe published "The Freeman's Dream" in the *National Era*. Subtitled "A Parable," this short sketch describes a prosperous, "thankful" farmer who is suddenly faced with the dilemma of choosing between human law and higher law. He turns away a family of struggling fugitive slaves, only to see them captured shortly thereafter. Following the scene, he has an apocalyptic dream in which he himself is turned away from the gates of heaven on judgment day: "An awful voice pierced his soul, saying 'depart from me ye accursed! For I was an hungered, and ye gave me no meat; I was thirsty, and ye gave me no drink; I was a stranger, and ye took me not in.'" Here the image of the family of fugitive slaves appears before the farmer, upon which the farmer awakens, "terrified" over the state of his soul. Stowe concludes by chastising those who "seem to think that there is no standard of right and wrong higher than an act of Congress"; she reminds readers that God's laws "are above human laws which come in conflict with them; and that though heaven and earth pass away, His word shall not pass away."[21]

Stowe develops this idea in much greater detail in *Uncle Tom's Cabin*. Gregg Crane concisely describes Stowe's purpose in writing the novel: to "place a fugitive at the door of every reader, challenging the reader to choose between lower and higher law."[22]

Stowe most pointedly illustrates this conflict between human law and higher law in the ninth chapter, particularly in the argument between Senator John Bird and his wife, Mary. The senator has returned home from the state capital, where he has recently helped pass legislation supporting the Fugitive Slave Law. He desires "a little comfort at home" following the "tiresome business" of "legislating," but he suddenly finds himself in an argument with his wife, who is upset by news of the law's passage and mortified by her husband's role in passing it. As the argument reaches an impasse between John's appeals to "great public interests" and Mary's appeal to the higher law of Christian hospitality, she finally demands, "I put it to you, John,—would *you* now turn away a poor, shivering, hungry creature from your door, because he was a runaway? *Would* you, now?" When John answers that he would, even though it would be "a very painful duty," Mary claims that she knows his heart better than he knows himself: "I know *you* well enough John. You don't believe it's right any more than I do; and you wouldn't do it any sooner than I."[23]

Remarkably, the senator has a chance to follow through on this "painful duty" that very night, when the runaway slave Eliza shows up, with her child, at the Birds' door, following her harrowing journey across the icy Ohio River. Faced with the living presence of the fugitive, the senator finds that he must follow his heart and the higher law of hospitality. He breaks the Fugitive Slave Law that he had helped to author. The senator encourages his wife to provide Eliza and her child with clothing, including garments worn by the Birds' recently deceased son. While the sudden visit of the fugitive immediately following the couple's debate may seem to be pushing the boundaries of verisimilitude, it in fact seems drawn from an incident in Stowe's own life, which she described in a letter to her sister Catharine Beecher. In the letter, written not long after the passage of the Fugitive Slave Law, Stowe recounts an argument she had with her neighbor, the Reverend Thomas Upham, who counseled obedience to the law. Stowe describes it as "that sort of an argument that consists in both sides saying over & over just what they said before." Frustrated by the impasse, Stowe finally asked Upham the very question that Mary Bird puts to her husband, would he obey the law if a fugitive appeared at his door? To this, the reverend's wife "laughed" while the reverend "hemmed and hawed," but according to Stowe, the Uphams' young daughter burst out, 'I wouldn't I know.'"[24] The very next day, Reverend Upham's hospitality would in fact be tested by the visit of a fugitive slave, and like Senator Bird in the novel, he would choose to abide by the higher law of hospitality rather than by the law of men that forbade it.

The Upham anecdote from Stowe's life, like the chapter from the novel, illustrates William Seward's contention that there would be "no public conscience" to uphold the Fugitive Slave Law in practice.[25] As Senator Bird finds himself taking an increasingly active role in Eliza's escape, Stowe offers a final reflection on the conflict between political duty and the higher law of hospitality, and in doing so, she engages her potential southern readers as well:

> And so, as our poor senator was not stone or steel,—as he was a man, and a downright noble-hearted one, too,—he was, as everybody must see, in a sad case for his patriotism. And you need not exult over him, good brother of the Southern States; for we have some inklings that many of you, under similar circumstances, would not do much better. We have reason to know, in Kentucky, as in Mississippi, are noble and generous hearts, to whom never was tale of suffering told in vain. Ah, good brother! Is it fair for you to expect of us services which your own brave, honorable heart would not allow you to render, were you in our place?[26]

Stowe's emotional appeal here is especially effective due to the central place hospitality holds in the overlapping antebellum discourses of domesticity and Christianity, but in her direct appeal to her southern readers, she also subtly engages the discourse of southern hospitality as well, using the South's proud reputation for hospitality to her advantage. Her closing appeal turns on the Golden Rule of loving your neighbor as yourself: she essentially asks southerners, would you want your right to exercise your famous hospitality to be infringed upon or compromised in any way? Would you be able to turn away a stranger in need if the law forbade it? Rather than putting the hypothetical southern reader in the position of the supplicant fugitive, she focuses the attention on the rights of the host. Southerners accused northerners of violating the Golden Rule by not respecting slave owners' rights to property, and Stowe here cleverly counters that southerners are violating the Golden Rule by not allowing northerners to exercise the sacred right of hospitality.

"I Dwell among Mine Own People":
Southern Hospitality and Transregional White Identity

Despite Stowe's appeals to southern readers, anti- and pro-slavery advocates generally operated under different assumptions when it came to the question of hospitality. If abolitionists and antirenditionists sought to persuade people that slaves were their Christian neighbors, pro-slavery and pro-rendition writers sought to persuade them that their true allegiance was with the white southern slave owner, and that runaway slaves were ultimately unworthy of their hospitality. For example, sermons that supported and counseled obedience to the Fugitive Slave Law (there were many) tended to avoid the plight of the slave altogether, instead emphasizing the unique political compact that existed between northerners and southerners, one that resulted in a sacred community of shared racial, political, and cultural heritage.[27] For example, in a sermon delivered in New York on Thanksgiving Day, 1851, a year after the Fugitive Slave Law had been enacted, John C. Lord begins with a passage from Matthew (including, "Render therefore unto Caesar the things which are Caesar's; and unto God, the things that are God's"), and goes on to depict the Constitution as ordained by God, a covenant that binds northerners and southerners together as brethren. Lord gives thanks for the legislative compromise that contained the Fugitive Slave Law, which he says has led to "the preservation of public tranquility, the adjustment of sectional difficulties, and the continuance of the bonds of [the] union, amid excitements which threatened its integrity." In his conclusion, he again notes the shared communal heritage and values of northerners and southerners: "I would appeal to the North and the South, by their common ancestry, by the august memories of the revolutionary struggle, by the bones of their fathers which lie mingled together ... by the farewell counsels of the immortal Washington, to lay aside their animosities and to remember that they are brethren. I would remind them that the Union has given us blessings which we enjoy ... [and] I would warn them of that abyss of ruin which fanaticism and treason are opening beneath them."[28] Like many other pro-rendition sermons of the period, as Lord appeals to patriotic duty and the sanctity of the union, he also portrays those who would disobey the law and take in the fugitive slave as fanatics with misplaced allegiances. This emphasis on a shared community of northerners and southerners is perhaps what prompted the Reverend Jonathan Stearns to base his pro-rendition sermon not on any of the numerous biblical passages dealing with slavery, but on 2 Kings 4:13: "I dwell among mine own people" (King James Version).[29]

In this same vein many Americans, North and South, invoked the discourse of southern hospitality during the crisis over the Fugitive Slave Law. They imagined southern hospitality to be a social practice that could cement the fraternal bonds between the North and the South. Just as literary renderings of the supplicant fugitive slave could mobilize Americans to favor abolition, renderings of gracious southern hospitality could rally them to defend slavery. Southern hospitality provided a way of reminding white Americans where their allegiances ought to lie. Even if one couldn't travel to the South and experience the hospitality of southerners firsthand, one could still read about it and imagine a national community based on the bonds of social manners and graces and on a shared racial and cultural heritage. Several of the proslavery texts written in the 1850s in response to the Fugitive Slave Law and *Uncle Tom's Cabin* provide good examples of the persuasive nature of southern hospitality and the essential logic of its appeal. In contrast to the absolute ethics of hospitality articulated in the antislavery texts just discussed, these pro-slavery texts express a politics of hospitality and a desire for exclusionary, discriminating boundaries that preserve hierarchies of race, class, and gender. Accordingly, these pro-southern texts emphasized characteristics such as gentility, refinement, benevolence, and civility; they portrayed abolitionists as ill-mannered, discourteous fanatics whose open-door policies toward fugitive slaves would inevitably lead to chaos in the form of racial amalgamation.

Martha Haines Butt's 1853 novel, *Anti-Fanaticism: A Tale of the South*, for example, sets out to correct the false impressions of the South created by "Mrs. Stowe and other fanatics," as she explains in the novel's preface, where she describes the "warm sympathy, glowing hospitality, and ... generous welcome, which makes the visitor at once feel at home under a Southern roof, and which assures him that the bosom warmed by such feelings cannot be the resting-place of cruelty and oppression." To accentuate this point, the author in the first chapter—titled "Southern Hospitality"—creates an imagined encounter between a northern stranger, Mr. I——, and a wealthy southern planter. Other than introducing the southern planter as one of the main characters, the chapter has little to do with the rest of the novel's action. It does, however, establish the main motif expressed in the chapter's title: if northerners could visit the South and experience its hospitality, they would come to a true and just appreciation of the southern way of life. In the scene a wealthy planter encounters a traveler from the North. Sensing the traveler's weariness and knowing there is no inn nearby, he invites the stranger to spend the night at his plantation mansion. The northern traveler also happens to be an abolitionist, but the exchange forces him to reflect on his misapprehensions regarding the character of southerners: "He felt deeply the kindness and hospitality of the South, and could not refrain from contrasting it with his northern home. 'Who,' thought he, 'would be kind enough at the North to invite a stranger, one of whom he knew nothing, to share his home?'" Ironically, many northerners were indeed opening their doors to complete strangers in the forms of runaway slaves, but as I illustrate below, southerners would not consider that a form of hospitality. In any case, the brief stay with the planter here quickly provides the stranger with concrete evidence of the blessings offered by the benevolent system of slavery: happy slaves serenading the master, a lavish meal prepared and served by slaves that featured "every delicacy the heart could wish," and a conversation with a contented house slave named Rufus, who scoffs at the idea of freedom in a dialect that makes him seem an absolute alien to the refined world of the white characters and readers: "'Caze den nobody would care for Rufus den—and when I be sick, no missus would be dar to tend poor Rufus. No! no! massa, me neber leab de souf in de world!" The northerner is forced to conclude "that the slaves at the South were certainly far happier than they had been represented to be."[30]

Having received the hospitality of the South, the traveler from the North later feels obligated to reciprocate the gift, specifically by defending slavery when he finds himself in a stagecoach full of northern abolitionists, telling them that the southerners "have only proved to [him], by their hospitality, and kind treatment to their slaves, that [he] was laboring under a wrong impression altogether."[31] Though this is a fantastically simple scene, it nonetheless illustrates the persuasive logic of southern hospitality from a southern point of view. Part of Butt's goal is to encourage southerners to entertain northerners with their proverbial southern hospitality and thereby sway public opinion in favor of the South. Many northerners did travel South—often for reasons of health—and many of them did in fact return to the North extolling the system of slavery in a manner that makes Mr. I——'s conversion seem, if not realistic, then at least plausible.

Abolitionists both derided and feared this persuasive power of southern hospitality and often felt compelled to attack it directly. The Reverend Philo Tower, for example, devotes an entire chapter in his 1856 book *Slavery Unmasked* to the phenomenon of northerners traveling south and being entertained by southerners. After arguing that the southern planters' penchant for hospitality is essentially selfish—the necessary consequence of a life of leisure and boredom—Tower offers a detailed analysis of the mixed motives and mutually beneficial exchanges between southern planters and northern tourists, whether they be "invalids," "pleasure seekers," or "business men." Masters offer their gracious hospitality to northern visitors, and these tourists, "on arriving North, ... make a good plea for the *dark institution* by way of extolling the hospitality of the Masters." These visitors, according to Tower, see only those scenes that the planters want them to see, and he concludes that the planters' expenditures on hospitality are simply a calculated investment, one that brings many "good returns" in the form of political allegiances on the slavery question.[32] One of the northerners whom Tower singles out for attack is the Reverend Nehemiah Adams, author of a travel narrative titled *A South-Side View of Slavery; or, Three Months at the South*, a conciliatory and decidedly prosouthern justification of slavery. Adams was a leading Congregationalist minister in Boston and, for much of his career, a professed opponent of slavery. In 1853, however, he traveled for three months to Georgia, South Carolina, and Virginia for his health and, while there, he began writing what would become *A South-Side View*.[33]

But for those who could not travel South, written accounts of the South and slavery—particularly fiction and travel writing—could provide positive images for northerners to consider, and many texts written about the South in this period often dwell in great detail on moments of interregional hospitality, as seen in the opening passages from *Anti-Fanaticism* cited above. Such domestic scenes of hospitality—of families, friends, and visitors around the table or the hearth—may do little to advance the plot, but they do create recognizable spaces for like-minded Americans to imagine their own social and cultural engagement with the South, southerners, and slavery. For example, fully half of the eighth chapter in Mary Henderson Eastman's *Aunt Phillis's Cabin; or, Southern Life as It Is*, is devoted to a detailed description of a dinner party at the plantation mansion of Exeter. Eastman's novel was written as a direct response to *Uncle Tom's Cabin* and was published by Philadelphia-based Lippincott, Grambo & Co., which published many pro-slavery texts, including the novel *Anti-Fanaticism*.[34] Eastman's dinner-party scene includes guests from the North and England, a situation that provides opportunities for outside perspectives on slavery to be expressed and, if needed, corrected.

This dinner-party scene is a set piece designed to emphasize white communal bonds, particularly by pointing to the country's shared history of white cultural elevation and refinement alongside black slavery. From Eastman's perspective, the spirit of the founding fathers lives on in slavery.[35] She opens her scene by describing in detail the conscientious efforts of the two slave waiters, Mark and Bacchus, as they prepare the sideboard and tables and create the appropriate atmosphere for the host and his guests. As the meal progresses, the reader is exposed to different conversations from around the table: gentlemen discuss the founding fathers and the current state of affairs in America, an elderly southern lady offers personal reminiscences of General Washington, and this anecdote in turn results in a series of toasts to the father of the country. Immediately following these patriotic toasts, the subject of the Fugitive Slave Law is brought up by one of the southerners, who puts the subject before a guest from the North, Mr. Perkins ("as you are not an Abolitionist, I suppose it will not be uncourteous to discuss the subject before you"). The southerner reminds Mr. Perkins of New England's own slaveholding past, which prompts some amiable joking about the probable severity of Puritan slave owners. Other threads of conversation follow, including discussions comparing the treatment of Irish laborers and free blacks in the North and comparing the plight of English factory workers to that of southern slaves, a recurring trope in pro-slavery literature of the period. One of the guests concludes, "If I must see slavery, let me see it in its best form, as it exists in our southern country." Mr. Perkins, the resident of Connecticut (and a stand-in for the northern reader), agrees, noting: "I am glad I am not a slave-holder, for . . . I should be knocking brains out from morning till night, that is if there are brains under all that mass of wool. Why, they are so slow, and inactive—I should be stumbling over them all the time; though from the specimens I have seen in your house, sir, I should say they made most agreeable servants."[36]

In this hospitable exchange of opinions, Eastman makes it acceptable for northerners to express their antipathy toward blacks, which is, for her and her ideal reader, the appropriate response. When Mr. Perkins goes on to express some misconceptions about the role of the overseer on the plantation, one of the southerners in attendance suggests an extended stay in the South, and the experience of a unique brand of southern hospitality, as a means of correcting his views: "Stay a little while with us.... You will not find us so bad as you think. We may roast a negro now and then, when we have a barbecue, but that will be our way of showing you hospitality. You must remember we are only 'poor heathenish Southerners,' according to the best received opinions of some who live with you in New England."[37] Eastman here directly engages the attacks of abolitionists who reported that slave punishments included such atrocities as being burned alive. For example, Theodore Dwight Weld's *American Slavery as It Is: Testimony of a Thousand Witnesses* includes several such accounts, and some of these incidents can be verified through other historical sources.[38] Eastman's dialogue, however, transforms such charges of barbarism into the fantasies of fanatical abolitionists. These charges now also become fodder for jokes at a dinner table by people in the know, including the northern and English guests. Perkins, the northerner, has admitted his own violent disgust toward blacks, and he can now join the company in laughing over the humorous idea of roasting a slave alive as an act of southern hospitality. Like the traveler from the North in *Anti-Fanaticism*, Mr. Perkins is being converted to the right attitudes on slavery through the social practices of southern hospitality, and presumably, some of Eastman's readers are also being convinced by this literary rendering of the South's unique tradition of hospitality.

Like Eastman's novel, Caroline Lee Hentz's 1854 novel, *The Planter's Northern Bride*, was written as a direct response to Stowe's *Uncle Tom's Cabin*. Hentz's novel details the budding romance between Eulalia Hastings, a simple and chaste village maiden from New England who happens to be the daughter of a firebrand abolitionist, and Russell Moreland, an aristocratic southern planter who is traveling in the North as he tries to recover from the emotional pain inflicted upon him by his first wife, the bewitching, exotic, and inconstant Claudia.[39] Eula and Moreland must overcome her father's prejudices in order to pursue their romance in marriage, but even after they succeed, they will face new challenges in the South, particularly at the hands of the novel's villains, Claudia and Brainard. In contrasting this pro-slavery novel with Stowe's text, it is worth keeping in mind that they were all aimed at roughly the same audience: white, middle- and upper-class Americans, especially women. A close reading of Hentz's novel and its representations of hospitality provides a more thorough and subtle picture of the nature of southern hospitality's appeal in antebellum America. While Stowe's novel assumes an ethics of hospitality that welcomes all equally, Hentz's book advocates a restrictive politics of hospitality emphasizing natural refinement and privilege to create a transregional feminine identity based on a hierarchy of supposedly natural racial *and* class identities. Hentz's novel exposes the decidedly antidemocratic and exclusionary sensibilities that motivated the discourse of southern hospitality in the antebellum period. The numerous rites, exchanges, and violations of hospitality described in the novel form a particularly meaningful subtext, helping to define characters' moral identities for Hentz's contemporary readers and creating the climactic crisis of the novel's plot.[40]

Early in the novel, for example, when we first hear of the heroine's abolitionist father, Squire Hastings, we are informed of his inappropriate practice of extending hospitality across the color line, particularly to a fugitive slave. Moreland, the ideal southern gentleman and plantation owner, is visiting the North, where he immediately falls in love with the pure, angelic Eulalia Hastings after seeing her in church. He inquires about her and her family and is disappointed to hear of her father's prejudices against the South and slaveholders. He is warned by his friend, a local architect, "You must not feel slighted if he invites your . . . slave . . . to come and break bread with him, without extending towards you the rites of hospitality."[41] Moreland is incredulous at the thought but is told of a past incident in which Hastings took in a runaway slave, which his informant describes as "one of the most repulsive objects I ever saw, —gigantic in stature, black as ebony, with coarse and brutal features, and manners corresponding to his appearance" (41). Yet Hastings, we are told, "gave him a seat in his carriage, brought him home, introduced him to his family, gave him a seat at table between his wife and eldest daughter, put him in the best bedroom, and appeared to feel himself honoured by having such a guest" (41). The thought of such liberal hospitality is repugnant to Hentz, and presumably to her implied readers as well, who are meant to identify with Eula Hastings, the novel's heroine. Pondering the incident, Moreland asks, "'But Miss Hastings, surely this must have been very repugnant to her feelings; she could not willingly submit to such an infliction.' He said this with a shudder of inexpressible loathing, as he looked on the delicate, graceful figure walking before him, and imagined it placed in such close juxtaposition with the rough, gigantic negro" (41). For Hentz, such liberal experiments are doomed to failure: we are further informed that Eula "happened to fall sick immediately after his arrival." Shortly thereafter, the runaway slave became "insolent" and unruly, so much so that "his host was at last compelled to turn him out of the house. Since then, he has had a double bolt fastened to his doors; and his dreams . . . are haunted by black spectres, armed and equipped for murder and robbery" (42). Later in the novel, Moreland and Hastings discuss this very incident, with Moreland admonishing Hastings, "I have heard the history of your hospitality to that vagabond. . . . I am sorry your hospitality was degraded so low. I do not wonder that Eulalia shrunk with horror . . . that her intuitive delicacy and purity felt the contamination and withered under its influence" (165). According to Moreland's—and Hentz's—perspective, racial antipathy is natural, and one's hospitality can be "degraded" if given too freely or to the wrong people. In this case, a fugitive slave is the worst possible recipient of one's charity or hospitality.[42] As discussed in chapter 2, etiquette and advice literature of the antebellum period often cautioned readers to be wary of the figure of the duplicitous beggar. Americans were warned that providing support for such unworthy poor would do more harm than good. In this passage, Hentz transforms the figure of the fugitive slave into just such a duplicitous beggar. Hastings mistakenly takes in this unworthy supplicant and pays the price. The fugitive's transformation into an insolent and unruly guest fills Hastings with nightmarish dread and causes his pure, delicate daughter to whither away under the specter of miscegenation.[43] The novel warns that fugitive slaves will become parasitical guests who overstay their welcome and create a growing burden for their hosts, a subtle caution to Americans concerned about the possibility of slavery's abolition and the consequent reality of having to absorb a population of former slaves into the social and economic order.

In addition to trading on fears regarding racial amalgamation, Hentz's novel also speaks to contemporary fears concerning class fluidity, both of which are expressed through the novel's politics of hospitality. The two villains in the novel—Moreland's first wife, Claudia, and Brainard, the itinerant preacher taken in by Moreland who turns out to be an abolitionist conspirator—violate the laws of hospitality as defined by Hentz, both by their actions and, perhaps more importantly, by their lower-class origins. Both of these characters violate social rites in ways that Hentz's readership would have easily recognized, but the author also implies that these social violations may be traced to their lower-class backgrounds.[44] Claudia, we are told, was born of Italian parents who lived a "gipsy life" as "itinerant minstrels" (373). She is rescued by a wealthy southern matron who, pitying her, purchases her from her parents and raises her as a lady. Similarly, Brainard was born of "obscure and indigent parents" and was early on incarcerated for theft. A "benevolent gentleman" takes pity on him, rescues him, and gives him all the benefits of a more respectable upbringing, including a college education. Hentz makes it clear, however, that these characters cannot overcome their lowly origins. Reflecting on Claudia, Hentz asserts, "Evil qualities, like physical diseases, are often hereditary, and descend, like the leprosy, a clinging, withering curse, ineradicable and incurable. The taint was in Claudia's blood. Education, precept and example kept down, for a while, her natural propensities, but when circumstances favoured their growth, they displayed a rankness and luxuriance that could proceed only from the strongest vitality. . . . Let the man who, infatuated by passion, is about to marry a woman taken originally from the dregs of social life, beware, lest he entail upon his offspring the awful judgment pronounced by a jealous God" (377). Hentz offers a similar assessment of Brainard. He is given the advantages of a stable upbringing and college education, "but the dark spot, for a time concealed, but never effaced, began to spread" (459). In short, the danger presented by both Claudia and Brainard is that they are not what they appear to be. While Brainard quite literally is in disguise as a preacher, the deeper implications surrounding both of these characters involve questions of class identity and upward mobility. Through the (misplaced) charitable acts of others, both of these characters have been provided ways of escaping the lowly class origins of their birth, but like Hastings's taking in the runaway slave, these charitable acts prove disastrous.

The message is quite clear: Hentz sees class distinctions as rigidly as she sees racial distinctions. There can be no equal social intercourse between blacks and whites or between the upper and the lower classes. Hentz's characterizations emphasize natural refinement and privilege in order to create a transregional feminine identity based on a hierarchy of supposedly natural racial *and* class identities.[45] As Hentz states elsewhere in the novel, "God has not made all men equal.... Inequality is one of Nature's laws.... It ... always will be felt, in spite of the dreams of the enthusiast or the efforts of the reformer" (305). This desire to make fixed castes of more fluid classes is seen in the numerous comparative representations of northern laborers and southern slaves in the novel but perhaps most notably in the character of Betsy Jones, the Hastings family servant. Betsy, we are told, "had none of the false pride which is often found in her class. She had no *ambition* to put herself upon a perfect equality with her employers. She did not care about sitting down with them at meal time, nor did she disdain the summons of a tinkling bell.... She had a just appreciation of herself" (66, emphasis in original). Betsy understands that her eternal role is to serve at the table, not to be served. Later, we are told that Betsy "was an uncommon instance of unchanging devotion to one family, in the midst of general fluctuation.... It is not often you find, among Northern servants, one who remains, as she had done, a fixture in the household, identified with the best interests of the family, and participating heartily in all its joys and sorrows" (548). How like a slave Betsy is, indeed, how like the paternalistic myth of the happy household of slavery transplanted to a northern setting! Advice literature of the day often lamented the difficulties women in the North faced in trying to find and keep reliable servants, and Hentz's portrayal of Betsy trades on the related fears and desires of her middle- and upper-class female readers. The novel suggests that every middle-class lady wants to be—and should be—an aristocratic lady, and that every American woman, North and South, would really rather have slaves than servants, or at least servants who acted like slaves. As we are told early in the novel, Eula's "exquisite sense of refinement" is rarely gratified in her New England village, but it is once she moves to her southern plantation home (56). Moreland provides Eula the life she deserves, and the slaves she deserves. She finally is given the appropriate environment in which to express her natural refinement. The rites of hospitality are a meaningful expression of this refinement, and considering the particular politics of southern hospitality advocated in Hentz's novel and in other pro-slavery texts, we begin to see that the degree to which the South boasted of its hospitality in the past was proportionate to the degree of subjugation existing in its social order.[46]

Overall, contrasting these anti- and pro-slavery responses to the controversy surrounding the Fugitive Slave Law shows that the discourse of southern hospitality provided southerners with a complex yet crucial way of imagining boundaries between foreigners or strangers from without (from whom the South often felt itself under attack) and the wholly other population of slaves that existed within (upon whose labor the aristocratic status of white southern planters depended and by whom they always felt threatened). In contrast to the progressive conceptions of hospitality articulated in anti-rendition texts, the politics of hospitality expressed in pro-slavery texts involve establishing and maintaining differences, as the discourse of hospitality and generosity effectively displaces the discourse of black rights as a way of maintaining the white, wealthy patriarchal order.

The Fugitives Respond: William Wells Brown and Frederick Douglass on Southern Hospitality and American Hostility

For most of its long history, the discourse of southern hospitality has functioned as just this sort of white exclusionary myth, produced by whites, directed to whites, and hostile to blacks (from subtly to blatantly so). The very persistence and proliferation of the myth in American culture indicates that throughout its long history, white Americans have generally been ready and willing consumers of this exclusionary racial message. In other words, the long persistence of the southern hospitality myth is to some extent a corollary of the broader persistence of American racism more generally. Writing in the wake of the national debate over the 1850 Fugitive Slave Law, the African American abolitionists and activists Frederick Douglass and William Wells Brown both offered critical interventions into the national debate over fugitive slaves and hospitality. Due to their notoriety as celebrated abolitionist activists who happened to also be fugitive slaves, both men were forced to travel abroad to be safe after the passage of the Fugitive Slave Law.[47] Both authors wrote about these experiences overseas in texts published in 1855: Douglass's *My Bondage and My Freedom*, which included significant revisions to and expansions of his original 1845 *Narrative of the Life of Frederick Douglass, an American Slave*, and Brown's *The American Fugitive in Europe: Sketches of Places and People Abroad*, which was a revised and expanded American edition of his 1852 travelogue, *Three Years in Europe*.[48] While both Douglass and

Brown echo the codified attacks on southern hospitality and the alternative themes of abolition hospitality discussed earlier, they also draw from their personal experiences traveling abroad to offer powerful attacks on American racism more generally. For both Brown and Douglass, southern hospitality was certainly a sham, but they also remind readers that the antebellum North was hardly a land of pervasive hospitality for free black Americans and would-be citizens.[49]

In publishing these 1855 texts, both Douglass and Brown drew on and made revisions to earlier slave narratives they had published in 1845 and 1847, respectively. Some of these revisions confirm the degree to which antislavery response to southern hospitality had been codified by midcentury and also indicate the degree to which hospitality was a critical discourse in the debate over the Fugitive Slave Law. Both authors revised aspects of their earlier writings to foreground the question of both slaveholder and abolition hospitality in ways that their earlier narratives had not. In *My Bondage and My Freedom*, for example, Douglass adds a new, extended description and analysis of southern hospitality as practiced on Colonel Lloyd's plantation, as well as a section on the religious hypocrisy of Master Auld's hospitality. These new sections that Douglass added to his 1855 text echo recognizable lines of abolitionist attacks that had become codified around southern hospitality in the decades of sectional conflict over slavery: he highlights the hypocrisy of slaveowner hospitality, underscores the slave labor and degradation that must pay for it (offering the perspective of the "big house" from the slave toiling in the field), and portrays southern hospitality as a propaganda tool.[50] In contrast to Douglass's narrative, some of the revisions made in William Wells Brown's 1855 work also offer a corrective to the discourse of "abolition hospitality." Brown celebrates the spirit of hospitality practiced by abolitionists in both his 1847 slave narrative and in his 1855 publication, *The American Fugitive in Europe*. In the latter text, however, he makes subtle yet meaningful changes to his narration of the hospitality exchange that resulted in his successful escape from slavery, and these changes work to alter the reader's perspective on the fugitive.

The theme of abolition hospitality figures prominently in Brown's 1847 narrative: a climactic moment in Brown's successful escape involves the hospitality he receives from the Quaker abolitionist Wells Brown, who takes the desperate fugitive in, provides for him, and sets him successfully on the path to freedom. This hospitality exchange is a formative moment in Brown's story: he consequently takes his host's name for his new identity as a free man and also dedicates his 1847 narrative to Wells Brown, invoking the biblical injunction to provide hospitality to those in need: "THIRTEEN years ago, I came to your door, a weary fugitive from chains and stripes. I was a stranger, and you took me in. I was hungry, and you fed me. Naked was I, and you clothed me.

Even a name by which to be known among men, slavery had denied me." But if we compare the way the scene of Wells Brown's hospitality is told in the 1847 narrative with its narration in the 1855 text, we can see subtle but important changes that direct the reader toward a different interpretation of the fugitive slave.[51] These changes reflect Brown's awareness that the discourse of hospitality, while pertinent to the plight of the fugitive slave, could potentially cloud the question of black rights, rendering fugitives only objects of pity and charity for the white reader rather than subjects worthy of respect, social equality, and full citizenship. For example, the tone and details of the 1847 narrative dwell much more on Brown's anxiety and awkwardness at finding himself sharing a social space with his white hosts, not unlike the depiction of the runaway slave in Whitman's "Song of Myself" (with "his revolving eyes and his awkwardness") mentioned earlier. Upon arriving at the Quaker's home, Brown emphasizes his timidity and embarrassment, noting, "It was some time before I could be induced to enter it"; he also explains, "I was not ... prepared to receive their hospitalities," for they were "too kind": "I had never had a white man to treat me as an equal, and the idea of a white lady waiting on me at the table was still worse!"[52] Brown even adds a slight element of humor as he describes his uncertain response to being provided a strong herbal tea by his hostess, who happens to be a practitioner of the Thomsonian system of botanical remedies popular in antebellum America. Overall, these details and sentiments make the fugitive an appropriate case for charity, but in doing so, they also run the risk of increasing the distance between whites and blacks, making the black figure an object to be pitied more than respected.

In contrast, Brown in the 1855 edition of *The American Fugitive* deleted all those lines just cited, as well as the element of humor. This, combined with the new third-person voice, results in a simpler, more direct treatment of the scene and arguably a more dignified representation of the black fugitive for the largely white readership to consider:

> He soon found that he was under the shed of a Quaker, and a Quaker of the George Fox stamp. He had heard of Quakers and their kindness; but was not prepared to meet with such hospitality as now greeted him. He saw nothing but kind looks, and heard nothing but tender words. He began to feel the pulsations of a new existence. White men always scorned him, but now a white benevolent woman felt glad to wait on him; it was a revolution in his experience. The table was loaded with good things, but he could not eat. If he were allowed the privilege of sitting in the kitchen, he thought he could do justice to the viands. The surprise being over, his appetite soon returned.
>
> "I have frequently been asked," says William, "how I felt upon finding myself regarded as a man by a white family; especially having just run away from one. I cannot say that I have ever answered the question yet."[53]

This revised scene downplays to some degree the sense of awkwardness and embarrassment in the 1847 narrative. While the earlier depiction of the slave's discomfort and social anxiety enhances the sense of white benevolence and charity for someone who may be perceived as a lesser being, the revised version makes it clearer that Brown deserves the equal treatment he is receiving as a natural right. Newly added phrases naturalize the sense of hospitality as an inherent right shared among equals rather than experienced as a gift bestowed by superiors; this is a "new existence," but an inherently just existence, a social "revolution" of natural equality. The closing lines, when Brown is asked to reflect on white hospitality, indicate that this revolution is still unfinished. Overall, these revisions reflect Brown's awareness that a strain of paternalistic benevolence in white abolitionism could too easily find itself aligned with assumptions of essential racial inferiority. The discourse of hospitality can sometimes blur the discourse of rights with ideas of benevolence and charity that place the host above the guest, and abolition discourse on fugitive slaves could occasionally betray such tendencies; it could nonetheless be useful at key moments for garnering greater support for the antislavery cause. Still, a great conceptual distance exists between accepting a fugitive slave as an object of charity and benevolence and accepting a free black man as a social equal.[54] Brown's revisions between the 1847 and 1855 texts attempt to shift the reader's response from the former to the latter.

Indeed, in their 1855 narratives, both Brown and Douglass remind their readers that while the fugitive slave may be a worthy object of compassion, benevolence, and charity, the free black American is also worthy of respect and entitled to equal treatment in all spheres of American life: social, economic, religious, legal, and political. Most notably, both authors draw on their personal experiences traveling abroad to delineate sharp, critical contrasts between the hospitality they receive as "foreigners" abroad and the hostility and racism they face as perpetual strangers or aliens in their native land. Both authors experienced a level of freedom abroad that was new to them, particularly freedom from the racism so prevalent in American culture. Brown, for example, relished his time abroad, traveling thousands of miles across Europe and the British Isles, taking in cultural sites one associates with a "grand tour," and hobnobbing with prominent diplomats, activists, artists, and reformers. He also delivered approximately one thousand public lectures in his five years overseas. As Ezra Greenspan puts it, the former slave Brown found this new sense of freedom—unrestricted for the first time by American forms of color prejudice or racism—"thoroughly exhilarating."[55] Indeed, Brown recounts how though he had originally felt himself a "foreigner in a strange land" upon arriving in England, five years of freedom and hospitable welcome had made him feel like "an Englishman by habit, if not by birth." Consequently, Brown feels conflicted when the time comes to return to his "native land," for he knows the racism and discriminatory practices that will greet him upon his return: "My heart became sad at the thought of leaving all these dear friends, to return to a country in which I had spent some of the best days of my life as a slave, and where I knew that prejudice would greet me on my arrival."[56] While Brown's narrative generally accords with the genteel, restrictive conventions of the travelogue genre to which *American Fugitive in Europe* aligns itself—a genre designed to give middle-class consumers a secondhand experience of cultural highlights and heritage—his reflections on his return to America provide nothing less than a full frontal assault on not just slavery but American racism more broadly.[57]

Near the end of his narrative, as he reflects on his time in England, Brown describes his ability to travel and visit, unmolested, such notable sites as St. Paul's Cathedral, Westminster Abbey, Temple Church, the British Museum and National Gallery, the Strand, and Piccadilly: "In all these I had been treated as a man. The 'negro pew,' which I had seen in the churches of America, was not to be found in the churches of London. There, too, were my daughters. They who had been denied education upon equal terms with children of a fairer complexion, in the United States, had been received in the London schools upon terms of perfect equality." In contrast, Brown experiences the veil of race and racism almost as soon as he returns to America and makes a trip to Philadelphia. He complains bitterly of the "Colorphobia" that reigns supreme in the "pro-slavery, negro-hating" cities of New York and Philadelphia, and he further characterizes this racism as an "unnatural" and "anti-christian prejudice." He narrates an incident that occurred in Philadelphia shortly after his return to America. Brown was with two companions from abroad—foreigners in America—and when the trio hailed an omnibus, Brown was gruffly informed, "We don't allow niggers to ride in here."[58] At the same time, his companions were offered seats. The incident lays bare the arbitrary logic of American hospitality and hostility: race governs the threshold, and whiteness is the passport to belonging. American racism overrides all other categories of identity and community, arbitrarily affording foreigners the privileges of citizens while simultaneously making aliens of native sons. Brown and his two foreign companions had traveled together from London to Liverpool and then across the Atlantic, but as Brown recounts:

> As soon as we touch the soil of America we can no longer ride in the same conveyance, no longer eat at the same table, or be regarded with equal justice, by our thin-skinned democracy. During five years' residence in monarchical Europe I had enjoyed the rights allowed to all foreigners in the countries through which I passed; but on returning to my NATIVE LAND the influence of slavery meets me the first day that I am in the country.... I had partaken of the hospitality of noblemen in England.... I had eaten at the same table with Sir

Edward Bulwer Lytton, Charles Dickens, Eliza Cook, Alfred Tennyson, and the son-in-law of Sir Walter Scott; the omnibuses of Paris, Edinburgh, Glasgow and Liverpool, had stopped to take me up... —but what mattered that? My face was not white, my hair was not straight; and, therefore, I must be excluded from a seat in a third-rate American omnibus. Slavery demanded that it should be so. I charge this prejudice to the pro-slavery pulpits of our land, which first set the example of proscription by erecting in their churches the "negro pew." I charge it to that hypocritical profession of democracy which will welcome fugitives from other countries, and drive its own into exile. I charge it to the recreant sons of the men who carried on the American revolutionary war, and who come together every fourth of July to boast of what their fathers did, while they, their sons, have become associated with bloodhounds, to be put at any moment on the track of the fugitive slave.[59]

As mentioned earlier in this chapter, many Americans were outraged by the Fugitive Slave Law's far-reaching effects in the North; these Americans felt that the 1850 Compromise essentially made slavery the law of the North as well as the South. Brown here rightly directs his readers to consider the broader American problem of racism. From his perspective, until America can move beyond its persistent forms of racism, slavery will always be the law of the land. According to Brown, slavery demands that he be treated as an inferior being not just in the South but in the North as well.

In *My Bondage and My Freedom*, Frederick Douglass recalls his experiences in England in much the same way, and he draws conclusions identical to those of Brown. His chapters that describe his experiences in the British Isles include a letter he composed for Garrison while abroad, and like Brown, he describes the newfound, exhilarating sense of freedom he enjoys living abroad, free from American racism. Both Brown and Douglass must leave America to discover a truer, more complete, and cosmopolitan sense of identity *and* hospitality:

> I have spent some of the happiest moments of my life since landing in this country. I seem to have undergone a transformation. I live a new life.... I find no difficulty here in obtaining admission into any place of worship, instruction, or amusement, on equal terms with people as white as any I ever saw in the United States. I meet nothing to remind me of my complexion. I find myself regarded and treated at every turn with the kindness and deference paid to white people. When I go to church, I am met by no upturned nose and scornful lip to tell me, "*We don't allow niggers in here!*"[60]

Like Brown, Douglass shows that race governs the threshold of belonging in American society. He continues with a devastating series of personal anecdotes from his life in America. In each anecdote he seeks entrance to the public entertainments and basic services that any white citizen and reader would take for granted—an exhibition, a religious revival, a lyceum lecture, a steamship cabin, a restaurant, an omnibus—and in each case he is met with this blunt and humiliating refrain, "*We don't allow niggers in here!*" After contrasting these experiences with his invitation to dine with the Lord Mayor of Dublin, Douglass sardonically reflects:

> What a pity there was not some American democratic christian at the door of his splendid mansion, to bark out at my approach, 'They don't allow niggers in here!' The truth is, the people here know nothing of the republican negro hate prevalent in our glorious land. They measure and esteem men according to their moral and intellectual worth, and not according to the color of their skin. Whatever may be said of the aristocracies here, there is none based on the color of a man's skin. This species of aristocracy belongs preëminently to 'the land of the free, and the home of the brave.' I have never found it abroad, in any but Americans. It sticks to them wherever they go. They find it almost as hard to get rid of, as to get rid of their skins.[61]

In short, both Brown and Douglass prod their American readers to entertain the possibility of a more inclusive form of American democracy, and ironically, they must return to the Old World for a usable model of behavior. At the same time, both authors push the discourse of hospitality in America beyond the recurring debates over the reality or unreality of hospitable slaveholders or the question of benevolence and charity toward fugitive slaves; their experiences beyond the nation's boundaries allowed them to frame a far more cosmopolitan ideal of hospitality and citizenship, a subject that I take up in the next chapter, where I consider the international contexts of southern hospitality.

CHAPTER FOUR

Southern Hospitality in a Transnational Context

The Geopolitical Logic of the South's Sovereign Hospitality

Writing against the backdrop of the civil rights movement in the 1960s, the historian and activist Howard Zinn offered the following assessment of what he described as the South's pervasive xenophobia, linking it to southern hospitality: "It is one of the curious paradoxes of Southern life that suspicion of strangers, of outsiders, goes along with what is called 'Southern hospitality.' The answer to the paradox is that there is a line of demarcation which separates the accepted person from the unaccepted. Within that line, the warmth is almost overwhelming. But outside it, the coolness can become hostility to the point of violence. The foreign-born is almost always outside that line in the South, as is, of course, the Negro."[1] Zinn was writing in the decade following the *Brown v. Board of Education* decision, when many in the South had grown increasingly suspicious of outside interference in southern affairs, part of the South's long history of navigating the relationship with outsiders from without and the outsiders within (African Americans). Of course, Zinn's assertion that the foreigner and the African American are both "outside that line" does not mean that they occupy the same position, for as Derrida has described it, the politics of hospitality help to maintain the difference between the "foreigner" and the "absolute other."[2] While the foreigner may (or may not) be welcomed, those deemed absolute strangers or aliens (for whatever reason a particular society defines) never can be.

Sarah Josepha Hale's 1853 novel, *Liberia, or Mr. Peyton's Experiment*, one of the many novelistic responses to the Fugitive Slave Law and *Uncle Tom's Cabin*, contains a unique scene illustrating this distinction between the foreigner and the absolute stranger, particularly as it relates to race and the discourse of southern hospitality. While the book is not exactly pro-slavery, it is pro-southern in its general sentiments and its representation of the book's titular hero, Mr. Peyton, whom Hale praises for his "hospitality, liberality, and true benevolence." Hale's novel details Mr. Peyton's freeing of his slaves and his various unsuccessful efforts to resettle them, first on nearby farms in Virginia, then in the urban North, and even in Canada. In each case his former slaves struggle to survive with the new responsibilities of freedom. They finally have a chance to thrive, however, when they join the newly established nation of Liberia on the west coast of Africa. As a longtime editor of *Godey's*, Sarah Josepha Hale was one of the most influential voices on all aspects of American domesticity. Though *Godey's* editorial policy was to refrain from engaging in political debate, her novel has a decidedly political goal in advocating the resettlement of slaves in Africa.[3] Hale makes it abundantly clear that, from her perspective, the African has no place in America. In her preface to *Liberia*, she describes those of African descent living in America as "the stranger within her gates," and declares that her goal in the novel is "to show the advantages Liberia offers to the African, who among us has no home, no position, and no future." In Hale's view, blacks living in America (whether slave or free) will forever be an unassimilable alien presence. Despite this inhospitable perspective on black men and women who had been born and lived their entire lives within the nation's borders, a strange turn occurs in one of the book's concluding scenes, where, in contrast to these unwelcoming sentiments toward the alien black population, a stranger visiting from Africa is deemed worthy of respect and hospitality. Moreover, when this man, the American-born president of Liberia, visits a group of philanthropists in Philadelphia, it is the southerner Mr. Peyton who shows the hypocritical northern philanthropists how to overcome their color prejudice in receiving the African. When Peyton arrives late to a reception for the Liberian president, he immediately understands and corrects an awkward social moment when the African is being ignored by the very men gathered to celebrate him ("they had assembled for the purpose of meeting; and each one of them was trying to appear unconscious of his presence"). The scene underscores what Hale perceives to be the inherent, natural color prejudice residing in all white Americans toward those of the African race, and only the aristocratic southern planter, armed with his social graces and his paternalistic knowledge of the African character, can step into this breach and show the way. Peyton immediately and gracefully enters into a lively conversation with the Liberian president, and soon the pair find themselves to be the life of the party, "the centre of an audience composed of all the persons in the room."[4] In this scene, the Liberian president's status as a "foreigner" gives him a recognizable identity, while *native-born* slaves and black freemen remain absolute strangers or aliens in Hale's view. Blacks living in America may be worthy of charity perhaps (in the form of being sent back to Africa) but not hospitality (which would imply the potential for reciprocity and even equality among the guest and host).[5]

This transformation from "stranger" to "foreigner" that occurs in Hale's novel raises questions regarding hospitality and how it relates to questions of race, national identity, and "foreignness" in the antebellum South. While previous chapters in this study have examined hospitality primarily within the domestic space, in this chapter, I put this question of southern hospitality in a broader, transnational context, particularly by exploring two case studies of southern xenophobia in the mid-nineteenth century, a xenophobia related specifically to slavery and race. Through the figures of free sailors of color (American and foreign) and of the revolutionary Hungarian freedom fighter Louis Kossuth, I trace the political logic of the South's jealously guarded sovereignty over slavery as it definitively overrides its claims of hospitality. In the case of the former, we see that, unlike Hale's conclusion, free citizens and foreign nationals of color were routinely quarantined and stripped of all legal status when they entered southern ports, even in the case of shipwreck. In the reception of Kossuth, we see that his status as a foreigner was a sliding identity contingent on slavery. As Kossuth's presence in America became even tangentially linked to the question of slavery, the southern reception evolved from admiration of a freedom fighter to denigration of a parasitical alien, with Kossuth himself figuratively transformed into the image of a fugitive slave. In these cases, we see the logical undercurrent of antebellum southern hospitality: driving fears regarding slavery and what the South perceived as external and internal threats to its peculiar social order. While historians and some literary scholars have provided thorough accounts of both the Negro Seamen Acts and the national and regional reception of Kossuth, they have yet to consider the extent to which these two national debates were informed by competing antebellum discourses of hospitality and to fully consider the fundamental relationship between the concepts of sovereignty and hospitality in the antebellum South. Southern sovereignty went hand in hand with southern hospitality, gauging threats and policing the borders of the prescribed social order.

Cosmopolitan Hospitality Meets the Negro Seamen Acts

Midway through "Civil Disobedience," his seminal essay arguing the existence of a "higher law" than mere governmental authority, Henry David Thoreau makes what today's reader would most certainly find to be an obscure reference to "an act of inhospitality" committed by South Carolina against Massachusetts:

> If my esteemed neighbor, the State's ambassador, who will devote his days to the settlement of the question of human rights in the Council Chamber, instead of being threatened with the prisons of Carolina, were to sit down the prisoner of Massachusetts, that State which is so anxious to foist the sin of slavery upon her sister,—though at present she can discover only an act of inhospitality to be

the ground of a quarrel with her,—the Legislature would not wholly waive the subject the following winter.[6]

The "esteemed neighbor" to whom Thoreau refers is Samuel Hoar, a Massachusetts politician and fellow resident of Concord who was sent by the state of Massachusetts to Charleston, South Carolina, in late 1844 to test the constitutionality of one of its laws that was negatively affecting free citizens of Massachusetts. The law in question, one of several such laws that had been adopted in southern coastal states since the 1820s, dictated that any free sailors of color who landed in southern ports be imprisoned, even in the case of shipwreck. Known collectively as the Negro Seamen Acts, the first of these laws was enacted in South Carolina in 1822 following Denmark Vesey's failed plot to spark a slave insurrection in Charleston.[7] In the wake of the uncovered conspiracy, South Carolinians worried about the possibility of free sailors of color, from either the North or foreign countries, mingling with and influencing their domestic slave population. The threat was so troubling that then–South Carolina governor John Wilson described free black sailors as being "afflicted with infectious disease." The "disease" in this case, would be freedom, and according to the logic of slavery, such a threat of infection must be effectively quarantined. Accordingly, the Act for Better Regulation and Government of Free Negroes and Persons of Color stipulated that any "free negroes or persons of color" who arrived on a ship in "any port or harbor" of the state are to be "confined in jail until said vessel shall clear out and depart from this State."[8] Moreover, the captain of the ship, and not the state, was responsible for covering the costs of the sailor's confinement. If a captain failed to pay such costs, the sailor would be considered a slave and sold. Over the next two decades, states across the coastal South—North Carolina, Georgia, Florida, Alabama, and Louisiana—would follow South Carolina's lead by adopting similar laws. Consequently, free citizens of color from around the world who entered southern ports were transformed into one of two identities: prisoner or slave.[9]

The laws were carried out with varying degrees of vigor and severity; South Carolina was considered especially notorious among black sailors. It is estimated that more than ten thousand free citizens of color—from both the United States and foreign nations—were jailed under these provisions across the South.[10] An untold number simply vanished into slavery, and because they lacked legal standing (South Carolina, for example, suspended habeas corpus for black mariners), there is little historical evidence of what essentially amounted to state-sanctioned kidnapping. Those allowed to return to their ships lost wages during their periods of confinement, and shipping companies routinely passed the cost of imprisonment on to them following their release. These laws had a profound effect on the livelihood of these *free citizens* of *both* the United States *and* foreign countries, often limiting their ability to sign on to vessels that might be traveling through southern waters. The laws also had a negative impact on free commerce with other states in the Union and foreign countries, as on many occasions black sailors either mutinied or abandoned ship rather than sail to southern ports.[11]

Southern states enacted and carried out these laws despite vehement challenges from state, federal, and foreign governments. Great Britain, for example, lodged protests with the United States over a full quarter century. Unable to obtain relief from the federal government, in the 1850s Britain discretely began to make direct appeals to the southern states through its consuls, a tactic that, when made public, aroused a good amount of controversy and suspicion in the North.[12] Those who protested the Negro Seamen Acts saw the southern practice of imprisoning foreign sailors of color as an outrageous violation of both the rights of free citizens and the "law of nations." On the one hand, the right to free interstate travel was a basic element of citizenship; on the other hand, the right to temporary sojourn (to visit a sovereign territory and not be treated with hostility) was a basic right in Immanuel Kant's cosmopolitanism. Southerners, in contrast, defended these practices, claiming that they were acting within their sovereign right and according to the first law of nature: self-preservation.[13] Southerners grew especially defensive of this example of state sovereignty as the sectional division intensified, as is evident in their inhospitable response to Samuel Hoar's mission, cited in Thoreau's "Civil Disobedience." Before Hoar could even begin to plead the case of Massachusetts, he was run out of Charleston by a mob that had been spurred on in part by both incendiary public declarations of South Carolina's governor, James Henry Hammond, and similar resolutions against Hoar passed by the state legislature.

While Thoreau's allusion to the Hoar affair may be lost on today's readers of "Civil Disobedience," among his contemporaries it was a well-known episode, widely reported in the press and frequently cited in the ongoing debates over slavery. The Massachusetts state legislature was so incensed by Hoar's treatment that it was considered a "plausible cause for war between the states."[14] In alluding to the affair as an "act of inhospitality," Thoreau, like many of the abolitionists and liberal reformers I have cited in previous chapters, challenges the pervasive myth of southern hospitality in a way that would have been understood by sympathetic listeners and readers of his day.[15] But Thoreau also directs his readers to both look beyond the surface of the Hoar affair and rethink their understanding of hospitality altogether. Thoreau, in line with liberal reformers discussed earlier, subtly prods his audience to see hospitality as a progressive state of mind, a form of empathetic human action, and a universal principle of equality.

If anything, Thoreau in the passage cited above chastises his audience for focusing too much attention on the treatment of Hoar and not enough on the plight of the black sailors themselves. Rather than focusing on legal maneuverings from a distance, Thoreau encourages his readers to take action by engaging in civil disobedience where they are, a program that places them in metaphorical proximity with the black sailors themselves.[16] As Thoreau explains, "Under a government which imprisons any unjustly"—as in the treatment of free black sailors in the South—"the true place for a just man is also a prison.... It is there that the fugitive slave, and the Mexican prisoner on parole, and the Indian come to plead the wrongs of his race...; on that separate, but more free and honorable, ground, where the State places those who are not *with* her, but *against* her." With this premise in place, Thoreau forcefully asserts that the prison is "the only house in a slave State in which a free man can abide with honor." Thoreau here utterly rejects the possibility of "southern hospitality," instead articulating his radical theory on resistance to government authority and its imperfect laws as a progressive form of universal hospitality. He is willing to forgo his privileged position as a protected citizen of a supposedly free society because he is aware that not all are invited to receive the same benefits. When Thoreau refused to pay his poll tax because the government was pursuing an unjust war in Mexico that would extend slavery, he placed himself, figuratively and—at least for the one night he spent in jail—literally, alongside the resident aliens, foreigners, and strangers in American society. Completely subverting the notion that hospitality is a matter of entertaining guests in one's own domestic space, Thoreau claims that there is more "honor" in breaking bread with the dispossessed in prison than in being feted by the social elites of an unjust society, in this case the wealthy aristocracy of the slaveholding South. Certainly, according to Thoreau's logic, there can be no hospitality where slavery exists.

Thoreau, again like many other progressives of his day, places this universal ethic of hospitality over the fallible laws of human institutions. For example, in the conclusion of "Civil Disobedience," when he attacks Senator Daniel Webster for his abiding faith in the Constitution and the laws of men, he criticizes Webster for a lack of *mental* hospitality: "Webster never goes behind government, and so cannot speak with authority about it. His words are wisdom to those legislators who contemplate no essential reform in the existing government; but for thinkers, and those who legislate for all time he never once glances at the subject. I know of those whose serene and wise speculations on this theme would soon reveal the limits of his mind's range and hospitality."[17] Through his references to the Hoar affair and the Negro Seamen Laws, his assertion that hospitality and slavery cannot coexist, and his criticism of Webster for his lack of mental hospitality, Thoreau subtly challenges the conventional discourses on hospitality in his day. For him, hospitality exists beyond social exchanges in domestic settings, conventional morality, and human law: it is the ethical horizon at which all strangers, foreigners, aliens, and outcasts are offered an unconditional and universal welcome. Thoreau's is a decidedly cosmopolitan vision of human society.[18]

The Negro Seamen Acts and the conflicts and controversies surrounding them place the question of hospitality squarely in the realms of international law and universal human rights. In these broad contexts, hospitality encompasses "all human rights claims which are cross-border in scope," as Seyla Benhabib concisely explains. Immanuel Kant in *Perpetual Peace* declares that cosmopolitan citizenship "shall be limited to conditions of universal hospitality," and Jacques Derrida has deconstructed Kant's assertion that hospitality is a matter of universal right by distinguishing between the absolute ethic of hospitality that demands a universal welcoming of the stranger and the laws that must limit this welcoming. Benhabib in *Another Cosmopolitanism* goes further to develop Kant's cosmopolitan philosophy in a way that both acknowledges and even embraces the paradoxes limned by Derrida. According to her, with the 1948 United Nations Declaration of Human Rights, "we have entered a phase in the evolution of global civil society, which is characterized by a transition from *international* to *cosmopolitan* norms of justice." International norms of justice develop from official relationships and obligations among various states and their representatives through negotiated treaties, trade agreements, guest-worker programs, and the like. In contrast, cosmopolitan norms of justice "accrue to individuals as moral and legal persons in a worldwide civil society." This transition, however, has necessarily resulted in tension between the particularities of law as articulated and enforced by states and their justice systems and the universal ethical obligation of human rights, which are often at odds with these laws but are nonetheless owed to each individual regardless of his or her state affiliation or "legal" status. In other words, the transition to cosmopolitan norms has created a conflict between the laws of nations and what may be described as the *higher* law of human rights. For Benhabib, this conflict conceptually boils down to two opposing terms: "sovereignty" and "hospitality." She observes, "Throughout the international system, as long as territorial bounded states are recognized as the sole legitimate units of negotiation and representation, a tension, and at times even a fatal contradiction, is palpable: the modern state system is caught between *sovereignty* and *hospitality*, between the prerogative to choose to be a party to cosmopolitan norms and human rights treaties, and the obligation to extend recognition of these human rights to all." Cosmopolitanism, then, cannot be seen as a transcendent end point or definitive destination toward which the world is inevitably headed. Instead, as Benhabib states, "Cosmopolitanism . . . is a philosophical project of mediations, not of reductions and totalizations."[19]

Though Benhabib rightly casts 1948 as a watershed moment in the transition from international to cosmopolitan norms of justice, we should also recognize that the inherent tension she identifies in this transition—the tension between sovereignty and hospitality—has always been present in organized human societies. In the case of the antebellum South, both of these terms were *essential* to how southerners defined and imagined their culture. Simply put, state sovereignty was the very core of the South's political philosophy; hospitality was likewise an essential, defining term in its social and domestic sphere. Both were inextricably tied to slavery and the racial order of the Old South. The example of the Negro Seamen Acts extends the consideration of southern hospitality beyond this domestic sphere and into the realm of international law and politics; indeed, one of the early legal defenses of the law in South Carolina used the example of the domestic space, where the master of the household governs who crosses the threshold, as a way of explaining the law:

> The civilized man can secure his family against the contagion of the dissolute or depraved, by closing his doors, or selecting his visitors;—So, every sovereign state, has the perfect right of interdicting all intercourse with strangers, or of selecting those whose influence or example she may fear, and confining the exclusion to them. A master of a family receives or excludes his visitors, according to the peculiar situation and feelings of his own household. A State must be the sole judge to decide what strangers may or may not enter.[20]

Here the South's restrictive politics of hospitality are extended to the broader sphere of intercourse with free citizens of other states and nations. In both of these spheres—the southern household and the domestic space of the state—hospitality involves determining who doesn't belong, with race serving as the common denominator governing the threshold. It is an exercise of sovereignty. What is particularly striking about the Negro Seamen Laws, from a contemporary perspective, is the manner in which the laws and politics of slavery violently transgressed the ethics of hospitality. While we have largely forgotten these contradictions in the passage of years, antebellum Americans and foreigners alike were well aware of them, and many found them utterly confounding. In fact, the existence of the Negro Seamen Laws created a decades-long, simmering controversy that mobilized abolitionists and also prompted transregional and international protests against them.[21]

Francis Colburn Adams's 1852 novel, *Manuel Pereira; or, The Sovereign Rule of South Carolina, with Views of Southern Laws, Life, and Hospitality*, is among the body of literature protesting the Negro Seamen Acts. It is a thinly fictionalized account of a particularly egregious case in which a shipwrecked sailor was imprisoned for fifty-four days in Charleston's jail, but Adams takes the opportunity to critique the entire South Carolina social order, making the case that southerners' social practices cannot be separated from this egregious law and its effects. The novel's subtitle underscores the very contradiction Benhabib describes between a state's right of sovereignty and the obligation of hospitality, but it also directs readers to think more broadly about how they define hospitality. Hospitality is not only embodied in a people's social life; it is also embodied—or not—in its laws. Adams's novel expresses a cosmopolitan view of citizenship and effectively illustrates Thoreau's contention that the prison is "the only house in a slave State in which a free man can abide with honor."

Francis Colburn Adams was a former resident of Charleston and had been an active member of the city's theatrical and literary communities. Many of the details of his life remain sketchy, but his writings show that he was an outspoken critic of slavery. In addition to *Manuel Pereira*, Adams published other books critical of the South: *Our World; or, The Slaveholder's Daughter* in 1855 and *Justice in the By-Ways* in 1856. He also published in 1853 a book titled *Uncle Tom at Home; A Review of the Reviewers and Repudiators of Uncle Tom's Cabin by Mrs. Stowe*.[22] In the prefaces to both his defense of Stowe's novel and *Manuel Pereira*, Adams directly appeals to southerners and claims that the books were written while he was in Charleston. In *Manuel Pereira*, he pointedly attacks the element of southern cultural identity that southerners held most dear: their hospitality. Through his depiction of the plight of Manuel Pereira, an olive-skinned native of Brazil who has no African blood and who swears allegiance to England, Adams extends hospitality beyond the merely social sphere and into the realms of universal law and cosmopolitan right. Manuel is a free citizen of the world, yet his natural rights are horribly violated by the peculiar laws of the South.

Adams endows his fictional version of the real-life Manuel Pereira with the qualities of Melville's Billy Budd: he is kind, generous, guileless, and incredibly well liked by the crew. But he also underscores Manuel's cosmopolitan identity, emphasizing the fluidity of *both* national *and* racial boundaries; more than a citizen of a particular nation, Manuel is a cosmopolite: "Manuel was born in Brazil, an extract of the Indians and Spanish, claiming birthright of the Portuguese nation. It mattered but very little to Manuel where he was born, for he had been so long tossed about in his hardy vocation that he had almost become alienated from the affections of birthplace. He had sailed so long under the protection of the main-jack of old England that he had formed a stronger allegiance to that country than to any other." In addition to his cosmopolitan identity, we are also informed of Manuel's cosmopolitan experiences as a sailor who "had sailed around the world" and "visited savage and semi-civilized nations." Among these varied travels, Manuel "had received the hospitality of cannibals, had joined in the merry dance with the Otaheitian, had eaten the fruit of the Hottentots, shared the coarse morsel of the Greenlander, been twice chased by the Patagonians—but what shall we say?—he was imprisoned, for the olive tints of his color, in a land where not only civilization rules in its brightest conquests, but chivalry and honor sound its fame within the lanes, streets, and court-yards."[23] The distinction Adams draws between the civilized and barbarous peoples of the world is the distinction between hospitality and hostility, and Manuel himself articulates his own sense of cosmopolitan rights, though they are still grounded in international law and the national status of England.[24] Unfortunately for Manuel—and for the thousands of black sailors imprisoned under the Negro Seamen Laws—it was just this sense of progress toward universal human rights that made free cosmopolitan citizens of color such a threat to the South's social order of race-based slavery.

When Manuel's ship is disabled in a storm and running low on fresh water, its captain, a Scotsman named Thompson, decides to head to the port of Charleston. His mate warns him of Charleston's unique laws concerning sailors of color and fears that they will apply to Manuel. The captain, however, expresses his confidence that, as a shipwreck, they surely must warrant an exception, particularly in light of southerners' reputation for hospitality: "Certainly, no nation in Christendom could be found, that wouldn't open their hearts to a shipwrecked sailor. I have too much faith in what I have heard of the hospitality of Southerners, to believe any thing of that kind" (24). Unfortunately, Captain Thompson's faith in southern hospitality proves unfounded. Shortly after their arrival, and despite the fact that Manuel is a free citizen and has no African blood, he is imprisoned in a decrepit, vermin-infested Charleston jail cell, where he withers away for most of the novel. The novel details the captain's and British consul's numerous efforts to have Manuel released and, when these efforts fail, to at least provide him some material comfort. Even these efforts are rebuffed by the manipulative and sadistic sheriff and constables, who seem dead set on asserting South Carolina sovereignty against any outside meddling.

While the plot of the novel is quite simple—with Manuel suffering increasing abuse at the hands of the sheriff and his lackeys—Adams often interrupts the narrative to provide anecdotes, scenes, and dialogues that, taken together, provide a more complete picture of life in Charleston, hence the breadth of the novel's subtitle. In contrast to the idyllic image of the paternalistic southern plantation with which Americans were familiar, Adams—in abolitionist fashion—portrays a southern legal, political, and social order based on arbitrary power and characterized by corruption, licentiousness, exploitation, violence, and barbarous cruelty. At the same time, he makes it clear that not all southerners are guilty of these crimes; instead, he includes some sympathetic southerners who attempt in vain to help Manuel or alleviate his situation. Adams cites and quotes from editorials from Charleston newspapers that decry the abuses of the Charleston judicial system, and some of the book's fictional southerners speak out against the law that lands Manuel in prison, criticizing in particular the law's negative effect on foreign trade with southern ports. All these critics, however, are ultimately ineffectual against the unbending law and the arbitrary power of politicians and officials sworn to uphold it. As Adams shows, the peculiar institution of slavery trumps everything in southern society, making the South's claims of hospitality ring hollow and their social manners seem utterly meretricious.

Despite the problems faced by Manuel, his captain, and the British consul, the Charlestonians repeatedly boast to the captain of the city's renowned hospitality. When the captain finally expresses his exasperation over the obvious contradiction between southerners' reputation for hospitality and the law under which Manuel is imprisoned, a Charlestonian replies, "Yes!—but society in South Carolina has nothing to do with the law" (51). Though the Charlestonian tries to separate sociability from law, Adams shows that a society's inhospitable laws override any claims of hospitality on the social level. It was, after all, the institution of slavery that gave rise to that "society"—its wealth, its capacity for leisure, and its development of its social habits and manners.

Today, we often forget this link between antebellum southern social life and slavery, and particularly between this social life and the laws designed to preserve the peculiar institution. To illustrate this forgetfulness—or selective remembering—I will briefly discuss Adams's novelistic treatment of the historical figure of Jehu Jones Sr. In the novel, the Jones anecdote offers a digression from the main plot, being related to Captain Thompson by a character named Colonel S——e, who "belongs to one of the first families" of Charleston (82). Jones was a prominent member of the free black community of Charleston and owned the Jones Hotel on Broad Street, the most popular and best-known inn of antebellum Charleston. Though today he is a relatively obscure historical figure, *Charleston Magazine* in 2007 included him in a feature titled "The Charleston 100," which celebrates the one hundred most noteworthy personages from Charleston's rich history. It is worth noting that the magazine portrays him as a sort of historical point of origin for the contemporary hospitality industry in Charleston. As the magazine feature concisely explains, "A free person of color, Jones began the tradition of fine hotels that catered to the white elite of the city now given over to the hospitality industry."[25] Without any irony, this simple statement encapsulates much of the essential history of southern hospitality, particularly its origins as an exclusively white practice founded on black labor. It also exemplifies the typical elisions of history that we see throughout the discourse of southern hospitality, for certainly Jehu Jones is a more fraught figure than *Charleston Magazine* here suggests.

First, Jones, though a free black, was himself an owner of slaves; in fact, his hotel prospered on slave labor. Moreover, as a member of the mulatto elites of Charleston, he wanted little to do with the "black" community as a whole.[26] But Jones's story, particularly as it relates to the South's traditions of hospitality, is even more complex; though he was something of a pioneer in the antebellum hospitality industry, he certainly was not a recipient of southern hospitality himself. Instead, he and his family were victimized by what Adams portrays as South Carolina's inhospitable laws. In addition to legislation designed to control the movements of free sailors of color, South Carolina also had laws that prevented free black residents of the state from leaving. If they did leave the state, they were subject to heavy fines and imprisonment upon their return. The colonel explains to Captain Thompson that Jones's eldest daughter, who "was fairer than seven-eighths of the ladies who term themselves aristocracy on Charleston," married and moved with her husband to New York. Thinking they were immune to the law, "for the family were very high-minded," Jones's second daughter went to visit her older sister in New York (89). While she was away, however, Jones was informed by authorities that the law would indeed be applied to his daughter should she attempt to return. She never was allowed to return to her native state even though several prominent Charlestonians attempted to intercede on her behalf. Later, when one of the daughters became gravely ill, Jones himself traveled in disguise to visit her. Unfortunately, while in New York he was spotted by another Charlestonian. Word of Jones's clandestine travels eventually reached Charleston authorities, and Jones, like his daughters, was denied the right to return to his home, again despite petitions signed by numerous prominent Charlestonians. Forbidden from ever returning, he was forced into a lengthy, costly process of settling his property and affairs through lawyers and his son, Jehu Jones Jr., who remained behind to run the family business for a period.

In light of the family's history of run-ins with antebellum South Carolina's notoriously inhospitable laws, *Charleston Magazine*'s portrayal of Jones as a pioneer of the southern hospitality industry is ironic indeed. In Adams's novel, in contrast, Colonel S——e acknowledges the severity of the law as it affected such a prominent and popular member of the free black community, concluding, "Such is our respect for the law, that we were compelled to forego our hospitality, and maintain it [the law], even though it was painful to our feelings. Thus, you see, we maintain the *point* and *spirit* of the law above every thing else" (90, emphasis in original). Historical evidence suggests Adams's portrayal of the Jones anecdote is accurate.[27]

As Adams shows, the Negro Seamen Laws ran counter to at least one segment of public opinion in South Carolina, namely, merchants whose trade with foreign nations was adversely affected. But the law was sustained even against such mercantile interests, not, according to Adams, because of some high regard for law, but because it benefited a handful of public officials and politicians. Most notably, the sheriff and the city constables received fees for each sailor they arrested and imprisoned. In the case of the sheriff, these fees amounted to almost $1,000 a year, "a nice little appendage to the sheriff's office," as Adams describes it (283). Perhaps most importantly, the law also carried potent symbolic value for the more radical politicians and citizens who were already advocating secession from the Union (and their repeated refrains of sovereignty over Constitution).[28]

Near the end of the novel, after detailing cases of three other victims of the law, Adams returns to the case of Manuel, describing in an incredulous and ironic tone the sailor's release after fifty-two days in prison. He again summarizes the inherent contradiction between southern hospitality and the South's social order: "Manuel Pereira, a poor, shipwrecked mariner, who, by the dispensation of an all-wise Providence, was cast upon the shores of South Carolina" was "imprisoned because hospitality to him was 'contrary to law'" (218–19). And Adams reminds readers that Manuel's story is "but a faint glimpse" of the ordeals suffered by sailors of color who land in Charleston or, by extension, the southern coastal states more generally. Throughout *Manuel Pereira*, Adams shows that southerners, rather than exercising the gracious hospitality of which they so often boasted, are more interested in displaying their sovereignty through the symbolic exercise of arbitrary power. Again and again, Adams's text illustrates the ironic contradictions between southern claims of being a hospitable people and southern laws, with the prevailing tones of the novel shifting back and forth between irony and outrage.

But the deeper relationship between the discourse of southern hospitality and the inhospitable, exclusionary laws regarding sailors of color is perhaps more complementary than ironic, for the discourse of southern hospitality for much of its history has served this same exclusionary function, policing the borders of white southern identity and cultural memory. This phenomenon can perhaps be understood by the distinction Seyla Benhabib describes between the *ethnos* and the *demos* in the construction of the nation-state. Benhabib defines the *ethnos* as a "community bound together by the power of shared fate, memories, solidarity, and belonging. Such a community does not permit free entry and exit." The *demos*, in contrast, is "a democratically enfranchised totality of all citizens, who may or may not belong to the same ethnos." As Benhabib explains, "All liberal democracies that are modern nation-states exhibit these two dimensions. The politics of peoplehood consists in their negotiation." Indeed, according to Benhabib's cosmopolitan perspective, "Democracies require porous borders" because the definition of the *demos* is a fluid process, as "aliens can become residents, and residents can become citizens."[29] It goes without saying that the antebellum South was no liberal democracy with porous borders; instead, it was constructed as an ethnos, a community bound together by a shared sense of "fate, memories, solidarity, and belonging"—both real and imagined. The discourse of southern hospitality was, in many ways, a symptomatic expression of this ethnos. As such, it was hardly a discourse of universal welcome; instead, it was an exclusionary discourse that reinforced cultural solidarity in the face of foreign threats from without and within. As Benhabib emphasizes, unlike the demos, the ethnos "does not permit free entry and exit." Antebellum discourse on southern hospitality, we might say, was as inhospitable and exclusionary as the Negro Seamen Acts themselves.

Insulting "The Guest of the Nation":
Sectional Divisions and the Reception of Louis Kossuth

In December 1851, a surprisingly contentious debate broke out in Congress over the obligations and limitations of the nation's hospitality. Louis Kossuth, the exiled Hungarian revolutionary, had just arrived on American shores, and the Senate was weighing how the government should officially receive him—or if he should be received at all. The December debate in the Senate over the reception of Kossuth was surprising for two reasons. First, the fact that any debate at all occurred ran counter to public opinion, for national sympathy for Kossuth and his fellow exiles had been extremely high since the Hungarian revolt began in 1848. Newspapers and periodicals were filled with thousands of articles and accounts of Kossuth, the revolt, and its aftermath, and hundreds of poems were published honoring the leader and his cause.[30] Second, and with abundant irony, the very same Congress that was now debating the propriety of receiving Kossuth was itself responsible for inviting him to America's shores. In response to Congress's inability to immediately pass even a simple resolution formally welcoming Kossuth, the *New York Daily Times* exasperatedly wrote, "No barbarians have yet been discovered who were insensible to the claims of hospitality. It has been reserved for the Congress of the United States to invite a guest and insult him upon his arrival."[31] Ten months before his arrival in America, in February 1851, Congress, spurred no doubt by popular sympathy for Kossuth, had taken the extraordinary step of passing a joint "Resolution for the relief of Louis Kossuth and his Associates, exiles from Hungary," which expressed sympathy for the exiles and encouraged them to immigrate to the United States, even offering a ship to transport them to America from their exile in Turkey.[32] This resolution and the subsequent debate that occurred in Congress ten months later again demonstrate that hospitality extends beyond the "domestic" realm of individual social practice and into the broader realms of politics, law, and international relations—in the official attitude a state or a people can assume toward the foreigner. The plight of Louis Kossuth in the years immediately following his failed rebellion provided Americans with a unique opportunity to consider—through both their imagined and their real relationship with an illustrious and admired foreigner—the obligations and limitations of just such national and international conceptions of hospitality. As Kossuth arrived in New York to a hero's welcome in early December 1851, the same Senate that had invited him degenerated into protracted bickering over the prospect of an official governmental reception. Importantly, this debate over extending American hospitality to Kossuth—carried out both in Congress and in print—would break down largely along sectional lines, with northerners enthusiastically welcoming Kossuth and southerners growing increasingly resistant to his presence in America. In short, national hospitality for a foreign freedom fighter could not be effectively separated from the South's peculiar institution of slavery; the arrival of the foreigner from without inevitably turned attention to the question of the "strangers" already living within, African slaves and free black Americans who were treated never as full citizens but rather as an alien presence.

Bonnie Honig's *Democracy and the Foreigner* provides a theoretical rethinking of foreignness that places it at the very center of how we define and construct democracy. Nationhood and citizenship are always constructed in relation to the foreigner; consequently, the traditional approach to foreignness sees it as a "problem in need of a solution," an approach that has developed quite naturally from the xenophobic model that considers the foreigner a threat to national identity and purity. Honig, however, switches the question; instead of approaching foreignness as a problem, she asks, "What does it mean? What sort of work does it do in cultural politics?" As she demonstrates through her readings of a variety of theoretical, literary, and popular texts, the more traditional xenophobic ideas of foreignness cannot be entirely separated from more positive, more cosmopolitan ideas and situations in which the foreigner is seen as a positive agent of renewal or "(re)-founding": "The novelties of foreignness, the mysteries of strangeness, the perspective of an outsider may represent the departure or disruption that is necessary for change." Honig shows how these xenophobic and cosmopolitan ideas of foreignness bleed into one another, and though she does not explicitly place the term hospitality at the center of her study, it is always there implicitly. Through the competing ideas of foreignness that Honig describes, we can think of hospitality quite simply as what takes place—or what doesn't take place—in the spaces between the citizen and the foreigner or between a national government and an outsider.

There was a lot at stake for Americans as they pondered the plight of the foreign freedom fighter Louis Kossuth, and they thought of him and wrote about him in terms that would certainly fit Honig's description of the symbolic value of "foreign (re)-founders," whose stories can revitalize a democratic community and "frame other issues of democratic theory and citizenship."[33] Not since the Marquis de Lafayette's visit to America in 1824–25 had the presence of a foreigner on American soil aroused such fervor and excitement in the American people, and Kossuth hoped to translate his celebrity status into support for his revolutionary efforts in Hungary.[34] For Americans in the mid-nineteenth century, Kossuth reflected back to them images of their own cherished national self-identity. On the one hand, he reminded them of their own origins in a fight for freedom against oppression, and on the other hand, his exile provided them the opportunity to exercise their identity as a hospitable people and a welcoming asylum for the oppressed of the world. Americans had watched rebellions spread across Europe—in Germany, France, Italy, and Hungary—in the late 1840s with keen interest and, given their country's own origins in revolution, with a sense of political kinship. They also felt themselves the model of republican democracy to which all these revolutionary movements aspired. The Hungarian cause was the most popular and closely watched of the 1848 revolutions among Americans, and during and after the failed revolution and prior to his arrival in America, Louis Kossuth enjoyed widespread popularity North and South.

Americans were deeply disappointed when the revolt in Hungary was put down by the combined might of Austria and Russia, and they continued to follow Kossuth's story closely. Upon the defeat of his revolutionary forces in 1849, Kossuth had fled to Turkey, where he and twelve hundred of his followers were living as exiles under house arrest. Russia and Austria had demanded his extradition, and Turkey offered permanent sanctuary only on the condition that the Hungarians convert to Islam. The February 1851 invitation from the United States government provided a way out of an untenable situation, and by September 1851 the Hungarians were on their way to the United States as exiles.

Even before Congress passed its resolution offering refuge to Kossuth in early 1851, Americans seemed eager to welcome Kossuth and his fellow revolutionaries following their 1849 defeat and subsequent exile. At the time, this included southerners as well as northerners. Southerners expressed their support in a variety of ways—by holding public rallies, by pledging financial support, and by supporting legislative action to support the refugees.[35] A passionate article titled "En Avant!" published anonymously in the *Southern Literary Messenger* in March 1850 similarly conveys this initial southern enthusiasm for Kossuth. The author reflects on the recently failed revolutionary movements in Italy and Hungary. Even though the revolutions in those countries ultimately failed, the anonymous author of "En Avant!" nonetheless takes them as evidence of the inevitable progress of human freedom and encourages his readers to "rejoice in the new birth of liberty on earth." He also expresses confidence that the names of Garibaldi and Kossuth, the revolutionary leaders in Italy and Hungary, respectively, will be justly honored by posterity despite the recent failures of their revolutions. As was often the case, the author links Kossuth to Washington as a reminder of the United States' own revolutionary origins. Note how as the author describes this ideal future world of liberty that will honor Kossuth and Garibaldi, he also invokes the idea of hospitality as the condition of universal freedom and cosmopolitan citizenship:

> Rome and Hungary, Garibaldi and Kossuth, have gloriously struggled to be free, and failing have fallen from the places of honour, but have fallen into the arms of the historic muse, to be crowned by her with the freshest laurels. And when, in future years, the day of the great social feast of free nations shall arrive, and all gates shall be opened, and viands for hungry souls shall be set out on the thresholds free for all comers, and strangers known and unknown shall be led to hospitality, and former foes shall converse in friendly words, and chains shall be knocked off from all captives, and all bickerings shall be composed, then ... shall there be suitable *pulvinaria* provided for Kossuth and Garibaldi, and they shall be borne about to feast rejoicing eyes in the same processions which bear images of the Wallaces, and the Tells, and the Dorias, and the Washingtons, of the world.[36]

These symbolic images of hospitality evoke Kant's call for "universal hospitality" as the condition of world citizenship. The author links freedom to hospitality in an important way; according to the passage, only the "free nations" of the world can offer such unconditional and universal hospitality to "strangers known and unknown," a curious phrase to which I shall return shortly. Considering that this article was published in a southern and pro-slavery literary magazine, there is also a certain irony in the author's imagining a day when all the "chains shall be knocked off from all captives." Still, the sympathy expressed here for Kossuth and his cause was typical of American sentiment toward the exiled leader from the 1848 revolution up until his arrival in America.

During this period, Americans followed his story through constant newspaper stories, and literally hundreds of poems honoring Kossuth and the Hungarian cause were published in American newspapers and periodicals. A typical example, a sonnet titled "To Kossuth," was published in May 1851 in the *Southern Literary Messenger*. The poem praises the "noble Kossuth" and hopes that

> the tears
> Of nations shed for thee .... [shall]
> Inspire the mailéd breasts of serried hosts,
> And flush ten thousand brows with proud disdain
> Of Austrian tyranny's vainglorious boasts.
> May once more wave thy fiery plume on high—
> A Morning star to night-steeped Hungary.

Against this backdrop of national sympathy, Kossuth in September 1851 stepped aboard the USS *Mississippi* and embarked on his journey to Amer-

FIGURE 13. *The Poor Organ Grinder from Hungary*, political broadside by T. W. Strong of New York, 1852. Courtesy of American Antiquarian Society.

ica. The American public eagerly followed every step of his journey, and the language of national hospitality and generosity dominated the discourse in anticipation of Kossuth's imminent arrival, with many calling for the government to do more for the exiled Hungarians.[37] This question of national hospitality carried out by the government is the subject of figure 13, a political cartoon by T. W. Strong of New York. The cartoon's caption reads, "The Poor Organ Grinder from Hungary," and it implies that the government is not doing enough to welcome Kossuth and support his cause. It shows Secretary of State Daniel Webster peering out from behind a well-locked door and giving two coins to a monkey (possibly a caricature of Charles Sumner), as the noble yet mute figure of Kossuth looks on. The monkey is apparently pleading Kossuth's cause (ostensibly support for his revolution), but the Treasury and Navy offices are closed and locked, with signs declaring, "Shut," "Closed," "No Admittance," and "Strangers Not Admitted." Despite favoring support for Kossuth, the cartoon illustrates the duality of foreignness as described by Honig. While the cartoon characterizes Kossuth in a noble manner, it also employs humor (Kossuth's bag reads, "Poor Hungary Man") and stock stereotypes of European immigrants through the organ grinder imagery.[38]

In part due to this doubleness of the foreigner, Kossuth's visit to America would remind Americans less of their republican ideals of freedom than of their failure to live up to them; it would also expose the ultimate double bind of hospitality. As suggested in the passage from "En Avant!" cited earlier, any talk of freedom must eventually turn on slavery, and any hospitable gesture to the foreigner from without seems hollow when it is not extended to the strangers already within the gates ("the strangers unknown and known"). Millions of slaves lived within the United States' borders, and the recently enacted Fugitive Slave Law made it a federal crime to extend hospitality to them, no matter how dire the circumstances.

Poems published in the progressive, antislavery newspaper the *National Era* soon after Kossuth's arrival forecast how the question of hospitality toward Hungarian refugees could not be separated from the question of hospitality toward fugitive slaves, the "alien" population already residing within the nation's borders. Catherine Ledyard's poem "Kossuth," published on December 11, 1851, links his struggle to American origins in revolution, but here his arrival also serves as a reminder of American deficiencies. Ledyard claims that unlike leaders such as Alexander and Napoleon, who fought "for love of power, lust of gold, or hope of glory," Kossuth wielded his sword "in the cause of Liberty, / That the fetters may be broken, and all the oppressed go free." The concluding lines suggest that Hungary has the potential to be a more perfect republic of freedom, one free from slavery: "Let it reign till Hungary's soil, home of the true and brave, / Freer than our own America, bears not a single slave."[39]

John Greenleaf Whittier had taken this implicit line of criticism further in his poem titled "Kossuth," which was published a week earlier in the *National Era*. In Whittier's poem, the arrival of the foreigner is a chance not so much to reflect on America's past and revolutionary origins as it is to make pointed criticisms regarding its political present—particularly its failure to abide by its own founding principles. Whittier implies that no one in America is worthy of welcoming this selfless freedom fighter while slavery still exists on American soil:

> Who shall receive him? Who, unblushing speak
> Welcome to him who, while he strove to break
> The Austrian's chain from Magyar necks, struck off
> At the same blow the fetters of the serf,
> And reared the altar of his Father-land
>   On the broad base of justice, and thereby
> Lifting to Heaven a pure and honest hand,
>   Mocked not the God of Battles with a lie!
> Who shall be Freedom's mouth-piece? Who shall give
> Her welcoming cheer to the Great Fugitive?

Whittier reminds Americans of the universal assumption behind Kossuth's revolutionary struggle; in addition to fighting for the Magyar nobility, he ended the system of serfdom in Hungary. It was not, according to Whittier, a "lie" but an act of universal justice. In contrast, Whittier implies that Americans are living a lie and have in fact betrayed the cause of freedom. When he refers to Kossuth as the "Great Fugitive," all Americans in 1851 would have understood the allusion to the recently passed Fugitive Slave Law. And as he responds to his own question ("Who shall receive him?"), he seems to be singling out for criticism Secretary of State Daniel Webster, who antislavery activists felt had sold his soul by supporting the 1850 compromises and particularly the Fugitive Slave Law: "Not he, who, all her sacred trusts betraying, / Is scourging back to Slavery's hell of pain / The swarthy Kossuths of our land again!"[40] The poem here transforms American slaves into "swarthy Kossuths," and by extension, slave owners and their political supporters (including Webster) are tyrannical despots like Austria and Russia, which crushed the Hungarian rebellion for freedom. Unable to find a suitable voice for liberty among present-day politicians, who are appeasers and compromisers, Whittier concludes the poem by conjuring up the spirit of the recently deceased John Quincy Adams, descendant of Puritan forefathers and a staunch, passionate critic of slavery. According to Whittier, only an uncompromising champion of universal freedom such as Adams is worthy of welcoming "the noblest guest," Kossuth.

While most Americans seemed to support Kossuth prior to his arrival, these poems make it clear that they could not easily ignore the connections between Kossuth's struggle for freedom and the fact of American slavery. How could southerners welcome someone whose cause could be so clearly and dramatically linked to the cause of the slave? And what would be the repercussions if the American government officially recognized and welcomed him?[41] On December 3, 1851, just days before Kossuth's much-anticipated arrival in America, a heated series of exchanges took place on the Senate floor, particularly among three southern senators—Henry Foote of Mississippi, Joseph Underwood of Kentucky, and William Dawson of Georgia—and an abolitionist senator from New Hampshire, John Parker Hale. Hale's clever rhetorical maneuvers would exacerbate divisions among the southerners and stall the resolution of welcome and hospitality for Kossuth. It was the first of many increasingly contentious exchanges that would develop in the coming weeks over the national reception of Kossuth. This lengthy and confrontational congressional debate over the reception of Kossuth was the result of the legal, political, and social contradictions inherent in the coexistence of American freedom and American slavery, but it was also the consequence of the inherent paradox of hospitality: any individual act of hospitality is also a violation of the ultimate ethic of hospitality that dictates the welcoming of all equally.

The trouble began as Senator Foote of Mississippi, acting on behalf of President Taylor, introduced a seemingly innocuous resolution concerning the "reception and entertainment of Kossuth." Foote had played a key role in the passage of the 1850 Compromise measures, but he was also known for his temper. During a heated argument over the 1850 Compromise, Foote had pulled out a pistol on the Senate floor and threatened to shoot Senator Thomas Hart Benton of Missouri; fortunately for Benton, Foote was wrestled to the floor and disarmed. Foote had introduced the February 1851 resolution providing for the transport of Kossuth to America, and now, ten months later, he was introducing a resolution that provided for a joint committee of the House and Senate to "be appointed ... for the reception of Louis Kossuth ... and to tender to him, on the part of Congress, and in the name of the people of the United States, the hospitalities of the Metropolis of the Union." Foote told his fellow senators that he expected a unanimous vote without any delay, for with Kossuth about to arrive, Congress should "receive him in a manner which [was] supposed to be proper by the Government."[42]

The propriety of a timely welcome did not seem to matter to Senator Dawson of Georgia, however, who raised the first objection to the resolution by questioning the prospect of an official government welcome. He noted that there was no precedent for such action, particularly for an individual who had never been "connected with [American] institutions" and had never "rendered any particular service to the country." He acknowledged, "[Kossuth] is a great man, but he is not greater than many men who now live, and who have lived." In conclusion, Dawson stated, "The American heart is open for his reception. It is the people who will receive him. It is the people and not the Government that ought to receive him."[43]

Senator Hale of New Hampshire immediately sensed a rhetorical opening in the reservations expressed by Dawson, and he offered what he characterized as a "friendly amendment" to assuage Dawson's concerns. Pointing out that Dawson objected to singling out Kossuth above all others, Hale offered to broaden the appeal by adding the following language to the end of the resolution: "And also to assure him [Kossuth] and his associates in exile of the sympathy of the Congress and the people of the United States with the victims of oppression everywhere, and that their earnest desire is that the time may speedily arrive when the rights of man shall be universally recognized and respected by every people and government of the world."[44]

The proposal was a good example of what Donald Spencer describes as Hale's "verbal guerilla tactics." Hale, a former Liberty Party nominee for president, was seen as the "most dedicated and consistent opponent of slavery" in the Senate, and he "impishly subscribed to the politics of disruption" as a way of keeping the injustice of slavery at the center of any Senate debate.[45] Hale and Foote had skirmished before. At one point Hale so incensed Foote that he threatened to lynch Hale should he ever venture South, a threat that earned him the name "Hangman Foote" among abolitionists. But Hale's proposal here goes beyond simple political maneuvering, for it also drew the debate to the inevitable double bind of hospitality as an ethical ideal of universal and unconditional welcome; he rhetorically extended the welcome to Kossuth to an exemplar of a universal ideal. Hale's proposal drew an immediate and stern response from Senator Foote; unfortunately for the Mississippian, he seemed to fall right into Hale's trap, a trap made possible only by this very double bind of hospitality.

Foote initially expressed his "deep grief" and "profound surprise" that the resolution was meeting with resistance, and he offered a passionate defense of Kossuth, at one point boldly equating him with Washington. Dawson seemed to bristle at the comparison, asking if Kossuth had ever distinguished himself in battle in the manner of Washington. To this Foote responded with a lengthy and increasingly hyperbolic defense of the resolution and of Kossuth, calling him "the author of achievements that must hand him down to future ages as *the man of the present age*." He reminded the senators that Kossuth would soon be arriving as "*the invited guest of the nation*" and that the proposed resolution was nothing more than a "simple and unavoidable act of national courtesy."[46] It was in his concluding remarks to Dawson, however, where Foote, a staunch defender of American slavery, fell—with fabulous dramatic irony—into Hale's trap:

> Sir, the gentleman from Georgia seems to overlook the fact, that there is a great struggle going on at this moment in all parts of the civilized world between the principles of freedom and the principles of slavery. The tyrants of the earth have combined for the overthrow of liberty. In some instances open attempts are made to break down political and religious freedom. In others, the means employed by the enemies of freedom are more disguised and insidious, but not at all less dangerous. At such a moment does it behoove the American people to join the side of despotism, or to stand by the cause of freedom? We must do one or the other. We cannot avoid the solemn alternative presented. Those who are not for us are against us. Those who are not for freedom are for slavery.[47]

To this, Hale simply responded, "Exactly." Hale had created a situation that placed Foote's resolution between two competing ideas of hospitality: Dawson's restrictive and somewhat xenophobic hospitality (which asks, what has the guest done for us in exchange, is he really better than anyone else, and does he really deserve special consideration?), and Hale's more expansive, cosmopolitan ideal of hospitality (which states, we welcome Kossuth as a representative of all oppressed strangers, and we only wish we could welcome them all in actuality).

Realizing he had fallen into Hale's rhetorical ambush and confronted with the unavoidable ironies of slavery's hospitality, Foote launched into a long tirade questioning Hale's true motivation. He characterized Hale (indirectly, of course) as an irrational fanatic and an "inflated demagogue" who was trying to raise the slavery question again, an issue that the 1850 Compromise was supposed to have laid to rest. Foote charged that Hale's use of the phrase "*the victims of oppression*" was a "sinister allusion" to American slavery, "obviously designed to be expressive of a very peculiar sympathy for the colored races of this continent."[48] Hale's proposal forced Foote to show that, for all his lofty talk of freedom and hospitality, his ideas of both were, as a southern supporter of slavery, limited and conditional.

With the subject of slavery now front and center in the debate over Kossuth's welcome, another southern senator, Joseph Underwood of Kentucky, ultimately derailed the discussion and doomed the resolution. Underwood flatly stated that he was opposed to the resolution altogether. He explained that if the Senate were to extend this unique welcome to Kossuth, "there is no end; there is no limit to the exercise of this power, from this time forth forever." More importantly, Underwood felt that extending hospitality to Kossuth was a first step down the slippery slope of "intervention in the affairs of other nations," in this case, Russia and Austria, which considered Kossuth a fugitive. As Underwood put it most simply, "I am not for intervening in any way. I think the soundest policy for any man, family, or nation, is to mind its own business and let the business of other people alone." Underwood's fears of intervention had less to do with international relations than it did with domestic sectional politics; he noted that Senator Hale from New Hampshire may "get up and say, 'I want to intervene a little; I think Kentucky has acted tyrannically; I think Georgia has rather a despotic system, and I want to express my sympathy with the oppressed?' Sir, I am against this whole measure."[49]

Following the objections of Underwood, other senators moved to postpone consideration of the resolution. Foote, clearly frustrated by the debate, withdrew his motion the next day, and the following week, Senator William Seward of New York put forward an even more moderately worded joint resolution: "*Resolved by the Senate and House of Representatives of the United States in Congress assembled*, That the Congress of the United States, in the name and behalf of the people of the United States, give Louis Kossuth a cordial welcome to the capital and to the country."[50] But even this simple resolution passed only after protracted debate. It would take another week and nearly one hundred thousand words spoken by senators for and against it before the resolution would ultimately pass on a 33 to 6 vote, with all 6 nays coming from southern senators. Thanks to parliamentary maneuvering, the House managed to pass the joint resolution of welcome without any debate, but the sectional divisions over the reception of Kossuth seen in the Senate debate would only deepen in the coming weeks and months. In early January, after another lengthy debate, the House voted 90–57 to receive Kossuth in an open session of Congress, with almost all the opposing votes coming from southern representatives. And while the Senate's December resolution to formally welcome Kossuth passed 33 to 6, a February resolution to enter Kossuth's reciprocal letter of thanks into the Congressional Record passed only by a 21 to 20 margin, with the opposition again coming primarily from southern senators (15 of 20 nay votes were from southerners, while only 2 of the 21 yeas were from southerners).[51]

During his time in America, Kossuth attempted to appease southern concerns by avoiding the slavery question altogether, claiming that it was an issue of states' rights and no concern for a foreigner such as himself. In March and April 1852, he traveled extensively in the South hoping to drum up support for his revolutionary cause. Yet in contrast to his experience in the North, where he received countless invitations from every state, in the South he came, for the most part, as an uninvited guest. He received only two invitations during his entire journey in the South. One came from Henry Foote, who had resigned from the Senate to become governor of Mississippi; Foote was one of the few southerners who remained supportive of Kossuth throughout his time in America. The other invitation came from the city of New Orleans, but this was undermined by the Louisiana state legislature, which renounced Kossuth and refused to consider him a guest of the state. As he traveled the South, southerners grew increasingly disdainful of him and his cause.[52] The *Mississippi Free Trader*, for example, referred to Kossuth as "the Great Hungarian Leech," a particularly harsh though effective metaphor for a parasitical, uninvited guest. Earlier, the same paper had included a parody of a newspaper notice for a fugitive slave, reading: "One Million Dollars Reward—Ran Away from the subscriber, on the 18th of August, 1849, a likely Magyar fellow, named Louis Kossuth.... He pretends to be free, but says he was robbed of his freedom.—Francis Joseph, Emperor of Austria."[53]

In the end, Kossuth's efforts to assure southerners that he had no interest in the slavery question did nothing to alleviate their suspicions. Although the *Southern Literary Messenger* had published pro-Kossuth items up until the month of his arrival, by mid-1852 its editorial stance had clearly changed. He received no more favorable press in the *Messenger*; instead the journal directed readers to anti-Kossuth and anti-intervention materials in other publications.[54]

To make matters worse, Kossuth's efforts to alleviate southern concerns only infuriated abolitionists, who initially had considered his arrival a potential boon to their cause. Both sides now openly admitted the parallels between Kossuth and the fugitive slave, and both sides projected onto Kossuth their own political anger, fear, and resentment. William Lloyd Garrison, for example, published his *Letter to Kossuth concerning Freedom and Slavery in the United States*, an attack that runs to over one hundred pages. As Timothy Mason Roberts notes, Kossuth's narrowly focused and ultimately nationalistic goal of Hungarian independence was "unsatisfactory to cosmopolitan American Abolitionists."[55] In truth, following this national debate over Kossuth, abolitionists had another potent contradiction to point to in their attacks on slavery.[56]

The extent to which these political debates over the obligations of hospitality pervaded the national consciousness may be seen in "Christian Duty to Emigrants," a sermon delivered in 1852 by Edward Everett Hale before the Boston Society for the Prevention of Pauperism. In this sermon Hale portrays hospitality as an ethical ideal that embraces all equally and universally, but he goes beyond the issues of Kossuth and the Fugitive Slave Law; in fact, he seems to berate his listeners for becoming overly concerned with these national political debates while neglecting the strangers who exist closer to home. The epigraph for his sermon, "I was a stranger and ye took me not in," is from Matthew 25:43 (King James Version), and the strangers he has in mind are the poor immigrants who arrive in the city from overseas every day. He asks his congregation, "How many who hear me have begun to attempt this duty? How many have ever stood upon the wharf to watch the unlading of one of these emigrant ships when she arrives?" In contrast, he notes, "If you knew that a hundred persons were coming into town who had been emancipated from Southern slavery by the success of whatever benevolence, you would be glad to watch their entry. Or if a handful of Hungarians, fresh from some last battle, sought a welcome, you would watch for their coming." And yet, according to Hale, the poor immigrants arriving every day "have fought a battle as hard, and have been rescued from slavery as oppressive."[57] Over the course of this sermon, he challenges his listeners and readers to overcome their fear of these strangers, and in doing so, to overcome their deep-seated ethnic, religious, and class prejudices. His description of these strangers implies just the sort of risk taking and discomfort required in acts of true hospitality, when we stand to receive no reciprocal benefit from our generosity:

> Do you tremble because you are afraid that there is a religious difficulty? Is your Protestantism wounded, lest they betray you to the Pope? ... They come to us. They come eager to work for us. They come darkened, ignorant, stupid, and untrained. They come, therefore, often poor; often wicked. Such are the strangers whom the Lord bids us entertain. It is not Hazael, servant of a distant king, with camels laden down with presents, who asks your hospitality. Ignorant men, thriftless women, neglected children, come to you; with no plea but that they are one blood with you, and one flesh; children of one father, heirs of one redemption, and bound to one heaven. Distasteful the care of them is, but it is not your taste which it is to gratify. Laborious it is, but it is not your love of ease which is to be trained. Unthankful they are, but it was not their gratitude that

was promised you. His gratitude it was who said, "Inasmuch as ye have done for the least of these my brethren, ye have done it unto me."[58]

With its references to his listeners' sense of taste, refinement, and leisure, with its unequivocal Christian precepts, with its allusions to Hungarian revolutionaries and fugitive slaves and foreign immigrants, Hale's sermon reminds us once again that antebellum discourse on hospitality informed many different cultural spheres, from the social to the religious to the political. His sermon also reminds us that this discourse was not simply a reflection of social practices and realities; it was also part of an ongoing ethical debate over the nature of American identity.

CHAPTER FIVE

Reconstructing Southern Hospitality in the Postbellum World
Reconciliation, Commemoration, and Commodification

In a sermon delivered at St. Mary's Church of Keyport, New Jersey, on January 27, 1867, the Reverend Telfair Hodgson, a Confederate veteran, made an emotional appeal to the northern congregation about charitable aid for his fellow southerners. Hodgson's "A Sermon in Behalf of Southern Sufferers" paints a dire picture of the South in the two years since the war had ended, with floods, droughts, and impending famines adding to the grim reality of an already devastated economy and a defunct social system. With this picture in mind, Hodgson reminds his audience of the Christian imperative of hospitality by citing Matthew 25:43: "I was a stranger and ye took me not in; naked, and ye clothed me not; sick and in prison and ye visited me not." Although Hodgson acknowledges that his northern listeners "may ... regard these people as enemies" and may feel that the southern sufferers have "made the bed upon which they lie," he urges them to remember the divine injunction: "I will have mercy, and not sacrifice."[1]

But Hodgson's persuasive appeal goes beyond biblical injunctions by trading on the legendary southern reputation for hospitality. After describing the Atlantans forced to live in tent cities in the dead of winter, he reminds the northern congregation of the privileged position hospitable southerners once enjoyed before they lost everything:

> Many of these same persons have been as well, or better off than you or I, and we would have esteemed it a privilege to enjoy their company, or to extend to them the hospitality of our table. These, too, were men noted for their generosity, for their hospitality to strangers. No one, I may safely assert, has ever been turned away by them hungry, when they had it in their power to feed them. And how low they have fallen now. Men of education, and women of refinement, with nothing to clothe their nakedness, with nothing to feed their hunger. Should it be that you hate these people, it seems to me that they have suffered enough to satisfy the animosity of devils. Even though you should regard them as your en-

emies, their fallen condition should reach your sympathy. If you are not moved by their distress, I fear that your hearts are hard indeed.[2]

In calling a southern reputation for hospitality to mind, Hodgson implies that northerners should likewise treat southerners—a recently foreign population forcefully taken back into the domestic space of the nation—with generosity and compassion. He cites the well-known legends of southern hospitality to help his listeners reimagine a national household following a fratricidal Civil War. His rhetoric promotes solidarity between northern audience and southern sufferers along the lines of religion and class, for his listeners would have recognized his characterization of hospitality as both an imperative of Christian morality and a pleasing social ritual carried out among people of refinement.

Hodgson's appeal, however, also has an underlying racial dimension. Elsewhere in his sermon he goes to great lengths to blame the freed black population for the current state of affairs in the South, concluding that the former slaves "are of no use to the social community at the South. They continue to be consumers while they are not producers. At length they begin to be in want, and when there is little restraint they unhesitatingly appropriate the effects of the white population, which is struggling for a bare subsistence."[3] For the faithful in New Jersey, Hodgson trades on recognized stereotypes that cast the former slaves as a shiftless, parasitical presence living off the white population. In short, he counterpoints fallen masters and freed slaves to suggest to his northern audience that, despite the white southerners' recent status as foreigners, the African Americans, and not the conquered whites, are the alien population residing within the nation's recently reestablished borders. With the end of the Civil War and the beginning of Reconstruction, the social order that generated such legends of the South's hospitality had collapsed, yet the discourse of southern hospitality persisted and eventually even proliferated in the postbellum period. Keeping in mind that hospitality is a philosophical question of how we both define and regulate borders between ourselves and others, it seems only natural that the discourses of hospitality generally and of southern hospitality more particularly would figure prominently in the national imagination at this particular moment, for national and regional identities had been formed, broken, and re-formed through sectionalism, the Civil War, and Reconstruction, and some four million slaves, a significant part of the nation's population, had suddenly been transformed from strangers or aliens living within the nation into citizens, members of the American body politic.

While the vaunted claims of southern hospitality had been vigorously and openly contested on ethical grounds in the antebellum period, these abolitionist critiques were largely forgotten after the Civil War, and between

Reconstruction and the early years of the twentieth century, the South increasingly came to be seen as the nation's official home of hospitality. These decades saw radical changes in the South's social and political order, as well as in the South's place in the national imaginary. Reconstruction had begun with a brief period of promise, and many Americans hoped for a successful transition to a new, racially inclusive republic, but this initial promise of Reconstruction would not be fulfilled. Faced with violent resistance from many white southerners and plagued by mismanagement and insufficient resources, the government's most progressive Reconstruction goals were essentially abandoned. With the end of Reconstruction in 1877, Jim Crow segregation settled in as the new culture of the South, a violent discriminatory culture that would eventually receive the Supreme Court's approval in the 1896 *Plessy v. Ferguson* case. Over these same decades that saw segregation emerge as the new culture of the South, the South itself assumed a new primacy in the national imaginary. As the Civil War receded into the distance, the way Americans remembered the conflict shifted away from its political causes and consequences—slavery and emancipation—and toward themes of national reconciliation and reunion. At the same time, positive and nostalgic representations of the South proliferated in print, popular culture, and the literary marketplace. As Americans turned their backs on the real plight of African Americans in the segregated South, a new rise in tourism and travel to the South increasingly brought northerners face-to-face with southerners, black and white. And in the emerging national marketplace of the late nineteenth century, the norms of middle-class consumerism were themselves predicated on the logic of segregation, with African Americans confined to the margins of the marketplace, not just regionally but nationally.[4]

In this rapidly changing postbellum world, the discourse of southern hospitality proved to be adaptable and useful in an increasingly wide range of endeavors. With the growth of tourism and travel in the South and in an emerging national consumer culture, southern hospitality evolved into a nostalgic image that could be adapted for both economic and political purposes, often in the same iteration. The growing popularity of literature about the South—particularly nostalgic plantation literature—only enhanced the power of the southern hospitality myth. To northerners facing industrialization and urbanization, this view of the South as a haven of hospitality provided an open field for the projection of their own nostalgic desires for a simpler, better time, while also carrying the promise of regional reconciliation following fratricidal war. To southerners, this reasserted self-image stood as a confirmation of regional pride, exceptionalism, and superiority even in the face of military defeat. To both, the gathering perception of southern hospitality provided an adaptable discourse for reimagining postwar political relations, particularly as the national way of remembering the Civil War shifted toward themes of regional reunion and reconciliation. At the same time, southern hospitality continued to encode a regressive racial ideology throughout this period from the Civil War and emancipation, through Reconstruction, and into the establishment of segregation as both a regional and a national cultural norm. Indeed, a rather blatant racism and white supremacy can be seen as a common denominator in most iterations of southern hospitality throughout these decades. More specifically, most postbellum versions of the discourse of southern hospitality continued to depict the now-free population of African Americans as an alien presence in America, as perpetual strangers incapable of being assimilated into American society, even as they simultaneously portrayed the South as a friendly land of perpetual welcome to white nonsoutherners. This picture of southern hospitality was especially at odds with the rampant racial violence occurring in the South, with some decades during this period averaging hundreds of lynchings of blacks annually.[5] Americans in this period somehow managed to live with and accept these obvious contradictions. Between the Civil War and the turn of the twentieth century, then, southern hospitality continued to function as an exclusive and exclusionary white myth, a virtual "race characteristic." In this chapter I focus on a range of texts that show how the southern hospitality myth was aligned with and generated by the development of tourism in the postbellum southern economy, the national cultural trends toward national reconciliation and unity following the war, and the increasingly popular field of plantation literature. As in the antebellum period of sectional tension, a regressive racial politics serves in these areas of cultural production as the ubiquitous subtext of southern hospitality. While some people questioned this perception of southern hospitality and offered alternative views of hospitality as a national ethic for a racially inclusive democracy, these voices were fewer and generally more muted than before the war. I begin and end this chapter with such alternative perspectives.

Reimagining Reconstruction as Hospitality in the Divided National Household

Just a few years before the Civil War, Abraham Lincoln famously used the biblical metaphor of "a house divided," drawn from Mark 3, to describe the moral and political effect of slavery on the nation: "'A house divided against itself cannot stand.' I believe this government cannot endure, permanently half *slave* and half *free*." Lincoln certainly was not alone in referencing this biblical metaphor to describe the sectional crisis. Many Americans had imagined the nation as just such an internally divided household before the Civil War, but the simple eloquence and the prophetic quality of Lincoln's 1858 speech to the Republican State Convention in Illinois make his the most enduring instance. Lincoln was correct in prophesying that the nation would eventually become "all one thing" (in this case, free), but emancipation alone would not be enough to heal the nation's internal divisions.[6] Following the war and emancipation, the national household would continue to be deeply divided, complicated now by the complex process of Reconstruction and by the addition of new or returning members to the household: the new population of freedmen and freedwomen, and the formerly "foreign" and increasingly recalcitrant population of white southerners.

Nineteenth-century discourses on hospitality and domesticity provided a meaningful lens through which to examine this divided domestic space of the nation in the years following the Civil War, and some women writers in particular elaborated upon this metaphor of a divided household in unique and powerful ways. While American women in the nineteenth century considered the domestic sphere as both a sacred space and the foundation for a virtuous republic, and while they generally saw hospitality as a pleasant social ritual founded on a biblically sanctioned moral imperative, nineteenth-century discourses of domesticity and hospitality were also more wide-ranging, bound up in broader conceptions of regional and national spaces and native and foreign identities.[7] Julia McNair Wright and Constance Fenimore Woolson both used these broader conceptions of hospitality as a way of reimagining the possibilities of the domestic national space and its shifting populations in the Reconstruction years. Wright was a prolific writer of literature promoting social reform; she was also a bona fide arbiter of domestic habits and taste and published a popular etiquette book in the postwar decade. Woolson was a popular author of fiction and travel writing whose sojourns throughout the South in the years following the war resulted in a significant body of work documenting from a northerner's perspective this period of the South's fitful postwar transition. Their works that I discuss here provide a glimpse of a brief period in which the possibility of a racially inclusive democracy was at least imagined by some, and hospitality provides the ethical principle to express this possibility. In these texts, the complex divisions within the national household—divisions of North and South, region and nation, male and female, black and white, slave and free, citizen and stranger—all seem to be in a state of constant flux around the question of hospitality.

Julia McNair Wright was a devoted Christian reformer and prolific writer who published numerous works of moral fiction and conduct literature for the National Temperance Society, the American Tract Society, and the Presbyterian Board of Publication. She also published a popular etiquette book titled the *Complete Home* in 1879, which I briefly discussed in chapter 2. Her chapter on hospitality from this volume indicates her wariness regarding the shifting cultural terrain surrounding hospitality—which she terms the "queen of the social virtues"—in the changing, postwar American marketplace. In particular, Wright's text shows increasing uncertainty regarding the impact that a growing culture of consumerism was having on the social habits of hospitality and particularly on what Wright saw as their foundation in Christian morality. But in 1867, in the early days of Reconstruction, Wright published a unique Civil War novel titled *The Cabin in the Brush* in which this Christian ethic of hospitality figures as perhaps the most prominent moral theme. Rather than focusing on the military side of the war, the novel details the plight of war refugees in the lawless border region between Missouri and Arkansas in the latter days of the war. Though set during the war, the novel promotes the ethic of simple Christian hospitality as a panacea for the numerous problems of identity politics facing the nation during Reconstruction, as Confederates were literally transformed from foreigners into countrymen, and slaves were transformed into freedmen and members of the American body politic. Given these shifting identities, Wright's novel proposes an ethic of hospitality that sees all strangers as one flesh and one body, and gestures toward the possibility of a truly integrated national household in which all stand equal before "the bar of God."

In a similar fashion, Wright blurs many of the typical divisions of identity that had dominated the nineteenth-century political landscape—race, class, North, South, black, white. The novel's preface, for example, reorients regional identities by substituting an East-West dichotomy for the North-South division that had obsessed the nation throughout decades of sectionalism. This reorientation seems to return the national agenda to a unifying effort of taming the western, uncivilized regions of the country, of bringing the light of Christian civilization into the darkness.[8] Significantly, rather than projecting the designations of savagery and ignorance onto blacks—a common practice during Reconstruction—the divide between the civilized and the savage and the enlightened and the ignorant exists within the white subject: the novel's heroine, Rachel Craig, a mother of five who is illiterate and without any knowledge of God. Rachel lives in "poverty and roughness" (9), raising her "uncouth flock of little ones," whose rough appearances are matched by "manners wild as those of young Hottentots" (12). By likening these white children to "Hottentots," Wright further blurs the distinctions between whiteness and blackness and civilization and savagery, particularly when we consider the novel's other genuinely positive representations of black characters. Despite her roughness, Rachel's domestic devotion to her children provides the basis for her regeneration. In Wright's view, she is a natural mother sans Christian foundation: "A very loving, devoted mother in her own way was Rachel, no mother more so; she lived but in her children, and would've defended the little group of white savages with her life" (12).

Rachel's life in the Brush during the war is one of constant trial and tribulation. Her husband is away fighting for the Union cause, leaving her to raise five young children on her own. She is barely able to scrape out a meager existence from the soil. Her oldest son, Jim, is sickly and dies early in the novel. The fact that her husband, James, enlisted with the Union puts her at odds with the majority of those in her region of the Brush, and as a result Rachel and her children are repeatedly harassed and raided by Confederate bushwhackers. The harassment becomes so devastating that Rachel is forced to flee to a refugee camp, reluctantly leaving one of her sons behind with a neighboring couple named the McQueens, a surly, unsavory pair who also happen to be Confederate sympathizers. Most of the novel is devoted to Rachel's journeys to and from the refugee camp: her first journey to escape the bushwhackers, and her second journey back to the Brush to retrieve her young son. Rachel traverses a war-torn, impoverished landscape populated primarily by fellow wanderers, and throughout her travails, Wright provides numerous scriptural allusions to frame these scenes. Up until her initial arrival at the refugee camp, Wright always follows these scriptural allusions by reminding the reader that Rachel has no knowledge of God and consequently can take no comfort from him in the way that her ideal Christian reader would. But this all changes with Rachel's arrival at the refugee camp. Through Wright's depiction of the refugee camp, Reconstruction is nothing less than a transformation of the national household premised on the ethic of Christian hospitality. Moreover, this transformation of the domestic space is led by the combined efforts of white *and* black Christian women. The title of the chapter in which Rachel arrives at this camp is "The Good Samaritan," and the Good Samaritans in this chapter figure as the unlikely pair of a former plantation mistress, Mrs. P——, and her former slave, Aunt Sally. The two welcome Rachel to the camp, and together they minister to both her physical and spiritual needs. A hopeful metaphor for the process of Reconstruction, the refugee camp itself is an erstwhile plantation whose slave quarters have been transformed into welcoming cabins and "kindly shelter" for an integrated population of refugee and former slave families. Mrs. P—— and Aunt Sally introduce Rachel to the Christian faith and also provide helpful domestic hints on cleaning and caring for her children. And in a deeply symbolic passage that has roots in ancient hospitality rites and resonates with numerous biblical scenes, Aunt Sally carefully cleans and binds the traveler Rachel's feet, which have been severely injured from her long journey. Aunt Sally also gives Rachel her very first introduction to "de good Lord Jesus Christ" who "come into dis worl', to bear our burdens an carry our sins" (119). Further, as Rachel and Sally share their difficult histories with each other (Sally's includes separation from five children and her husband), the slave's narrative is symbolically laid beside the white refugee's narrative, with Sally reassuring Rachel that the Lord will "bring good out ob all de ebil" in the world, offering her own current state of freedom as proof (120).

    Hospitality also figures prominently in Rachel's arduous journeys to and from the refugee camp to retrieve her young son Bill; in fact, nearly every scene described during these journeys revolves around the question of hospitality. Reflecting the fluidity of the postwar political moment, identities always seem uncertain in repeated scenes where Rachel must approach a campfire to ask for succor from fellow refugees (both Confederate and Union sympathizers), from newly freed blacks, from Union scouts, and even from some of the very bushwhackers who burned down her cabin (in this instance, a gray-haired bushwhacker does her a kindness, and he later figures in the novel's resolution). These encounters are usually filled with trepidation for both the guest *and* the host, as the simplest exchanges of hospitality become fraught with uncertainty and risk in the war-torn landscape. The understated simplicity of Wright's descriptive and narrative style lends these scenes an almost biblical, parable-like quality. Rachel is enlightened and transformed by these exchanges, particularly when she desperately seeks the hospitality of a stranger who turns out to be an itinerant preacher named Parson Murray:

> "May I sit by your fire? I am all alone, wet and tired," said Rachel.
> "Come in, and welcome," replied the man, "it is an old story that misery loves company; I'm all alone, too, and besides the Lord has said, 'Be not forgetful to entertain strangers,' and so here is such entertainment as I got."
> This was a new speech, and Rachel entered the shelter of the branches, overwhelmed at the goodness of the Lord. (158)

Following this encounter with Parson Murray, which occurs during Rachel's return journey to the Brush to retrieve her son Bill, the novel takes on new themes of postwar reconciliation and regeneration. This stranger becomes a fellow traveler and seeker, with Rachel's anxious search for her son paralleling Parson Murray's search for his long-lost brother Matt, a bushwhacker whom he hopes to "turn from his ways" (158). It soon becomes clear to Rachel that the gray-haired bushwhacker who had treated her with some kindness earlier in the novel is in fact Murray's brother, a fact that gives the parson hope for Matt's redemption. Somewhat enigmatically, Parson Murray seems to embody the theme of regional reconciliation: he originally hails from Vermont yet he is described as being clad in "a suit of threadbare butternut," a de facto badge of the Confederate soldier (162).

Wright uses Parson Murray as a mouthpiece to express a generally progressive attitude toward Reconstruction racial politics. For example, in the midst of his "godly conversation" with Rachel, the parson tells her of his experiences ministering to blacks; in contrast to the mixed results of his preaching to whites, he says, "Negroes is pretty generally ready to learn 'bout the Lord. I'se spent many happy hours in their cabins, feelin' we was all one in the Lord" (174). Rachel concurs, noting, "It was a good old black woman first told me of the Lord lovin' folks, and folks lovin' the Lord" (174). Though the novel at times betrays a patronizing attitude regarding black spirituality—common for much of the nineteenth century—Wright nonetheless is progressive in her repeated symbolic representations of the national household as a racially integrated space governed by Christian principle. She immediately follows this passage with a scene in which Rachel and Parson Murray accept the hospitality of a small party of black refugees. This is one of the longest, most detailed of such scenes in the novel, with the white and black travelers dining, praying, worshiping, singing, and eventually sharing tents together.

Though the novel is set near the end of the Civil War, it is clearly directed to the cultural and political climate of Reconstruction. For example, in this exchange with the black refugees one of the anecdotes related through the narrative seems to allude less to the violence that occurred during the war and more to the racial violence and intimidation already under way in the South at the time of the novel's publication. As the black refugees depart, one of them relates his hopes to arrive at a "colored church" recently established by a preacher known as Uncle Lucius, but Wright interrupts the narrative with this editorializing aside:

> Alas for his expectations! Already had the humble edifice been fired by lawless hands, because a school for colored children had been opened there, and while the unhappy blacks were violently prevented from doing aught to save their property, the place so dear to their simple hearts crumbled to blackened ashes. The black women wept from fright, Uncle Lucius wrung his hands from his pulpit and big Bible, and hymn book, and the children filled the air with cries for their books and slates; a rich ovation, all this grief and lamentation, to the cruel hearts who had done the deed. Who will build again the walls of this little outpost of Zion, where Christ was indeed preached with zeal and sinners were led to him? (182–83)

Rather than alluding to some fictional church established during the Civil War, Wright's direct question to the reader seems to refer to the current violence taking place in the South, as white southerners who rejected black progress and black social equality launched a successful and lawless campaign of violence and intimidation against black citizens and white Republicans alike.

But in the story of Matt Murray, the gray-haired bushwhacker and the parson's brother, Wright's narrative also holds out the hope for the possibility of Confederate regeneration. After finding her son, Rachel and the parson come upon his brother Matt, who is being held prisoner by a troop of Union scouts who had earlier offered Rachel their hospitality. With Rachel's testimony and Matt's promise of loyalty, the parson's brother is spared. Still, the troop does proceed with the execution of the bushwhacker Sime, Matt's malevolent commander who had seemed to take genuine pleasure in his persecution of Rachel's family earlier in the novel. As a Civil War parable for the Reconstruction era, the novel offers equal status for both freedmen and reconstructed

Confederates within the national household, but lawless, unregenerate guerillas like Sime (a stand-in perhaps for the lawless insurgent groups such as the Ku Klux Klan that emerged during Reconstruction) do not. The novel ends with a scene of life back at the integrated refugee camp. Parson Murray departs with the now "subdued," ex-Confederate brother, while Aunt Sally acts as an agent in the transformation of Mrs. McQueen, the former Confederate and bushwhacker sympathizer who, we are told, "came out in an entirely new character, and behaved herself quite decently" in this newly integrated domestic setting (248).[9]

While Julia McNair Wright's *The Cabin in the Brush* is direct and unwavering in its advocacy of the Christian ethical imperative of hospitality in the context of Reconstruction, Constance Fenimore Woolson's writings of the South and the ethics of hospitality are more probing, circumscribed, and realistic in their moral expectations. Woolson spent six years living in and traveling throughout the South from 1873 to 1879, and her fiction and travel writing that resulted from these sojourns are kaleidoscopic, offering wide-ranging, nuanced views of the South as it was in the process of being reinvented both in the world of politics and in the national imagination. While some of Woolson's writings on the South view the southern aristocracy with a type of nostalgic fascination that seems to both conserve and celebrate the class and racial distinctions implicit in the discourse of southern hospitality, two of her "Southern Sketches"—"Old Gardiston" and "Rodman the Keeper"—provide remarkable rereadings of southern hospitality in the context of Reconstruction and national reconciliation.[10] While these texts interrogate the motivating politics of southern hospitality, they also explore and reimagine interregional hospitality as an ethical imperative with national political consequences in the context of Reconstruction and reconciliation. More than once in these stories southerners are forced to either extend hospitality to or receive hospitality from northern military men.

As the last of her family and thus the last protector of the family home following the war, Gardis Duke, the central figure in "Old Gardiston," believes in social practices that are pointedly exclusive rather than politically inclusive. Gardiston House had been in decline well before the war, and the South's defeat has ironically raised the family's social status by reducing everyone to the same low level. This allows Gardis's aunt, Miss Margaretta, to open her doors to her new peers, and while a subsequent visit of "two ancient dames" is a hollow and pathetic parody of the lavish ways of the past, the "little stories" they tell of earlier generations fill "Gardis with admiring respect."[11] Later in the story, when the military officers David Newell and Roger Saxton first visit Gardiston House to inform the household of the Union regiment's encampment in the area, Gardis immediately faces a conflict regarding her supposed heritage of hospitality: "'Shall I ask them in?' she thought. 'What would Miss

Margaretta have done?' The Gardiston spirit was hospitable to the core; but these—these were the Vandals, the despots, under whose presence the whole fair land was groaning. No; she would not ask them in" (111). Unfortunately for Gardis, she later becomes beholden to the occupying troops after they protect the house from a mob of rioting freedmen, and she is forced to extend them the hospitality she first denied. A deeply conflicted Gardis extends an invitation to the officers, but with the caveat that it is a "mere dinner of ceremony, and not of friendship" (119). Gardis seems acutely aware of the obligations entailed in the gift of hospitality, and receiving aid from her sworn enemies carries a sense of degradation for her, particularly since she had earlier denied them hospitality. Following the dinner, she is further horrified when Saxton extends his hand in friendship. She does not deign to acknowledge his efforts, and later she melodramatically burns the "desecrated" clothes she wore for the dinner.[12]

But "Old Gardiston" does not simply debunk southern hospitality by portraying it as a hypocritical and self-serving myth. If that were the case, Woolson would not have given voice to Gardis's aging Cousin Copeland, who rebukes her when she initially fails to welcome the northern officers: "Hospitality has ever been one of our characteristics as a family.... It is a very sad state of things, my dear—very sad. It was not so in the old days at Gardiston House; then we should have invited them to dinner" (114). Rather than simply dismissing southern hospitality out of hand, then, Woolson here offers two contrasting dimensions: Gardis's sense of hospitality's recent politics and Cousin Copeland's sense of hospitality's abiding ethics. In "Old Gardiston," politics and ethics seem peculiarly at odds.

Can northerners and southerners move beyond the trauma and resentment of the war and see one another as equals? This enduring ethical possibility is illustrated in the humble exchange of hospitality that takes place between Captain Newell and Cousin Copeland later in the story. When the family loses its one remaining source of income—rent from a warehouse tenant—Copeland is forced out of his house to seek employment in town. Newell comes upon the dejected and impoverished Copeland sitting on the steps of a church after a degrading and unsuccessful job search. In contrast to Gardis's politically charged efforts to maintain a sense of superiority, the present exchange is marked by equality and mutual respect. Newell takes a seat beside the dejected Copeland as though "a church-step on a city street was a customary place of meeting" (127), and Copeland offers Newell a portion of his meager rations—a small piece of cornbread—as he proceeds to tell his story of failure. The exchange, however, ends "in the comfortable eating of a good dinner at the hotel, and a cigar in Captain Newell's own room" (127). Since the two men can see each other as equals, Copeland has no qualms about accepting Newell's offer of assistance in finding a new tenant. He even goes so far as to invite Newell to spend the night during a later visit, much to the chagrin of his cousin Gardis. Anticipating the promise of a budding romance between Newell and Gardis, Copeland helps bring the story to a permanently hospitable close. The story concludes by incorporating the sort of intersectional marriage plot that proliferated in postbellum fiction as a symbol of national reconciliation.[13]

The politics of hospitality were not so easily banished, however, even in the South that Woolson imagined. In "Old Gardiston," the reconstructive pressure of new black citizens intrudes only briefly with the rioting freedmen and only to encourage white solidarity and a grudging "noblesse oblige" that brings Gardis and Captain Newell together. Old resentments can be eased through a newly national ethic of hospitality, it seems, as long as new political burdens do not frustrate a sense of well-heeled resolution. But in "Rodman the Keeper," the title story of her 1880 collection of "Southern Sketches," prejudices run too deep for characters to move forward, particularly when the politics of hospitality are tied to a more complex handling of race than "Old Gardiston" allows.

At first, a similar but more dramatic instance of the ethics of hospitality occurs in "Rodman the Keeper" when the Union veteran John Rodman grudgingly takes in the dying Confederate veteran Ward De Rossett, caring for him in his small cabin at Andersonville National Cemetery.[14] The story's exposition underscores the absolute sense of alienation and hostility between victorious northerner and the defeated South. Rodman feels little but contempt for the defeated South, and his sectional prejudices only harden through his daily task of memorializing the Union dead: he is charged with "transcribing day by day" the names of the fourteen thousand dead Union soldiers that surround him. Not surprisingly, the townspeople likewise resent his presence and the entire initiative of the national cemetery within the conquered South: "Everything was monotonous, and the only spirit that rose above the waste was a bitterness for the gained and sorrow for the lost cause. The keeper was the only man whose presence personated the former in their sight, and upon him therefore, as representative, the bitterness fell, not in words, but in averted looks, in sudden silences when he approached, in withdrawals and avoidance, until he lived and moved in a vacuum." Like the Union dead in the southern cemetery, Rodman is a "Stranger ... in a strange land," yet the southerners in the story also feel a sense of alienation, having been forced back into the nation (12).

But Rodman is able to overcome his own sectional prejudices—or at least momentarily suspend them—and open his door to his former enemy, the dying Confederate veteran Ward De Rossett. Rodman comes across De Rossett when searching for a cold spring on an abandoned plantation near the cemetery grounds. De Rossett is a pitiful specimen of the defeated planter class, starving and slowly wasting away from his war wounds in a dilapidated plantation mansion, tended to by an aging former slave named Pomp. Rodman feeds and cares for De Rossett, and with Pomp's assistance, eventually moves him to the keeper's cabin at the cemetery so that he can care for him, much to the chagrin of De Rossett's proud but impoverished niece, Bettina. As the following passage indicates, Rodman's benevolent actions create a "remarkable" new existence for De Rossett, Rodman, Bettina, and Pomp within the confines of the national cemetery:

> Then began a remarkable existence for the four: a Confederate soldier lying ill in the keeper's cottage of a national cemetery; a rampant little rebel coming out daily to a place which was to her anathema-maranatha; a cynical, misanthropic keeper sleeping on the floor and enduring every variety of discomfort for a man he never saw before—a man belonging to an idle, arrogant class he detested; and an old black freedman allowing himself to be taught the alphabet in order to gain permission to wait on his master—master no longer in law—with all the devotion of his loving heart. For the keeper had announced to Pomp that he must learn his alphabet or go; after all these years of theory, he, as a New-Englander, could not stand by and see precious knowledge shut from the black man. So he opened it, and mighty dull work he found it. (28)

For at least a tenuous moment, the "house divided" by sectionalism and war is momentarily made whole under one roof, but this is a household that comes into existence only after Rodman can accept the risk of suspending his sectional prejudices and extending his hospitality to Ward De Rossett. Moreover, the resulting situation puts every party at some risk of similar discomfort, but this is essential if we think of hospitality from an ethical perspective.

Even though Woolson in this metaphorical passage can imagine the possibilities of a national ethic of hospitality, the story cannot sustain such possibilities through to its conclusion. Old resentments and new political burdens frustrate any sense of resolution. Unlike the conclusion of "Old Gardiston," which follows the dominant cultural patterns of reconciliation and reunion, "Rodman the Keeper" offers no sense of closure. Instead we see that prejudices run too deep to move forward. Bettina Ward cannot bring herself to sign the cemetery's registry of visitors. This more pessimistic—and realistic—conclusion can be tied directly to the story's more complex handling of race. Though the imagined household of reunion described a moment ago does include an African American presence, Pomp's role in the household is a mere projection of white desires. For De Rossett he plays the part of faithful slave, and to Rodman he remains the subject of missionary zeal. But a third alternative is offered through the events that occur on Memorial Day. Ironically, Rodman had totally forgotten the day until he is reminded of it by the arrival of a parade of freed blacks who have come to honor the dead.[15] As the line of former slaves moves among the Union graves, Woolson describes the "new-born dignity of the freedman" and portrays the African American community in this scene as a more vital, self-directed presence and the former slaves as potentially equal partners in the American political landscape. Even Pomp momentarily steps out of character by sneaking out later that evening to honor the dead, unbeknown to his former master. Unfortunately, the possibility of black equality and political agency is something that Bettina Ward, like so many southerners, is unwilling to accept. When racial difference is a factor, they cannot accept the risk that unconditional hospitality requires. After the parade, Rodman ruefully notes to himself, "Not a white face." Bettina Ward coolly responds, "Certainly not" (34). Indeed, if we compare the African American presence in both stories, the results are telling. In "Old Gardiston" the African Americans pose a threat in the form of a rioting mob that in turn brings the northern and southern characters together; in contrast, envisioning the freed African Americans as potentially equal partners in the political process drives a divisive wedge between the northern and the southern characters. With this juxtaposition, Woolson's stories here subtly prod her readers to imagine the possibilities of a civil society in which hospitality is a national ethical principle because national politics have been transformed.

In these fictions, Constance Fenimore Woolson and Julia McNair Wright both adapt nineteenth-century discourses of hospitality to conceptually open up the national domestic space around issues of identity and citizenship in Reconstruction, articulating complex and often shifting fault lines between self and other, region and nation, upper and lower classes, and, inevitably, white and black Americans. However, at the same time as Wright and Woolson were reimagining the ethical possibilities of hospitality, others were resurrecting the discourse of southern hospitality in ways that foreclosed these more democratic and racially inclusive possibilities.[16] Ranging from the emerging tourism and hospitality industries, to Civil War memorialization, and to developing genres of regional literature, these iterations of southern hospitality evolved in the postwar decades into a wide-ranging, exclusionary white myth, all at the very moment when African Americans were struggling to define and assert themselves in their new roles as citizens in the national household and before an increasingly skeptical American public.[17]

Southern Tourism and the "Social Reconstruction" of Whiteness: Edward A. Pollard's *The Virginia Tourist* (1870)

Published in 1870 in the midst of Reconstruction, the journalist Edward A. Pollard's *The Virginia Tourist* shows how the discourse of southern hospitality was easily adapted to a new economic agenda of tourism and travel in the postbellum South; it also reveals the historically situated racial and political dimensions of these emerging discursive practices.[18] In the concluding chapter, titled "Practical Hints," Pollard goes to great lengths to reassure his northern readers of the warm and hospitable reception they will receive from southerners, who customarily make "a special and sedulous effort" (277) to accommodate northern visitors:

> Persons in the North . . . will be received there with the most cordial welcome, will enjoy the advantages of marked efforts to please them, and will have the satisfaction of assisting in a social "reconstruction," in which the people of the South are prepared to meet them with gracious readiness and with grateful alacrity. . . .
> To the peaceful and richly-endowed spaces of her springs and mountains and scenery the State invites all comers; and what nature has bestowed, a generosity that does not encumber with its obligations, and a hospitality that never wearies of its offices, unite to dispense. (277)[19]

Not only would the immediate needs of northern tourists be met, but "the social reunion of the two sections" would naturally ensue (277). Through the genres of popular fiction and travel writing, Americans of the nineteenth century would have recognized the long-held assumption of southern hospitality, which Pollard here rhetorically transforms into both an enticing tourism pitch and a patriotic call to the duty of social reconstruction. On the one hand, Pollard's rhetoric reflects the post–Civil War culture of reconciliation, which increasingly described the South in romantic and nonpolitical terms. On the other hand, his specific allusions to southern hospitality also forecast the more modern tendency to transform southern hospitality into both a compelling advertising strategy and a consumable product.[20]

At the same time, when Pollard suggests that visiting northerners will be participating in the "social 'reconstruction'" of the nation, the reconstruction he has in mind is decidedly retrograde. It was Pollard who coined the phrase "the Lost Cause," and following the publication of *The Lost Cause* (1866), his history of the rebellion from a chauvinistically Confederate perspective, he had written *The Lost Cause Regained* (1868), a work that outlines a comprehensive national political agenda based on the doctrine of white supremacy. For Pollard, the end of slavery only clarified the central political issue facing the country, that of white racial purity and dominance: "When [the South] defended Slavery by her arms, she was single-handed, and encountered the antipathies of the world; now, when she asserts the ultimate supremacy of the white man, she has not lost her cause, but merely developed its higher significance, and in the new contest she stands, with a firm political alliance in the North, with the binding instincts of race in her favour, and with the sympathies of all generous and enlightened humanity drawn upon her."[21] With this political agenda in mind, we can look at his comments in a new light; for Pollard, the "social reconstruction" that southern hospitality can help to secure is the reconstruction of the white race on a national level.

Significantly, this depiction of southern hospitality as a statement of white solidarity is sometimes seen in a more blatant manner in texts promoting northern and foreign emigration to the South after the Civil War. In Frederick B. Goddard's *Where to Emigrate and Why*, for example, the introduction to the book's southern section concludes that "the Southern people will extend to the immigrant of every land and condition, their far-famed hospitality and welcome." This promise is echoed in the numerous letters from southern officials that follow, detailing the South's climate, social customs, and economic opportunities. For example, in a letter describing the potential for immigration in Virginia, the state agent for immigration, J. D. Imboden, writes that there is a "universal" desire for immigration in the state, whether immigrants are foreign-born or from the North, and he promises these potential immigrants a "cordial welcome." But again this promise of southern hospitality involves a racial logic. Tellingly, he draws his letter to a close with a promise of white supremacy that includes the potential immigrant (even the foreign-born) in its power structure: "This too will always be a white man's State. The white male population of voting age exceeds the negroes more than 40,000 in the State, and the majority will rapidly increase as white population flows in, and the negroes move southward, as is now their tendency. They will be harmless here. No immigrant need fear any trouble from them, and the whites will welcome all you can send with open arms."[22] For Pollard and like-minded southerners, then, the discourse of southern hospitality was about establishing boundaries of community and political power. While the sense of who could belong is fluid and depends largely on political or economic needs, the notion of who does not belong—the black population—remains constant.[23]

Even a simple call for the economic development of southern plantations into hunting resorts betrays this same dynamic. An 1879 article in *Forest and Stream* titled "A Hint to Southern Plantation Owners" encourages owners of southern plantations to open their lands to well-heeled sportsmen from the North. The article complains that too often these abundant hunting grounds only supply "entertainment for friends and an unlimited supply of 'sport' to our colored hero of the dollar shot gun." Like Pollard, the pitch here joins economic benefits with sociopolitical ones. By charging "gentlemen visitors" for their "proverbial and long time-honored Southern hospitality," southern landowners will gain economically while still providing important opportunities for the sort of social reconstruction advertised by Pollard:

> Hundreds of gentlemen who read this journal would eagerly embrace such an opportunity.... There would be many very pleasant attendant features of such

visits of Northern sportsmen to their brothers in the South.... All such social interchange is to be encouraged. Its results are happy.... The dollar shot gun hunter of colored complexion would doubtless have his enjoyment somewhat marred and his privileges curtailed. But the proprietor who employs efficient game wardens will find ample reason to congratulate himself upon the new order of things.[24]

Importantly, in this case, the "new order" includes the displacement of the heretofore usurping black population and the happy reunion of southern and northern brothers-in-(sporting) arms. The article concludes by recommending a particular plantation in Virginia and reminding readers that they are already "familiar with the beauty of the scenery, the hospitality of the people, and the abundance of game, for all of this ha[d] been repeatedly written of in [the journal's] columns."[25]

With the war lost, the old social verities largely destroyed, and the free black population exerting an unforeseen pressure, Pollard's *Virginia Tourist* tries to imagine just such a "new order," both social and political. As David Blight writes in *Race and Reunion*, Pollard's *Lost Cause Regained* "counseled reconciliation with conservative Northerners on Southern terms." It is not surprising, then, that his tour book published only two years later is primarily addressed to northerners, but particularly those of the white upper classes.[26] His representation of life at the Springs resorts emphasizes conspicuous consumption, elegance, refinement, and exclusive society. At the same time, Pollard is noticeably ambivalent about the possibilities of more fluid relationships among the middle and upper classes. So while he insists on white solidarity in the face of a free black population, he also wants to maintain clear class distinctions among whites.

In his introductory chapter, for example, Pollard describes at great length the opportunities for economic development and speculative investment in the Springs, which he believes can compete with northern resort areas such as Saratoga Springs and Cape May. A factor preventing this is the southern one-rate system, which puts all guests on the same level as consumers. Pollard urges Virginia's resort hotels to favor a more northern model of "adaptation to different classes of customers." As things currently stand, Pollard complains that there are "no degrees of comfort, or what is more, degrees of privacy."[27] Later, in a description of social life at the Montgomery White Sulphur Springs, he hints at a fear of class fluidity infecting the life at the Springs, particularly in the form of the newly wealthy from the North: "The social life here, high as it is, is peculiarly Southern, drawing its animation from the principal Southern cities, such as New Orleans, and having little of that Northern shoddyism which it has been attempted to import into some of our summer resorts in Virginia" (122).[28] Pollard's comments on "Northern shoddyism" carried a particular meaning in the years after the war, for the word was "first used in the United States with reference to those who made fortunes by army contracts at the time of the Civil War, it being alleged that the clothing supplied by the contractors consisted largely of shoddy," a type of cheap, recycled woolen yarn.[29] Pollard, then, is criticizing the nouveau riche of the North. More specifically, he points to those whose sly wartime trickery enabled their social climb, and his critical comments here reveal the anxiety running beneath his desire for social reconstruction with the North. Pollard desires white political solidarity, but he fears the loss of rigid class distinctions in the more fluid postwar economy. Yet Nina Silber's assessment of bourgeoning travel and tourism industries in the South following the war reveals that this criticism of northern shoddyism actually could prove effective with northerners: "The South held a unique class appeal which other tourist spots seemed to lack ... [for] the South could offer an association with true aristocracy, even if it meant the remnants and ruins of an aristocratic past.... Consequently, for middle- and upper-class northerners, the South became a land in which the class tensions of their own industrializing and stratified society could evaporate."[30]

At another point in *The Virginia Tourist*, romantic visions of the aristocratic antebellum past are counterpointed with the postwar threat posed by a free black population. Pollard describes traveling in a remote and mountainous area of Bedford County, where he unexpectedly comes across a mansion in the mountains:

> It is a wild and desolate country immediately around me. I ride for miles with no sign of human life by the roadside but what some hut contains; some dogs bark at the horse's heels, and an old, half-nude negro glares at the traveler with savage curiosity, ceasing his work in a half-scratched field of withered corn. Suddenly, and as if by a magical translation, the road that has hesitated in such scenes, comes out upon a broad shoulder of the mountain, in sight of a pleasing mansion, and where are noticed, with infinite surprise, all the evidences of the broad and garnished farm of a wealthy planter.
>
> It was indeed a surprising revelation to have displayed here something like a vision of feudal proprietorship.... It was a picture of the old plantation life of Virginia hid away in the niche of a mountain; the romantic home of a modern feodary suspended in the clouds. The hospitality of the proprietor detained me; and it was indeed as refreshing as it was unexpected to dismount at a house which would have been of no mean pretensions even among our lowland gentry. (62–63)

In this scene, Pollard draws pointed contrasts between black and white, former slave and former master, savagery and refinement, and failure and success. These binary oppositions reinforce the desire for the aristocratic associations of the Old South while subtly warning readers of what Pollard sees as the potential disaster and dysfunction that would come with black political power. The hospitality and refinement of the planter he describes reaffirm white identity and provide an ethereal refuge from the grim realities Pollard sees in the shacks of black subsistence farmers. Like Telfair Hodgson, Pollard reinforces the myth of southern hospitality while simultaneously reminding readers of the perpetual strangers or aliens, the African American population.[31]

Reconciliation, Reunion, and Southern Hospitality: A Northern Regiment Returns South for Mardi Gras

That northerners were *both* willing consumers *and* producers of this reconstructed discourse of southern hospitality may be seen in John Franklin Cowan's *A New Invasion of the South* (1881), which illustrates the adaptability of the discourse of southern hospitality in the hands of northerners and southerners desirous of regional reconciliation and national unity in the decades following the Civil War. The book chronicles the 1881 expedition of the Seventy-First New York National Guard to New Orleans to participate as invited guests in the festivities of Mardi Gras and to commemorate the twentieth anniversary of the beginning of the Civil War.[32] Within the national contexts of reunion, reconciliation, and commemoration, the Seventy-First's trip to New Orleans at the invitation of the Royal Host of Mardi Gras was a self-consciously symbolic performance of southern hospitality. In Cowan's depiction of the trip we see this performance of southern hospitality translated into discursive practices that parallel those of Hodgson, Pollard, and others cited above, namely, by advocating national solidarity among the sections while simultaneously alienating or marginalizing black citizens. It also shows that as a way of commemorating or connecting with the past, the discourse of southern hospitality is as much about forgetting as it is about remembering. As David Blight shows in *Race and Reunion: The Civil War in American Memory*, in the decades after the Civil War, the national way of remembering the conflict shifted away from slavery and emancipation (its political cause and effect) and toward themes of regional reconciliation and mutual sacrifice. This changing way of remembering (and forgetting) was accomplished through rituals, memorials, and histories, and the discourse of southern hospitality was particularly well suited to this cultural work.[33]

In the "Dedicatory Note" and opening chapter of the text, Cowan pointedly underscores the national importance of this act of southern hospitality, noting that "there was an underlying principle of greater import than the mere interchange of courtesies."[34] Cowan explains that he has written this account so that "the generous treatment of Northern men by Southern men may be known, and to commemorate an event, that it is hoped, by all who participated, will be but that forerunner of that era of national fraternity on which so much of the future of our great country depends" (1). In the first chapter, titled "A New Invasion," Cowan portrays southern hospitality as having nothing less than transformative powers, turning the military invaders of twenty years earlier into a new invasion of appreciative guests and tourists: "In 1861 they met with crossed bayonets. In 1881 they met with clasped hands. It was a new invasion of the South, but the olive branch and the magnolia twined about the rifles and the old flag rose and fell over all" (6). The Seventy-First had been formally invited by the Royal Host of Mardi Gras, which Cowan claims is "probably the most powerful society in the Southern States, having for its object the development of the financial and commercial interests of the South" (7). Describing the society as "knowing no politics," he notes that they "headed the invitation with the offer of generous hospitality" (7). Cowan interprets for the reader the logic and meaning of the invitation from the southerners' perspective: "We of the South are anxious to show you of the North that the war is over. The throbbing of the war drums is hushed, the rancor of the past is gone forever. The soldiers of the South are Americans like yourselves, they have been and are misrepresented by designing men, and they are tired of misrepresentation. The old sectional bitterness is swallowed up in the desire for a new era of peace and brotherly love. Come and visit us that we may show you how sincere we are" (7).

Like Pollard, Cowan interprets the extending and receiving of hospitality between northerners and southerners as evidence of national reconciliation and reunion. Throughout the text, he reminds his readers of their warm reception in the South with numerous anecdotal examples and hyperbolic interpretations: the men of the regiment experienced "not a single instance of unfriendliness," they were "overwhelmed with kindness," they experienced the "true hospitality" of southerners, and the "social attention" they received "was unprecedented in the history of any body of travelers" (8, 42). Significantly, in a passage that elides the causes of the war and seems very much in line with Lost Cause ideology, Cowan proclaims, "It was nearest the heart of the old confederacy that the reception was warmest" (8).

But again as with the writers cited earlier, Pollard's representation of southern hospitality has an implicit racial meaning. His vision of national unity restored through hospitality does not include the population of former slaves. Despite all the references to the military action of the war, he does not include the causes of the war. For one thing, slavery is never even mentioned in the text, and the overall representation of the black population in the South is hardly sympathetic. Instead, the free black population merely hovers in the background, occasionally adding a sense of exotic local color interest to the narrative, as laboring "darkies," half-naked "pickaninnies," or rough-and-tumble roustabouts: "Several old darkies stood about the cars," or

"Three or four little pickaninnies were playing before the door," or "A little darkey, black as coal, and lively as a rat" who performs for the officers "a genuine plantation dance ... that would make our 'variety specialists' turn green with envy" (33, 35, 36). By the time Cowan was writing, many of the political, legal, and social gains that African Americans in the South had experienced under Reconstruction had already been eroded or dismantled by white lawmakers, and segregation was evolving as a way of life that would become the law of the South by the 1890s.[35] Instead of confronting the complex political questions surrounding race in the post-Reconstruction era, Cowan's text approaches race through the stock conventions of minstrelsy and local color writing. Moreover, these exoticized and dehumanizing depictions of the black population are consistently juxtaposed with contrasting images of hospitable exchanges among white northerners and white southerners. These contrasting representations, which taken together underscore national solidarity and reconciliation along racial lines, culminate in two episodes related at the end of chapter 9 and in chapter 10.

The first of these passages relates what is meant to be a humorous anecdote about a black servant of one of the officers. The servant, known as Jep, was brought along on the trip to wait on his employer. Cowan describes how Jep, enamored of the "dusky belles" of the city, dreamed what it would be like to be an officer like his employer, Commissary Hess: "He saw himself among the colored girls—the lion of the evening, petted and feasted and admired above all his comrades" (76). Following his dream, Jep comes up with a plan to turn it into reality, to which Cowan cannot resist the aside, "Of course it took Jep some time to form an idea in its entirety, but with hard work and determination he succeeded" (76). As Cowan sarcastically describes Jep's thought process as he decided to steal his employer's uniform and sneak out for a night on the town, it is clear that he finds Jep's aspirations ludicrous, and this message is underscored by the illustration that accompanies the passage. Captioned "Ambitious Jep," the illustration features a black figure in full uniform and with facial features drawn from the caricatured expression of blackface minstrelsy (grossly exaggerated lips, bulging eyes), as a white sentry recoils in surprise and horror. After his ruse is exposed, Jep is returned to his "proper sphere," stripped of the uniform and incarcerated until Commissary Hess secures his release. The anecdote seems to be a gratuitous and superfluous digression in the scheme of the overall narrative, but its placement in the text is perhaps calculated, appearing as it does immediately before the volume's climactic chapter, titled "Across the Divide," which details the regiment's trip to Greenwood Cemetery to honor the Confederate war dead. Cowan explains that the conciliatory gesture was "born of a desire to do something in return for the kindnesses heaped upon" the regiment during its time in New Orleans (78). The hospitality of the southerners has created a sense of indebtedness and obligation in their northern visitors. Later, Cowan describes a Mardi Gras ceremony honoring the regiment as a similarly reciprocal act of kindness: "The salute to the dead was a tribute of the North to the South; the ceremonies at the Opera House were a tribute from the South to the North" (82). Reflecting on these exchanges, Cowan again interprets the southerners' intentions for his reader: "In every action that day—in every word—those men and women gathered to do honor to a Northern regiment—breathed but one hope: *that the past might be hidden* by the weal of the present and the golden promises of the future" (83, italics added for emphasis).

These lines from Cowan hint at the dual nature of this commemorative trip and his written record of it, for acts of memory are also, necessarily, acts of forgetting, as certain details of the past are brought to the foreground and others are allowed to recede into the background, to be forgotten. The acts of hospitality celebrated in Cowan's text remind readers of the shared cultural identity of northern and southern whites while simultaneously obfuscating the historical fact of slavery and avoiding the difficult racial politics of the present. Writing against the backdrop of post-Reconstruction politics in the South, which included the calculated disenfranchisement of the African American population and the systematic development of Jim Crow segregation, Cowan's text shows no concern with these contemporary political issues or with questions of African American rights, equality, or justice. Instead, he expresses a sense of indebtedness toward his southern hosts and passes along to his readers the southern message regarding the happy condition of "colored" people in the South.[36]

While these negative representations of the newly freed black population are not really surprising for this period, what generally hasn't been considered is how these representations work *in tandem* with the persuasive appeal of southern hospitality. The contrasts drawn between the civility, generosity, and hospitality of white southerners and the savagery, ignorance, and barbarism of the freedmen are recurring discursive patterns in the decades following the Civil War and into the early twentieth century. Paternalistic, offensive, and racist images of African Americans were commonplace through cultural forms such as minstrelsy, cakewalks, newspaper reports and editorials, commercial advertising, and popular fiction and travel writing. At the same time, Americans were increasingly exposed to nostalgic images of the Old South as the war and its causes receded in public memory. Feeling a sense of nostalgia in the face of industrialization, immigration, urbanization, and the like; desiring reconciliation and peace following the devastation of the war; and accustomed to seeing negative stereotypes of African Americans, white Americans proved ripe and willing consumers for these racially inflected fictions of southern hospitality.[37] In contrast to the antebellum period of sectional crisis when the claim of southern hospitality was hotly contested on ethical grounds, the South now emerged as the nation's official home of hospitality. As an Atlanta tourism promoter would later put it in a 1914 *Atlanta Journal*, "Every Southern city and every Southern state is joined in a new confederacy, not of arms, but of hospitality"—a statement that still cites the theme of regional reconciliation nearly a half century after the war.[38] The ethical dimensions of hospitality largely disappeared or were muted in the new postwar economy and amid the emergence of a new hospitality and tourism industry. Indeed, the discourse of southern hospitality seemed perfectly suited to this new endeavor and new economy, providing a renovated and favorable image of the South after the war and in the face of continuing strife around racial issues. Americans could either face the stark political questions surrounding a newly freed population struggling for equality, or they could sink back into imagining themselves guests of the refined hospitality of the old southern aristocracy. Nostalgia was the easy choice for many, made easier by a Lost Cause ideology that reframed the conflict of the Civil War, by an honest desire for reconciliation, by growing fatigue over the difficult terrain of the so-called Negro question, and by a burgeoning school of plantation literature.

"The New South is . . . simply the Old South": Plantation Literature, Hospitality, and the Example of Thomas Nelson Page

As the nation progressed fitfully toward the modern era in the last decades of the nineteenth century, regional writing increasingly provided fodder for Americans' imaginations and particularly their nostalgic desires for pleasanter, simpler ways of life. Plantation literature of the South was perhaps the most popular and certainly the most ideologically potent school of this growing field of regional and local color writing.[39] Writers in this field helped to renovate the image of the Old South after the war, providing a sanitized, favorable view of slavery, and popularizing a nostalgic, sentimental image of southern hospitality. Many of our perceptions of the South today are still filtered through the lens created by this late nineteenth-century plantation literature and its fictions. As Americans navigated the accelerated rate of social change and flux that came with modernity, this sentimental view of southern hospitality allowed them to project onto the South their own desires for social ideals they may have felt were slipping away. But these imagined hospitable social relationships did not include the African American population. Instead, while white Americans faced the increasingly complex racial politics of the so-called Negro question—including the development of segregation culture and disenfranchisement of the free black population of the South—southern plantation literature encouraged them to retreat into sunny pastoral landscapes filled with hospitable southerners and happy-go-lucky slaves who exhibited a doglike fidelity to their white masters. The "New Negro" may have been agitating for political rights or making inroads into the middle class at the end of the century, but in these fictions, the "Old Negro" of the plantation days was still alive and well.[40] So while these positive representations of the Old South were steeped in nostalgia, they also went hand in hand with a racist doctrine of white supremacy. The overarching ethical ideals of hospitality were utterly displaced as southern hospitality became a prevailing signifier of white civilization, white solidarity, and white supremacy.

Thomas Nelson Page was by far the most influential and popular writer in this growing field of plantation literature, and his most significant extended statement on southern hospitality occurs in the sketches that comprise *Social Life in Old Virginia before the War*. *Social Life in Old Virginia* was originally included in Page's 1892 collection *The Old South: Essays Social and Political*, and it was also published in book form in 1897, with illustrations by Genevieve and Maude Cowles. Page labored relentlessly in his writings and public appearances to alter the American public's perception of the Old South, and many of the sketches and essays from these works were originally either delivered as lectures or published in periodicals as he strove to reach the widest possible audience. Page knew this world of the Old South firsthand, having spent his boyhood years on a plantation in Virginia. But the world he writes about had essentially disappeared by the time he was twelve with the South's defeat in the Civil War, so perhaps not surprisingly Page's representations of the Old South betray a sense of arrested development. He earnestly wants to believe, and desperately wants his audience to believe, that all his idealized, romantic notions of the Old South existed in the first place *and* that they still exist. Page wants no distinction drawn between the postbellum and the antebellum South. As he writes in the title essay to *The Old South: Essays Social and Political*, "The New South is, in fact, simply the Old South with its energies directed into new lines."[41] Whether in his fiction or nonfiction writing, Page channels his nostalgic representations of the Old South toward a deeply conservative and ultimately racist political agenda. Whether in lectures or on the printed page, his ultimate goal was to reconcile his audience to the sort of Lost Cause ideology articulated by Pollard and others, and to convert his national audience to a doctrine of white racial solidarity and supremacy.

In the introduction to *Social Life*, Page explains that he wrote the book to correct "the absolute ignorance of the outside world of the real life of the South in old times" and out of "the desire to correct the picture for the benefit of the younger generation of Southerners themselves."[42] An emphasis on gentility, refinement, and social graces runs throughout the text, and for Page, these qualities assume an important racial dimension. In an America that was experiencing radical social changes and pressures at the close of the nineteenth century, Page's version of the Old South becomes a haven for all the traditional values that many Americans felt were slipping away: manners, civility, courtesy, secure and happy social relations, and, of course, hospitality. Indeed, hospitality is both an important theme *and* a subtle governing principle of the narrative. By the end of the volume, Page has naturalized this social habit into the essential characteristic of the southern (read: white) race.

Social Life in Old Virginia is a series of sketches that essentially takes the reader on a tour of an archetypal southern plantation as Page imagines it to have existed before the war. The narrative logic accords with that of a friendly visit, moving from the exterior scenes and sweeping panoramas of the plantation's fields and grounds to the interior world of the mansion, with particular details of the household, its furnishings, and its inhabitants. Page essentially makes the reader a guest of the plantation in its days of glory. As the narrative enters the domestic space, Page introduces us to the characteristics and habits of the archetypal figures of the plantation household (with special emphasis on the "Southern Lady") and eventually to particular social customs and rituals on the plantation. Throughout, he appeals to his readers' senses, immersing them in a dreamlike ambience of the sights, sounds, and smells of plantation life. The accompanying illustrations by the Cowles sisters only underscore this atmosphere, as many seem to be viewed through a hazy, romantic lens that softens the subject. For example, consider the frontispiece portrait for the volume, which portrays the figures of a mother and daughter standing among lilies in a garden before an imposing, white-pillared mansion (see figure 14). The caption reads, "Tall lilies, white as angels' wings and stately as the maidens that walked among them." The downcast eyes of the women create a somewhat mournful tone, perhaps hinting at a loss in the family or perhaps just nostalgically mourning the loss of the old order of things: the images of white pillars and white women and white lilies work in tandem to create this mood. Page likewise acknowledges that his verbal pictures are "perhaps . . . idealized by the haze of time" (7).

The slaves themselves are an important part of the romantic atmosphere that Page creates, adding a "picturesque" quality to the scenes being described. He presents the reader with a picture of pre–Civil War racial harmony, with "servants" (according to Page, they were only referred to as "slaves" in legal documents) in their proper sphere under the paternalistic institution of slavery: "The life about the place was amazing. There were the busy children playing in groups, the boys of the family mingling with the little darkies as freely as any other young animals, and forming the associations which tempered slavery and made the relation one not to be understood save by those who saw it" (22). Unlike the New Negro, who was attempting to assert himself politically and economically, here the young slaves assume the docility and quaintness of barnyard animals under the budding paternalistic supervision of the young, future master. Typically, Page later describes happy slaves singing as they labor in the fields, a sign that "the heart was light and the toil not

"*Tall lilies, white as angels' wings and stately as the maidens that walked among them.*"

FIGURE 14. Frontispiece for Thomas Nelson Page's *Social Life in Old Virginia before the War*, 1897. Courtesy of American Antiquarian Society.

too heavy" (28). Even harvest time, which in reality was a period of arduous, tedious labor, is transformed by Page into a carnival: "The severest toil of the year was a frolic" (28). When it comes to representing slaves in the antebellum South, Page's strategy typifies plantation literature and southern travel writing of the last decades of the century. Nina Silber has described how writers from both the North and the South "helped to soften and sentimentalize the 'negro problem' amidst an abundance of flowery prose," particularly by portraying African Americans as "a 'picturesque' element on the southern scene" or "simply another feature of the landscape." In short, the picturesque provided a "formula to render possibly threatening features of society ... safe and amusing."[43]

As Page's narrative turns to the inward life of the plantation household, hospitality becomes a more overt and prominent theme, with perpetual guests and entertainments and what Page characterizes as an abundant, wasteful generosity. He emphasizes hospitality as perhaps the most dominant characteristic of the Old South. Of the master, for example, he writes, "To a stranger he was always a host, to a lady always a courtier. When the house was full of guests, he was the life of the company. He led the prettiest girl out for the dance" (48). It is for the women of the South, though, that Page reserves his most lavish praise, and in these depictions he combines long-standing notions of an inherent southern aristocracy with a fallacious combination of Darwinian thinking and pseudo-scientific racism. His language calls to mind what Nina Silber has described as a "cult of Anglo-Saxonism" that developed in America at the end of the century, a discourse employed by white Americans to describe "their sense of national will ... as the working out of the Anglo-Saxon destiny."[44] Of the archetypal Southern Lady, Page emphasizes bloodlines and an innate sense of gentility:

> She was gently bred: her people for generations (since they had come to Virginia) were gentlefolk.... She was the incontestable proof of their gentility. In right of her blood (the beautiful Saxon, tempered by the influences of the genial Southern clime), she was exquisite, fine, beautiful; a creature of peach-blossom and snow; languid, delicate, saucy; now imperious, now melting, always bewitching.... She had not to learn to be a lady, because she was born one. Generations had given her that by heredity. She grew up apart from the great world. But ignorance of the world did not make her provincial. Her instinct was an infallible guide. When a child she had in her sunbonnet and apron met the visitors at the front steps and entertained them in the parlor until her mother was ready to appear. Thus she had grown up to the duties of hostess. (52–54)

Page here depicts the Southern Lady as a unique product of biological inheritance and environmental influence. Her Anglo-Saxon blood combines with the southern environment and social habits to produce the perfect hostess, one immune from the unseemlier "ways of the world." Her social graces are the result of instinct. Moreover, she becomes an object of desire and allegiance for Page's ideal reader, for by the time he was writing, the intersectional marriage plot featuring a southern woman and a northern man had become a recurring trope in popular fiction. And at a time when the old-time virtue of hospitality was being supplanted by a bourgeoning hospitality and tourism industry and commodified in a developing national marketplace, Page offers the Southern Lady as the last bastion of this ancient domestic ideal.[45]

For Page, though, hospitality is no moral imperative or ethical ideal; rather, it is both a marker of whiteness and an idealized form of consumption: excessive, lavish, and wasteful (an appropriate attitude for the Gilded Age audience for whom Page was writing). The Virginian Lucian Minor in the 1830s complained of the wastefulness and conspicuous consumption of the antebellum planter class. Page likewise describes their way of life as extravagant and wasteful—but wonderful for this very reason. Life within the house, writes Page, "was like the roses, wasteful beyond measure in its unheeded growth and blowing, but sweet beyond measure, too, and filling with its fragrance not only the region round about, but sending it out unmeasuredly on every breeze that wandered by" (32). Page casually obscures the link between the labor of the slave and the leisure of the master; he only briefly describes the supporting cast of the household—presenting them as members of "one great family in the social structure now passed away"—before going on to detail the social habits and typical entertainments of the plantation: festivals, balls, friendly visits that stretch on for days, and, of course, fox hunts (64). Here Page's narrative reaches a crescendo, and he expresses some exasperation over his inability to convey the wonders of this antebellum world to his contemporary reader. At this point he offers his boldest claims regarding southern hospitality:

> I am painfully aware of the inadequacy of my picture. But who could do justice to the truth! . . . Hospitality had become a recognized race characteristic, and was practiced as a matter of course. It was universal; it was spontaneous. It was one of the distinguishing features of the civilization; as much a part of the social life as any other of the domestic relations. Its generosity secured it a distinctive title. The exactions it entailed were engrossing. Its exercise occupied much of the time, and exhausted much of the means. (77)[46]

What is unique in this passage is the manner in which Page completely naturalizes this social habit of hospitality by describing it as a "race characteristic."[47] Thirty years before the Civil War, and only a few years after the phrase "southern hospitality" had been invented, Lucian Minor could acknowledge that southerners' reputation for hospitality was contingent on slave labor, a product of the unique social circumstances of the South; thus Minor characterized it as an "easy virtue." He also acknowledged that Yankees could be just as hospitable in spirit, even if the circumstances of their culture (the lack of slave labor) dictated different social practices. In contrast, Page, writing thirty years after the war, naturalizes southern hospitality in the Old South so that it becomes a race characteristic, a matter as attributable to blood as to custom. While some may argue that with his use of the term "race" Page may simply mean a group of people sharing a common history rather than a group of people genetically linked, both the conclusion of *Social Life* and Page's other writings dictate otherwise.

Indeed, in the conclusion of *Social Life*, Page lays bare the racial assumptions and racist underpinnings of his portrayal of the South and its valorized social habits. Here he wistfully reflects on the changes that have taken place in the South since the war, and for the first time, he directly links his hyperbolic praise and nostalgic romanticism for the Old South's culture and social habits to his underlying racist assumptions and political agenda. This connection is accomplished both textually and visually in the 1897 illustrated edition. Having taken his readers on a virtual tour of the Old South plantation, encouraged them to nostalgically long for the simpler times of the past, and allowed them to imagine themselves as guests of the hospitable plantation household, Page offers the following conclusive remarks on the Old South's social habits:

> That the social life of the Old South had its faults I am far from denying. What civilization has not? But its virtues far outweighed them; its graces were never equalled. For all its faults, it was, I believe, the purest, sweetest life ever lived. . . . It largely contributed to produce this nation; it led its armies and its navies; it established this government so firmly that not even it could overthrow it; it opened up the great West; it added Louisiana and Texas, and more than trebled our territory; it christianized the negro race in a little over two centuries, impressed upon it regard for order, and gave it the only civilization it has ever possessed since the dawn of history. It has maintained the supremacy of the Caucasian race, upon which all civilization seems now to depend. It produced a people whose heroic fight against the forces of the world has enriched the annals of the human race,—a people whose fortitude in defeat has been even more splendid than their valor in war. It made men noble, gentle, and brave, and women tender and pure and true. It may have fallen short in material development in its narrower sense, but it abounded in spiritual development; it made the domestic virtues as common as light and air, and filled homes with purity and peace.
>
> It has passed from the earth, but it has left its benignant influence behind it to sweeten and sustain its children. The ivory palaces have been destroyed, but myrrh, aloes, and cassia still breathe amid their dismantled ruins. (106–9)

Notice how Page here drifts from a wistful reflection on social graces to a harder, more chauvinistic stance on white supremacy and Lost Cause idealism ("fortitude in defeat," "valor in war") before slipping back to his more nostalgic, softer emphasis on the "domestic virtues." This passage concisely exemplifies the fact that white supremacy was the hard center of Page's nostalgic vision of the South and, more particularly, this narrative. Indeed, the entire narrative has gently tried to direct the reader to this ideological conclusion. And the slightly alarmist tone here ("It has maintained the supremacy of the Caucasian race, upon which all civilization seems now to depend") is reminiscent of Page's polemic titled "The Negro Question," where he describes blacks as "an ignorant and hostile race," repeatedly rails against "negro domination" and the "evil ... race-degeneration" that will result from any social contact between the races, and alarmingly warns that the "only thing that stands between the North and the negro is the people of the South."[48] Moreover, his overtly racist statement on white supremacy in *Social Life* is underscored visually in the 1897 edition of the text. In this edition, at the very moment in the text when Page mentions the "supremacy of the Caucasion race," a full-page illustration appears on the opposing page depicting "A Typical Negro Cabin" that features an African American couple before a quaint, ramshackle plantation cabin (see figure 15). The quaint and "picturesque" quality of this image contrasts sharply with the volume's numerous romantic images of white gentility and refinement. Indeed, if the frontispiece picture (figure 14) may be said to stand for the pillars of Page's constructed Old South ideal of white purity and civilization, this final illustration is the necessary antithesis of that picture. With the rustic, earthy, quaint, and disorderly image of the "Typical Negro Cabin" and its inhabitants, the text exiles African Americans to the backgrounds of a bygone era, reducing them once again to "picturesque" elements of the plantation landscape.[49]

Hospitality, Hostility, and Transgenerational Trauma
in Charles Chesnutt's *The Marrow of Tradition* (1901)

Standing on the outside of the southern hospitality myth, African Americans in the late nineteenth and early twentieth centuries continued to offer critiques of this white exclusionary discourse, but their more critical voices were at odds with the prevailing trends of the literary marketplace and their overwhelmingly positive representations of the old plantation South. Frederick Douglass, for example, continued his criticism of the hospitality of the Old South in his later autobiographies, and W. E. B. Du Bois followed suit in *The Souls of Black Folk*, offering an ethical critique of southern hospitality that is very much in line with abolitionist critiques before the Civil War. Paul

A Typical Negro Cabin.

FIGURE 15. "A Typical Negro Cabin," illustration from Thomas Nelson Page's *Social Life in Old Virginia before the War*, 1897. Courtesy of American Antiquarian Society.

Laurence Dunbar offers one of the more imaginative literary renderings in his story "Nelse Hatton's Vengeance" from *Folks from Dixie*.[50] In this story, a fallen, impoverished master is forced to seek the hospitality of his former slave, Nelse Hatton, who is now living prosperously in Ohio. Upon meeting, initial reminiscences between the two are wistful and nostalgic, but Nelse's wife eventually pulls him aside and reminds him of the abuse he had suffered at the hands of his master. Recalling that pain and humiliation, Nelse momentarily contemplates violence against his former master, but in the end he restrains himself and gives the former master money and a suit of Nelse's own clothes before sending him on his way. Given the way the economy of gift exchange functioned among planters in the antebellum South, one could say that Nelse's choice is an act that essentially humiliates the former master. Still, the story's resolution leaves an uneasy balance among the narrative's competing currents of nostalgia, truth, and justice: the encounter dredges up traumatic memories for Nelse, but the master is never forced to remember his own brutality, that he was the source of Nelse's trauma. A similar tension among truth, justice, and memory exists in Charles W. Chesnutt's 1901 masterpiece, *The Marrow of Tradition*. The question of southern hospitality figures in very subtle but meaningful ways in the novel, becoming intertwined with these questions of (collective) remembering and forgetting. Most notably, the ethics and politics of hospitality figure prominently in the parallel and climactic scenes in which the white supremacist Major Carteret first refuses and then later is forced to seek out the assistance of the black physician, Dr. Miller, in order to save his dying son (chapters 7 and 36–37).[51] But this conclusion also suggests that for the South to move into a meaningful future will require hospitality of mind, namely, a willingness to acknowledge the full trauma of the past.

Chesnutt was keenly aware of the popularity of romance and nostalgia when it came to depictions of the South, but he also believed that American readers could be swayed by compelling moral and ethical arguments. So in an age where much of the literary marketplace put a premium on the romantic "moonlight and magnolias" depictions of the South, Chesnutt opted instead for a heavy dose of realism in *The Marrow of Tradition*, which he based on the recent Wilmington, North Carolina, "race riot" of 1898 ("massacre" or "coup" are actually more appropriate terms).[52] Two years before Du Bois would declare the color line "the problem of the Twentieth Century," Chesnutt's novel paints a comprehensive and nuanced picture of slavery's legacy and the debilitating consequences of southern and indeed American racial thinking.[53] This panoramic view of southern society at the turn of the twentieth century cuts across classes of black and white characters, across varying positions of the racial-political spectrum, and, perhaps most importantly, across generations. As one of the novel's white characters is forced to reflect on the lasting legacy of slavery, "The weed had been cut down, but its roots remained, deeply imbedded in the soil, to spring up and trouble a new generation."[54]

The plotlines of the novel are held together by the shared, interwoven, and interracial history of two families, the Carterets and the Millers, and the fate of their two male children. The two families embody the historical reality of a racially integrated South and of the shared histories of white and black southerners more generally. This is the truth of the South, but it is one that the white southerners in the novel work hard to forget. Indeed, Major Phillip Carteret is a proud and ardent white supremacist whose main obsession in the novel is restoring his bloodline to its former dignity, and according to his Lost Cause worldview, this requires racial segregation and white dominance of southern culture and politics. The major's white supremacist blustering and obsession with racial purity cannot, however, erase the fact that his wife, Olivia, has a mulatto half-sister, Janet Miller, who is married to William Miller, a successful black doctor who is committed to uplifting his race. Particularly galling to Major Carteret is the fact that the self-sufficient and upwardly mobile Millers live in the former Carteret family mansion, Carteret's boyhood home. Both the major and Olivia forcibly repress these blood ties, despite the fact that Olivia's younger half-sister, Janet, is so similar in appearance as to sometimes be mistaken for Olivia on the street. This repression of the racially integrated reality of the South produces outbreaks of hysteria in the white characters—including Olivia's induced premature labor at seeing her sister on the street, her later nightmares, the major's rabid, race-baiting editorials, and the mass hysteria of the lynch mob and climactic white riot later in the novel.[55] For Olivia Carteret, though, the full truth asserts itself over the course of the novel: she comes to learn that her father had in fact legally married Janet's mother, his former slave Julia, and that Janet is thus her lawful sister and heir to a significant portion of the family estate. Deeply troubled by this revelation, Olivia initially decides to keep this secret to herself, but the truth will out, and in this case, it emerges under extraordinary circumstances in the novel's closing pages.

A year before *The Marrow of Tradition*, Chesnutt had made his skepticism regarding southern hospitality readily apparent in his novel *The House behind the Cedars*. Here he directly links the boasted claims of southern hospitality to the South's hostility toward its black citizens. More specifically, at one point in the narrative as one white gentleman welcomes another into his home, he opines: "Strangers are rare birds in our society, and when they come we make them welcome. Our enemies may overturn our institutions, and try to put the bottom rail on top, but they cannot destroy our Southern hospitality. There are so many carpet-baggers and other social vermin creeping into the South, with the Yankees trying to force the niggers on us, that it's a genuine pleasure to get acquainted with another real Southern gentleman, whom one can invite into one's house without fear of contamination, and before whom one can express his feelings freely and be sure of perfect sympathy."[56] Here southern hospitality can only exist among whites; indeed, it becomes a sort of defense mechanism that maintains hierarchies and inoculates the right sort of white citizens against blacks and their political supporters, who carry with them the possibility of "contamination." Chesnutt develops this line of criticism more comprehensively and in more nuanced ways in *The Marrow of Tradition*, particularly with juxtaposed scenes early in the novel that carefully link southern laws with southern social practices to show that the South has no hospitality for African Americans, whether in the public space of a railway car or the private space of a front parlor. This linking of southern laws and southern social practices is reminiscent of F. C. Adams's *Manuel Pereira*, discussed earlier.

Dr. William Miller is introduced in the novel's fifth chapter, titled "A Journey Southward," and here Chesnutt details the gross indignities faced by African Americans forced to endure segregated rail travel, as well as the coercive effect that these southern laws had on all outsiders, including white citizens. Miller is returning to Wellington after a trip north to acquire equipment for his new hospital, and he's pleased to run into one of his mentors from medical school, Dr. Burns, who happens to have been called to Wellington to perform a delicate operation on Major Carteret's son. Unfortunately for Miller, once the train crosses into Virginia he must face the humiliation of being sent to the "colored" car in front of his mentor and professional peer. Miller and Burns both protest but to no avail. For Chesnutt, this obsession with defining the color line is a peculiarly American phenomenon, and it trumps all other aspects of one's identity when considering the social worth of an individual: class, intelligence, wealth, cultural refinement, public service, and so forth.[57] Chesnutt goes into detail in describing the painful psychological effect that this experience has on Miller. Musing on the fact that he, as a gentleman and a doctor, had been sent to the colored car, while a black nurse was allowed into the white car with her mistress, Miller utters the simple, universal truth that informed the discourse of southern hospitality in the nineteenth century: "'White people,' said Miller to himself, . . . 'do not object to the negro as a servant. As the traditional negro,—the servant,—he is welcomed; as an equal he is repudiated'" (59). Further reflecting on the logic of segregation, Miller, with a particularly apt allusion, compares it to the violent practices of Procrustes, the duplicitous host of Greek myth who invited guests into his home in order to murder them:

> Surely, if a classification of passengers on trains was at all desirable, it might be made upon some more logical and considerate basis than a mere arbitrary, tactless, and, by the very nature of things, brutal drawing of a color line. It was a veritable bed of Procrustes, this standard which the whites had set for the

negroes. Those who grew above it must have their heads cut off figuratively speaking,—must be forced back to the level assigned to their race; those who fell beneath the standard set had their necks stretched, literally enough, as the ghastly record in the daily papers gave conclusive evidence. (61)

Closely following on this chapter on the segregated railcar, Miller finds himself again repudiated, this time at Major Carteret's home, where his professional peers in Wellington have gathered to witness Dr. Burns perform his operation to save Carteret's son. While on the train, Burns had invited Miller, a former star pupil, to assist with the delicate operation, but Burns has yet to learn of the racist logic that governs the major's hospitality: "It was traditional in Wellington that no colored person had ever entered the front door of the Carteret residence, and that the luckless individual who once presented himself there upon alleged business and resented being ordered to the back door had been unceremoniously thrown over the piazza railing into a rather thorny clump of rosebushes below" (68). As the scene unfolds, we see just how deep Carteret's obsessive racism runs, for he is willing to argue with Dr. Burns about Miller's presence even while his son is awaiting the doctor's care: "Carteret was deeply agitated. The operation must not be deferred; his child's life might be endangered by delay. If the negro's presence were indispensable he would even submit to it, though in order to avoid so painful a necessity, he would rather humble himself to the Northern doctor. The latter course involved merely a personal sacrifice—the former a vital principle" (72). Luckily for Carteret, another "way of escape" comes to mind. Considering his wife's deep anxiety regarding her half-sister, he informs Burns that there are "personal reasons, apart from Dr. Miller's color," that would make Miller's presence "distasteful" (73). With this new information, Burns eventually relents and agrees to proceed with the operation, never learning that Carteret's "personal reasons" still essentially revolve around Miller's race and the uncomfortable fact that the two families are bound by a common bloodline. Just as in the train scene, Dr. Burns, who holds genuinely progressive views on race, is coerced into conforming to the South's racist assumptions and correlating social practices.[58] The white supremacist Carteret gets his way, and Miller is humiliated when he learns the truth from one of Carteret's servants. Even better for Carteret, Burns is able to remove the obstruction in his son's windpipe without a surgical procedure.

This repudiation of Miller during the operation scene is a defining moment in the novel, particularly in the way it foreshadows the novel's provocative conclusion, which essentially replays the operation scenario under more extreme circumstances to pose a fundamental question to the white reader. In the concluding chapters, Carteret and his political counterparts have successfully staged their riot and coup, but things spin out of Carteret's control as the white mob's destruction in the city exceeds what he had imagined, and even his family's faithful black servant, Mammy Jane, is among the victims. Worse yet, when he returns home he finds that his young son has fallen deathly ill with membranous croup, in part because his black nurses have fled the violence and left him unattended. None of the white doctors in town are available to attend to his son. Some had been forewarned of the planned coup and left ahead of time, while others are already attending other victims of the violence or have been themselves injured. Carteret finds his wife hysterical and inconsolable and his son attended only by an inexperienced medical student who is unable to perform the tracheotomy his child needs. Under these desperate circumstances, the major is finally willing to seek out the assistance of Dr. Miller, his de facto brother-in-law whom he has never met or acknowledged as such due to the color of his skin.

In creating this closing scenario, Chesnutt prods his contemporary white readers to explore the limits of their own sense of racial superiority and prejudice. Given the contrast with the earlier scene in which Miller is excluded, Chesnutt essentially asks the reader, *Would you be willing to let a black man into your house if your child's life depended on it?* Chesnutt proposes that in such a situation, even an ardent white supremacist like Carteret would relent. Unfortunately for Carteret, as he approaches Miller's door for assistance he is unaware that Miller's child lies dead inside, an innocent victim of Carteret's orchestrated violence. In considering the exchange that takes place between the two men, it is important to remember that Miller lives in the former Carteret family mansion, so when Carteret knocks on the front door, it is in fact the door of his own past. And in returning to his family's antebellum mansion, the scene behind the door that is revealed to Carteret is not some plantation idyll of Thomas Nelson Page; instead, the major is met with the lifeless form of an anonymous black child. Unlike the Carteret baby, who has a name and even a nickname in the novel, the Miller child remains nameless throughout the book. The death of this unnamed black child could perhaps be said to signify a lost generation of black southerners who have seen the promise of emancipation go unfulfilled as they struggled unsuccessfully for equality in the segregated South. Returning to the scene of his own past, then, Carteret must face an uncomfortable truth in the form of the Millers' dead child. He is suddenly forced to fully comprehend his own complicity and must face the consequences of his own actions; he may even sense the toll that slavery and its legacy of segregation have taken on black citizens of the South. Moreover, when Miller refuses his desperate pleas for assistance, Carteret is ultimately forced to accept the justice of Miller's decision:

> Carteret possessed a narrow, but a logical mind, and except when confused or blinded by his prejudices, had always tried to be a just man. In the agony of his own predicament,—in the horror of the situation at Miller's house,—for a moment the veil of race prejudice was rent in twain, and he saw things as they were, in their correct proportions and relations,—saw clearly and convincingly that he had no standing here.... Miller's refusal to go with him was pure, elemental justice.... As he had sown, so must he reap! (321)

But rather than opting for such an eye-for-an-eye sense of justice at the end of this novel filled with racial hostility, Chesnutt chooses to put a thematic emphasis on truth instead. Indeed, justice and truth seem particularly at odds with each other in this novel. The black child is dead, but the white child will live, though this is only possible after Olivia is forced to reveal the truth of the past and her familial bond with Janet Miller. Following the major's return home after Dr. Miller's refusal, Olivia runs to the Miller household and throws herself at the doctor's feet, begging for his aid. Momentarily swayed by the strikingly similar appearances of the pleading Olivia and his own grieving wife, Miller tells Olivia that she must take her appeal to his wife, the younger sister she has never acknowledged, and that he will abide by Janet's decision on whether he should act to save the Carteret child. Driven by her fear for her child's life, Olivia finally acknowledges her younger half-sister and reveals the full truth that she had learned regarding her father's marriage and Janet's legal standing as her sister. In response, Janet rebukes this "sisterly recognition," which comes like "apples of Sodom, filled with dust and ashes," but she does release her husband to save the Carteret child, her de facto nephew (328–29).

The novel's resolution, we might say, hinges on a profound act of "good Samaritan" hospitality performed by the Millers. Despite Carteret's earlier repudiation of Miller, despite the South's inhospitable system of racial segregation, despite the racist terrorism of the Wellington riot, and despite the death of their own child, the Millers open their door to these white family members who have heretofore scorned them. In the closing scene, the Carterets in turn allow Miller to cross their jealously guarded threshold to save their son, a possibility they had earlier denied. However, this moment of hospitality results in thematic tension where truth and justice particularly seem at odds. One could even argue that the novel seems to privilege a sense of forgiveness without justice, for while the black child dies, the white child will live if Miller acts in time. Carteret himself had acknowledged that the death of his own son would be a just result of his actions, but the plot involving the two families does not offer this eye-for-an-eye justice of the Mosaic code. Instead, we might say that the just payment made in exchange for their son's life has come in the form of truth—more specifically, in the white characters' acknowledgment of a truth they had heretofore repressed. This honest acknowledgment carries consequent emotions of remorse and guilt, and it also brings about the most difficult of reconciliations between the families, one marked by trauma, tragedy, and irrevocable loss.[59] Carteret knows and now must live with the consequences of his own racism and actions, and Olivia has revealed all to Janet. So unlike "Nelse Hatton's Vengeance," the truth of the past in the novel's conclusion is at least acknowledged equally by both black and white characters, even though the trauma experienced by the two families is profoundly unequal. Considered more broadly, Chesnutt's conclusion suggests that given the white and black South's shared though unequal histories of trauma, acknowledging the full truth of the past may be more important than justice. Such a resolution seems particularly prescient, as it forecasts both the practices and the complications of "truth commissions" in modern states like South Africa.[60] Despite William Dean Howells's assessment that the novel was too "bitter," *The Marrow of Tradition* is in fact a novel of hope: acknowledging the full truth of the past is the only way to move into the future. The Carteret child represents the future generation, and he is able to live only after his parents face and acknowledge the full truth of the past, including their complicity in the racial injustice of slavery and segregation.

As Matt Wilson explains in *Whiteness in the Novels of Charles W. Chesnutt*, "one of the major cultural tensions with which Chesnutt had to contend as a writer was that he was producing his race fictions in a period when Americans wanted to forget what he insisted they remember, when the national consensus was one of active forgetting."[61] Chesnutt felt it was essential that the nation remember the truth of slavery and that it face the fact of the continuing racial injustice of segregation. His novel ends with a moment of hope that comes only at a terrible cost. While racial hostility had been the prevailing mood of the novel, culminating in the white riot, the novel's final pages give way to an act of hospitality in which both the Millers and the Carterets are willing to put themselves at some risk. With the closing words of the novel—"There's time enough, but none to spare" (329)—Chesnutt implies that the complex and violent racial divisions and injustice in America were an urgent problem requiring immediate action. Unfortunately, when it came to the South and the legacy of slavery, most Americans at the time preferred romance and nostalgia over realism and truth.[62] Over one hundred years later, many would say that we still have not faced the full truth of this past; instead, we have had more than a century of repression and active forgetting about slavery and its legacy. And unlike the acts of hospitality in the novel's conclusion, which open the characters up to the full truth of this difficult past (acts of "mental hospitality" we may say), the discourse of southern hospitality has provided a pervasive and recurring mechanism for the repression of this past.

CHAPTER SIX

The Modern Proliferation of the Southern Hospitality Myth

Repetition, Revision, and Reappropriation

> Now some of our guests ain't sure yet what this shindig is all about, so we better get started with our centennial, right folks? Yessirree! Now, it's been a hundred years, but what we celebratin' ain't important. What we need are guests, and you all are it! Now for the next few days y'all gonna be guests of the town. You gonna have the best hotel rooms, the best food, the best entertainment, and it's all on the house! Yessir, y'all our guests, and we gonna show you some SOUTHERN HOSPITALITY!
>
> —Mayor Earl Buckman,
> from the 1964 film *Two Thousand Maniacs!*

Unfortunately for his tourist guests from the North, when Mayor Earl Buckman promises them the best of southern hospitality, what he actually has in mind includes torture, mutilation, dismemberment, burning, cannibalism, and ritualistic mob violence. The shock film *Two Thousand Maniacs!* was screened in drive-in theaters around the country, North and South, in the summer of 1964, and it was ardently promoted and particularly popular in southern markets. I begin this concluding chapter with *Two Thousand Maniacs!* for a number of reasons. First, like perhaps no other text, the film shows the incredible, even absurd, ranginess of the myth of southern hospitality as it proliferated through twentieth-century mass media, popular culture, and advertising; one can hardly be more removed from the refined social practices of antebellum planters that first spawned the myth than the gore and destruction of this cult classic of American pop culture. With the twentieth-century development of new forms of popular culture, mass media, and mass marketing, the southern hospitality myth proliferated as never before, reaching wider audiences with an increasingly consistent, repeated message that the South was the nation's home of hospitality.[1] Not surprisingly, this discourse of southern hospitality was perfectly suited to an overall "branding" of the

South as a consumable product and marketable identity in twentieth-century economic endeavors such as tourism, lifestyle and leisure industries, and even manufacturing.[2] These consistent repetitions of southern hospitality increasingly made it seem like a "natural" condition and attribute of southern culture, something that just goes without saying when one thinks about the South. Second, I begin with this film because it was produced at a unique juncture in the modern South's political, cultural, and economic history. On the one hand, the film was originally screened as the South was in the midst of its most profound cultural change since the Civil War: the erosion and eventual elimination of legalized segregation. White southern resistance to desegregation efforts had been unfolding in the national spotlight for a full decade since the *Brown v. Board of Education* decision of 1954, and the landmark Civil Rights Act was finally passed on July 2, 1964, the same summer as the film's original screenings across the South. On the other hand, the film also appears at an important juncture in the South's economic history. By the early 1960s, decades of sustained effort had firmly established a thriving tourism industry across the region, making it the "second or third largest generator of wealth in the South," one that was growing annually by 5 percent a year.[3] Shortly after the film's release and just after the legal end of segregation, *Southern Living* magazine would be successfully launched across the South, ushering in a new era of profitable lifestyle branding around southern identity. Both of these economic endeavors relied heavily on the southern hospitality myth as both a recognizable framing narrative and a virtual thematic center. As I will show later in this chapter, these iterations are characterized by pervasive habits of repression and repetition. The history of the southern hospitality myth in the twentieth century could easily be the subject of a book in itself, whether focusing on pop culture, literature, or even African American reappropriations of the myth post–civil rights. But I conclude my study by focusing on tourism and lifestyle because they have been major generators of economic wealth for the South and for some southerners in the twentieth and twenty-first centuries. Consequently, more is perhaps at stake from an ethical perspective in these endeavors, particularly when we think about the long history of the southern hospitality myth and its racial dynamics.

You may recall that in chapter 1 I considered the original social practices of antebellum planters—which generated the southern hospitality myth—through the lens of Pierre Bourdieu's theories of social capital. There I argued that the rituals of hospitality exercised by the antebellum planter class could be seen as an investment strategy for enhancing their social and cultural capital, a reproductive and legitimating tactic that enhanced and extended their own power and influence. The emergence and development of the southern hospitality myth had a multiplier effect on these original social practices, extending the planters' network of connections and consequently their influence and power. In short, the proliferation of the southern hospitality myth ensured that the investment made in these limited social practices paid off for generations of white southerners, as well as for the legacy of the original planters themselves: the southern hospitality myth helped legitimate white supremacy and privilege long after slavery, helped shape American cultural memory of the slaveholding class in a laudatory way, and provided future generations of white southerners with an effective branding strategy for some of the modern South's most important economic endeavors. At the same time, modern iterations of the southern hospitality myth inevitably erase the fact that it was the slave's degradation and labor that paid for the master's hospitality. But these contemporary iterations of southern hospitality cannot be entirely separated from the past of slavery, for they achieve their recognizable meanings only within the framework of this long history of repetition and citation. Consequently, even modern iterations of "southern hospitality" can be haunted by this past, as can readily be seen in *Two Thousand Maniacs!*, which provides one of the most uncannily incisive resignifications of the southern hospitality myth in its centuries-long history.

Two Thousand Maniacs! is a cult classic among B-movie aficionados, a breakthrough film in the shock and exploitation genres. Producer David Friedman, a former Paramount Studios executive, and director Herschell Gordon Lewis, a former English professor, had collaborated on a number of soft-porn exploitation films in the early 1960s, but as the market for such films became glutted, the pair sought to create some other form of cinematic exploitation. They struck gold with their 1963 film *Blood Feast*, which invented new standards and a new genre of cinematic gore. Of the groundbreaking nature of the film, Lewis was known to quip: "*Blood Feast* is like a Walt Whitman poem. It's no good but it's the first of its kind, therefore it deserves recognition."[4] With the success of *Blood Feast* behind them, the pair became more ambitious; Lewis hoped to make a "better" gore film (that is, one that would actually tell a story): the result was *Two Thousand Maniacs!*. In contrast to *Blood Feast*, which was produced on a $7,500 budget and a fifteen-page script that took six hours to write, *Two Thousand Maniacs!* was shot on a $65,000 budget following a seventy-page script. Lewis even created a tie-in novelization of the screenplay in an attempt to capitalize on the film's anticipated success. Sixty-three copies of the film were originally created and circulated mainly in the South and the Midwest in the spring and summer of 1964. The novel version of the film may still be found today.[5]

Against a theme song whose refrain repeats, "The South's gonna rise again," the film opens with two cars of northern tourists being purposefully detoured off the main highway and directed toward the small town of Pleasant Valley, Georgia—population two thousand. As they arrive in the town, they are greeted by smiling locals who quickly surround the cars and hail the strangers with whoops and hurrahs, waving Confederate flags. A banner hanging across the street reads, "Welcome to Pleasant Valley Centennial, April 1865–April 1965," and the locals repeatedly tell the six northerners that they are the celebration's "guests of honor." The northerners, who alternately seem arrogant and naive, are clearly mystified and initially even unsettled by the crowd, but the southerners' congenial warmth and good spirits eventually win them over. Even so, when Mayor Buckman stands before the crowd and gives his promise of southern hospitality cited in the epigraph, the crowd of locals responds with knowing, even mocking, laughter. The nature of this insider's joke soon becomes apparent as one by one the northerners are separated from one another and meet their unfortunate ends at the hands of the southern mob. Later in the film, we learn that the town's residents are the hapless ghosts of a Civil War massacre who, in an odd twist to the Broadway musical *Brigadoon* that inspired it, will come to life once every one hundred years to seek vengeance against unsuspecting northerners.[6]

While the film is trashy, cheap, and exploitative, it is also unnerving. Perhaps the most disturbing element is that the violence is usually carried out at the center of a mob of smiling and cheering faces, and as the victims are led along to their unhappy ends, they are repeatedly reminded that they are the town's special guests. Simply put, the film shockingly juxtaposes two recognizable images of the region: the hospitable South and the violent South, or the South that claims a unique tradition of gracious hospitality, and the South that historically has been the site of ritualistic mob violence, particularly with the lynchings of thousands of African Americans, many of which took place in public squares before hundreds and even thousands of people. The unique reversal in the film is that, in contrast to the historical black victims, it is the white northern tourists who are victimized by the white southern mob.[7] Similarly, the film's plotline offers an interesting twist on the historical trajectory of the myth of southern hospitality. The film's tourists from the North are on their way to Florida and Atlanta, both important icons of the New South ideals of progress and development and centers of the New South's expanding tourism and hospitality industries, but they are detoured away from these destinations and toward a site of repressed regional conflict, where they are literally confronted by ghosts of a traumatic past. By the time *Two Thousand Maniacs!* was produced and screened in 1964, "southern hospitality" had proliferated through popular culture and mass media and had also become a familiar, even incessant, branding mantra for all sorts of southern economic and corporate endeavors. Through decades of concerted efforts, many southern states had already developed successful heritage and recreational tourism industries. Not surprisingly, promotional campaigns for these growing industries often hinged on the South's reputation for hospitality.[8] At the time of the film's production, tourism ads placed in northern newspapers for southern resorts and vacation destinations routinely promised their potential visitors "true southern hospitality" or "real southern hospitality" or "warm southern hospitality."[9] Southern hospitality was also often cited in ads trying to lure professionals and businesses to the South. A 1960 ad in the *New York Times* for the Norfolk Industrial Park reads, "New Housing, new businesses, new growth, all added to Norfolk's old southern hospitality make Norfolk the perfect place for you to expand and grow." Similarly, a Fulton County Commission ad trying to lure businesses to Atlanta promises "just the right blend of Southern hospitality and hustle."[10] And Atlanta's own Delta Air Lines emphasized southern hospitality as an effective marketing tool and as the thematic basis for its culture of customer service.[11] In short, by the time of the film's initial screening in 1964, American consumers had long been conditioned to think of the South as the nation's home of hospitality.

Rather than having these consumer desires fulfilled, however, the film's northern tourists are detoured away from their target destinations of Florida and Atlanta and toward the site of an earlier, repressed historical conflict. Indeed, the film's genre—a southern Gothic tale featuring literal ghosts from a violent past—is particularly appropriate for addressing the unresolved regional conflicts facing the nation for a full century since the Civil War, particularly those surrounding race and the long struggle for civil rights. In Pleasant Valley, the regional strife and conflict of the past continue to haunt the present. The northerners, however, are unsuspecting; their view of the South as a hospitable vacation destination (along with their condescending attitudes toward the southerners) prevents them from seeing the ghosts for what they are, and the only northerners who survive are the ones with a fifth-grader's basic knowledge of American history:

> TOM WHITE: Has it occurred to you that nobody has told us what this centennial is all about? Now, this is 1965, and a hundred years ago it was 1865, right? So, what happened in 1865?
> TERRY ADAMS: It was the ending of the Civil War. The war between the states!
> TOM WHITE: Well then you tell me why would a southern town want northerners as guests of honor at the centennial? It must have something to do with what happened a hundred years ago. So, something is very wrong with this town.[12]

Even though the film can offer a counternarrative to traditional views of southern hospitality, particularly by suggesting that the myth of southern hospitality obscures lingering and repressed historical conflict, it does not directly address the racial element of this historical conflict between the North and the South. The entire cast and all extras are white, and the only seemingly overt allusion to the subject of race occurs in the opening credits. As the crowd gathers, waving their Confederate flags, a number of rambunctious youngsters scurry about the crowd; a perceptive viewer might notice that all of them seem to be carrying small nooses. In a sudden shift near the end of the opening sequence, the camera cuts to a small group of the boys who use one of the nooses to strangle a black cat. A close-up shows that the cat wears a tag reading "Dam [sic] Yankee" (a detail meant to confirm the negative stereotype of southern illiteracy), and after the cat is killed, the camera holds a long still shot of the noose as the credits roll to a close.[13]

When it comes to race, the film operates according to what Tara McPherson describes as the "lenticular logic" that typically regulates the representation of race in the imagined South. According to McPherson, "a lenticular logic is a monocular logic, a schema by which histories or images that are actually copresent get presented (structurally, ideologically) so that only one of the images can be seen at a time. Such an arrangement represses connection, allowing whiteness to float free from blackness, denying the long historical imbrications of racial markers and racial meaning in the South."[14] In other words, just because the South's bifurcated racial history is invisible does not mean that it is not there. Indeed, in addition to the lynching of the black cat, the images of violence in *Two Thousand Maniacs!* seem haunted by the complex history of racial strife and violence in the South. For example, in a modern incarnation of the trope of interregional romance, which figured prominently in reconciliation efforts following the Civil War, the first female victim from the North is easily seduced away from her husband by one of the locals. The interregional romance here, however, is just a mask for repressed regional hatred. The tryst takes a savage turn when the man abruptly and inexplicably cuts off the woman's thumb, and the film erupts into several minutes of violence as the victim is taken into a cabin where Mayor Buckman and others are waiting for her. Against a backdrop of a hearth and mantle decorated with Confederate flags, she is held down on a table and her right arm is chopped off with an axe. In a revenge fantasy with real historical antecedents, the woman from the North is here victimized in a manner analogous to the way southerners often imagined Reconstruction and black political power: as a threat to white southern womanhood (see figures 16 and 17). In what becomes standard practice for the film, several shots counterpoint close-ups of the victim's bloody corpse with close-ups from low and side angles of her crazed yet gleeful tormentors. Later that evening, the victim's severed arm is seen roasting on a spit at the centennial barbeque while the crowd enjoys a rollicking rendition of Flatt and Scruggs' "Rollin' in My Sweet Baby's Arms."

Fans of this classic of cinematic gore often laud what they see as the particularly original forms of death meted out to the rest of the northern victims, but these scenes are likewise haunted by the South's history of racial violence during slavery and segregation. One victim is dismembered by having his arms and legs tied to four horses, which are then driven in opposing direc-

FIGURE 16. *Murder of Louisiana Sacrificed on the Altar of Radicalism*, political broadside by A. Zenneck, 1871. Courtesy of Library of Congress Prints and Photographs Division.

tions. Another is placed in a barrel lined with sharp nails and rolled down a hill. And finally, in a macabre variation on a carnival dunking booth, the last victim is tied up beneath a teetering boulder as a crowd of townspeople take turns trying to hit the target that will trigger the boulder's fall. While these certainly are creative methods for murder and mayhem, they are not necessarily original. The first two of these three death scenes actually have historical antecedents in the legacy of slavery, and even the carnival-like death scene featuring the teetering boulder, while original, nonetheless calls to mind the atmosphere of the modern "spectacle lynching" described by Grace Elizabeth Hale and others.[15] The South's history is replete with competing and contradictory images, and the film's novelty is that it manages to conjoin contradictory images of the South and resignify them in unusual ways: hospitality becomes hostility, the romance of reunion becomes repressed regional hatred, and the white visitor from the North assumes the position so often occupied by the black victim.

Given the timing of its release in 1964, the film's ironic resignification of southern hospitality is especially evocative, for it occurred when this idea of the South was under intense pressure. Indeed, you could say that the resulting irony and tension in the film's juxtaposition of southern hospitality and hostil-

FIGURE 17. Scene from the 1964 shock film *Two Thousand Maniacs!*

ity accurately reflects the cognitive dissonance then circulating in American culture over the South's image. While the plotline and violent images in the film are haunted by the past, viewers of the film in 1964 must have felt strong resonances in the present. The summer in which this film was screened in drive-ins throughout the country coincided with the Student Nonviolent Coordinating Committee's Summer Project of 1964, a campaign that marked an increase in white involvement in the southern civil rights movement. It was the summer that came to be known as "Mississippi Burning," the FBI's code name for the violence and intimidation taking place in response to these concerted efforts by white and black civil rights workers to register black voters. It was also the summer in which three civil rights workers—Michael Schwerner, Andrew Goodman, and James Chaney—were kidnapped and murdered by the Ku Klux Klan. With this more immediate context in mind—and knowing that this violence unfolded under a national media spotlight—the film's plotline and violence, and particularly its juxtaposition of southern hospitality and hostility, seem somewhat less fantastic. We can only wonder how audiences in this immediate context would have reacted to the film's details—its violence directed at northerners, the theme song's refrain of "The South's gonna rise again," the insiders' joke about southern hospitality, and the image of the hangman's noose and the "lynching" of the black cat that occurs in the film's opening credits. Might some southerners have taken satisfaction

FIGURE 18. Political cartoon by James Dobbins, originally published in the *Boston Traveler*, 1961.

at seeing the arrogant northerners meet their horrible ends? And what of nonsouthern viewers? Did the film provide comfortable confirmation of their assumptions about southern abjection, backwardness, and violence, thereby confirming their own sense of moral superiority?

Significantly, the film's ironic resignification of southern hospitality is not an isolated or aberrant example in this particular moment. Against the backdrop of the increasing tension and violence of the civil rights movement of the early 1960s, and at a moment in which the very image of the South in the national consciousness was in a constant state of flux, the myth of southern hospitality was both cited widely and deeply contested. The same newspapers that were advertising southern hospitality as a commodity were also printing numerous stories and images that challenged this claim of southern hospitality. A 1961 editorial cartoon originally published in the *Boston Traveler*, for example, has a freedom bus driving past the barred windows of a jail; the caption simply reads, "Southern hospitality." Similarly, a 1963 cartoon in response to the strife in Birmingham, Alabama, shows an imposing Birmingham city jail with a dripping water hose, sleeping guard dogs, and a "No vacancy sign." The caption again ironically reads, "Southern hospitality" (see figures 18 and

"Southern hospitality."

FIGURE 19. Political cartoon by Pierre Bellocq (PEB), originally published in the *Philadelphia Inquirer*, 1963. Courtesy of Pierre Bellocq (www.pebsite.com).

19).[16] Other news stories made similarly ironic allusions to southern hospitality.[17] In short, simply uttering "southern hospitality" in this particular context of racial strife and violence in the segregated South is enough to challenge the myth, reminding readers that the concept of hospitality has important moral and ethical dimensions, and that these dimensions don't seem operational in the South at this moment in its history. Importantly, this sense of irony in both the film and these other media instances runs throughout the history of this discourse. Indeed, *from an ethical perspective*, it is fair to say that southern hospitality could not exist until after the civil rights movement, for segregation, like slavery, is antithetical to the ethics of hospitality. Despite this contradiction, the southern hospitality myth has been successfully deployed throughout the twentieth and twenty-first centuries to market the southern tourism industry, and since the 1960s, to promote a range of lifestyle industries based on southern identity. The end of segregation might have provided a day of reckoning for the southern hospitality myth, particularly given the examples just cited that point to the ethics of hospitality amid the politics of segregation. Instead, however, the myth continued to follow familiar patterns of repetition and repression of historical connections, though some have challenged, resignified, or reappropriated it in ways that expose the South's repressed histories of conflict and trauma.

Historical Conflict and the Southern Hospitality and Tourism Industries

Anyone familiar with *Two Thousand Maniacs!* may very well have felt a little uneasy had he or she pulled into one of South Carolina's eight official welcome centers over a series of weekends in the spring of 2002. Not only had a trashy remake of the film (titled *2001 Maniacs!*) been released the previous year, but had they arrived at one of the welcome centers in March or April of that year, visitors entering the state whose tourism motto at the time was "Smiling Faces, Beautiful Places" would likely have been welcomed—or confronted—by groups of smiling individuals enthusiastically waving Confederate flags and holding signs with slogans like "Welcome to South Carolina, We Love You," "Southern Heritage is American Heritage!" "Stop hate against the South!" "We love our flag and we love our state!" and "Southern Hospitality."[18] Unlike the film, though, these individuals were not ghosts from the past; rather, they were primarily members of the European-American Unity and Rights Organization (EURO), a white rights group organized in 2000 in Louisiana by David Duke, former Grand Wizard of the Ku Klux Klan and former Louisiana state representative. In March and April 2002, EURO organized a series of "welcome patrols" to counter the NAACP boycott of South Carolina's tourism and hospitality industries over the state's continued display of the Confederate flag on state house grounds.

The NAACP had initiated the boycott of South Carolina's tourism industry in January 2000 in an effort to remove the Confederate flag that had flown on the state house dome since 1962. This boycott was launched following a fifty-thousand-strong march on the state capitol protesting the flag. Later that year, after an estimated loss of 500 million in tourism dollars, the state legislature voted to remove the Confederate battle flag from the state house dome and instead place it on the state house grounds with the Confederate Memorial, which had originally been erected in 1879. This proposal, however, did not satisfy the state chapter of the NAACP. As Dwight C. Jones, executive director of the NAACP South Carolina State Conference, explained, "They took it [the flag] from one prominent place, the dome and placed it in another—in front of the Capitol with the 24-hour guard and illuminated it so that now you can see it day and night."[19] According to the state chapter of the NAACP, the boycott would remain in effect until the flag was removed from official state sites. In the spring of 2002, as a way of highlighting the fact that the boycott was still in effect, NAACP "border patrols" established "informational pickets" at the state welcome centers to protest the state's continued display of the Confederate flag on the state house grounds. EURO had organized and manned its own "welcome patrols" within a week. Vincent Breeding, EURO's national director, told reporters that his group's presence at the welcome centers was not an act of protest but instead was "just a display of Southern hospitality." Breeding went on to say, "The NAACP's divisive policies must give way to understanding in South Carolina.... It is time to begin accepting that the people of the South have every right to their faith, symbols, heroes, monuments, and beautiful cultural heritage. Tolerance is not a one-way street. These policies of divisiveness and ethnic cleansing must end."[20]

These competing protests staged at the welcome centers during March and April 2002 caused state officials a great deal of consternation. Some officials described the NAACP boycott as "economic terrorism," an emotionally charged phrase given the very recent 9/11 terror attacks. Attorney General Charlie Condon, a flag supporter, threatened to sue both the NAACP and EURO to stop the protests at the welcome centers. All of this played out as travelers continued to pass through the state welcome centers, with some expressing support for the NAACP efforts, and others showing solidarity with the flag supporters, if not exactly with EURO.[21] No doubt many unsuspecting travelers were simply mystified by the controversy. As one resident of New York State on his way to vacation in Hilton Head put it, "This has been going on awhile. It hits the news from time to time, but it seems like it's never settled. It's basically whoever yells the loudest."[22] While the competing protests at welcome centers eventually faded away, the Confederate flag would continue to fly on the state house grounds until July 2015, when a young white supremacist's terrible massacre of nine black members of the historic Emanuel African Methodist Episcopal Church in Charleston prompted a nationwide debate over the flag and its meaning. Nine months before the massacre, Governor Nikki Haley had downplayed the significance of the flag in a gubernatorial debate, claiming that it wasn't hurting the state's economic development and noting that in her time in office she had "not had one conversation with a single CEO about the Confederate flag."[23] Following the massacre, however, and to her credit, Haley strongly advocated for the removal of the flag. After weeks of public outcry, the state legislature finally took action, and the flag was removed on July 10, 2015.

Repeated calls to remove the flag and the NAACP boycott were too often seen as momentary and local flashpoints or derided as outbreaks of "political correctness"; instead, we should view the debate surrounding the flag as an ethical problem involving cultural memory. For the episode really speaks to a long, complicated history in which African Americans have been repeatedly displaced from the "official" public memory and heritage of the South, in part through the very efforts of the South to develop itself as a popular and hospitable tourist destination for Americans. While the NAACP probably chose to boycott the state's tourism industry for its calculated economic impact, its choice had profound historical resonances and implications as well. The boycott was an effective means of injecting the ethics of public memory into state economics and thereby revising perceptions of the South Carolina tourism industry. When we think about the commodification of southern hospitality in the twentieth century and particularly its role in branding the South as a desirable tourist destination, we should always keep in mind that these concerted efforts by southern states to develop the tourism economy had their origins in the segregated South in the early and middle part of the twentieth century. Moreover, this fledgling industry's most significant period of growth in the postwar decades *coincided with* the period of major struggle for African American civil rights in the South. In short, the success of this myth of southern hospitality in branding the southern tourism industry shows that American consumers—North and South—were willing to either overlook or forget the fact that African American citizens were not welcome guests of this growing tourism economy in the South. From the beginning of the century through at least the end of segregation, then, southern hospitality continued to function as an exclusionary white myth for both marketers and consumers of the South's flourishing industry, and the negative consequences of this exclusionary history linger to this day.

Like many southern states, South Carolina experienced exponential growth in its tourism and hospitality industries over the course of the twentieth century. Today, tourism is by far the most important industry in South Carolina, generating $18 billion annually for the state's economy. As Nicole King notes, the state's long-used marketing slogan, "'Smiling faces. Beautiful places'—evokes both mythologized southern hospitality and the beautiful landscapes that make tourism so popular in the South."[24] South Carolina is not alone in the important place tourism holds in the state's economy and in the way that it trades on the myth of southern hospitality to promote that industry. Tourism generates more revenue than agriculture in many southern states, and it is "one of the top three economic activities in every state of the former Confederacy."[25] Indeed, the South's unique blend of heritage attractions, mild climate, and recreational landscapes has historically made it a popular tourist destination. Given its economic impact, it is no wonder that so many portray the South's tourism and hospitality industries as a sign of its progress and development. However, the history of southern tourism is richly varied and complicated, and these economic endeavors can seem to pull the South in opposing directions.

While the origins of tourism in the South go back to the antebellum period, particularly with northerners traveling South for health reasons, it was in the post-Reconstruction decades and through the development of railroad lines and travel that the South first began to market itself specifically as a tourist destination, increasingly appealing to northerners as a land of "leisure, relaxation, and romance."[26] With the advent of the automobile in the twentieth century, the South became even more accessible, with boosters launching new strategic efforts not only to make the South an appealing destination but also to tell visitors a particular story about the South. This development of heritage tourism in the early twentieth century drew heavily on the stock images of plantation fiction and Lost Cause ideology. In 1914, John Temple Graves, a prominent newspaper editor whom many considered one of the great orators of the age, concisely captured the emerging sensibility of the South's nascent tourism economy in an editorial reflecting on the success of a major Shriners convention held in Atlanta: "Every Southern city and every Southern state is joined in a new confederacy, not of arms, but of hospitality."[27] But like Edward A. Pollard before him, even as Graves promoted a vision of the hospitable South, he publicly advocated a retrograde agenda when it came to racial politics, making headlines for his public defenses of white southern lynch mobs, arguing for castration as a means to thwart potential black rapists, and whipping up racial unrest in Atlanta through caustic, fearmongering editorials. Ida B. Wells singled Graves out for particular criticism for his defense of lynch mobs, and an editor of a black Atlanta newspaper called Graves "one of the most vitriolic enemies of the negro race."[28]

While someone like Graves could boast of and welcome this new "confederacy of hospitality," the development of the southern tourism industry had profound implications for African Americans living in the South. In a repetition of the antebellum racial dynamics of the southern hospitality myth, this new tourism industry essentially excluded African Americans from the South's mythic hospitality even as it depended on them to fulfill many of the emerging industry's low-paying service jobs. The tourism industry alternately fixed them in subordinate positions, portrayed them through degrading stereotypes, and even erased their presence from history and the landscape. In *The Southern Past: A Clash of Race and Memory*, W. Fitzhugh Brundage traces the evolution of how the South's tourism industry commercialized the southern past through heritage tourism. According to Brundage, the period between the world wars "marked a watershed in the self-conscious commercialization of the southern past. The struggle to cultivate and perpetuate historical memory in the South was incorporated into the commerce of tourism." Memorialization groups such as the United Daughters of the Confederacy played an important early role in both promoting and setting the tone for the development of southern tourism around southern heritage, and combined with fortuitous market forces and consumer demands, these concerted efforts created a powerful, though conflicted, sense of collective memory of the South. Brundage points to Charleston, South Carolina, as a quintessential example of this process. Charleston city and society leaders early on saw the potential to cash in on tourism as the city became more accessible through the development of new roads such as the Dixie Highway. They put resources into effective marketing, the creation of a coherent "historic district," and the development of a tourism infrastructure that could support growth in the industry. They effectively transformed the tourist's experience of the city into a form of "memory theater" that offered "a magical suspension of time: these tourists experienced an enchanting, innocent, exotic, and seemingly timeless past while simultaneously escaping the perceived tedium, emptiness, and artificiality of modern life."[29] Other cities across the South developed similar strategies in the 1920s, including Richmond, Savannah, Natchez, and New Orleans, each of which modified the prevailing nostalgic vision of the Old South to meet its particular New South economic goals around tourism.[30]

Of course, this "New South" wasn't so new for African Americans living in or traveling through the region. Because the development of tourism was occurring during segregation, African Americans could not participate in this new welcoming South, but they could nonetheless be exploited by it. African Americans were typically confined to marginal roles in this cultivated memory theater, primarily in servile positions as service or domestic workers or as picturesque, exotic elements in the touriscape, pushing flower carts or weaving handmade baskets. As Brundage puts it, "Tourists could enjoy the picturesque spectacle created by servile African-Americans without needing to understand them.... As the southern past became one of the region's leading generators of wealth, it shaped and perpetuated pernicious representations of blacks in places that became icons of regional identity."[31]

This complex intersection between tourism, nostalgia, and racism becomes readily apparent in a short piece from *Life* magazine in 1923. The article, titled "Hints for Our Native Southerners: What They Should Do before the Winter Tourist Comes," was certainly meant at the time to be a lighthearted, humorous list (like, say, a David Letterman "Top Ten" list), but from today's perspective it provides a disturbing glimpse into what then were prevailing expectations and desires as northern consumers prepared to travel South, particularly regarding the subject of race. Notice how the list playfully engages nostalgic stereotypes of the plantation myth but also how blacks can be imagined only in subservient roles:

1. Teach all Negroes to call all white men "boss."
2. Learn to drink liquor only in mint juleps.
3. Find out what is meant by term, "old plantation melodies," and memorize words and air of at least one.
4. Discover, if it can be done upon such short notice, a bald Negro with a fringe of snow white hair.

5. Learn what is expected of you to justify term, "Southern hospitality."
6. Start immediately growing white mustache and goatee.
7. Let each family come to an agreement now as to battles of Civil War in which grandfather received wounds.
8. Training Negro servants in following points:
   (*a*) (negro men) Answer only to Biblical names, preferably Moses, Abraham, Daniel and Ezekiel.
   (*b*) (negro women) Wear at all times red bandanna handkerchief round head.

The list—and particularly items 1, 4, and 8—indicates that the development of the modern consumer version of southern hospitality in the twentieth-century tourism industry simply repeated the dynamics of earlier iterations: southern hospitality here is still a message from whites to whites, with the marginalized African American presence only reinforcing that exclusive sense of white privilege. There is little subtlety about it: the humiliating etiquette of Jim Crow segregation as experienced by African Americans (item 1) becomes the stuff of humor for white consumers visiting the South and expecting to experience "southern hospitality."

A certain irony can also be detected in the statement "Learn what is expected of you to justify the term, 'Southern hospitality,'" for the list's negative racial stereotypes suggest that this hospitality exchange is a two-way street: northerners demand southern hospitality, but they reciprocate this gift by abiding by the South's Jim Crow assumptions. Northern consumer desires for constructed ideals of southern romance, gracious living, and history override any concern for African Americans demanding justice while living under the daily degradations of Jim Crow segregation. To give the list more context, the article appeared after a significant number of well-publicized mob lynchings had occurred across the United States and particularly in the South between 1917 and 1923. Moreover, earlier in 1923, the infamous Rosewood massacre had occurred in Florida, and 1923 also marked yet another failed attempt by Congress, with the support of the NAACP, to pass the Dyer Anti-Lynching Bill.[32] The idea of experiencing southern hospitality, drinking mint juleps, and laughing at stereotypes of "Uncle Tom" and "Aunt Dinah" may have proven more appealing to many Americans than considering African American demands for justice, equal rights, or even personal safety.

But beyond promoting such pernicious forms of representation, the forces of the developing heritage tourism industry could literally wipe the black presence from public spaces, the landscape, and history. In Charleston, for example, through the development of the city's historic district, the city cited "preservation" as a reason to "move black residents away from the 'Old and Historic District' and into African-American public-housing projects.... The 'restoration' of historic Charleston effectively purged black residents from the tip of the Charleston peninsula for the first time in the city's history."[33] A subtler form of erasure took place in the way various states privileged white southern history in "official" historic routes and heritage markers along roadways. As states across the South developed more modern road and highway systems, they linked these efforts to historic preservation and commemoration. States such as Mississippi, Virginia, Alabama, and South Carolina developed "historic routes," interpretive maps, and systematic methods for marking landmarks of historical significance for the new tourist consumers. Virginia was an early leader in these efforts, and by the middle of the 1930s the state had erected over one thousand official state landmark signs commemorating significant events in the state's history.[34] Promotional literature of the time described the heritage landmarks as "history written on iron."[35]

These early efforts to mark the landscape with historical significance generally elided the African American presence in the South's history. About ten years into the state of Virginia's efforts in erecting these historical markers, the African American poet and literary scholar Sterling A. Brown was working on the Negro Affairs Project of the WPA's Federal Writers' Project. Despite Brown's efforts to record the history of the African American presence in Virginia, he clearly was dismayed by what he saw in the state's memorialization of an exclusively white history. His 1939 poem, "Remembering Nat Turner," laments the utter annihilation of black history and, consequently, black identity.[36] Brown describes following the trail of Turner's failed uprising and encountering both misinformed white perspectives on his historical significance and African American ambivalence and ignorance, though the poem makes clear that the latter is more the result of oppressive social and economic structures than of choice. Despite the obvious historical significance of Nat Turner in the history of the antebellum South, Brown's poem laments that there is no sanctioned reminder of that past. At the end of the poem, Brown imagines Turner's ghost haunting the landscape even as signs of "New South" progress—highways carrying trucks, buses, and tourists—infiltrate the Virginia countryside:

> As we drove from Cross Keys back to Courtland,
> Along the way that Nat came down upon Jerusalem,
> A watery moon was high in the cloud-filled heavens,
> The same moon he dreaded a hundred years ago.
> The tree they hanged Nat on is long gone to ashes,
> The trees he dodged behind have rotted in the swamps.
> The bus for Miami and the trucks boomed by,

And touring cars, their heavy tires snarling on the pavement.
Frogs piped in the marshes, and a hound bayed long,
And yellow lights glowed from the cabin windows.

As we came back the way that Nat led his army,
Down from Cross Keys, down to Jerusalem,
We wondered if his troubled spirit still roamed the Nottaway,
Or if it fled with the cock-crow at daylight,
Or lay at peace with the bones in Jerusalem,
Its restlessness stifled by Southampton clay.[37]

As Mark Sanders notes, Brown's poem "identifies a tragic breakdown in continuity and community between generations of African-Americans." Only through a continuity of memory and cultural identity can the African American community maintain the "psychological and physical resistance" necessary to its own survival—particularly under such pressures as disenfranchisement and Jim Crow segregation—but here the vital connection to the past has been lost. While a historical figure such as Nat Turner has the potential to be interpreted among African Americans as a revolutionary figure, as a self-directed and self-empowering freedom fighter, "whites reconstruct" that history so as to "delimit its political potential."[38]

In light of such historical patterns of repression and segregation in the development of the South's hospitality and tourism industries, the target of the NAACP boycott in South Carolina makes perfect sense, injecting as it does an important ethical debate over cultural memory into a state-sanctioned economic endeavor that rarely, if ever, considers its own troubled past. From an ethical perspective, the development of the southern hospitality and tourism industry subtly repeated the dynamics of the planter class's original social practices, which likewise relied on black subordination and labor to support white privilege, status, and economic power across the South.

An Underground Railroad for the Twentieth Century

During this same period when the South was graciously welcoming white American tourists, travel for black American citizens in the segregated South was always a fraught endeavor. To them, the South was anything but hospitable; instead, they were unwelcome strangers and aliens to this invented image of the South as a hospitable tourist destination. A 1941 "Bungleton Green" comic strip titled "Southern Hospitality" concisely conveys an African American perspective on the ubiquitous southern hospitality myth as it relates to the black tourist or traveler (see figure 20).[39] "Bungleton Green" was a comic that ran from 1920 to 1964 in the African American *Chicago Defender* newspaper. Given the significant influx of southern blacks in the city as part

FIGURE 20. 1941 "Bungleton Green" comic strip from the *Chicago Defender*.

of the Great Migration of African Americans fleeing the Jim Crow South, this particular 1941 strip titled "Southern Hospitality" would have seemed a pedestrian form of realism to many of its contemporary readers. The opening frame establishes that Bungleton and his new bride are on their honeymoon traveling "thru Virginia and Maryland and up thru Washington and Baltimore." "This is a swell honeymoon Bung," she notes, "but it's not keeping me from getting hungry." Bungleton, however, cautiously reminds her that there are other forms of discomfort besides hunger: "We're in the South now, so let's wait till we get to Baltimore and save ourselves embarrassment," to which his bride responds, "I'd rather be embarrassed than hungry!" She instructs him to stop at a roadhouse diner that advertises "Southern Barbeque," with Bungleton still warning, "We're sticking our necks out." Sure enough, the penultimate frame shows some already-seated white diners looking on as a white waitress, standing over empty tables, informs the couple, "I'm so sorry sir. All the tables are reserved out here ... but we do have a lovely private dining room." The final frame shows the newlyweds in a back room, with Bungleton's wife sardonically commenting, loud enough for the waitress to hear, "Isn't it nice to be such 'honored' guests?!" The simple irony of the comic points to a general consensus among African American readers regarding travel in the South, and caustically places black experiences of white southern hostility directly alongside the South's vaunted claims of being a hospitable tourist destination.

As Cotten Seiler makes clear in *Republic of Drivers: A Cultural History of Automobility in America*, fear of embarrassment and humiliation was a constant for African Americans traveling in the segregated South, but it was only one of many uncertainties, as they could never be sure where they would be welcome to stop, rest, refuel, eat, use the bathroom, or spend the night. If their car broke down, they could not be certain of finding a mechanic willing to serve a black customer. And they also had to be mindful of the real possibility of white intimidation and violence against "uppity" blacks who did not know their "proper" place. Automobiles were a sure sign of upward mobility, but such an indicator of prosperity could be dangerous. As an example of this all-too-real possibility, Cotten Seiler points to the 1948 case of Robert Mallard, who was "attacked in his car by a Georgia mob (allegedly for being 'too prosperous' and 'not the right kind of negro') and murdered in front of his wife and child." Given this range of negative possibilities, Seiler concludes that, "for black drivers, the road's only constant was uncertainty."[40]

The uncertainties associated with travel in an era of segregation and discrimination (not only in the South but *across America*) were pervasive enough to prompt Victor H. Green, a New York travel agent, to create in 1936 *The Negro Motorist Green Book*, which would become an essential companion for black travelers until it ceased publication in 1964, the year that the Civil Rights Act was passed, making it illegal for businesses such as gas stations, hotels, and restaurants to discriminate against potential customers. As the cover typically and somewhat ominously warned, "Carry your Green Book with you—you may need it." In an age when "southern hospitality" was being used as a mantra to lure white Americans to the South, the *Green Book* formed a sort of alternative underground hospitality network for African Americans living and traveling under the pressures of Jim Crow and in the shadows of the South's flourishing tourism industry. The first *Green Book* was modest in scope, but Green continually solicited black travelers, asking for personal recommendations of every sort that business travelers may need: hotels and motels, garages and service stations, barber shops and beauty parlors, restaurants and taverns, liquor stores and drugstores. Scanning the pages of a *Green Book* provides a stark reminder of just how circumscribed African Americans were in their mobility and their citizenship, the open hostility they often faced, and the constant anxiety they must have felt as they tried to map out their journeys by connecting stops from the often sparse options for welcome and assistance. At the same time, the *Green Book* provides equal evidence of the power of their community, social networking, *and hospitality* in the face of these obstacles.

More particularly, one thing that stands out in scanning these pages is the significant number of "Tourist Homes" in the listings of accommodations, where private homeowners would provide lodging to African American travelers. In some towns and cities, these were the only accommodations available for African Americans. For example, even though by 1949 Charleston, South Carolina, was in the midst of a successful tourism boom following decades of civic effort and investment, the *Green Book* entry for Charleston that year lists four tourist homes as the *only* accommodations willing to cater to black travelers. No hotels or motels were listed as available to them. At the same time, however, the *Green Book* reminds us that some white businesses and individuals made the conscious choice to respect the African American traveler and welcomed their business, whether motivated by profit or justice or both. The Esso Standard Oil Company provided support for the *Green Book* and became known as a safe haven for African American travelers, and Green notes in his introduction to the 1949 edition that "the guide contains 80 pages and lists numerous business places, including whites which cater to the Negro trade." Significantly, Green does not distinguish white-owned businesses from black-owned. In the same introduction, he concludes with the following prophetic words: "There will be a day sometime in the near future when this guide will not have to be published. That is when we as a race will have equal opportunities and privileges in the United States. It will be a great day for us to suspend this publication for then we can go wherever we please, and without embarrassment." The quotes on the cover also suggest that Green saw his travel guide as helping to effect this change; they read: "Travel is fatal to prejudice" (Mark Twain), and "Travel makes America stronger."[41]

During its twenty-eight-year publication history, the *Green Book* was very much an underground endeavor—crucial to African Americans yet unknown to most white Americans—and after 1964, it fell into oblivion, largely forgotten even in the African American community that had relied on it. However, the *Green Book* has received renewed attention in recent years from scholars and artists who increasingly have come to see this as an important, though largely unrecognized artifact of the long struggle for civil rights. A particularly noteworthy example is the African American playwright and writer Calvin Alexander Ramsey, who has written both a play and an award-winning children's book based on the *Green Book*'s important role in the African American community during segregation. Tellingly, Ramsey's explanation of why he felt compelled to write about the *Green Book* (and particularly a children's book about it) makes important connections to an even earlier underground hospitality network that assisted African Americans: "Most kids today hear about the Underground Railroad, but this other thing has gone unnoticed.... It just fell on me, really, to tell the story."[42] With realistic oil-wash illustrations by Floyd Cooper accompanying Ramsey's narrative, *Ruth and the Green Book* tells the simple yet poignant story of Ruth, a young girl from Chicago who is initially filled with excitement to set out on a journey to visit her grandmother's house in the family's new car. Her excitement, however, soon turns to confusion, disappointment, and sadness as the family begins to encounter the discriminatory practices of the Jim Crow South: stopping for gas they are refused access to the restroom and must resort to the woods; stopping at a hotel they are turned away and must continue to drive through the night. Following the incident at the gas station, Ruth tells her mother that she was embarrassed, but her mother replies, "The people who should be ashamed of themselves were those service station owners."[43]

Ruth is truly distressed at the experiences and particularly at seeing the effect they have on her parents—their growing frustration and impotent anger. She feels out of place in the South and consequently homesick. Thankfully, though, the family learns of the *Green Book* after spending the night with family friends in Tennessee. Having been told that they can purchase it at any Esso service station, Ruth is given the job of lookout. Ruth spots an Esso station near the Georgia border, and the travel guide they acquire steers them to safe havens along the rest of their journey. With the *Green Book* now in hand, the family first finds a "tourist home" run by Mrs. Melody: "We reached the tourist home in the early evening. Mrs. Melody, the owner, gave us a big smile when she opened the door. It was like coming home. And she wouldn't let Daddy pay her. She said she welcomed Negro travelers because it was right to help each other out. I'm going to do the same one day!" As the official keeper of the *Green Book*, Ruth can't stop reading and rereading it, finding reassurance in "all those places in all those states where [she and her family] could go and not worry about being turned away."[44] Rather than take the *Green Book* as evidence of the family's degraded status in the South, Ruth sees it as evidence of communal strength and support. With the *Green Book*'s help, the family is able to service their car when it breaks down and find another hotel to stay in during the resulting delay, where they spend time sharing stories with other African American travelers and users of the *Green Book*. They successfully make it to the home of Ruth's grandmother, but what had originally begun as a trip to reconnect with immediate family has become a trip to reconnect with the larger African American community. Ruth finds comfort in the underground network of African American hospitality in the Jim Crow South, and young readers are successfully introduced to this important though neglected episode in American history. On the last page of the book, Ramsey provides a concise history of the *Green Book* and also directs readers to a web link where they can view an online digital copy of a real *Green Book*.

While Ramsey's children's book is geared toward memorializing this underground hospitality network for a young generation of readers, his 2010 play, *The Green Book*, extends and complicates the ethical question of hospitality in significant ways.[45] Set in 1953 at a tourist home in Jefferson City, Missouri, the play brings together Keith Chenault, a cynical, self-serving young African American salesman from Harlem, and Stefan Lansky, an older Polish Jew and concentration camp survivor. Chenault is initially incredulous and outraged that the Davises, the owners of the tourist home, would admit a white man. Lansky, however, has arrived at the Davises' after refusing to stay at the town's "whites-only" hotel. Notably, upon his arrival at the Davises' he offers thanks for their "southern hospitality." We later learn that Lansky owes his life to an African American soldier who saved him at Buchenwald, and through both Lansky's story and the unfolding events in the play, Chenault comes to see the limitations of his narrow pursuit of economic self-interest in an era of racial segregation and injustice. The play illustrates the fluidity of hospitality as an ethical ideal, extending it from a local to a cosmopolitan scale, while also resignifying "southern hospitality" by retroactively recasting this historical African American institution of private tourist homes as a form of "true" southern hospitality.

Overall, the case of the *Green Book* provides an alternative narrative of hospitality that contrasts sharply with the perceptions and practices of southern hospitality that prevailed during the growth period of southern tourism, not unlike the way that nineteenth-century abolitionist discourse and activism around the Fugitive Slave Law or the Negro Seamen Laws had challenged the antebellum claim of southern hospitality more than a century earlier. In contrast to the consistently restrictive politics of southern hospitality, these alternatives are governed by a more expansive ethics of hospitality, premised on a more egalitarian ideal of welcoming all equally. Why have these American narratives of a more ethical form of hospitality been forgotten while the myth of southern hospitality has prevailed? By revisiting a forgotten document of the past and transmitting it to the future generation, Ramsey's award-winning children's book and play are examples of what Paul Ricoeur terms "telling otherwise."[46] In recent years, this "telling" has also been occurring through the development of newer, more inclusive forms of heritage tourism in the South, particularly those involving the history of civil rights and slavery in the South, which are in many cases being revisited and recognized.[47] Take, for example, the case of Nat Turner discussed earlier. In contrast to the marginalization of the Nat Turner insurrection from a variety of earlier efforts to mark the Virginia landscape's history, and despite a long history of conflict over this past among local black and white populations, in February 2013 the Southampton County Board of Supervisors, in conjunction with the Southampton County Historical Society, announced its sponsorship of a proposed Nat Turner/1831 Southampton Insurrection Trail. The county was awarded a $420,000 Transportation Enhancement Grant "to connect travelers, tourists, students and residents with sites associated with the Nat Turner rebellion."[48] While the county may or may not have mixed motives involving economic development, its willingness to engage this traumatic history in its fullness requires an acceptance of risk and an awareness of the contradictions, conflicts, injustices, and competing values of the South's past.

But even as progress is being made, the legacy of the segregated racial history of southern tourism can linger across this aspect of the South's economy in subtle ways. A 2013 article by Derek H. Alderman and E. Arnold Modlin Jr. published in the *Journal of Cultural Geography* provides a case in point. Alderman and Modlin's comprehensive study of North Carolina tourism brochures, funded in part by the Center for Sustainable Tourism at East Carolina University, revealed that "racial inequalities ... characterize the seemingly harmless arena of southern hospitality and tourism promotion," and they link this to the long history of racial injustice in the South. The authors forcefully argue that "it is essential that the tourism industry recognize its involvement in the politics of representation" and that it also "recognize that current racial patterns in travel are not simply the product of the contemporary market but also the product of a racialized history of southern mobility and hospitality and the traditionally limited access that minority travelers have had to destinations."[49] Alderman and Modlin's study is particularly notable for their willingness to see an ethical dilemma in the way "southern hospitality" is used to promote the South; moreover, their approach also suggests that southern hospitality can be reframed as a progressive ethical imperative that can have sustainable and just socioeconomic benefits.

Southern Hospitality, "Lifestyle" Choices, and White Southern Sublimation

> We Southern women have been forced by the ever-growing global economy to become just as fast-paced as our counterparts in the North. The days of sipping mint juleps on the porch are long gone, and in many cases so are the porches. Although we may slave over our computers eight hours a day, we still have an innate need to entertain and be hospitable. It's a characteristic that forms at the instant of conception.
>
> Rebecca Lang, *Southern Entertaining for a New Generation*

So begins Rebecca Lang's 2004 cookbook *Southern Entertaining for a New Generation*. At the time of the book's publication, Lang was a food columnist for several newspapers in the Southeast, and she was on her way to a successful career as a food writer, cooking instructor, and eventually a contributing editor at *Southern Living* magazine. Her words embody one of the most typical rhetorical strategies associated with the southern hospitality myth, as she here affirms the notion of southern tradition and continuity of identity even in the face of change, in this case the social changes wrought by globalization. It's worth considering her explanation of southern hospitality alongside the earlier explanations offered by Lucian Minor and Thomas Nelson Page, for across these three writers we can see the discourse of southern hospitality becoming increasingly naturalized as an essential cultural trait of the South and southerners. While Minor in the 1830s could acknowledge the fact of slavery's role in southern hospitality, and Page in the 1890s attributed southern hospitality to the combination of "Anglo-Saxon" bloodlines and the unique southern social environment, Lang here attributes southern hospitality to the genetic code of southerners. In reality, and as I hope I have shown, southern hospitality is more a matter of discursive practices than social habits (or even genetics); it is a phrase that has been repeated so often that many have come to accept it as a natural fact.

From the 1960s through the early twenty-first century, this assumption that the South and southerners are inherently hospitable has formed a narrative frame and thematic center for a variety of successful lifestyle industries built on southern regional identity, seen most prominently in the remarkably successful *Southern Living* magazine and its numerous related spinoff industries, and in the national popularity and success of a southern celebrity chef like Paula Deen, who offered American viewers and readers a folksier—even crass—alternative to the more genteel, refined representations found in *Southern Living*. In such economic endeavors built on southern identity, the southern hospitality myth seems alive and well, even as "the South" and "southerners" are becoming ever more difficult to define. On the one hand, new demographics and mobile populations have both destabilized and simultaneously expanded the potential definition of "southerner." Almost a third of the population in the contemporary South consists of migrants who came from outside the South, and this migrant population includes significant numbers of African Americans who have returned South since the civil rights movement, many as southern suburbanites, as well as Latin American immigrants who have simultaneously complicated the notion of a racially bifurcated (black/white) South.[50] On the other hand, this is the age of late capitalism and globalization, when local or regional cultures lose their aura of authenticity as they are repeatedly absorbed, reproduced, and commodified by market forces. Scott Romine explains that in this age of cultural reproduction and simulation, "the real South" has been replaced by "the 'real'/'South': a set of anxious, transient, even artificial intersections, sutures, or common surfaces between two concepts that are themselves remarkably fluid." As for the effect on southern identity itself, Larry J. Griffin and Ashley B. Thompson studied trends through a decade of Southern Focus Polls and described the emergence of what they term "symbolic southerness," an identity that "need not rest on an actually existing distinctive South." Instead, "symbolic southerners are able to proclaim their heritage and differentiate themselves from the mass of Americans by grounding their sense of who they are in a mythic place existing mainly in cultural memory—the South as an imagined community—rather than in a 'real' space." According to the cultural logic of late capitalism, consumption is the primary method of affirming such an imagined identity, which can raise a host of intersecting questions about who or what is defining southern identity and with what consequences. As Amy Elias asks, "Is regional identity being created by multinational outsiders now marketing Southerners to themselves as lifestyle products as well as lifestyle producers? Are Southerners, in other words, now products rather than consumers in the global market?"[51]

When such business interests begin driving the identity of southerners, one might expect a certain level of historical amnesia around sensitive or unpleasant topics and unresolved historical tensions. This is especially true in the way southern hospitality has been commodified in lifestyle industries, as these iterations of southern distinctiveness inevitably elide the complex racial dynamics that were foundational to the origins of the southern hospitality myth. Indeed, to return to the quote from Rebecca Lang with which I began this essay, there is something ironic and awkward in her description of contemporary southern women "slaving over computers." One might even be tempted to read Lang's word choice as a Freudian slip, for while her description tries to make her southern identity as a refined, gracious hostess seem natural (presenting it as a biological fact), her words also point to unacknowledged traces of the historical past, namely, the fact that black women performed the labor (first as slaves and later as domestics) that allowed white southern women the leisure to be such gracious and attentive hostesses.[52]

If the discourse of southern hospitality is largely used to affirm a sense of tradition and continuity of southern identity in the face of change, then certainly the greatest change that white southerners faced in the twentieth century was integration. The end of segregation might have provided a day of reckoning for the southern hospitality myth or, more optimistically, an opportunity to recast it as an inclusive ethical principle for the newly integrated South, but the southern hospitality myth continued to follow familiar patterns of repetition and repression. More particularly, the details and timeline surrounding the creation of *Southern Living* magazine in 1966 indicate the ways that the southern hospitality myth provided white southerners a defensive means of sublimation and substitution in response to the new social reality posed by integration. For the generation of white southerners who lived through this profound and often violent cultural change in the late 1950s and 1960s, integration was a traumatic experience. Segregation was built on the assumption of white supremacy, and these white southerners had to cope with a range of emotional and psychological conflicts when this change finally came. Depending on whether or how deeply a southerner believed in the assumption of white supremacy, integration could have prompted feelings of rage, fear, and impotence, on the one hand, or profound feelings of guilt, shame, and regret, on the other.[53] As a long-standing affirmation of white southern exceptionalism and superiority, the southern hospitality myth provided a way for these southerners to both contain and transform the trauma they experienced with the end of segregation. Integration was a world change much more traumatic than the globalizing forces to which Lang alludes in the epigraph above, and many white southerners were desperate to hold on to a sense of their own felt exceptionalism and superiority in the face of these changes. The southern hospitality myth provided a way to affirm "the good life" and continue traditions of the South even as its foundational tradition of racial segregation and white supremacy gave way. More specifically, if this generation of southerners lost the public markers and blatant expressions of white supremacy (separate schools and water fountains, segregated lunch counters and buses, police dogs and water cannons, lynchings and church bombings, etc.), they could still find other, more acceptable, more subtle ways to express their superiority and exceptionalism, such as an exaggerated emphasis on hospitality, gracious living, and manners. *Southern Living* attempts to embody and reinforce such domestic virtues, and the fact that it was created at the very same moment that segregation was ending in many ways assured its success.

Today *Southern Living* is by far the most successful regional magazine in the country and one of the most successful American magazines overall, ranking in the top twenty for overall circulation. To put that in perspective in relation to magazines with more "national" target audiences, this is just above *Glamour* and *O, The Oprah Magazine*, and close behind *Cosmopolitan* and *Sports Illustrated*.[54] Its profits amount to over $300 million annually, and it boasts approximately 3 million subscribers and more than 15 million monthly readers. The readership is mostly female (77 percent) with a median age in the early fifties. Southernliving.com, the online division of the magazine, claims another 1.2 million unique visitors and 11 million page views annually. As the *Southern Living* 2013 Media Kit notes to potential advertisers, "1 in 5 Southern Women Read Southern Living." Today, *Southern Living* is much more than a magazine: for many southerners, it is a tradition, a connective web for an incredibly wide range of consumerism around southern identity, and "a kind of imagined community."[55] The idea of southern hospitality has been essential to this community since the magazine was founded in 1966, but the motivation behind its founding belies any true sense of hospitality from an ethical perspective.

Southern Living was developed in the early 1960s as an offshoot of the long-standing *Progressive Farmer* agricultural magazine, and its early success and incredibly loyal readership were very much a matter of timing: it entered the marketplace just as segregation was ending, and it offered its readers relentlessly positive images of the white, suburban South at just the moment when they were feeling most threatened and under attack. *Progressive Farmer* had been a successful agricultural magazine based in Birmingham, Alabama, since its founding in 1886 by Confederate veteran Leonidas L. Polk. *Progressive Farmer*'s subscription list peaked at 1.4 million readers in the post–World War II decade, but by the late 1950s, its readership had declined as more southerners were living in and around cities than on farms. *Southern Living* was conceived and launched in response to these changing demographics, essentially casting the emergence of the southern suburban landscape as a marker of white identity. The concept for *Southern Living* magazine was first brought before the Progressive Farmer Board of Directors meeting on May 22, 1963, and it was immediately embraced. The board decided that the "Home Section" of *Progressive Farmer* would be retitled "Southern Living" and that the editorial staff would begin the transition to a stand-alone magazine. The first issue of *Progressive Farmer* to include the new "Southern Living" section appeared in October 1963. Following a successful transition period, the board definitively decided to move forward with the magazine launch in March 1965. The first stand-alone issue of *Southern Living* magazine was published in February 1966, and it included features on food and entertaining, gardening, home projects, and travel, along with general interest stories. The first issue featured stories, for example, on azalea trails across the South, Mardi

Gras, cornbread, and the carving of the Confederate icons on Stone Mountain in Georgia.[56]

To put the time line of *Southern Living*'s inception into some context, the year in which the board initially decided to pursue the project was one of the most tumultuous periods in the civil rights movement, and much of the nation's attention that year was focused on events unfolding in Birmingham, Alabama, the home city of *Progressive Farmer* and its offshoot, *Southern Living*. In January of that year, Alabama governor George Wallace had delivered his inaugural address, in which, in response to national pressure to integrate, he staunchly promised Alabamans "segregation now, segregation tomorrow, segregation forever." Under Martin Luther King Jr.'s leadership, the Southern Christian Leadership Council launched its "Birmingham Campaign" in early April of that year and was met with Birmingham public safety commissioner Bull Connor's violent tactics, including police dogs and fire hoses eventually being used against demonstrating students, all under a national and world media spotlight. Martin Luther King Jr. was jailed early in the campaign, prompting him to write his "Letter from Birmingham Jail" to the white clergy of the city who had made it clear that they did not want outsiders meddling in the city's business. These events were unfolding only weeks and days before the initial decision was made to launch *Southern Living*. Indeed, on May 10 the City of Birmingham, under the pressure of nonviolent protest and increasing national outrage, acceded to the protestors' demands, effectively ending the most overt and discriminatory practices of segregation in the city. This was only twelve days before the board decision to launch *Southern Living*. And some months later, the first "Southern Living" section of *Progressive Farmer* was published only weeks after what is surely among the most infamous acts committed in response to the civil rights movement, the bombing of the Sixteenth Street Baptist Church in Birmingham, which left four black girls dead and many others injured.[57]

Given this context of political turmoil and violence, it is difficult to imagine today what those editorial meetings must have been like or how readers would have responded to the new "Southern Living" section of *Progressive Farmer*. As Diane Roberts observes in her critical analysis of the early years and development of *Southern Living*, from our contemporary perspective, the total avoidance of any mention of politics in a southern magazine in the 1960s now seems "strange, even perverse," but as she goes on to explain, this is precisely the point: *Southern Living* "thrives on denial." Particularly for its early readers, it provided "a haven from the world turning upside down around them."[58] The editorial staff in those early years seemed to know precisely what they were doing. Publisher Emory Cunningham was one of the main proponents of the *Southern Living* launch, and he later offered a frank assessment of the magazine's agenda and consequent success:

Everybody was running down the South.... I felt that keenly, and a lot of other Southern people did, too, people with their hardships going all the way back to the Civil War. The Depression hit us harder. Everybody up North thought the racial unrest was an Alabama and a George Wallace problem only. It hadn't hit Watts in Los Angeles and Chicago. Southern people were thirsting for something to make them feel good about themselves.[59]

It is interesting to note the way that the magazine's habits of denial and repression are mirrored in Cunningham's own memories. Even while recounting the context of the magazine launch many years later, he fails to directly acknowledge the context of the civil rights movement, which was the main reason why everybody was "running down the South" at the time. Moreover, his comments here oddly turn white southerners into victims, noting first the "hardships" (white) southerners have faced since the Civil War and the Depression and indirectly suggesting that it was unfair to criticize the South for its racial unrest of the times because the North had racial problems as well. In reality, Jim Crow segregation was a matter not of "racial unrest" but of racial oppression, one in which white southerners figured in the role of oppressors and not victims.[60]

Southern Living quickly developed an intensely loyal readership, due largely to the fact that it repressed any reminders of the South's fraught racial history and civil rights conflicts. Instead the magazine offered readers optimistic images of a refined, contemporary southern lifestyle that revolved around entertaining, traveling, gardening, and maintaining southern "traditions." Howell Raines has referred to the magazine's editorial approach and "relentlessly cheerful" content as "the Southern Living disease," which obscures the historical past and recasts the region as "one endless festival of barbecue, boiled shrimp, football Saturdays and good old Nashville music."[61] By avoiding the world of politics and offering such content to its readers, *Southern Living* has successfully transformed itself into a "tradition" in the South. This conflict between the pressure of political realities and the pull of escapist fantasies was there from the start of the magazine's history. Indeed, the magazine's sublimation of white supremacist desires may be gleaned from the editorial wrangling that took place leading up to publication of the first issue in 1966. John Logue and Gary McCalla describe how this first issue unfolded in their joint memoir, *Life at Southern Living*, which traces their experiences working at the magazine from the period leading up to its creation in the early 1960s through its eventual purchase in 1985 by Time, Inc. Logue and McCalla describe the editorial conflicts that took place between the "Old Guard" of the *Progressive Farmer* who wanted to pursue a more overtly political editorial agenda and the younger generation of editors who had experience in modern advertising and marketing and were consequently savvier to the subtle workings of the contemporary media marketplace. Dr. Alexander Nunn, the president of the Progressive Farmer Corporation, insisted on having absolute editorial control over the launch of the first issue. According to Logue and McCalla, Nunn was an ardent segregationist who "thought two things will ruin the South, or ruin the country: integration and a decline in agriculture, city people not appreciating farmers. He felt those were fundamental problems and were going to ruin the country."[62] Nunn hoped to use *Southern Living* as a way to bolster white political solidarity, and he went so far as to offer the cover of the first issue to Lurleen Wallace, wife of then–Alabama governor George Wallace. While the editorial staff somehow managed to nix the idea of Lurleen Wallace on the cover, they could not control the contents of the opening editorial message of the first issue, a bizarre statement, complete with Scripture, that preached the need for unity between the rural and urban people of the South and on the need to avoid the urban problems (read: racial problems) of the North.[63]

Appearing in the context of segregation's simultaneous demise, the magazine allowed southerners to maintain a sense of regional pride and (white) superiority. Directed to a target audience of white middle- and upper-middle-class southerners (as well as to those who aspired to be), the magazine's features and stories guided the performance of white southern identity post–civil rights. It also reinforced white privilege in subtle (and sometimes obvious) ways, as may be seen in the way the magazine coded racial identity. Especially in the early years of the magazine's publication, the only blacks who appear among the pages are in service roles for white subjects, as hotel attendants, domestics, or waiters.[64] While Martin Luther King Jr. had dreamed in 1963 of the day when "the sons of former slaves and the sons of former slave owners will be able to sit down together at the table of brotherhood," the images of blacks in the early years of *Southern Living* show that the magazine's editors and readers were still much more comfortable with having blacks appear in adjunct service roles to the white southern hospitality myth. This is certainly not to say that all the early readers of *Southern Living* magazine were consciously looking to have their sense of white supremacy maintained when they perused the magazine's pages, but there is little doubt that some were. In 1973, for example, a cover photograph featuring an integrated picnic apparently resulted in approximately five thousand subscription cancellations from outraged readers.[65]

Even though today *Southern Living* has made progress in its representations of race and its acknowledgment of the South's civil rights history, it still struggles with the past racial history of the South and the racialized meaning of the southern hospitality myth it draws upon, where blacks have historically been confined to service roles in the white imagination. In a fairly recent (2009) interview, a *Southern Living* travel editor was asked specifically about the magazine's relationship to the South's racial history, prompting a rambling and at times conflicted response. At first, the editor assures the interviewer that the magazine strives for diversity, but his answer also suggests that some things may not be so different from the 1960s:

> We are very, very deliberate here about trying to put diversity in the magazine, so that's something I look for when we're going through the pictures. Do we have black faces in our magazine? And not just the help. That sounds harsh, and I don't mean it to sound harsh. But a lot of times when you go to look through the pictures for any particular month, sometimes the only minority faces you'll see are the hotel maid or the hotel waiter, and I believe—this is not based on any research—but I believe if you're looking through a magazine and you don't see any people who look like you, whether you're a woman or you're young or you're old or you're black or white or whatever, that you will internalize that and say, "That magazine is not for me."[66]

Maybe the problem now is that the world that *Southern Living* strives to represent is still a world where minorities too often figure only as "the help." Here the notion of diversity seems superficial at best. As the editor goes on to discuss the way the magazine engages the South's history of racial politics, we also see that things haven't progressed much. He provides an oscillating description of editorial choices and reader desires:

> We cover the history of the South. We don't talk a lot about history at *Southern Living* because it's not a huge interest of our readers. They're interested in today. How do I make my meal tonight better? How do I make my garden grow next spring better? How do I plan my next vacation? So they're really not that interested in history, but when we do talk about the racial tensions in Birmingham and Mississippi, we're really proud of those moments in our history. A lot of southerners are very sheepish about what happened here.[67]

From here the editor shifts rather abruptly and strangely to talk about racism in other regions in the country, noting, "The worst racist jokes I've ever heard in my life were in New York." To his credit, he goes on to acknowledge the complex and difficult racial history of Birmingham and the South more generally, noting that "the institutionalized racism in the South that existed prior to the Civil Rights Movement is certainly a very dark, dark spot on our history." While it is somewhat troubling that such a statement portrays institutional racism as a thing of the past (it isn't), at least the editor speaks quite openly about the subject in relation to the magazine. He concludes by saying that the South's racial history is "not something [he's] ashamed of," commenting, "I don't think my colleagues here are ashamed of it. We write about it at least once a year. There's a new civil rights trail, a new museum opening up on a regular basis around the South, and so we cover that and we're proud of it."[68]

The editor's tightrope-walk response is perhaps understandable for someone whose primary motivation is increasing market share for advertisers and profits for stockholders, but still, the way the magazine has historically repressed the fullness of southern history—warts and all—can have pernicious effects. By softening the rough edges and injustices of the historical past, and by severing the links of complicity between past and present, you may make the past more palatable for modern readers of a "lifestyle" magazine, but you also encourage a dangerous sense of complacency. As Diane Roberts succinctly and poignantly concludes in her analysis of the magazine: "*Southern Living* admits no sense that race has been the great sorrow and burden of the south."[69]

As a modern iteration of the southern hospitality myth, we can associate *Southern Living* magazine with Paul Ricouer's discussion of melancholia and cultural memory. In his analysis of the processes and pathologies of collective memory, Ricoeur draws on Freud's concepts of melancholia and mourning to contrast two different responses to the traumas of the past. Melancholia, the undesirable response, results from resistance, repression, and a general unwillingness to accept the losses of the past. Melancholia is based not in reality but in sentiment and nostalgia. The subject is compelled to simply repeat these symptoms "and is barred from any progress toward recollection." In contrast, mourning, the healthier though more difficult response, is the result of "a *travail*," a patient and difficult "working through" that results in an acceptance of loss and a reconciliation with the reality of past. According to Ricoeur, "What is preserved in mourning and lost in melancholia is self-esteem, of the sense of one's self. This is so because in melancholia there is a despair and a longing to be reconciled with the love object which is lost without the hope of reconciliation."[70]

Paula Deen, White Southern Melancholia, and the Dilemma of "Southern Foodways"

To illustrate how melancholia can provide a useful framework for understanding the relationship between white southerners' experience of integration and the persistence of the southern hospitality myth, let us briefly consider passages from Paula Deen's memoir, particularly where she describes growing up during integration, alongside one of the more controversial details from a deposition she provided in a 2013 workplace lawsuit, namely, her expressed desire to have a "southern, plantation style wedding" for her brother featuring an all-black waitstaff. Paula Deen's rise to fame from the early 1990s to 2013 was remarkable; despite her relatively humble background, a difficult first marriage, financial uncertainties, and a battle with agoraphobia, she would eventually advance from small-time caterer to entrepreneurial restaurateur to a TV star celebrity chef. She did so by combining a folksy brand of southern hospitality with a particularly deep-fried, butter-baked, mayonnaise-laden version of southern cuisine. Deen built her business empire by trading heavily on the coupled concepts of southern hospitality and southern comfort food; in fact, her original TV show was successfully pitched to Food Network executives as a way to help Americans cope with the trauma following the terrorist attacks of 9/11.[71] By early 2013, Deen was seemingly on top of the culinary entertainment world with popular TV shows, numerous cookbooks, a magazine, her own line of culinary products, and profitable sponsorships. For much of the American public, she had come to embody the very idea of southern hospitality, but in June of that year, the story broke that Deen had admitted to using racist language in a deposition she gave in a lawsuit filed by former employee alleging a hostile work environment that included sexist and racist behavior.

Deen's fall from grace was remarkable for its rapidity. She gave her deposition on May 17, details of the transcript were leaked by the *National Enquirer* on June 19, and a media feeding frenzy ensued that resulted in the crumbling of her empire in a matter of weeks. Despite two video apologies and a tearful live TV interview, by July 1 the Food Network had fired Deen and she had lost her sponsorship with Smithfield Foods and her role as spokeswoman for Novo Nordisk. Numerous retailers, including Target, Home Depot, Sears, Kmart, and Walgreens, also dropped her products from their shelves and severed their ties with her. Despite strong pre-sales on Amazon.com, Ballantine Books canceled the publication of what was to be her fifteenth cookbook. Random House also canceled a multibook contract that Deen had signed the previous year. Among Deen's transgressions revealed in the deposition: admitting to using the N-word, telling racist jokes, and perhaps most startlingly, desiring a southern plantation–style wedding for her brother that would feature an all-black waitstaff.[72]

I choose to focus on Deen here not to simply denigrate her or because she is an easy target, but because I think there is something to learn in this controversy about the southern hospitality myth post–civil rights. In other words, Deen's constructed southern identity—as it exists within her generation, within the region, and within the nation—reflects larger cultural patterns of repression and repetition around the southern hospitality myth. When considering the details of this deposition alongside her memoir's account of living through the South's transition to integration, the relationship between melancholia and mourning is thrown into sharper focus, revealing unresolved historical tensions around race in the white imagination and suggesting the complex psychological motivations behind the historical persistence of the southern hospitality myth post–civil rights. Deen was nineteen at the time *Southern Living* was first published in 1966, so she embodies the same sort of cultural and psychological experiences I have described regarding that generation of white southerners who lived through integration and who consequently experienced this loss of an explicit white supremacy. Indeed, Deen's hometown of Albany, Georgia, was the site of the high-profile Albany Movement of 1961–62, whose tactics of boycott and protest, while unsuccessful at the time, nonetheless paved the way for the successes of the Birmingham Campaign in 1963. Deen's high school was integrated during her senior year in 1965, when five black female students were admitted.

Deen's 2007 memoir, *It Ain't All about the Cooking*, which was a *New York Times* best seller, provides a brief but telling glimpse into her experiences of segregation, and these recollections hint at the sort of traumatic psychological effects that the process of integration would have had on many white southerners. While most of Deen's memoir details her various personal struggles and eventual rise to fame, one early chapter goes into some detail regarding her experiences growing up in the segregated South as it was moving toward integration. On the one hand, Deen at times seems to downplay the day-to-day experience of living through these changes as they occurred, noting that the "civil rights movement belonged to the nightly radio news" and that "we lived a pretty unexamined life in terms of politics or civil rights." At other moments, however, and I would argue to Deen's credit, her memories reveal a burden of guilt, remorse, and even shame. For example, as she recalls the visible signs of segregation that informed her world (such as separate bathrooms and drinking fountains), she claims the memory "shocks" her and that she is "plain horrified that things could have been that way and [she] was so blind [she] didn't get that it was wrong." Later, when Deen recalls the experience of her senior year, when five African American girls integrated the high school, she is similarly disturbed by the memory of her own indifference. She remembers her self-centered teenage amazement that someone's parents would be willing to put her through something as difficult as the isolation the black girls faced. Deen is "embarrassed and ashamed" to admit that she felt this way at the time, and she later claims to be "mortified" over the fact that she did nothing to assuage the obvious loneliness of the five girls, whom Deen describes as "five small black faces in a sea of unthinking teen-aged white faces."[73]

The most difficult memory Deen recalls, however, comes from earlier in her life, and it involves her experience with a "real nice black woman" who looked after her and her sister. This episode, which occurs when Deen is about ten years old, is especially powerful because it involves a greater degree of culpability and complicity on her part, and a sort of initiation into the true implications of segregation, as well as her place of power in the system:

> Everybody would be so busy working over at River Bend and at the gas station that sometimes I would be told to stay with a real nice black woman who often babysat Trina and me. I remember this one day she had brought her little girl

to work, and that child had many big, fat blisters on her hand, probably from helping out her momma. Something about those blisters just attracted me and I remember hitting those little hands with a bolo bat, and it busted her blisters good. It was pretty satisfying. I don't know why I did it. I have a hard time thinking I did it out of meanness. But her mother—I can't remember if she slapped me across the face or she spanked me, or both—but either way, now I know I sure had it comin'. Well, still, I was heartbroken, and I went running to find my Grandmother Paul and Granddaddy and my momma. And my granddaddy had the woman arrested for hitting me. The little black girl's momma went to jail. All this time it's bothered me. It was me who deserved to be sittin' in that jail for breaking a little black girl's blisters in 1957.[74]

Here Deen experiences the power of her own white privilege in a way that produces profound guilt and remorse. Her impulsive act, which may or may not have been done simply "out of meanness," has unintended and very real consequences for others. A "real nice black woman," a grown woman and mother, lands in jail because of Deen's impulsive act and is consequently separated from the child whom Deen hit. Whether Deen had a conscious realization of this at the time or not, the incident shows that even as a ten-year-old girl, she had more social standing than a grown black woman who also happened to be her caretaker. If this incident occurred as Deen describes it, it would certainly be a traumatic initiation into the complicated and unequal world of segregation, one that reveals her own complicity in the unjust system. The lack of many details surrounding the scene suggests a possibly incomplete process of coming to terms with this past event: Did the little black girl cry? Was she hurt? How much younger was she than Deen? What steps led to her mother being jailed? What happened next? Why did she find hitting the little girl's hands to be a "pretty satisfying" experience at the time?

These uncomfortable memories of segregation, though brief, stand in stark contrast to all the scenes of "comfort" she describes in her recollections on family, friends, and home-cooked meals, which provide the bulk of her other childhood memories. Remorse, guilt, shame, embarrassment, and mortification are the emotions Deen describes feeling as she recalls her experiences in the segregated South, and they are appropriate and understandable responses, part of what is necessary in a successful "working through" of memory and an acceptance of the losses of the past. But they are also difficult and painful emotions to confront, so it is no wonder that individuals try to avoid them. In the case of southerners and the South, acknowledging such emotions can be a particularly complicated process because there are so many ready-made and long-standing cultural myths to draw on as a way of protecting the self from difficult truths of the past. As Ricouer explains, personal memory and collective memory interact and inform each other constantly and in a "reciprocal and interconnected" manner as identity is continually formed and re-formed over time.[75]

Deen in her memoir seems to know and acknowledge something about the injustice of segregation and even her own complicity in it, but in other instances she relies instead on jaded explanations of the South and race that can be traced back to the nineteenth century. These are myths that can protect one from the uncomfortable truths of the past and from one's own experience of trauma and loss. Moreover, they can at times subtly reinforce a lost sense of white superiority. In a *New York Times* video interview with Deen in October 2012, Kim Severnsen notes that Deen has a "pride about the South" and goes on to ask her how she places the South's history of racism and slavery "within that." It's a fair and natural question to ask of a celebrity who trades so heavily on her southern-ness, and one would expect that it's a question Deen or her handlers would have prepared her to answer at some point. Deen, however, seems utterly flummoxed by the question, and her response is awkward to watch. She's hesitant and halting and seems to be searching for words: "I do. You know, it's funny. I think. I feel like the South is almost less prejudiced because black folks played such an integral part in our lives. They were like our family. Ummm. And we didn't see ourselves as prejudiced."[76] It's hard to reconcile Deen's comments on "black folks" being "like family" with her more direct expressions of her memories growing up during segregation. Her response here trades on the old paternalistic myth of slavery as a way of protecting herself from the truth of segregation. Given her standing at the time as one of the most recognizable southern celebrities in America, one might have hoped for something better. One might have hoped that she had actually reflected on the issue at some point.

But if we consider details from Deen's 2013 deposition, and particularly her desire to have an all-black waitstaff at her brother's wedding, we can see that Deen is even more rooted in the past than the personal anecdotes in her memoir would lead one to think. Indeed, they suggest a deeper, impossible longing for that past. The exchanges regarding these wedding plans are surely one of the more remarkable moments in the deposition, for by expressing this desire so blatantly, Deen makes overt the unacknowledged historical meaning of the southern hospitality myth itself: blacks are to serve whites, first as slaves, later as domestics, and now as waitstaff. In response to Deen's admission of using the N-word in the past, some were willing to accept or defend her, noting that many people of her generation would have used it as a matter of course. The wedding anecdote, however, is more pathological and, I would suggest, more revealing, especially if we keep in mind her uncomfortable recollections of segregation in her memoir. In the deposition, Deen describes going to a restaurant in the South where "the whole entire wait staff was middle-aged black men, and they had on beautiful white jackets with black bowties. I mean it was really impressive. And I remember saying I would love to have servers like that... but I would be afraid somebody would misinterpret." When the plaintiff's lawyer asked, "The media might misinterpret it?" Deen replied, "Yes, or whomever is so shallow that they would read something into it." As the lawyer pressed Deen on details, asking, for example, whether she could not achieve the same desired effect with "people of different races," she replied, "Well, that's what made it. That's what made it so impressive. These were professional. I'm not talking about somebody that's been a waiter for two weeks. I'm talking about these were professional middle-aged men, that probably made a very, very good living.... It was the whole picture, the setting of the restaurant, the servers, their professionalism." When asked if she could possibly have used the N-word in referring to these men, she replied, "No, because that's not what these men were. They were professional black men doing a fabulous job."[77]

While her earlier explanation of seeing blacks as "family" may be understood as a way to deflect the real, though unacknowledged, guilt or shame from complicity in segregation, this pathological desire for an all-black waitstaff seems to reveal an unconscious longing to recover or hold on to a lost ideal, in this case, a sense of one's own white supremacy that was lost with integration. Deen, however, seems to not see the historical associations that such an image of black men might conjure up, and in the deposition transcript, the lawyer almost acts like an analyst, asking questions to help a patient trace these connections and thereby relocate the lost object of desire:

> LAWYER: Why did that make it a—if you would have had servers like that, why would that have made it a really southern plantation wedding?
> DEEN: Well, it—to me, of course I'm old but I ain't that old, I didn't live back in those days but I've seen the pictures, and the pictures that I've seen, that restaurant represented a certain era in America.
> LAWYER: Okay.
> DEEN: And I was in the South when I went to this restaurant. It was located in the South.
> LAWYER: Okay. What era in America are you referring to?
> DEEN: Well, I don't know. After the Civil War, during the Civil War, before the Civil War.
> LAWYER: Right. Back in an era where there were middle-aged black men waiting on white people.
> DEEN: Well, it was not only black men, it was black women.
> LAWYER: Sure. And before the Civil War—before the Civil War, those black men and women who were waiting on white people were slaves, right?

DEEN: Yes, I would say that they were slaves.

LAWYER: Okay.

DEEN: But I did not mean anything derogatory by saying that I loved their look and their professionalism.[78]

Deen was certainly correct in stating that the media wouldn't understand her desire to have an all-black waitstaff at a "southern style" wedding, because it's simply hard for anyone to understand this peculiar desire in the twenty-first century. For a woman who both grew up in the segregated South and later made a fortune in the restaurant industry not to be able to see the uncomfortable historical associations that such an image conjures up is really quite remarkable. Deen here seems entirely too comfortable in her historic position of privilege as a white southerner. According to her, if her wanting an all-black waitstaff is a problem, it is due to the misunderstanding of people who would be so "shallow" as to read something into it. In other words, from Deen's perspective, the desire itself is not problematic. This strange desire to surround oneself with an image of the past exemplifies the habits of melancholia described above, revealing a hopeless longing to hold on to the lost love object of this past. The love object in this case would be Deen's own white superiority where blacks are confined to serving whites. But it is also worth noting that her language makes the image a timeless one: it reminds her of a time "after the Civil War, during the Civil War, before the Civil War." Indeed, this is the essential fact of the southern hospitality myth itself: it has created a seemingly timeless, "natural" image through which white southerners and white Americans more generally have either consistently accepted or conveniently forgotten the long history of subjugation and alienation of black Americans. In other words, if there's something pathological in Deen's personal memories and desires, it is also a reflection of something pathological in the broader, collective, cultural memory. Southern hospitality has historically celebrated white superiority and southern exceptionalism, and when integration disrupted this myth of white supremacy, it created new anxieties and desires for white southerners and thereby breathed new life into the myth, a sublimation of white supremacy. The southern hospitality myth survives through a pernicious habit of forgetting: forgetting the realities of slavery, of black domestic servitude, of racial inequality, and, importantly, black contributions to southern culture itself.

The national media reaction to Deen's transgressions are perhaps as telling as the transgressions themselves, revealing a national desire to purge ourselves of racism in one simple act, rather than acknowledging more pervasive habits of inequality and forgetfulness in American culture. Paula Deen momentarily showed us the racism that could reside within the southern hospitality myth, but it has been there from the beginning. Significantly, and in contrast to the knee-jerk media reaction, some of the most thoughtful responses to the controversy came from black southerners working in the culinary fields, particularly those devoted to preserving the history and traditions of southern foodways, a rapidly growing endeavor in the twenty-first century. Some took umbrage at the fact that Deen, whose celebrity status made her a de facto spokesperson for southern cuisine, had shown little interest in honoring the complex history of southern foodways and particularly the many contributions made by slaves and later domestic servants who did the cooking and in many instances were responsible for the traditions. As a *New York Times* article reported, the controversy around Deen "stirred up long-simmering issues in the culinary business, including accusations of industrywide racism and sexism; class divisions; and the fight over the true heritage of the region's food."[79]

Perhaps the most impassioned statement in this regard came from African American culinary historian Michael W. Twitty, who published an "Open Letter to Paula Deen" on his website, Afroculinaria, which is devoted to "preparing, preserving and promoting African American foodways and its parent traditions in Africa and her Diaspora and its legacy in the food culture of the American South." In the letter, which went viral on the web and was picked up by the Huffington Post, Twitty speaks to Deen as a "fellow Southerner" and notes, "As Southerners our ancestors co-created the food and hospitality and manners which you were born to 66 years ago and I, thirty-six." Given his ancestors' contributions of labor to the making of the "southern hospitality myth," Twitty reappropriates this tradition as his own. Still, this doesn't stop him from chastising Deen for drawing attention away from much more vital issues than her use of the N-word; according to Twitty, Deen's celebrity status as the de facto spokesperson for southern cuisine speaks to a long tradition of "culinary injustice": "In the world of Southern food, we are lacking a diversity of voices and that does not just mean Black people—or Black perspectives! We are surrounded by culinary injustice where some Southerners take credit for things that enslaved Africans and their descendants played key roles in innovating." This lack of diversity and the consequent loss of culinary traditions is, for Twitty, "far more galling than you saying 'nigger,' in childhood ignorance or emotional rage or social whimsy." Twitty goes on to point to the long-unacknowledged African American labor that made the southern hospitality myth possible:

> Culinary injustice is what you get where you go to plantation museums and enslaved Blacks are not even talked about, but called servants. We are invisible. Visitors come from all over to marvel at the architecture and wallpaper and windowpanes but forget the fact that many of those houses were built by enslaved African Americans or that the food that those plantations were re-

nowned for came from Black men and Black women truly slaving away in the detached kitchens.⁸⁰

Twitty's critique in his "Open Letter to Paula Deen" exposes the historical elisions that lie at the heart of the southern hospitality myth, but he also closes the letter on a note of true hospitality, one that would offer Deen a "reconciliation" with the truth of the region's past and perhaps her own. Reminding Deen of King's dream of the future day when "sons of former slaves and the sons of former slave owners would sit down at the table of brotherhood," Twitty closes by inviting Deen to "bake bread and break bread" at a fund-raising dinner for African American farmers to be held at Historic Stagville, an antebellum plantation and state historic site in North Carolina. In contrast to the repression and repetition of melancholia, such a meeting would amount to the travail associated with mourning, an appropriate "working through" and proper reconciliation with the past, warts and all. In short, Twitty's open letter reappropriates and resignifies the southern hospitality myth in important and significant ways: by claiming the heritage of black labor that produced the southern hospitality myth, by alluding to King's futural vision of full equality and justice, and by extending this invitation for reconciliation to Deen. Twitty's version of hospitality has a hard ethical edge, demanding a sense of future justice that can come only through a full and honest reckoning with the past.

Discourse around this growing field of southern foodways has often attempted to recast or reimagine southern hospitality as an inclusive cultural practice, but due to the way the field fetishizes southern food *as tradition*, it may simply, in the long run, further naturalize the repressive patterns of the southern hospitality myth of old. For example, consider the way the Southern Foodways Alliance incorporates hospitality as a "cornerstone" of both its own subject and its entire enterprise. Devoted to preserving and celebrating the South's culinary heritage, the Southern Foodways Alliance is an academic endeavor sponsored by the Center for the Study of Southern Culture at the University of Mississippi, and its mission statement and website seem to accept the notion of southern hospitality—here expressed as the "welcome table"—at face value: "The Southern Foodways Alliance documents, studies, and explores the diverse food cultures of the changing American South. Our work sets a welcome table where all may consider our history and our future in a spirit of respect and reconciliation." Striving to be racially and ethnically inclusive, willing to tell "honest and sometimes difficult stories about our region," motivated by a sense of justice and sustainability are all stated goals of the SFA, and they are indeed laudable goals.⁸¹ However, the tone and tenor of the SFA's discourse on hospitality is ultimately problematic. For example, the SFA's website includes a "Southern Food Primer" that historicizes the various cultural influences that shaped southern cuisine, including its African and ethnic connections, and this is immediately followed by the following statement on "Community in the South":

> Hospitality is a cornerstone of Southern foodways.
>
> John Egerton asserts, "Whether in the home or in public places, the food traditions that had become a part of Southern culture by the 1940s could be summarized under a single descriptive heading: hospitality. As overworked and ambiguous as the word may have been to many, it had meaning for most Southerners.
>
> It was not a myth, nor was it a hallmark of the rich alone; it was simply the way people were. Twice in their history since the Revolutionary War—in the aftermath of the Civil War and in the depths of the Great Depression—Southerners had known hunger, even starvation, and that knowledge had taught them to enjoy the moment, to feast when food was available, and to keep a wary eye on the future. Among all the classes—those who had plenty and those who had nothing and all the others in between—food was a blessing, a pleasure, a cause for celebration. The tradition of hospitality, of serving large quantities of good things to eat to large numbers of hungry people, of sharing food and drink with family and friends and even strangers, proved to be a durable tradition in the South, outliving war and depression and hunger."[82]

The quote is drawn from SFA founding member John Egerton's *Southern Food: At Home, on the Road, in History*, considered a classic text on southern cuisine, but it could come from just about any of a thousand southern cookbooks published in the last fifty years, for it is little more than a jaded echo of the southern hospitality myth. Despite the way that modern southern cookbooks throw around the word "hospitality" as a sort of hallowed essence of southern tradition, classic southern cookbooks of the nineteenth century never even mention it; they do, however, allude to slave labor and the need for management systems for effectively organizing such labor.[83] To his credit, Egerton in *Southern Food* discusses at some length the reality of the slave labor that created the planter's wealth and hospitality, and he notes slave contributions to southern cuisine, but he just as often describes the hospitality of antebellum southerners in the sort of uncritical, breathless terms that might be associated with Thomas Nelson Page.[84] This excerpted quote on the SFA website once again obfuscates historical connections as it attempts to naturalize southern hospitality *as tradition*. Indeed, there is something particularly awkward in suggesting that "food traditions" in "public places" in the 1940s South could be said to embody hospitality: from an ethical perspective, even a children's book like *Ruth and the Green Book* speaks a more powerful truth than this statement by Egerton.

Scott Romine and Fitzhugh Brundage have both offered insightful critiques of this growing field of southern foodways and the motivations behind it. According to Brundage, interest in the movement is fueled, in part, by a pervasive desire for authenticity as well as by a desire "for a usable past of multicultural adaptation and exchange." But as Brundage points out, in looking to the southern past, these "champions of southern syncreticism are prone to overreach and exaggeration." Romine has effectively described the way the movement fetishizes southern food as tradition and has offered a sharp critique of the "irrepressibly upbeat" nature of its iconography and discourse, including Egerton's notion of "one great Southern table": "Aspirational rather than historical, this discourse of the southern table suppresses the racial taboos and prohibitions that for generations dictated the protocols of food consumption. The pleasures of consumption predominate, while accounts of hunger and lack—Frederick Douglass's or Richard Wright's, say—are lost to history."[85] The problem here is that, considered from an ethical perspective, *there is no usable past* when it comes to the southern hospitality of slavery and segregation. In short, as well-intentioned as the Southern Foodways Alliance may be in its stated principles, its recurring emphasis on tradition runs the risk of simply further naturalizing long-standing habits of repression. Indeed, given both its standing as an academic institution and the sometimes breezy nature of its discourse (as described by Brundage and Romine), the work of the SFA might simply end up creating an aura of seeming legitimacy and authenticity for "symbolic southerners" who fetishize southern food and southern hospitality and who can move seamlessly from a Paula Deen cookbook to the pages of *Southern Living* to the websites or workshops of the SFA, repeating the mantra of tradition, tradition, tradition.[86] But from an ethical perspective, hospitality is not in the past, and it is not a tradition. It is an ethical imperative whose obligations always lie in the future arrival of the stranger. To repeat (and slightly modify) Jacques Derrida, "We do not yet know what [southern] hospitality is."

EPILOGUE

New Strangers of the Contemporary South

> All the strangers came today,
> and it looks as though they're here to stay.
>
> —David Bowie

Today, the discourse of southern hospitality is so burdened with a long history of jaded, empty, and meaningless repetitions that it perhaps seems impossible to reconstruct it as a meaningful regional ideal. Take, for example, the "Southern Hospitality Experience" program developed in 2006 by *Southern Hospitality* magazine, a Florida-based trade magazine for hoteliers and restaurateurs in the southeastern United States. Here we see the crass commercialization of southern hospitality at perhaps its worst. The Fall 2006 issue of the magazine announced this "certification program" as "an unparalleled opportunity to brand your property as a provider of the authentic Southern Hospitality Experience. Your guests will look for the SOUTHERN HOSPITALITY EXPERIENCE seal and then make their reservations with confidence."[1] As the program announcement goes on to proclaim, "Your guests expect Southern Hospitality: Warmth, courtesy, care, and comfort—the special welcome and attention of the South. And, you deliver on that Promise through superb service, high quality product and unique, satisfying venues. Let's elevate that message and your distinctive Brand by certifying your Performance through the 'Southern Hospitality Experience' program." After listing the program details (which includes a "professional hospitality assessment," the awarding of a "seal of distinction," and consequent marketing benefits), the announcement displays the "Southern Hospitality Experience" seal of certification, emblazoned, of course, with a pineapple. Is it possible to be any further removed from the moral and ethical dimensions of hospitality? Beneath the seal of certification on the program announcement, large bold red letters announce, "EVERYONE WINS."[2]

Typically, though, not everyone is a winner in the contemporary hospitality industry in the South (or anywhere, for that matter); the industry is known for low-paying, menial jobs, and it relies heavily on an international labor force of migrant workers. As the Southern Poverty Law Center reports, these workers often are unaware of their rights and fearful of deportation or other consequences, making them easy to manipulate by some employers and contractors who do not abide by industry standards and fair labor practices. In the worst cases, these workers are so consistently and thoroughly exploited that they exist in a state "close to slavery."[3] What role might such service laborers play in the "Southern Hospitality Experience" I just described? The program's assessment check sheet, to be filled out during the reviewer's unannounced visit, includes the following clues:

ROOM ATTENDANT'S ATTITUDE

Upon encountering guest(s), the room attendant should be friendly, polite and prepared to answer questions.

ROOM ATTENDANT'S ATTIRE/APPEARANCE

Room attendants should be appropriately dressed for the task and have a neat appearance. Reasonable grooming standards should be demonstrated....

MANAGEMENT INVOLVEMENT

Management and supervisory personnel should be... setting the proper example of Hospitality to the guests as well as evaluating and correcting employees' deficiencies. Discipline should be carried out away from the guests' view; however, praise should be given where guests can observe it.[4]

These guidelines suggest a nagging fear of what may go wrong when the obligation of carrying out "authentic southern hospitality" has to be entrusted to low-wage workers, largely from minority and immigrant communities. And this nagging fear seems to go beyond just this example. In 2004, for example, the city of Columbia, South Carolina, in conjunction with its newly minted city slogan, "Where Friendliness Flows," launched a new "Hospitality course" for "Columbia tourism's first responders: hotel desk clerks, waiters and cab drivers." The Columbia Metropolitan Convention and Visitors Bureau funded the classes with proceeds from restaurant taxes. In the profile in the Columbia newspaper the *State*, a bellman and shuttle driver enrolled in the course noted, "I think I'm friendly naturally." However, the paper stated that once the course was complete he would "officially be 'certified friendly.'" An official of the Hospitality Association of South Carolina expressed hope that the program could be developed to "generate more friendly employees."[5] These examples suggest that these generally low-wage service laborers, many of them immigrants, are being placed under new disciplinary practices of the southern hospitality myth, and this raises an important ethical question. We see here that the myth of southern hospitality can make demands of these laborers, but what is owed to them? Can they likewise be imagined as subjects of southern hospitality?

The intense debate that occurred in 2011 over the state of Alabama's immigration law (Alabama HB 56) provides a possible answer to these questions. The debate over this law marks an important contemporary episode in the history of southern hospitality, on the one hand, providing a reminder of the tension between politics and ethics in the southern hospitality myth and, on the other hand, offering a glimpse into how hospitality in the South *can* still function as a meaningful ethical ideal, one directed toward the challenges of both the present and the future.

Like many other southern states, Alabama cashes in on its reputation for "southern hospitality" with a thriving travel and tourism sector: Alabama's official travel site, like the "Southern Hospitality Experience" program described above, is keen to emphasize the "authenticity" of hospitality in the South as it announces the following to its potential visitors (and their tourism dollars):

> *Wherever you're from, you'll feel welcome in Alabama. Politeness and generosity are the norm, and there's always plenty of space around the dinner table.*
>
> Southern Hospitality:
>
> A truly authentic Southern experience is about something far more memorable than a stately plantation or frosty mint julep. While you'll find plenty of those in Alabama, the moments that best define our state are far more personal. The firm handshakes, the warm smiles, the generations of stories behind each delicious dish and handmade craft. Our famous Southern hospitality goes far beyond the warm welcome and fond goodbyes you'll hear across the state—although its always nice to hear "Come on in!" and "Y'all come back!" More than anything, we love telling stories about times gone by and the traditions passed down through our families. We share these stories to keep the memories alive and remind the world that the most meaningful interactions still happen face-to-face.[6]

These warm words of welcome seemed hopelessly ironic after the state passed Alabama HB 56 in June 2011, which at the time became the toughest set of anti-illegal immigration regulations in America. Bill sponsor Representative Micky Hammon (R-Decatur) told legislators that the bill "attacks every aspect of an illegal alien's life" and "is designed to make it difficult for them to live here so they will deport themselves." Representative Kerry Rich (R-Albertville), a supporter of the bill, portrayed illegals as parasites and a physical threat to the "household" of the state of Alabama: "The illegals in this country are ripping us off.... If we wait for the federal government to put this fire out, our house is going to burn down."[7] Still, state senator Scott Beason, another supporter of the law, had no problem reconciling southern hospitality with the nation's toughest crackdown on illegal immigrants, stating, "We expect people to be here in the state of Alabama legally. We have open arms, we have all the hospitality we can muster for the people who come to the state of Alabama legally. But if you are here illegally, it's going to be a challenge."[8]

The law's provisions challenged illegals (and to some extent, anyone who could be mistaken for one) in a wide variety of ways. Following Arizona's suit, the law required "state and local police officers to determine the immigration status of anyone they stop based on a 'reasonable suspicion' the person is an illegal immigrant," a provision that critics claimed amounted to racial profiling.[9] But Alabama went much further than Arizona as it sought to put pressure on every possible aspect of an illegal's life.[10] Among its numerous provisions, the law required schools to identify and report any students who were illegal aliens, prohibited illegals from attending any public university, required businesses to determine the legal status of all employees, and made it illegal to knowingly rent properties to illegals or knowingly transport, harbor, or assist them in any way. Moreover, it required all state employees to assist in the enforcement of these laws; failure to do so would be seen as a punishable criminal offense.[11] These provisions together created, in theory at least, a panoptical system of surveillance where almost anyone could be a potential informant for the state and could consequently present a threat to an illegal alien: a teacher or school administrator, a police officer, a social worker, a courthouse clerk, a landlord, even a member of one's church if he or she happened to be a state employee.

Passage of the law had profound and immediate consequences, with schools reporting high rates of absenteeism among immigrant populations, farmers left with crops rotting in fields, and hotels and restaurants suddenly short-staffed. Reports indicated that many *legal* aliens also left the state due to the new law. The state also had to endure the prospect of economic losses, boycotts, and embarrassing public relations moments. For example, a representative from a major medical convention that canceled its scheduled convention in Mobile, cited the law, saying, "We had people who felt they would not be able to jog without identification if they did not appear to be American."[12] An early study of the law's potential economic effects predicted the state would lose billions annually as a result. The cost-benefit analysis conducted by the Center for Business & Economic Research at the University of Alabama determined that the law would "annually shrink Alabama's economy by at least $2.3 billion and ... cost the state not less than 70,000 jobs." Job losses would come in part "from reduced demand for goods and services provided by Alabama businesses patronized by immigrants" but also because low-wage labor performed by immigrants inevitably is connected to and supports jobs in other sectors and industries: "Those positions support other jobs, leading to a net employment loss of 70,000 to 140,000." Dr. Samuel Addy, who carried out the study, "estimated that the state's gross domestic product [would] decline by $2.3 billion to $10.8 billion for every year the law is in effect and [would] cost $56.7 million to $264.5 million in tax revenue." Significantly, the departure of immigrant laborers under the law did not suddenly create new jobs for natives, as the law's supporters had promised; rather, "the four job categories that once hired most of the state's immigrants—agriculture, construction, food service, and hospitality—" were found to "employ fewer people than they did before the law went into effect." As Addy noted, "Many Alabamans have rejected hard, dirty, low-paying jobs that immigrants once performed.... Now employers struggle to fill those positions."[13] So while proponents of the law portrayed immigrants as parasites or thieves, the reality is much more complex, with both legal and illegal immigrants contributing to the overall economy in a variety of unseen but impactful ways, as producers, consumers, and taxpayers.

While the law succeeded in creating a pervasive sense of threat to immigrants in low-paying industries, its dragnets did not discriminate, making for some embarrassing moments for the state. In November 2011, the case of a German executive from Mercedes-Benz arrested for failing to produce proper paperwork during a traffic stop made the national headlines. A similar incident occurred the following month with a Japanese executive from Honda. Like many southern states, Alabama had gone to great lengths to woo foreign auto manufacturers to the state, but with these cases, it found itself essentially insulting the corporate guests after initially putting out the welcome mat. In response to these incidents, a *St. Louis Post-Dispatch* editorial gleefully skewered the state for its lack of hospitality and encouraged Mercedes to move to Missouri.[14] As the *Decatur (AL) Daily News* ruefully noted in an editorial, "The people of our once-hospitable state should send a thank-you card to the Mercedes Benz executive arrested Friday for violation of the immigration law.... The German did more to demonstrate the idiocy of the immigration law in one day than the law's opponents have managed in months."[15]

All in all, the story of HB 56 would seem to be just another anecdote that illustrates the disparity between politics and ethics in the southern hospitality myth, but the debate and protests that followed suggest otherwise. With grassroots protests and challenges to the law coming from a wide range of Alabamans, the state suddenly found itself in a significant debate on the obligations and limitations of hospitality itself, one not unlike the antebellum debate over the Fugitive Slave Law a century and a half earlier. These grassroots efforts to repeal the law involved interdenominational clergy and churches; industry representatives; public policy and political organizations such as the NAACP, the Center for American Progress, the Southern Poverty Law Center; and ordinary Alabama citizens. This coalition was also integrated across lines of race and class and included groups historically seen as "strangers" to the southern hospitality myth, specifically Latinos and African Americans.[16] These activists and protestors routinely drew on the South's reputation for hospitality as a way to bolster their arguments, but they also viewed hospitality through a moral and ethical lens. Early on after the law was passed, for example, the state's United Methodist, Episcopal, and Roman Catholic churches joined forces and filed suit against the law, claiming that the law's provisions violated their religious freedom and particularly the biblical imperative of hospitality. As Methodist minister Melissa Self Patrick of Birmingham noted, "The new legislation goes against the tenets of our Christian faith—to welcome the stranger, to offer hospitality to anyone."[17] Similarly, Reverend Fred L. Hammond, a Unitarian minister from Tuscaloosa, invoked the Christian ideal of the Good Samaritan in speaking out against the law: "The work of people of faith lies here in attending to the people in the shadows, including those who are immigrants among us. HB 56 criminalizes the ability of faithful people to provide sanctuary, transportation to needed services, and the basic care that the despicable Samaritan offered to one injured by society. This law needs to be repealed ... so people of faith can bring everyone out of the shadows and truly be whole and upright living in the noonday light of love."[18]

In addition to invoking the biblical imperative of hospitality, critics of the law also invoked Alabama's civil rights history as a way of framing the debate. Lawton Higgs, a retired Methodist minister from Birmingham who supported the church's lawsuit challenging the law, likened the current debate over immigration in Alabama to the earlier civil rights movement that he had lived through, noting that this time the clergy who stood up against the law were going to be on the right side of history. Indeed, it was to the conservative, gradualist clergy of Birmingham that Martin Luther King Jr. had addressed his famous "Letter from the Birmingham Jail" a half-century earlier. Like many others, Higgs compared the new immigration law to Jim Crow and candidly noted that he had been on the wrong side of the earlier debates: "And I'm a recovering racist, transformed by the great fruits of the civil rights movement in this city." Just as many Alabamans strongly supported the law, not all clergy and church members agreed with the suit; however, the emerging immigration debate in the state suddenly put the question of hospitality in the South in stark terms, making it a pressing ethical dilemma for many Alabamans. As one Methodist minister from a "very conservative" congregation in north Alabama filled with supporters of the law noted, "You cannot tell a church that if there's a man hungry out there, a family hungry out there, that they can't feed them just because they don't have a green card.... That's just not Christian."[19]

Interestingly, the ethics of hospitality articulated in these grassroots political efforts had much more in common with the abolitionists than with the long history of iterations of "southern hospitality." Take, for example, the case of a resolution submitted to the Alabama Baptist Convention, an association of Baptist churches affiliated with the Southern Baptist Convention, during its annual meeting in November 2012. The resolution was submitted by the Reverend Alan Cross, pastor of Gateway Baptist Church in Montgomery, Alabama. Though Alabama Baptists provided a significant bloc of support for the Republican legislature that passed the immigration law, Cross's resolution shows that their support of the law was not universal. What is perhaps most notable in the resolution is the way that Cross so closely echoes abolitionist discourse around hospitality and the Fugitive Slave Law from a century and a half earlier, with the stranger or alien transformed from the runaway slave to the illegal immigrant. The resolution cites the very same biblical passages most often cited by abolitionists, and it portrays hospitality as part of God's "higher law."[20] When human law runs counter to God's higher law, Cross, like the abolitionists before him, contends that we must follow the former ("we seek to be good citizens in our state and nation only because we are first citizens of the Kingdom of God who represent Christ as His ambassadors"). In a series of blog posts leading up to and following the convention, Cross explained his reasons for submitting the resolution. After noting that Alabama Baptists are close supporters of the Alabama Republicans who created the law, Cross declared, "[My] simple hope was that we could send a clear message to Alabama Baptists that when they met a Hispanic person in need, they should first seek to love and minister to them instead of worrying about if they might get in trouble with the state if that person is here illegally. We could have done that today."[21] Moreover, Cross goes on to describe the real dilemma many Alabama Christians faced in light of the law's provision regarding state employees and the legal obligation to report illegals:

> Our church is in the state capitol of Alabama. We have a lot of state workers who are members of our church. If our church is helping a Hispanic family in need, are the state workers to try and figure out if the people are here legally or not? If we do ministry in a nearby community that we know has illegals living in it, will the state workers not engage in the ministry for fear that they might come in contact with illegals and be forced to report them or report other church members who help them in any way? ... My concern is that Christians be free to help people in need who live in our community without fear that they are breaking the law.... Private citizens, whether they work for the state or not, should not be called upon to act as law enforcement or as an immigration agent.[22]

The dilemma posed to Christians by the Alabama law can indeed be likened to the Fugitive Slave Law, particularly in the way it criminalizes acts of hospitality to illegals and also in the way it requires state employees to uphold the law even though they may find it morally objectionable. The Fugitive Slave Law required citizens to assist federal officers in the capture of fugitives when called upon, and it made the act of extending hospitality to a runaway slave a federal crime, punishable with excessive fines and imprisonment.

But Cross goes beyond simply critiquing the law. In a later blog post, he proposes the possibility of Alabama Baptists—and Christians more generally—taking a leading role on the issue of immigration reform in the United States, based again primarily on this moral and ethical approach to the question of hospitality. Motivated in part by the frustration of not having his resolution make it out of committee, Cross wonders whether "it might not be possible for Alabama Baptists to tell a better story than [they] have" on the issue of immigration. The title of this post asks, "Could Alabama Baptists Lead the Way in Immigration Reform in America?" Cross's answer to the titular question returns to the question of hospitality and hinges on how we define the immigrant—either as a neighbor and brother and sister or as a stranger and alien. And again, the scriptural text he cites and his approach to it are more in line with abolition hospitality than with southern hospitality. In this particular case, he cites Paul's Letter to Philemon as evidence that we have a duty to minister to immigrants, whether they are illegal or not.[23] The parallel between his progressive reading of Philemon and that of the abolitionists' 150 years earlier shows that while the historical and political contexts have changed, the underlying ethical questions and dilemmas surrounding hospitality remain constant. Whether we are speaking of the runaway slave in biblical times or the runaway slave in antebellum America or the contemporary illegal immigrant in Alabama, similar points of tension emerge between the ethics and the politics of hospitality, between higher law and human law, between the claim of hospitality and the claim of sovereignty, and between strangers cast as guests, neighbors, or brothers and strangers cast as aliens, parasites, and criminals. These parallels show that the ethical question of hospitality in the South (and in the nation as a whole) is as urgent today as ever, perhaps even more so, given the new pressures of a global economy and the demands that go along with an increasingly mobile population of immigrants, aliens, and strangers.[24] While so many iterations of "southern hospitality" are simply jaded echoes of an exclusionary historical politics, in this debate over HB 56 we see that hospitality in the South can perhaps be renovated as an ethical principle oriented toward the future and the arrival of new strangers.

NOTES

Introduction. What Can One Mean by Southern Hospitality?

1. Isaac, *Transformation of Virginia*, 303. Scholars who have written about southern hospitality have limited themselves almost exclusively to the antebellum period and have concerned themselves only with determining its origins and cultural meanings. For representative examples, see Genovese, *Political Economy of Slavery*; Luraghi, *Rise and Fall*; Wyatt-Brown, *Southern Honor*; Greenberg, *Honor and Slavery*; and Isaac, *Transformation of Virginia*.

2. See Kreyling, *Inventing Southern Literature*; Duck, *Nation's Region*, 3; McPherson, *Reconstructing Dixie*, 1; Greeson, *Our South*, 1; G. E. Hale, *Making Whiteness*; Bone, Ward, and Link, *Creating and Consuming the American South*), 1; and Lassiter and Crespino, *Myth of Southern Exceptionalism*, 7.

3. Wilson and Ferris, *Encyclopedia of Southern Culture*, 1133, 1134. Volume 4 of *The New Encyclopedia of Southern Culture*, also edited by Charles Reagan Wilson and published in 2006, includes a more nuanced and critical discussion of southern hospitality's origins, evolving meanings, and motivations. Still, the tone of this excerpt from the 1989 edition is in many ways more typical of the way many people think about southern hospitality and its relationship to the past, as many examples in the pages that follow will illustrate.

4. Wallerstein, "What Can One Mean?," 1, 3, 7. The scholars Wallerstein discusses as examples are George Brown Tindall, Clement Eaton, William Nicholls, Richard Weaver, F. Garvin Davenport, John Egerton, Richard Current, and Barrington Moore.

5. Ibid., 8.

6. Ibid.

7. Ibid., 9.

8. By approaching southern hospitality as a form of cultural memory, I seek to build on the scholarship on cultural memory and the American South that has been produced in recent years, such as Hinrichsen, *Possessing the Past*; Kreyling, *South That Wasn't There*; Brundage, *Southern Past*; and Brundage's earlier edited collection, *Where These Memories Grow*. While much of this work has focused on more "official" or at least discretely defined forms of cultural memory—histories, monuments, rituals, museums, landmarks, literary texts—the southern hospitality myth as I define and trace it is a more pervasive yet subtler form of cultural memory, one that has persisted and evolved for over two centuries, functioning consistently as a narrative form of southern community, to borrow Scott Romine's phrase. See Romine, *Narrative Forms of Southern Community*.

9. For the seminal work on "imagined communities" and the construction of national identities, see Anderson, *Imagined Communities*.

10. See Foucault, *Archaeology of Knowledge*.

11. African Americans in the post–civil rights South have often reappropriated this myth of southern hospitality according to the logic of what Zandria F. Robinson terms "country cosmopolitanism." Robinson posits, "Country Cosmopolitanism is a best-of-both worlds blackness that addresses the embattled notion of racial authenticity in a post-black era by hearkening back to and modernizing rural, country tropes." This version of black identity is "both performed and performative." While informed by traditional notions of southern manners, politeness, and hospitality, it also "calls for seemingly paradoxical approaches to race, class, and gender realities" and provides "the theoretical validation for black southern cultural superiority relative to both whites and non-southern blacks." To the extent that this performed identity draws on the discourse of southern hospitality, it marks an important reappropriation of a myth originally generated by black labor. See Robinson, *This Ain't Chicago*, 17, 18, 21, 22.

12. Given my thesis, it should be apparent that in using the terms "southerners," "non-southerners," and "northerners" I am generally referring to different groups of "white" Americans.

13. Benedict Anderson comments on the roles memory and forgetting play in the national imaginary of Americans faced with the historical trauma of the Civil War: "A vast pedagogical industry works ceaselessly to oblige young Americans to remember/ forget the hostilities of 1861–1865 as a great 'civil' war between 'brothers' rather than between—as they briefly were—two sovereign nation-states" (*Imagined Communities*, 201). My point here is that the discourse of southern hospitality is just such a form of memory and forgetting that responds to this fraught, often traumatic history.

14. Also see Duck, *Nation's Region*, especially part 1, titled "Imagining Affiliation," where she provides a theoretical model for rethinking the role of region in U.S. nationalism, a model in which white supremacy similarly serves as "a source for not only regional but national passions" (11).

15. Henry Wiencek offers a powerful description of the slave activity that generated Jefferson's hospitality and the way Jefferson consciously designed Monticello to conceal that activity from guests:

> In designing the mansion, Jefferson followed a precept laid down two centuries earlier by Palladio: "We must contrive a building in such a manner that the finest and most noble parts of it be the most exposed to public view, and the less agreeable disposed in by places, and removed from sight as much as possible."
>
> The mansion sits atop a long tunnel through which slaves, unseen, hurried back and forth carrying platters of food, fresh tableware, ice, beer, wine and linens, while above them 20, 30 or 40 guests sat listening to Jefferson's dinner-table conversation. At one end of the tunnel lay the icehouse, at the other the kitchen, a hive of ceaseless activity where the enslaved cooks and their helpers produced one course after another.
>
> During dinner Jefferson would open a panel in the side of the fireplace, insert an empty wine bottle and seconds later pull out a full bottle. We can imagine that he would delay explaining how this magic took place until an astonished guest put the question to him. The panel concealed a narrow dumbwaiter that descended to the basement. When Jefferson put an empty bottle in the compartment, a slave waiting in the basement pulled the dumbwaiter down, removed the empty, inserted a fresh bottle and sent it up to the

master in a matter of seconds. Similarly, platters of hot food magically appeared on a revolving door fitted with shelves, and the used plates disappeared from sight on the same contrivance. Guests could not see or hear any of the activity, nor the links between the visible world and the invisible that magically produced Jefferson's abundance. (Wiencek, "Dark Side of Thomas Jefferson")

16. Gray, "Foreword," xvi–xvii, xvii–xviii.

17. Ibid., xxi.

18. As some scholars have noted, there are no doubt many limitations to the corpus, which only represents about 4 percent of all the books ever published, and to the program. I am not hanging my argument on this data, but I do find it worthwhile to mention here that the data patterns revealed in the n-gram viewer at least echo the findings of my research in this project. See Michel, "Quantitative Analysis"; and Geoffrey Nunberg, "Google's Book Search."

19. The earliest use in print of the phrase "southern hospitality" that I have found is in 1824. As Michael O'Brien points out, in the early decades of the nineteenth century, "the South" was in many ways "a moving target, a thing in process, never what it had been ten years before, never what it would be ten years later." At the beginning of the century, it "was not yet habitually called the South" (O'Brien, *Conjectures of Order*, 5).

20. See Loughran, *Republic in Print*, 3, 345. Also see Jennifer Greeson's discussion of the emergence of the concept of the "Slave South" in the national imaginary, which coincides with this emergence of the discourse of southern hospitality (*Our South*, part 2). Greeson traces three major shifts in the national conception of the South as an "internal other"—the Plantation South, the Slave South, and the Reconstruction South—all of which worked to constitute evolving notions of American exceptionalism.

21. For discussions of the centrality of *Gone with the Wind* to the contemporary imagined idea of the South, see McPherson, *Reconstructing Dixie*, 47–68; and Romine, *Real South*, chapter 1.

22. See Bone, *Postsouthern Sense of Place*; and Romine, *Real South*. See also see Griffin and Thompson, "Enough about the Disappearing South."

23. Since colonial times, the pineapple has been a symbol of hospitality. In the colonial era, pineapples were exotic, rare, and expensive to obtain; consequently, to serve a pineapple to guests or to have it as a centerpiece was seen as a sign of status for both the host *and* the guest. Pineapples were so prized by hosts and hostesses that they could even be rented for parties. See, for example, A. F. Smith, *Oxford Encyclopedia*.

24. The print by Kevin Liang provides an interesting example of the marketability of "southern hospitality": the painting is available online under two different titles: "Sun Room" and "Southern Hospitality."

25. See McPherson, *Reconstructing Dixie*, 150–57.

26. Tracy McNulty, for example, claims that "the problem of hospitality is coextensive with the development of Western civilization, occupying an essential place in virtually every religion and defining the most elementary of social relations: reciprocity, exogamy, potlatch, 'brotherly love,' nationhood. In almost every Western religion, hospitality is the attribute or special domain of the principal divinity ... who evaluates the character of the human hosts by appealing for hospitality disguised as a supplicant.

In ancient Greece, one could even argue that hospitality *is* religion, the defining social ethics of *Zeus Xénios*, Zeus god of strangers. Similarly, Christian 'eucharistic hospitality' is the medium through which Christians are invested with a transcendental identity, made 'equal' to their fellows through the love of Christ, the supreme Host" (McNulty, *Hostess*, vii). In addition to its classical and Judeo-Christian religious origins and traditions, hospitality has figured as an important concept in both philosophy and political theory. In the Enlightenment, Immanuel Kant reenvisioned hospitality as the universal right of the world citizen, an essential precondition for cosmopolitan law and the premise for a state of perpetual peace. More recently, Seyla Benhabib has revisited Kant's cosmopolitan theories in light of our current debates on globalization, international law, and universal human rights. She explains that in these realms, hospitality encompasses "all human rights claims which are cross-border in scope" (Benhabib, *Another Cosmopolitanism*, 31).

27. Quoted in McNulty, *Hostess*, xvii.

28. Derrida and Dufourmantelle, *Of Hospitality*, 25.

29. See Phillipson, *International Law*, 214–16. The unusual title of the essay by Derrida cited in the epigraph ("Hostipitality") points to this shared origin.

30. Derrida, "Hostipitality," 3.

31. In *Perpetual Peace: A Philosophical Sketch*, Immanuel Kant outlines a series of six "preliminary" and three "definitive" articles necessary for the achievement of perpetual peace among the nations of the world. The third definitive article addresses the question of hospitality and marks a seminal moment in philosophical thinking about the ethics of hospitality. Kant's third definitive article reads, "The Law of World Citizenship Shall Be Limited to Conditions of Universal Hospitality." Significantly, Kant maintains that hospitality is not a matter of a host's "philanthropy" toward a guest; instead, it is the inherent "right" of the stranger: "Hospitality means the right of the stranger not to be treated as an enemy when he arrives in the land of another." Kant considers this to be a natural right that all humans have "by virtue of their common ownership of the surface of the earth, where, as a globe, they cannot infinitely disperse and hence must finally tolerate the presence of each other. Originally, no one had more right than another to a particular part of the earth." But this right is, for Kant, not without limitations. He offers many conditions that limit this "universal" right; the stranger can be turned away, as long as he or she is not harmed, and the stranger cannot demand the "right to be a permanent visitor.... It is only a right of temporary sojourn, a right to associate, which all men have." Since Kant's outlining of "universal hospitality" is already conditional and limited, it isn't surprising that Derrida uses Kant's concept of "universal hospitality" as a starting point for some of his deconstructive reading of the paradoxes of hospitality. See Kant, *Perpetual Peace*, 21.

32. See, for example, Derrida and Dufourmantelle, *Of Hospitality*, 147–50.

33. Derrida, "Hostipitality," 14.

34. Quoted in Rosello, *Postcolonial Hospitality*, 11–12.

35. Derrida, "Hostipitality," 6.

36. Ibid., 14.

37. Ricoeur juxtaposes individual and collective memory, which exist in a complementary relationship. Collective memory antedates an individual's memory, serving

as a backdrop. History mediates between the two. Ricoeur's monumental work *Memory, History, Forgetting* provides an incredibly detailed synthesis and summation of his career-long engagement with these issues. For my purposes here, and for the sake of concision, I am relying on his earlier essay, "Memory and Forgetting," published in *Questioning Ethics: Contemporary Debates in Philosophy.*

38. In outlining what he describes in *Memory, History, Forgetting* as this "pathology of collective memory" (71), Ricoeur transposes several principles from Freud. In particular, he draws on Freud to contrast two different responses to the traumas of the past: melancholia and mourning. Melancholia, the undesirable response to the traumas of the past, results from resistance and repression, which prevent one from "progress towards recollection, or towards a reconstruction of an acceptable and understandable past." Instead, the subject is compelled to simply repeat symptoms "and is barred from any progress toward recollection." In contrast, mourning, the healthier though more difficult response, is the result of "a *travail*," a patient and difficult "working through" that results in a reconciliation with the past. This idea of the *work* of memory is especially important to Ricoeur, who claims that "it is quite possible that the work of memory *is* a kind of mourning, and also that mourning is a painful exercise in memory." Ricoeur draws the following important distinctions between the two responses to such trauma and loss: "What is preserved in mourning and lost in melancholia is self-esteem, of the sense of one's self. This is so because in melancholia there is a despair and a longing to be reconciled with the love object which is lost without the hope of reconciliation." Narratives of collective memory can betray such negative symptoms as the compulsion to repeat and the tendency to manipulate or block memory, all abuses of memory linked to melancholia rather than proper mourning. Ricoeur claims that we can see evidence of such abuses of memory in "the excess of certain commemorations, their rituals, their festivals, their myths which attempt to fix the memories in a kind of reverential relationship to the past" (Ricoeur, "Memory and Forgetting," 6, 7, 9).

39. It should also be noted that neither of these groups—black and white—are homogeneous; rather, each contains a variety of possible affiliations, including distinctions such as rich and poor; rural, urban, and suburban; male and female, and so on.

40. See also Lisa Hinrichsen's recent book, *Possessing the Past*. Hinrichsen challenges the traditional function of "memory" in southern studies, where it has figured as a "knowable object" that can be possessed and mastered. According to Hinrichsen's analysis—which draws on Sigmund Freud, Slavoj Žižek, and Lauren Berlant, among others—the narrative of southern hospitality would qualify as a "fantasy" that "forms a suture between political forms and the subjective understanding of historical experience, and, as such, it is fundamental to the formation of the public sphere" (7).

41. Ricoeur, "Memory and Forgetting," 8–10.

42. See Benhabib, *Another Cosmopolitanism*, 31.

43. A number of scholars have turned their attention in recent years to the effects of globalization on the South; see Peacock, Watson, and Matthews, *American South in a Global World*; Cobb and Stueck, *Globalization and the American South*; and Peacock, *Grounded Globalism*.

44. See Benhabib, *Another Cosmopolitanism*; and Appiah, *Cosmopolitanism*.

45. Benhabib, *Another Cosmopolitanism*, 31, italics in original.

Chapter 1. A Virginian Praises "Yankee Hospitality"

1. Minor, "Letters from New England—No. 2," 166. Minor is not named as the author; instead, the letters are simply attributed to "A Virginian." Also, the series was originally published in the *Fredericksburg Arena*.

2. A short sketch titled "The Wedding" that appeared in 1835 in *The Lady's Book* makes essentially the same points as Minor does in contrasting northern and southern hospitality, locating the origins of the differences in the "political conditions" of the region (i.e., slavery). With slaves to serve in the South, hospitality is "free from care," while in the North it is "full of anxiety." See Ogle, "Wedding," 205. For a later version of the same argument, see Atwater, *Incidents of a Southern Tour*, especially chapter 3. Atwater's tone suggests how the legend of southern hospitality proliferated in the decades of sectional crisis. Regarding southern hospitality, he notes, "We have most of us heard this lauded to the skies," but like Minor, he points to the "different circumstances" provided for by slavery (9).

3. Minor, "Letters from New England—No. 2," 166.

4. "Editorial Remarks."

5. L. Jackson, *Business of Letters*, 36.

6. Minor, "Letters from New England—No. 5," 425.

7. Thomas Willis White felt that Minor's views on Liberia were too progressive for the *Messenger*'s readership and ordered Edgar Allan Poe to edit out passages that could be deemed controversial or offensive to southern readers. Minor came from a slaveholding family whose history had something of a progressive streak; in the late eighteenth century, for example, his grandfather had sponsored an emancipation bill in the Virginia legislature, and for over three decades a female cousin recorded a journal she titled "Notes Illustrative of the Wrongs of Slavery." Minor certainly seems to have inherited at least some of the family's progressive leanings regarding slavery. At the same time that his "Letters from New England" were appearing in the *Southern Literary Messenger*, he had undertaken to teach one of his father's slaves to read, keeping a "journal of Elisha's learning" and apparently rousing the ire of neighbors. These efforts seem especially remarkable when we consider that the memories of Nat Turner's bloody rebellion in 1831—which resulted in the deaths of fifty-five whites and the hangings of seventeen blacks, as well as the wanton killing of an untold number of slaves—were still fresh in the minds of Minor's fellow Virginians. See Whalen, *Edgar Allan Poe and the Masses*, 297n38, and his discussion of the editorial changes made to Minor's essay "Liberian Literature," 124–25.

8. Quoted in Isaac, *Transformation of Virginia*, 71.

9. For example, Daniel R. Hundley in *Social Relations in Our Southern States* also includes the "yeomen farmer" as a practitioner of true southern hospitality. He divides southerners into eight distinct social types or classes, with "The Southern Gentleman" at the top, and the "Poor White Trash" and "Negro Slaves" at the bottom; the "Yeoman" figures in the middle. Of the yeomen he writes, "So far as hospitality goes, the Yeomen of the South are not a whit behind the Southern Gentleman" (207). Hundley's text also suggests the degree to which idealized stories of southern hospitality had proliferated in the antebellum period. Describing northerners who travel south, he writes,

"They have been so accustomed from infancy to hear and read of Southern hospitality and wealth, as well as of the splendors of natural scenery in all Southern latitudes, they seem to anticipate at every step a princely mansion, and at every turn magnolia groves. Filled with such ideal conceptions of the Summer Land, it is not at all strange that such persons can not refrain at times from expressing their disappointment, when they come to realize the facts" (23–24).

10. See Wyatt-Brown, *Southern Honor*, 327–29; and Isaac, *Transformation of Virginia*, 302–3. See also D. B. Smith, *Inside the Great House*, for a detailed discussion—drawn from diaries—of the visiting habits and open house rituals of eighteenth-century planters (21–22, 175–78, and 198–230). For a discussion of the experiences of southern women within these rituals and traditions, see Fox-Genovese, *Within the Plantation Household*, 140–41, 213–15, 223–28; and Weiner, *Mistresses and Slaves*, 23–28, 33–34, and 48.

11. Wyatt-Brown, *Southern Honor*, 332–33.

12. S. M. Stowe, *Intimacy and Power*, xv, 162, 252.

13. Wyatt-Brown, *Southern Honor*, 337.

14. Mauss, *Gift*, 3.

15. Greenberg, *Honor and Slavery*, 70.

16. See, for example, Luraghi, *Rise and Fall*, 74–75; and Genovese, *Political Economy of Slavery*, 16–18, 28–36, and 245–46.

17. Isaac, *Transformation of Virginia*, 71.

18. Bleser, *Secret and Sacred*, 174.

19. Ibid., 170.

20. Greenberg, *Honor and Slavery*, 3. Wyatt-Brown cites this same passage from Hammond in his discussion of the sense of deep competition underlying hospitality among southern gentleman, but he does not mention the entire context of the letter regarding his sexual indiscretions, one that further underscores what Greenberg would describe as the "superficial" quality of southern honor. It is also worth noting that Hammond alludes to hospitality as one of the "high and noble qualities" that the system of slavery promotes in southern society. See his "Letters on Slavery," where he dismisses abolitionists' charges that the sexual exploitation of female slaves by their masters was rampant: "But I have done with this disgusting topic. And I think I may justly conclude, after all the scandalous charges which tea-table gossip and long-gowned hypocrisy have brought against the slave-holders, that a people whose men are proverbially brave, intellectual and hospitable, and whose women are unaffectedly chaste, devoted to domestic life and happy in it, can neither be degraded nor demoralized, whatever their institutions may be. My decided opinion is, that our system of slavery contributes largely to the development and culture of these high and noble qualities." It should be noted that Hammond did make at least two female slaves his mistresses, first a seamstress named Sally Johnson and, later, her twelve-year-old daughter, Louisa. See "Hammond's Letters on Slavery," 120–21; and Bleser, *Secret and Sacred*, 17–20.

21. Minor, "Letters from New England—No. 2," 167, emphasis in original.

22. For an example of this early tendency to identify particular social habits with a more localized community, see Dr. Ladd, "Sketch of the Character," which was re-

printed in the *Massachusetts Magazine* in 1791. While the article warns of the dangers of luxury and ostentatious display and also suggests the potential for "savage brutality" among slave owners by alluding to the West Indies, the author concludes that when it comes to "the exercise of hospitality, and all the social virtues ... no country on earth has equalled Carolina" (231). In contrast, an 1837 sketch in the *Southern Literary Journal* shows the ways that these particulars eventually tended to be generalized more broadly as "Southern hospitality." The sketch details a day of entertainments, including a hunt, in Summerville, South Carolina, but even as the writer focuses on the more particular habits of "the Carolina planter," the anecdotes are also generalized to extend the traits to the entire region of the South: "Every thing was in accordance with Southern hospitality." See "Day at Summerville," 228.

23. Foster, "Visit to a Southern Plantation."
24. Ibid.
25. Ibid. A unique early use of an anecdote of southern hospitality is included in the preface of *Learning Is Better Than House or Land*, a popular children's book by Irish-born classicist John Carey that went through several editions between 1808 and 1864. In the preface the author praises American hospitality and notes that it "shines more conspicuously in the southern states of the union, where any decently dressed man may travel a thousand miles without ever entering an inn." He goes on to recount when he was lost in Virginia in a snowstorm and was forced to seek the hospitality of a plantation. At the end of the preface, he makes special note that, in retrospect, upon his arrival at the home, "there was not the smallest necessity for [him] to stand parleying with the negro at the door," observing, "I might at once have commanded him to take my horse ... walked in without hesitation, and experienced precisely the same reception." The book tells the comparative stories of two orphan immigrants to the United States—one industrious and one indolent—to emphasize the virtues of persistence and hard work as the keys to one's social rise, so it is somewhat ironic that the book begins with an anecdote featuring slavery. Given the book's popularity, many young American children may have first learned of the South's reputation for hospitality from it. They also learned that a "negro" was someone who could be "commanded" (vi, xi).
26. Bourdieu, "Forms of Capital," 87.
27. Ibid., 86, 87.
28. Jennifer Greeson describes how the emergence of abolitionism resulted in a "newly configured" image of the "Slave South" in the national imaginary. As she understands it, this was "not evolution but rupture"—hence, the palliative nature of the emergent discourse of southern hospitality. See Greeson, *Our South*, 118.
29. Minor, "Letters from New England—No. 1," 87.
30. Ibid., 87–88.
31. Minor, "Letters from New England—No. 5," 426.
32. Bourne, *Picture of Slavery*, 86.
33. X Y Z, "Letters from the South West."
34. Ibid. For a similar report from a northern clergyman traveling in the South and expressing discomfort with the conflict between southern hospitality and slavery, see "Scenes from Louisiana." Sarah M. Grimke also makes similar observations in "Narrative and Testimony of Sarah M. Grimke."

35. Bourdieu, "Forms of Capital," 89.
36. "SOUTHERN ARGUMENTS," emphasis in original.
37. "Pro-Slavery as It Is."
38. "Report of the Committee on Slavery." Southerners often expressed confidence in the persuasive powers of southern hospitality to sway northerners to their cause, and abolitionists routinely expressed anxiety and outrage at this prospect. For an example of the former, see Hutchinson, "Mrs. Hutchinson's Letter"; for an example of the latter, see "Pro-Slavery as It Is."
39. Barker, *Influence of Slavery*, 10, emphasis in original.
40. Redpath, *Roving Editor*, 139.
41. Fox-Genovese and Genovese, *Mind of the Master Class*, 96.
42. Redpath, *Roving Editor*, 82.
43. Ibid., 139.
44. Ibid., 140.
45. Only a year later, Redpath would offer the following direct criticism of southern hospitality in his *Southern Notes*: "Down South where the Slave-holders so loudly boast of their hospitality, they nevertheless have changed all that; and 'Be *in*hospitable to strangers, for some have entertained Abolitionists without knowing it,' seems now to be the rule that governs them." Quoted in McKivigan, *Forgotten Firebrand*, 58.
46. For an analysis of Genovese's scholarly and political shifts in the latter part of his career, see Lichtenstein, "Right Church, Wrong Pew."
47. Fox-Genovese and Genovese, *Mind of the Master Class*, 5.

Chapter 2. The Amphytrion and St. Paul; the Planter and the Reformer

1. See Scott, 6:227.
2. Carothers, "Modern Hospitality," 120–21, hereafter cited parenthetically in text.
3. For example, the story that follows "Modern Hospitality" in this issue of *Godey's* is an installment of a five-part nostalgic tale of plantation life titled "Sketches of Southern Life," by Pauline Forsyth. The five installments appeared between May 1852 and August 1853.
4. See Lehuu, "Sentimental Figures," 82.
5. McNulty, *Hostess*, viii.
6. To return to Carothers's story from *Godey's* for a moment, as Lehuu points out, "*Godey's* epitomized the nineteenth century shift from a primarily devotional to an increasingly secular literature, blurring in a single medium the sacred and profane" ("Sentimental Figures," 83).
7. Wright, *Complete Home*, ix.
8. The titles of these various sketches published under the pseudonym Hermes include "The Mysteries of Bona Dea," "The Reformer," "The Mysterious Countess," "Gaston De Foix," "The Ghostly Banquet," "The Death of Chevalier D'Assas," and "The Prophecy"; all were published in the *New-York Mirror* during 1833, with the exception of "Gaston De Foix," which was published serially in the *Philadelphia Album* that same year.
9. Hermes, "Science of Hospitality."
10. C.C.O., "On Hospitality," emphasis in original.

11. Ibid.

12. Ibid.

13. Mireille Rosello has argued that the discourse of hospitality often "blurs the distinction between a discourse of rights and a discourse of generosity, the language of social contracts and the language of excess and gift-giving." See *Postcolonial Hospitality*, 9.

14. In light of the contrasts drawn in these two essays, I would also direct the reader's attention to an essay published in the *New-York Mirror* in 1838 that discussed the negative effects that fashionable or ostentatious practices of hospitality could have on the moral development of children in the household, warning that children "should be sheltered from the ostentatious and heartless intercourse that fashion authorizes." See "Family Circle."

15. Rosello, *Postcolonial Hospitality*, 14, 15.

16. See also McNulty's discussion of Derrida's reading of the story of Lot in *Hostess*, 15–22.

17. As Christie Anne Farnham explains, "young, unmarried women from the North" were largely responsible for the education of the female population of the southern social elite, and one of the most appealing features of this northern population of educators was that "these women were in a position to train their charges in the minutiae of etiquette by which distinctions could be drawn between the elite and others. In this regard they were essential in the socialization of the Southern belle." See Farnham, *Education of the Southern Belle*, 113.

18. Hartley, *Ladies' Book of Etiquette*, 3.

19. Etiquette books proliferated in nineteenth-century America, particularly from the 1820s onward, and several cultural historians have provided interesting analyses of etiquette and domestic advice literature of the nineteenth and, to a lesser extent, twentieth centuries. For examples, see especially Kasson, *Rudeness and Civility*; Hemphill, *Bowing to Necessities*; and Leavitt, *From Catherine Beecher to Martha Stewart*.

20. *Art of Good Behaviour*, ix.

21. Kasson and Hemphill both argue that the development of increasingly restrictive codes of manners in nineteenth-century America was an anxious response to the excesses of American democracy and class fluidity. See for example, Kasson, *Rudeness and Civility*, 6; and the third section of Hemphill, *Bowing to Necessities*. Hemphill claims that restrictive manners guided "behavior in a supposedly democratic but increasingly unequal society. The resulting rules allowed Americans to deal with the contradiction, largely by espousing one set of values while nonverbally communicating another" (9).

22. *Art of Pleasing*, vi–vii.

23. The following passage appears on pp. 28–29 of *The Art of Pleasing*; it is plagiarized from Calabrella, *Ladies' Science of Etiquette*:

> To receive visitors with ease and elegance, and in such a manner that everything in you, and about you, shall partake of propriety and grace—to endeavor that people may always be satisfied when they leave you, and be desirous to come again—are the obligations of the master, and especially of the mistress, of the house.

> Everything in the house ought, as far as possible, to offer English comfort, and French grace.
>
> Perfect order, exquisite neatness and elegance, which easily dispense with being sumptuous, ought to mark the entrance of the house, the furniture, and dress of the lady.
>
> In a house where affluence abounds, it is indispensable to have a drawing-room; if that can not be afforded, then let the receiving-room be the parlor. To receive company in a dining-room is not allowed, except among those who can not bear the expense of furnishing a parlor or drawing-room.

The Baroness de Calabrella's etiquette book was republished in varying forms in America between the 1840s and 1860s, including a T. B. Peterson edition in cheap paper wrappers that cost only twenty-five cents. This edition includes numerous advertisements inside its covers, and the back cover boldly announces: "BOOKS FOR EVERYBODY, PRINTED FOR THE 'MILLION,' AT GREATLY REDUCED RATES." The cheap material presentation contrasts sharply with the aristocratic tones of the text (as well as with frontispiece portrait of the baroness), suggesting that this particular edition probably provided its readers with fodder for daydreams rather than any useful etiquette guidance. Americans in the middle and even lower classes could at least fantasize about living like exclusive aristocrats or perhaps like hospitable southern planters, the closest thing we had to a natural aristocracy. Sarah A. Leavitt has argued that domestic advice literature has "always been the stuff of fantasy," and this particular edition provides excellent evidence of this. See Leavitt, *From Catherine Beecher to Martha Stewart*, 5. For more details on the publication history of the baroness's text, see Bobbitt, *Bibliography of Etiquette Books*.

24. *Art of Pleasing*, 47–48, 52. Conduct-of-life literature such as *Anecdotes for the Family and Social Circle* often included numerous stories warning against ostentatious display and emphasizing simplicity at the table when entertaining guests. They also included many tales of Christian hospitality either being rewarded or having the power to convert nonbelievers. See, for example, "A Widow and Her Son," "The Worldly Family," "Luxury," "William Wilberforce, Esq.," "An Innkeeper's Family," "A Christian Family" (24–25, 139, 140–41, 142–43, 250–53, 258–61).

25. Kirkland, "Chapter on Hospitality," 224, 225.

26. C. E. Beecher, *Treatise on Domestic Economy*, 257.

27. Ibid.

28. Ibid., 257–58.

29. Quoted in O'Brien, *Conjectures of Order*, 1:58.

30. Ibid., 1:2, 5, 7.

31. Calvin Henderson Wiley's *Roanoke, or, Where Is Utopia?* was first published serially in *Sartain's Union Magazine of Literature and Art* in 1849. It was subsequently republished under several other titles between 1849 and 1866. It appeared in London in 1851 under the title *The Adventures of Old Dan Tucker and His Son Walter*. Following the sensation over *Uncle Tom's Cabin*, it was published in 1852 by T. B. Peterson of Philadelphia under two different titles: *Life in the South: A Companion to Uncle Tom's Cabin*, and *Utopia, a Picture of Life in the South*. After the Civil War, Peterson published

it again under the original title of *Roanoke, or, Where Is Utopia?* See Johnson, "Southern Fiction Prior to 1860," 104–5. In the pages that follow I cite from the 1852 T. B. Peterson edition, *Life at the South: A Companion to Uncle Tom's Cabin*; citations are made parenthetically in the text.

32. See Jarrett, "Calvin H. Wiley"; and *Dictionary of North Carolina Biography*, 6:196–97. Though he is considered an important historical figure in southern educational history, very little scholarship has been devoted to Wiley's work as an author. Still, Wiley did figure in nineteenth-century literary debates on the question of the South's literary tradition: a deeply critical and satirical article that appeared in *Putnam's Monthly Magazine* in 1857 lambasted Wiley for censorship, namely, for his elimination from the North Carolina common schools any book that "tended to disseminate the heresy of human brotherhood." See "Southern Literature," 209–10. The article heaps scorn on efforts among southern writers and editors to create a distinctly southern literary tradition, and it also ridicules Wiley's public statements on North Carolina's literacy rates, noting that the state's mostly illiterate slave population does not figure in his statistics.

33. In the opening pages of his novel, Wiley directly and unapologetically states his goal in writing: to defend and celebrate North Carolina history and culture, and the southern way of life more generally. Noting that the lack of "commercial facilities" in North Carolina has at times led to "ridicule abroad," Wiley asserts that this very lack of commerce has in fact been a blessing. He goes on to draw familiar contrasts between the more progressive, industrial North and the more traditional, agrarian South; indeed, his contrasts forecast the statement of principles outlined by the Southern Agrarian group in their 1930 manifesto, *I'll Take My Stand*; see Wiley, *Roanoke*, 11–12.

34. As if his rants against the aristocracy were not ironic enough in a pro-slavery novel, Walter later meets up with a notorious runaway slave named Wild Bill and enters into a debate with him on the arbitrary nature of power and the relative rights of oppressed groups to revolt. Walter's lengthy dialogue with Wild Bill is unique among pro-slavery literature of the period, for Wiley creates a black character who argues with both logic and passion for his own freedom. Bill condemns the white race's treatment of the Indians and the African slaves, and his comments on the arbitrary nature of power echo Walter's own attitudes toward the aristocracy articulated only a few pages earlier. Bill goes on to argue that slaves have as much right to revolt against their masters as the colonists have a right to revolt against their king. Walter, however, claims that "the case is altogether different" because, first, the slaves have no chance of success, which would make it "useless bloodshed" (81); second, and more importantly, whites and blacks "are two distinct nations living in the same country, and one or the other must be masters of it" (81). Amazingly, Bill accepts Walter's argument as having the greater merit, acknowledging, "I know very well what you mean, and you need not apologize. My people were the lowest barbarians in Africa: they have been slaves here; and are, I know it well, vastly inferior to the whites" (81–82).

35. Robert Bladen, another survivor of the shipwreck at Utopia, serves as something of a foil to Walter Tucker. Walter earns his place in aristocratic society through his actions, while Robert is born into it. Robert takes advantage of his position, growing increasingly dissipated over the course of the novel and eventually making impure advances toward Utopia, who spurns him.

36. "Hospitality of the Olden Time."
37. Ibid.
38. Fox, "Mental Hospitality," 5.
39. Ibid., 6.
40. An 1856 column in the Unitarian *Christian Inquirer* magazine is similarly titled "Mental Hospitality" and follows a nearly identical pattern of development. It likewise begins by alluding to the same passage from Paul's Letter to the Hebrews, adding, "But why not heed it in respect to guests of the mind, as well as to those of the house? There is no inhospitality so full of suspicion, so determined to bar all newcomers, as that which is extended to ideas and truths having a strange aspect. There are many persons at the gates of whose minds a new truth might sit in a supplicatory attitude forever, ere they would ask it to come in." Echoing Fox's sentiments, hospitality here is more a state of mind than a set of social practices: "The liberal mind is courteous, it will avoid everything that looks like insult, coarse attack, and coarse ridicule." More importantly, the liberal mind's hospitality is absolutely essential if we are to have access to God's truth: "Truth is divine; it has a divine message; but it will have no message for us if we shut our minds and hearts against it because it is a stranger." See "Mental Hospitality."
41. Frothingham, "Christian Hospitality."
42. Ibid.
43. Ibid.
44. Ibid. Channing was no radical abolitionist and was in fact sharply criticized by William Lloyd Garrison for not being radical enough on the slavery question. He did adopt a stronger position near the end of his life, though. By the time Frothingham delivered this sermon (only two years before the Civil War), the abolition of slavery was a more mainstream position. The "look" of the "stranger" described here could be taken as the public's view of the American abolitionist movement's early days in the 1830s, when it was seen by many as "vulgar," ridiculous," and "fanatical."
45. Derrida writes, "To take up the figure of the door, for there to be hospitality, there must be a door. But if there is a door, there is no longer hospitality. There is no hospitable house. There is no house without doors and windows. But as soon as there are a door and windows, it means someone has the key to them and consequently controls the conditions of hospitality. There must be a threshold. But if there is a threshold, there is no longer hospitality. This is the difference, the gap, between the hospitality of invitation and the hospitality of visitation. In visitation there is no door. Anyone can come at any time and can come in without needing a key for the door. There are no customs checks with a visitation. But there are customs and police checks with an invitation. Hospitality thus becomes the threshold or the door" ("Hostipitality," 14).
46. Frothingham, "Christian Hospitality." As these examples have largely been from Unitarian ministers, it's worth noting that the general question of the hospitality of the church itself and of particular congregations toward strangers was also a matter of pressing concern at times. Several essays in the Unitarian *Christian Register* lament what the writers feel is a want of hospitality at some of Boston's most prominent churches. See, for example, "Hospitality of 'The Church,'" *Christian Register*, February 1, 1845; "Hospitality," *Christian Register*, August 29, 1846; and "Church Hospitality."
47. "Abolition Hospitality." See also "Hospitality," *Liberator*, November 26, 1847, for an

article that criticizes northerners both for accepting the claims of southern hospitality and for believing the common charge "that they are stingy and mean in comparison."

48. For a contemporary discussion of hospitality and the oppressed stranger as theorized by Levinas, see Zylinska, *Ethics of Cultural Studies*.

49. Kant, *Perpetual Peace*, 21. For an insightful discussion of the ambiguity behind the abolitionist motto "Our County Is the World" and its broader implications, see Greeson, *Our South*, 118–20.

50. While the industrial experiment of Lowell was a popular topic of discussion at the time among politicians, economists, and capitalists, Whittier warns his readers in the preface that his writings on Lowell were "influenced by no special considerations of practical utility"; instead, he simply wrote with "his heart open to the kindliest influence of nature and society." Whittier, *Stranger in Lowell*, v–vi, hereafter cited parenthetically in text. Whittier himself developed a considerable reputation for his practices of liberal hospitality. An 1883 article in the *Friends' Intelligencer* praises him for practicing "the truest type" of hospitality, which placed "all on equal terms," and particularly notes that "his home was a well-known refuge for fugitive slaves" (Rowe, "Quaker Poet," 12).

51. Jennifer Greeson describes how the growing anonymity of urban industrial life in the North led to northern nostalgia and a consequent fixation on traditional aspects of southern culture. According to Greeson, by the end of the 1830s the concept of the "Slave South" produced by the emergence of abolitionism had evolved to become an "indispensable cultural register" for handling the trauma of rapid modernization. By the early 1840s, "these two realms—industrial city and Slave South— . . . were bound together imaginatively for U.S. writers by their shared contradiction of the ideals of the republic, their joint location of power extremes, and their fundamental hostility to the very existence of the nation according to the terms of its founding." Published in 1845, Whittier's text bucks this trend by fully embracing the northern, urban-industrial environment, portraying it as a leveler of social distinction and a path to a more inclusive republic. See Greeson, *Our South*, 118–44; quotations from 133, 142.

52. For a thorough cultural history of the antebellum American response to Catholicism, see Franchot, *Roads to Rome*.

53. The chapter title is an allusion to George Henry Borrow's book, *The Zincali; or, An Account of the Gypsies of Spain* (Philadelphia: James M. Campbell, 1843).

54. As Susan M. Ryan explains, "In addition to their codes of manners, . . . antebellum Americans developed an etiquette of charity, one that identifies the duplicitous beggar as its enemy." See Ryan, *Grammar of Good Intentions*, 51.

55. Antislavery almanacs provide a good indication of the way the issue of hospitality could pervade a range of topics in abolitionist discourse. These almanacs contain numerous anecdotes, facts, and talking points, and they routinely derided southern social habits, expressed outrage and exasperation over the fact that southerners have a reputation for hospitality, drew on Scripture and the Constitution to advocate aiding runaway slaves and treating free blacks as equals, and criticized the inherent racism and inhospitality of the colonization movement and particular northern laws and social practices toward free black citizens. For examples, see *American Anti-Slavery Almanac for 1836*, 34–35, 37; *American Anti-Slavery Almanac for 1837*, 26; *American Anti-Slavery Almanac for 1839*, cover, inside cover, 23, 29, 46; *American Anti-Slavery Almanac*

for 1840, cover, 25; *American Anti-Slavery Almanac for 1841*, 9–15, 18, 19; *Liberty Almanac for 1850*, 34–35; *Liberty Almanac for 1852*, cover, 18–19.

Chapter 3. Making Hospitality a Crime

1. The U.S. Constitution contained a fugitive slave clause (article 4, section 2, clause 3): "No Person held to Service or Labour in one State, under the Laws thereof, escaping into another, shall, in Consequence of any Law or Regulation therein, be discharged from such Service or Labour, but shall be delivered up on Claim of the Party to whom such Service or Labour may be due." The 1793 Fugitive Slave Law, signed by President Washington, was meant to close loopholes in the original constitutional provision, but by 1850 the 1793 Law had become ineffectual and haphazard in its application. See Hamilton, *Prologue to Conflict*, 21–23. Hamilton's work remains the classic historical study of the 1850 Compromise.

2. See Laura L. Mitchell's analysis of religious discourse surrounding the Fugitive Slave Law, "'Matters of Justice.'"

3. For representative examples, see J. T. Randolph, *Cabin and the Parlor*, 182; Eastman, *Aunt Phillis's Cabin*, 20; D. Brown, *Planter*, 216, 273; Evangelicus, *Onesimus*. The *Liberator* includes scores of references to the Epistle to Philemon, including the following representative examples: Whittier, "Sabbath Scene"; "Puzzle for Philemon"; "Philemon and Onesimus."

4. See, for example, Ralph A. Keller's study of Methodist newspapers' responses to the Fugitive Slave Law. His study surveys five northern Methodist newspapers with a combined circulation of over seventy thousand Americans, showing that, in regard to the 1850 Compromise, "it was the Fugitive Slave Law which aroused the greatest anxiety. Not only did the Methodist weekly press give attention to the fugitive slave portion of the Compromise of 1850 far out of proportion to the attention given it in Congress, but also the attention was unanimously negative, even by conservative editors who ordinarily sought to avoid political issues" (Keller, "Methodist Newspapers," 322).

5. Seward, *Works of William H. Seward*, 1:65–66, 74.

6. As Julie Roy Jeffrey explains, the "growing discomfort with the Fugitive Slave Law provided an opening for abolitionist propaganda, while the enforcement of the law created the material for a persuasive case against slavery" (Jeffrey, *Great Silent Army of Abolitionism*, 176).

7. Scanning the pages of the *Liberator* for 1850 and 1851 reveals how the debate over the Fugitive Slave Law brought the subject of hospitality to the forefront of abolitionist consciousness at the time and also how it intersected with other issues such as the plight of black sailors in southern states and, by early 1851, the arrival of Louis Kossuth (both subjects I discuss in the next chapter). During this period, the *Liberator* made constant references to the moral, biblical, political, legal, and constitutional claims of hospitality. For a range of examples in a variety of forms—essays, letters, anecdotes, news reports, poems—see "Daniel Webster"; "Fugitive Slave to the Christian"; "Mr. Webster's Speech on Slavery"; "Letter to Henry Clay"; "Puzzle for Philemon"; Whittier, "Sabbath Scene"; Bungay, "Scene in Boston"; "Colored Seamen in South Carolina"; "Imprisonment of Colored Seamen"; "Declaration of Sentiments"; "Did Willie Do Wrong?"

8. "Fugitive Slave to the Christian."

9. According to Jeffrey, the passage of the Fugitive Slave Law "brought the plight of the fugitive slave into the foreground of abolitionists' consciences and shaped the activities they undertook during the decade" of the 1850s, providing women with a "tangible purpose" in the broader cause of abolitionism. See Jeffrey, *Great Silent Army*, 179, 188–89.

10. *Liberty Almanac for 1852*, 18–19.

11. Emerson, "Fugitive Slave Law," 11:219.

12. Crane, *Race, Citizenship, and Law*, 17.

13. Whitman, *Leaves of Grass*, 28.

14. For a thorough consideration of Whitman's complex and evolving views on race, slavery, and the South, see Reynolds, *Walt Whitman's America*.

15. Charles Beecher, *Duty of Disobedience to Wicked Laws*, 14.

16. Ibid.

17. Ibid.

18. Ibid., 21–22.

19. Pointing first to the "Golden Rule" of "Do unto others as ye would that others should do unto you," he asks the members of his congregation to imagine that, while on a cross-country journey to California, they have been taken prisoner by hostile Indians and reduced to "the most servile condition." Later the Indians threaten to separate parents from children, which prompts them to attempt an escape. After describing their successful escape and travails as fugitives, Arvine asks his congregation to imagine reaching the door of a "Home missionary" who nonetheless turns them away due to the provisions of law that prevent him from receiving them: "So he shuts the door in your face, and leaves you and your family faint, hungry, and cold, to bide the winter storm and drag on your weary way further. What think you? Would not your head and heart at once and utterly condemn him as one who so poorly understood the law of love, that instead of being a teacher of the heathen, he had 'Need that one teach' him which be the first principles of the gospel of Christ? You feel, you *know* that such conduct, in such a case, would be most palpably unjust, most infamously cruel." Arvine asserts that this scenario is completely parallel to the situation of fugitive slaves fleeing from the South: southerners have no greater right to enslave Africans than Indians have to enslave white settlers. See Arvine, *Our Duty to the Fugitive Slave*, 15–16.

20. Ibid., 19–20.

21. H. B. Stowe, "Freeman's Dream."

22. Crane, *Race, Citizenship, and Law*, 60.

23. H. B. Stowe, *Uncle Tom's Cabin*, 118–19, 121–23.

24. Quoted in Hedrick, *Harriet Beecher Stowe*, 205–6.

25. Seward, *Works of William H. Seward*, 1:66.

26. Stowe, *Uncle Tom's Cabin*, 133–34.

27. As Mitchell explains, pro-rendition ministers from the North "justified the reenslavement of fugitives by establishing the Union as the most important community for Christian citizens and ultimately, the most important community in the world.... In numerous sermons, northern Protestant ministers from nearly every denomination preached that the Union, the white citizenry's community, was divinely or-

dained and that the Constitution was its divinely inspired set of laws. The Constitution was to the Union what, in effect, the Ten Commandments had been to the Hebrews" (Mitchell, "'Matters of Justice,'" 150–51).

28. Lord, *"Higher Law,"* 4, 15–16.

29. Quoted in Mitchell, "'Matters of Justice,'" 152.

30. Butt, *Anti-Fanaticism*, v, 15, 16, 17.

31. Ibid., 23.

32. Tower, *Slavery Unmasked*, 410.

33. See Drew, *Refugees from Slavery*, ix–xi. According to Tilden G. Edelstein, editor of this modern reissue of Benjamin Drew's 1855 collection, *A North Side View of Slavery*, the 1854 publication of Adams's account created something of a crisis in the abolitionist movement already demoralized by the passage of the Kansas-Nebraska Act, for Adams, a well-known Boston minister, directly challenged the veracity of *Uncle Tom's Cabin* and drew conclusions regarding the paternalistic institution of slavery similar to those outlined by George Fitzhugh in *Sociology for the South; or, the Failure of Free Society*, published that same year. Adams was repeatedly attacked in the *Liberator*.

34. The Philadelphia publishing houses of T. B. Peterson and Lippincott, Grambo both published extensive lists of pro-southern texts throughout the sectional crisis and even after the Civil War. These publishing houses exploited a niche market and political controversy, and they perhaps felt complementary economic and political motivations for their production and distribution of these texts. They also enjoyed closer proximity to southern markets than Boston and New York publishing houses.

35. Eastman opens the chapter by downplaying her capacity to adequately portray this scene, comparing her meager efforts to those of the "master," James Fenimore Cooper. She alludes in particular to his 1821 Revolutionary War romance *The Spy*, and the opening chapter where General Washington, in disguise, seeks out the hospitality of the Wharton family as a storm approaches: "It was in the olden time that Cooper described a dinner party in all its formal, but hospitable perfection. Washington was a guest there, too, though an unacknowledged one." This allusion to Cooper's novel—and particularly to the founding father Washington—places her own domestic scene amid a broader, national political and cultural context, subtly underscoring the theme of a shared heritage of hospitality. Eastman, *Aunt Phillis's Cabin*, 88. See also Cooper, *Spy*, 23.

36. Eastman, *Aunt Phillis's Cabin*, 91, 95, 96.

37. Ibid., 96.

38. See Weld, *American Slavery as It Is*.

39. In addition to being perhaps the most famous novelistic response to *Uncle Tom's Cabin*, the novel is notable for its early treatment of the subject of divorce.

40. Caroline Lee Hentz was actually a native of Massachusetts who moved to North Carolina following her marriage and subsequently lived most of her adult life in states across the South. Hentz was a highly successful author of several novels, and she was also personally acquainted with Harriet Beecher Stowe from time spent in Cincinnati earlier in her career. For a thorough discussion of her career and standing in the literary marketplace, see Moss, *Domestic Novelists of the Old South*.

41. Hentz, *Planter's Northern Bride*, 40, hereafter cited parenthetically in text.

42. Later, Hastings further violates the laws of hospitality even when extending them to Moreland, who is invited to the house for dinner. After enjoying a meal and conversation, Hastings ruins the visit by presenting Moreland with copies of the "Emancipator," edited by Mr. Hastings himself. In short, Hentz portrays Hastings's hospitality as motivated by selfishness rather than generosity of spirit: "Mr. Hastings, like most men, was actuated by mixed motives. He believed in the good old scripture injunction of hospitality to strangers, and he was exceedingly fond of making impressions, and enlarging the bounds of his influence.... He loved to have strangers call at his house, assured that when they left the place, they would carry the impression that Mr. Hastings was the greatest man in the village" (60).

43. A similar scenario occurs in the novel *Mr. Frank, the Underground Mail-Agent*, another pro-slavery response to Stowe published under the pseudonym "Vidi" in 1853 (also by Lippincott, Grambo). Mr. Frank, an abolitionist and agent for the Underground Railroad, has helped Tom run away from slavery, even giving him money to establish himself in Canada, but when Tom and his wife show up again at Mr. Frank's door to ask for additional assistance, Mr. Frank learns a sad lesson regarding his misplaced charity: "When he left his master, some two years previously, through the persuasions of Mr. Frank, [Tom] ... was a well-dressed, obedient, steady man—now he was dirty, ragged, and saucy; and presented, in every respect, most unquestionable appearances of leading a drunken, vagabond life. Mr. Frank seemed to be fully impressed with this truth, and a painful cloud passed over his countenance." Mr. Frank is much like the character of Squire Hastings in Hentz's novel: both are portrayed as hypocritical idealists who devote themselves to the distant cause of the southern slaves while neglecting the worthier, whiter objects of charity in their own, more local sphere. Mr. Frank's daughter Emma, who is more vocal than Eula Hastings, questions him directly on these apparent contradictions of character in chapter 3 (36–45). See Vidi, *Mr. Frank, the Underground Mail-Agent*, 47.

44. Claudia, for example, violates the laws of hospitality by boldly allowing herself into Eula's home unannounced in order to confront Eula. Later, we find that when she had been married to Moreland, she and her mother were in the habit of "introducing... unprincipled companions into his household during his absence, and making his home a scene of midnight revelry" (375). Brainard also violates the laws of hospitality, though much more dramatically, by taking advantage of Moreland's hospitality in order to carry out his plans for a slave insurrection (see p. 457). This notion of duplicitous abolitionists taking advantage of southern hospitality is a recurring trope in pro-slavery novels of the period. As a character in Robert Criswell's *"Uncle Tom's Cabin" Contrasted with Buckingham Hall* states, "If those Northern abolitionists were to stop their meddling in our concerns, the condition of the slaves would be much improved. They come among us as friends—and while enjoying our hospitality, whisper sedition and conspiracy into the ears of our slaves, and often go so far as to steal them from us. If they were to let us alone, there is no doubt that, in the course of years, not a slave State would be in existence; and for my part I should rejoice to see that time arrive" (58).

45. Carme Manual Cuenca sees Eulalia as a figure who represents "literary democratization" and suggests that the nationalistic model of womanhood presented in the

novel is "the American middle-class lady, not the Southern aristocratic lady." Critics such as Cuenca and Kathryn Seidel have been right to argue that the novel's intersectional marriage of Eulalia Hastings, a village maiden of Massachusetts, and the aristocratic southerner planter Russell Moreland, stands as a proffered solution to the intersectional political impasse; however, they have failed to sense the important point the novel makes regarding class. See Cuenca, "Angel in the Plantation," 97; and Seidel, *Southern Belle in the American Novel*.

46. Novels and travel narratives about the South written in this period often dwell in great detail on the social details of hospitality—of families, friends, and visitors around the table or around the hearth. These scenes often do little to advance the plot or story line, but they do create a recognizable space for like-minded Americans to imagine an amiable social engagement with the South, southerners, and slavery. That these depictions are taken seriously is seen in one of the most pointed criticisms David Brown offers of Stowe's *Uncle Tom's Cabin* in his book, *The Planter*. In particular, Brown singles out a scene in which Shelby, Uncle Tom's first owner, dines with a slave trader. Brown is absolutely incredulous that Stowe would depict a high-born planter such as Shelby entertaining a lowly slave trader at the dinner table (32–35).

47. While Douglass traveled to England even before the passage of the 1850 Fugitive Slave Law, Brown happened to be abroad when the law was passed and was consequently forced to remain in England for nearly five years, with his daughters eventually joining him there as well. While living abroad, both Douglass and Brown had their freedom purchased for them by English supporters, allowing them to return to the United States in relative safety.

48. *The American Fugitive in Europe* includes an abbreviated, revised version of Brown's 1847 slave narrative, *Narrative of William W. Brown, a Fugitive Slave, Written by Himself*, this time written in the third-person and presented as a "memoir."

49. Rights of citizenship were tenuous for free blacks in the antebellum period and up until the passage of the Fourteenth Amendment in 1868. Only some states granted citizenship rights to blacks, and the Supreme Court's 1857 Dred Scott decision declared that no black resident living in America could be deemed a citizen, whether slave or free. For an insightful discussion of the role travel and mobility played in the construction of antebellum American identity—including the travel narratives of slaves and runaways—see John D. Cox, *Traveling South*. According to Cox's readings of American travel narratives, "travel is constitutive of American freedom and identity, serving as proof of . . . [the authors'] status (or lack thereof) as American citizens" (18). While Cox focuses on travel within the boundaries of the United States, it's interesting to consider how these narratives of fugitive slaves traveling abroad both extend and perhaps complicate his thesis.

50. For example, according to Douglass, the hospitality practiced on the Lloyd plantation "would have astonished and charmed any health-seeking northern divine or merchant, who might have chanced to share it. Viewed from his own table, and *not* from the field, the colonel was a model of generous hospitality." Douglass goes on to describe the "magnificent entertainments" for visitors, which created a graceful veneer over the institution of slavery. The plantation home was transformed into "a hotel, for weeks during the summer months," and the goal was always to "dazzle"

and "charm"—as well as to persuade—the visitors. Reflecting on the effects produced on visitors by the figure of the gracious, paternalistic master surrounded by well-trained, well-dressed, and graceful house slaves (the only scene shown to guests), Douglass states that only "a fanatic" could be expected to feel any sympathy for the slave. But according to Douglass, the scene is only "a sham at last! This immense wealth; this gilded splendor; this profusion of luxury; this exemption from toil; this life of ease; this sea of plenty; aye, what of it all?" "The poor slave" in the field or "on his hard, pine plank, but scantily covered with his thin blanket" remain out of sight for the visitors. It's also worth noting that Douglass, as a self-made black man who raised himself out of slavery, presents, in many ways, a more recognizably "American" version of identity for the reader than the idle, aristocratic slave owner, whose life free from work breeds nothing but "restless discontent" and "capricious irritation." Later Douglass also adds a new critique of the false hospitality that Master Auld provides for pro-slavery ministers. These pro-slavery ministers who come "to share Master Thomas's hospitality" are fed "on the fat of the land," while his slaves are "nearly starving." See Douglass, *My Bondage and My Freedom*, 110–11, 197–98. For a detailed analysis of the way that Douglass self-consciously re-creates his personal narrative in *My Bondage and My Freedom* as that of a representative American, see chapter 3 of Levine, *Martin Delany, Frederick Douglass*. The passage just cited on Lloyd's dissipated form of hospitality figures in Levine's analysis of Douglass's temperance agenda in *My Bondage and My Freedom*, 120–21.

51. Brown's 1852 travel narrative, *Three Years in Europe*, also included the "memoir" of Brown in the first section of the text, but for this English edition, the scene of Wells Brown's hospitality is less developed than in either his 1847 slave narrative or in the 1855 *American Fugitive in Europe*, both published for American audiences. See W. W. Brown, *Three Years in Europe*, xvii–xviii.

52. W. W. Brown, *Narrative of William W. Brown*, iii, 102–3.

53. W. W. Brown, *American Fugitive in Europe*, 26.

54. For a thorough analysis of these complicated issues regarding essentialist racial thinking and abolitionism, see Levine, *Martin Delany, Frederick Douglass*. In the case of Douglass and Delany, these issues become especially fraught in regard to their contrasting responses to Stowe's *Uncle Tom's Cabin* and their conflicting stances on black emigration to Africa (and, in Delany's case, the Caribbean).

55. See Greenspan, *William Wells Brown Reader*, 130–35, 130.

56. W. W. Brown, *American Fugitive in Europe*, 303, 305.

57. See Greenspan, *William Wells Brown Reader*, 134.

58. W. W. Brown, *American Fugitive in Europe*, 306, 312.

59. Ibid., 312–14.

60. Douglass, *My Bondage and My Freedom*, 372–71.

61. Ibid., 372.

Chapter 4. Southern Hospitality in a Transnational Context

1. Zinn, *Southern Mystique*, 249. Zinn's overall point is to also challenge the American habit of projecting undesirable attributes on the South, and he goes on to

critique the xenophobia of America more generally, citing several examples of national xenophobia. He concludes, "It ill becomes us to let the South bear the burden of the charge of nativism or xenophobia" (252).

2. Derrida and Dufourmantelle, *Of Hospitality*, 25.

3. Hale in the preface describes the Liberian experiment as the Union's act of charity on behalf of the slave. A native of New Hampshire, Hale was sympathetic to southerners, as she made clear in her preface to the 1852 fifth edition of *Northwood*, written in the wake of the Fugitive Slave Law, where she openly admonishes abolitionists: "The great error of those who would sever the Union rather than see a slave within its borders, is, that they forget that the *master* is their brother as well as the *servant*." But for Hale, the master certainly had the greater claim of being treated like a brother. S. J. Hale, *Northwood*, iv.

4. S. J. Hale, *Liberia*, 6, iv, 191–93.

5. For another example of the racial underpinnings of Sarah Josepha Hale's domesticity, see her *Manners*. Published a few years after the end of the Civil War, the structure of the book appeals to ideals of national unity by focusing on national holidays (Washington's Birthday, Independence Day, and Thanksgiving), but it also links domestic manners to a specifically white identity. As Hale states in the preface, "When we study domestic life in its influence on national characteristics, it seems as if the two Anglo-Saxon Peoples were intrusted with the holy duty of keeping pure the home of woman and the altar of God.... The Anglo-Saxon peoples have another bond of unity,—they represent home life, in its highest characteristics among the nobility of England, and in its best aspects of purity and happiness in America. These characteristics and virtues of the Princely and the Popular are united in the MANNERS that form the most perfect standard for social life and home happiness" (5–6).

6. Thoreau, *Essays of Henry D. Thoreau*, 134.

7. See Hamer, "Great Britain," 3.

8. Both sources—the comment from Governor Wilson and the excerpt from the law—are quoted in Bolster, *Black Jacks*, 194.

9. As Edlie Wong explains, these coastal states in the South "seized on their sovereign power to decide on the value and nonvalue of life as they effectively deemed certain individuals outside the political community and, therefore, alienable as property. Only two legal identities existed for black sailors under the specific provisions of such police laws: they were either prisoners or slaves. And the prisoner quickly became a slave if the jail fees went unpaid" (Wong, *Neither Fugitive nor Free*, 184).

10. See Bolster, *Black Jacks*, 206.

11. See Wong, *Neither Fugitive nor Free*, 188–91.

12. See Hamer, "British Consuls," 146–52.

13. See Hamer, "Great Britain," 5–7.

14. Thoreau, *Essays of Henry D. Thoreau*, 335.

15. Thoreau's essay was first delivered as a lecture in January 1848 and was first published in essay form the following year. See Thoreau, *Essays of Henry D. Thoreau*, 330.

16. Ibid., 335. This logic is consistent with the message of the "Abolition Hospitality" advertisement discussed in chapter 2.

17. Ibid., 134, 143.

18. See Fanuzzi, *Abolition's Public Sphere*, for a thorough discussion of cosmopolitanism and abolitionism. Of Thoreau's cosmopolitanism in *Walden*, Fanuzzi states that Thoreau "looked forward to... the arrival of cosmopolitanism in the wake of town's destruction. In the 'Conclusion' to *Walden*, he recommended the model of the 'cosmopolite' over the life of the provincial village, whose residents would 'think if rail-fences were pulled down, and stone-walls piled upon our farms, bounds are henceforth set to our lives and our fates decided'" (177).

19. Benhabib, *Another Cosmopolitanism*, 15–16, 19–20, 31.

20. Quoted in Wong, *Neither Fugitive nor Free*, 197.

21. In *Neither Fugitive nor Free*, Wong traces the decades-long controversy surrounding these laws from the time they were enacted up until the Civil War, noting that when legal appeals were regularly blocked,

> Antislavery activists and opponents of this police regulation increasingly turned to the 'bar of public opinion.'... Black and white abolitionists and merchants, southern reformers, and free blacks within the Atlantic world forged unexpected alliances as they endeavored to push the issue to the top of the political agenda. In the failure of law, they turned to newsprint, pamphleteering, and literature as they sought to enlist the 'public mind' to do the work that legislators and jurists refused to do. These writers and orators, such as [David] Walker, drew forth a revolutionary black consciousness from the law's negativity and limits, creating an oppositional agenda over these many decades of intermittent transatlantic protest. (Wong, *Neither Fugitive nor Free*, 185)

22. Only two scholars have written on Adams's antislavery writings: Harold Woodell and Edlie Wong. Woodell, drawing on earlier reference works, identifies Adams as an American author, but Wong, pointing to contemporary reviews of his novel, identifies him as an Englishman. Woodell describes Adams's temporary successes as a theater professional in Charleston and traces subsequent legal proceedings against Adams that resulted in his incarceration in the Charleston jail for the inability to pay his debts. Here he may have come face-to-face with mariners jailed under the Negro Seamen Laws. In contrast, Wong also discusses Adams's work as editor of a Savannah, Georgia, newspaper and cites an unverified early review that traces his point of increasing activism to his time in Charleston, where he saw the Samuel Hoar affair unfold. See Wong, *Neither Fugitive nor Free*; and Woodell, "Justice Denied in the Old South."

23. Adams, *Manuel Pereira*, 15, hereafter cited parenthetically in text. As Wong notes, "Free black mariners... best typified the cosmopolitanism" outlined in David Walker's incendiary text, "An Appeal to the Coloured Citizens of the World," and such "black maritime circulation... threatened slaveholding localisms in a world where freedom seemed to inch westward" (Wong, *Neither Fugitive nor Free*, 183, 185).

24. After describing to a shipmate his close encounter with Patagonia savages, Manuel explains that he prefers to "always sail in English ship, because [he] can get protection from flag and consul, where [he goes]—any part of the globe" (19). His shipmate in responding casts England and America as the guiding powers in the world's progress toward universal human rights, and he also portrays this progress as inevi-

table: "It's a glorious thing, this civilization, and if the world keeps on, there'll be no danger of a fellow's being imprisoned or killed among these savages.... Men neither imprison nor kill strangers, that don't fear the injustice of their own acts" (19).

25. Greene and Hoffius, "Charleston 100."

26. Koger, *Black Slaveowners*, 147, 153–54.

27. A petition for Jones asking that he be allowed to return to South Carolina was submitted to the South Carolina Senate by former governor John L. Wilson, who served as Jones's "Guardian at Law" and was also the very governor who had supported the creation of these laws in the first place; no action was taken by the senate in response to the petition. For the text of this petition, see Schweninger, *Southern Debate over Slavery*, 1:87. It should also be noted that Jones's son, Jehu Jones Jr., also found himself subject to the law some years later. The younger Jones, a free black and Lutheran minister, had left South Carolina in preparation for immigrating to Liberia with other free blacks from Charleston. When he attempted to return to South Carolina, he was arrested and expelled from the state. An 1840 petition from Jones to the South Carolina Senate was denied. See Schweninger, *Southern Debate over Slavery*, 173. See also Aaseng, *African American Religious Leaders*, 125.

28. As Philip M. Hamer summarizes, "In one sense this law represented, not only an attempt to protect the institution of slavery, but an assertion of the state's rights to exercise police power.... Some stubbornly defended the law because it was so roundly criticized by 'outsiders.' Others were opposed to making any concession because northerners desired it. In some quarters there existed a feeling of antagonism to Great Britain, ... in part ... a reaction against Britain's antislavery tendencies.... In part it was the result of provincial dislike of foreigners in general" (Hamer, "British Consuls," 144–45).

29. Benhabib, *Another Cosmopolitanism*, 65, 68.

30. As Donald S. Spencer explains, "So convinced was the nation of Kossuth's virtue that it became hazardous to attack him publicly or to question his dedication to those principles Americans claimed as their own" (Spencer, *Louis Kossuth and Young America*, 43).

31. "Kossuth and Congress."

32. The text of the resolution reads as follows:

> Whereas the people of the United States sincerely sympathize with the Hungarian exiles, Kossuth and his associates, and fully appreciate the magnanimous conduct of the Turkish Government in receiving and treating these noble exiles with kindness and hospitality; and if it be the wish of these exiles to emigrate to the United States, and the will of the Sultan to permit them to leave his dominions: Therefore,
>
> *Be it resolved by the Senate and House of Representatives of the United States of America in Congress assembled,* That the President of the United States be and he hereby is requested to authorize the employment of some one of the public vessels which may now be cruising in the Mediterranean to receive and convey to the United States the said Louis Kossuth and his associates in captivity. (Cong. Globe, 31st Cong., 2nd Sess., Senate Special Session, 710 [1851])

33. Honig, *Democracy and the Foreigner*, 2, 4, 39, 7.

34. See T. M. Roberts, *Distant Revolutions*, 18.

35. See T. M. Roberts, *Distant Revolutions*, 131. See also Roberts's discussion of southerners' initial response to the revolutions of 1848 (125–29).

36. "EN AVANT!," 142–143.

37. In typical fashion, an article titled "Kossuth" from *Gleason's Pictorial Drawing-Room Companion* predicted, "In America, wherever ... [Kossuth] goes, his welcome will be as enthusiastic and general as it is sincere, and every arrangement made to give him a generous reception." *The National Era* went further by calling on Congress to provide material refuge for the exiles: "Will not Congress ... signalize its devotion to the great cause of republicanism in Europe, and its appreciation of the services of these, its gallant, but unfortunate champions, by giving them homes upon our soil? We are all brethren in the sacred cause of liberty; but, while we won a continent by striking for freedom, they have lost a country. Let us, then, impart to them freely of our blessings. We have sent a national vessel to bring Kossuth to our shores. Shall our hospitality cease with this?" See "Liberation of Kossuth."

38. The title of an article published in the *New York Daily Times* also plays on this stereotype. See "'Organ' upon Kossuth." The article offers a liberal response to a recent *Washington Republic* story on Kossuth and laments the emerging sectional divisions regarding his national reception.

39. See also Julian, "America's Welcome to Kossuth."

40. Whittier, "Kossuth." For a more typical poem of welcome for Kossuth, see Julian, "America's Welcome to Kossuth."

41. See Spencer, *Louis Kossuth and Young America*, 65–81.

42. Cong. Globe, 32nd Cong., 1st Sess., 21 (1851).

43. Ibid., 22.

44. Ibid.

45. Spencer, *Louis Kossuth and Young America*, 72–73.

46. Cong. Globe, 32nd Cong., 1st Sess., 22 (1851), emphasis in original.

47. Ibid., 23.

48. Ibid., 23–24, emphasis in original.

49. Ibid., 25–26.

50. Cong. Globe, 32nd Cong., 1st Sess., 34 (1851).

51. See Komlos, *Louis Kossuth in America*, 81–84. For an example of northern media exasperation over the South's growing resistance to Kossuth and the idea of intervening in foreign affairs, see "South and Intervention." As the article summarizes, "The prominent politicians of the South seem determined to make the policy of nonintervention a sectional issue. They proclaim the hostility of the South to any diplomatic action on the part of our Government concerning Russian intervention in the domestic affairs of Hungary. Southern politicians in Congress and their leading presses throughout their section of the Union, are generally hostile to Kossuth and his cause."

52. See Spencer, *Louis Kossuth and Young America*, 147–48. See also T. M. Roberts, *Distant Revolutions*, 148, 162–63. The visit to New Orleans included other uncomfortable moments for Kossuth; as Timothy Mason Roberts notes, "City officials escorted

Kossuth both to the battleground of Andrew Jackson's victory over a British force in 1815 and to a slave auction, scenes awkwardly suggesting Southerners' tension at hearing a Hungarian preach self-determination for his own country" (162).

53. *Mississippi Free Trader* excerpts quoted in Spencer, *Louis Kossuth and Young America*, 103–4, 148.

54. See, for example, "Whimsicalities"; and "Outlines of English Literature." The latter, for example, points readers to a scathing attack on Kossuth and the idea of intervention in the *Southern Quarterly Review*. The article calls Kossuth "a sort of political Jenny Lind" who "would have done vastly better, if he had placed himself ... under the charge and management of Mr. Barnum." Regarding the notion of universal rights that Kossuth had come to symbolize, the writer dismisses the notion and calls Kossuth a "political pedlar of unsound wares." See "Kossuth and Intervention," 226, 228.

55. T. M. Roberts, *Distant Revolutions*, 154.

56. For example, following her description of the heroic fugitive slave George Harris in *Uncle Tom's Cabin*, Harriet Beecher Stowe pointedly chastises Americans for their inconsistent support of freedom fighters:

> If it had been only a Hungarian youth, now bravely defending in some mountain fastness the retreat of fugitives escaping from Austria into America, this would have been sublime heroism; but as it was a youth of African descent, defending the retreat of fugitives through America into Canada, of course we are too well instructed and patriotic to see any heroism in it; and if any of our readers do, they must do it on their own private responsibility. When despairing Hungarian fugitives make their way, against all the search-warrants and authorities of their lawful government, to America, press and political cabinet ring with applause and welcome. When despairing African fugitives do the same thing,—it is—what *is* it? (H. B. Stowe, *Uncle Tom's Cabin*, 284)

57. E. E. Hale, *Christian Duty to Emigrants*, 21.

58. Ibid., 22.

Chapter 5. Reconstructing Southern Hospitality in the Postbellum World

1. Hodgson, *Sermon in Behalf*, 11.

2. Ibid., 16.

3. Ibid., 12.

4. For a detailed history of the way the initial promise of Reconstruction was undermined and eventually extinguished, see Foner, *Reconstruction*. For a study of the changing way the Civil War was remembered in American culture, see Blight, *Race and Reunion*. Nina Silber also considers the themes of reunion and nostalgia, with attention paid to the emerging southern tourism industry, in *Romance of Reunion*. Grace Elizabeth Hale describes the contemporaneous development of segregation culture and the national consumer marketplace in *Making Whiteness*, while more recently, K. Stephen Prince outlines the various ways popular and print culture redefined the South in the American imagination in his book *Stories of the South*.

5. For a detailed analysis of causes, contexts, and complex social codes in the southern practice of lynching during the late nineteenth and early twentieth centuries, see

Brundage, *Lynchings in the New South*. Brundage offers a sweeping, comparative analysis of nearly six hundred lynchings that occurred in the two states over this period. See also chapter 5 of Grace Elizabeth Hale's *Making Whiteness*. Hale focuses on the emergence of "spectacle lynchings," showing that even as the numbers of lynchings began to decrease, their symbolic potency was enhanced as lynchings became increasingly commodified through postcards, photographs, advertising campaigns in the media prior to lynchings, and national press coverage.

6. Lincoln, "House Divided," 372–73.

7. Amy Kaplan radically challenges traditional scholarly readings of nineteenth-century feminine domesticity by showing how antebellum discourses of domesticity and empire were inextricably linked and how both were "dependent upon racialized notions of the foreign." Domesticity has traditionally been understood as an "anchor" or "feminine counterforce to the male activity of territorial conquest," but as Kaplan shows, nineteenth-century domesticity was "more mobile and less stabilizing" than we typically think, moving along often "contradictory circuits both to expand and contract the boundaries of home and nation and to produce shifting conceptions of the foreign." More specifically, Kaplan shows that part of the "cultural work" of domesticity was to "unite men and women in a national domain and to generate notions of the foreign against which the nation can be imagined as a home." The discourse of hospitality was similarly mobile—ranging from inclusive and progressive to exclusive and reactionary—in its construction of otherness. See Kaplan, "Manifest Domesticity," 183–85.

8. Wright in the preface directly addresses the book to those readers "who spent the last few years in the peaceful East" and assures them "that there is in this enlightened land such a region of darkness" as that depicted in the novel, a region populated by "bushwhackers" and "guerrillas" but also by families who have faced "trials that have pressed hard on living hearts." In the novel's opening pages, Wright defines "the Brush" as the border region between southwestern Missouri and Arkansas populated mainly by "uncouth children" and "men and women, with scarcely a thought rising above the earth they live upon." These uncivilized inhabitants of the western frontier are the antithesis of Wright's domestic middle-class readership in the East, but she nonetheless reminds her readers of their common humanity: "Here, nevertheless, poor, degraded, and outcast, live those bound to us as kindred by common descent, bodies that must moulder, as we shall, under the sod, and souls that shall meet us at the bar of God" (Wright, *Cabin in the Brush*, 5, 8–9, hereafter cited parenthetically in text). The first edition of the novel was published by J. A. Moore in 1867; J. P. Skelly published editions in 1870 and 1872. I cite here a copy of the 1870 edition housed in the American Antiquarian Society in Worcester, Mass. It is likely that the same plates were used for all these editions.

9. For a sharply contrasting use of the hospitality trope in relation to Reconstruction politics, consider the obscure white supremacist book by A. C. Harness, *The Great Trial*, with its lamenting of the passing of southern hospitality, its use of the trope of the "good "Samaritan," and its apocalyptic views of miscegenation (9–25, 88).

10. For evidence of Woolson's shrewd nostalgia, which quietly incorporated white northerners of a certain class, see her travel sketch of Charleston, "Up the Ashley and

Cooper." Woolson seems to celebrate the class distinctions implicit in the discourse of southern hospitality; she also reminds her readers that the original Charlestonians included "the only bona fide United States nobility of which we have record"(3), and she goes on to paint a romantic picture of the "great magnificence" and "lavishness" of the planter lifestyle. There is little mention of the war or slavery and no hint of the complicated politics of Reconstruction. Instead, Woolson's narrative, like much of the period literature described by Silber, seems "directed to the potential tourist" (73). Her travel account opens with a detailed picture of Charleston from the aerial view of St. Michael's Church spire, where it is possible to make out the Battery, Fort Sumter, Morris Island, and "the old ridge of Battery Wagner," though Woolson does not elaborate. Instead, after briefly describing the "picturesque" qualities of the city streets and architecture, her narrative moves "up the two rivers to search out the old manors, with their legends and history, now almost forgotten, of colonial times and of the Revolution" (4). Published on the eve of the nation's centennial year, "Up the Ashley and Cooper" turns away from the present—from the fresh memories of the Civil War and the stubborn political uncertainties of Reconstruction—and back toward the shared mythology of the colonial era and the Revolutionary War, when northerners and southerners stood united against the British.

11. Woolson, *Rodman the Keeper*, 108. Quotations from the stories "Old Gardiston" and "Rodman the Keeper" are drawn from this text and hereafter cited parenthetically in the text.

12. In "Rodman the Keeper," which I discuss later, Bettina Ward has a similarly melodramatic reaction when she finds out that her cousin, a dying Confederate veteran, has been taken in by a Union soldier who maintains the National Cemetery. She cannot address Rodman as an equal; instead, "she spoke to him as though he was something to be paid and dismissed like any other mechanic" (26). She in fact does attempt to pay Rodman for his services to her cousin, but she is humiliated even further when Rodman knowingly states a price that she cannot afford.

13. See Silber, *Romance of Reunion*, especially chapter 2, 39–65.

14. Though the exact location is never indicated, one might presume that it is Andersonville based on the numbers of dead specified in the story. Also the description of the landscape accords with the area around Andersonville in Georgia. For an alternative reading of the story and setting, see Buinicki, "Imagining Sites of Memory." For a history of the government's efforts to create the National Cemeteries following the Civil War, see Faust, *This Republic of Suffering*.

15. The story may be subtly reminding readers that the first "Decoration Day" following the Civil War was actually performed by African Americans in Charleston, South Carolina, on May 1, 1865. The event was covered in the national press at the time and is discussed in Blight's *Race and Reunion*, 68–71. Also it should be noted that Woolson provides mixed representations of the freedmen in other stories. In "King David," for example, the main character, David King, a northern teacher working with the freedmen, invites two of his students to dine in his home, yet he refrains from eating with them, going so far as to fix an entirely new supper after they depart. The representations of African Americans in this text stand in sharp contrast to this Memorial Day scene from "Rodman the Keeper." Overall, Woolson's writings contain conflicting

representations of race, and it can be difficult to precisely locate her position among the views articulated by her characters and narrators.

16. A fictional sketch by Sarah Annie Frost published in 1878 provides a concise and pointed contrast to the fictions of Wright and Woolson and illustrates the remarkable adaptability of the discourse of southern hospitality, how it could be easily renovated to suit the new political climate and serve the ideology of the Lost Cause. Frost was a managing editor at the influential *Godey's*, a frequent contributor to genteel periodical magazines, and also an author of children's books, guides to domestic parlor games and family entertainments, and perhaps the most popular etiquette book of the period, *Frost's Laws and By-Laws of American Society*. She was, in short, an arbiter of public sentiment and a prominent public voice for the values and social mores of American middle-class domestic culture. Writing under her married name, S. A. Shields, Frost provides an assessment of the black population of the South similar to that of Telfair Hodgson in her sketch titled "Sambo." Published just a year after Reconstruction had ended, Frost's recasts the exploitative contract and sharecropping systems that emerged after the war as evidence of the hospitality and generosity of the planter classes, transforming the planter classes into the overly generous hosts and their former slaves into a parasitical population, surviving off the planters' limitless generosity. History certainly tells us otherwise: former slaves were perpetually indebted through exorbitant pricing systems and exploitative loan practices. See, for example, W. E. B. Du Bois's devastating analysis of the tenant and sharecropping system in *Souls of Black Folk*, especially chapters 7 and 8, "Of the Black Belt" and "Of the Quest of the Golden Fleece." For a discussion of the conflict between the North's free-labor ideology and the contract system that emerged in the South under Reconstruction, See Foner, *Reconstruction*, especially chapter 4.

17. The abolitionist James Redpath, whom I discussed briefly in chapter 1, provides an interesting example of this increasing sense of skepticism regarding black rights in the Reconstruction era and later. In 1876, Redpath traveled to the South as part of a congressional committee to investigate political violence and intimidation in state elections. According to John R. McKivigan, these travels produced a sense of "grave despair" in Redpath over the failure of Reconstruction, and he went on to criticize both white *and* black southerners in a series of letters published in the *New York Independent*. His comments on abolitionism seem to accord to a certain extent with Frost's sketch: "Sentimental abolitionism was well enough in its day; but Mississippi owes its present condition as much to sentimental abolitionism as to fiendish Negro-haters" (quoted in McKivigan, *Forgotten Firebrand*, 145). At the same time, Redpath still believed that education was the key to the freedman's citizenship, and he also continued to criticize the coercive political tactics of the Democratic Party in the South. See McKivigan, *Forgotten Firebrand*, 144–46.

18. See Pollard, *Virginia Tourist*; further references are cited parenthetically in the text. Directed to potential visitors from the North, Pollard's volume provides a comprehensive tour of the mineral springs resort areas of Virginia, combining detailed information on hotels, travel arrangements, the medicinal qualities of the springs' waters, descriptions of natural scenery, overviews of local and natural history, discussions on the possible economic development of the region, and a large number of local color

scenes and sketches based on firsthand experience and secondhand knowledge. Pollard's travel guide was also serialized in *Lippincott's Magazine of Literature, Science and Education* that same year. The Lippincott publishing house had strong ties to southern markets both before and after the war and published many pro-southern titles; for discussions of the Lippincott house, see Derby, *Fifty Years*, 381–89; and Mott, *History of American Magazines*, 396–401.

19. The 1873 edition of Jones, *Appleton's Handbook of American Travel*, quotes extensively from Pollard's travel guide, including from this particular passage on the warm reception that northerners will receive (91–93). For a similar assurance that northerners, particularly those who desired to travel South for reasons of health, need not be anxious about southern travel following the war, see Brinton, *Guide Book*, 136.

20. According to Nina Silber, for example, both the tourism experience and tourism literature allowed middle- and upper-class northerners "to view the South and reconciliation through a romantic and depoliticized prism" (*Romance of Reunion*, 92). Still, the manner in which Pollard presents the South as open for the tourist's business so soon after the war stands in stark contrast to some of the travel narratives published in the immediate aftermath of the war, such as Reid, *After the War*; Andrews, *The South since the War*; and Kennaway, *On Sherman's Track*.

21. Pollard, *Lost Cause Regained*, 155.

22. Goddard, *Where to Emigrate and Why*, 336, 358, 359.

23. See also Atkinson and Loring, *Cotton Culture*. In contrast to Pollard, some letters from southern officials in these emigration texts warn upper-class northerners that they will not be well received in the South; see, for example, Goddard, *Where to Emigrate and Why*, 420–21. For a series of widely conflicting impressions on the reception of northerners in the South, see Atkinson and Loring, *Cotton Culture*, 67–84.

24. "Hint to Southern Plantation Owners."

25. Ibid. As Bertram Wyatt-Brown and others note, in the antebellum period, many southerners already charged for their hospitality to travelers in need of a place to spend the night.

26. Blight, *Race and Reunion*, 260. See also Maddex, *Reconstruction of Edward A. Pollard*. Maddex describes Pollard's remarkable evolution from Old South secessionist to New South unionist. Even as Pollard moved away from his southern nationalist ideology, however, he remained committed to the doctrine of white supremacy and the social separation of the races.

27. Pollard, *Virginia Tourist*, 28, hereafter cited parenthetically in text.

28. The passage goes on to contrast the inherent character of northern and southern women in ways that were typical of the day: "Our Southern belles might, perhaps, improve their taste in decoration, but we are sure that people of fashion in the North might improve their own style by imbibing some of that earnest and natural gayety and enthusiasm, that unconcealed sense of happiness and enjoyment, which characterizes the more impulsive and demonstrative people of the South in places designed for pleasure and recreation" (122). A very similar contrast is drawn between the women of northern resorts like Saratoga and the women in the springs resorts of Virginia in an 1874 article published in a phrenological journal, which notes that while the women of the South may dress "less fashionably" and "less tastefully," they have more natural

and graceful manners, which can be traced to the "English ancestry" of their antebellum forebears. The article also discusses the habits of hospitality in the South. See M.L.C., "Women at the South," 174–75. For a more thorough phrenological interpretation of southern character and hospitality based on the "effects of climate," see "Signs of Character." The article notes that in the "sunny South" the "black man is there in his element," while the white man is compelled to "seek the shade," where he grows "cadaverous," "attenuated," "indifferent and careless," which in turn contributes to his "hospitality, generosity," and "excessive prodigality" (59).

29. *Oxford English Dictionary*, http://www.oed.com/.

30. Silber, *Romance of Reunion*, 69. Considering this aristocratic appeal, we should not be surprised that Pollard subsequently turns to a long description and "knightly" defense of a "Grand Tournament" held at the White Sulphur Springs, a spectacle hearkening back to antebellum plantation practices and what Twain termed the "Sir Walter Scott disease."

31. For a similar scene that compares the former grandeur of southern hospitality with the vaguely threatening prospects of black freedom, consider the following description of Charleston written by English novelist and travel writer Lady Duffus Hardy in *Down South*:

> Occasionally, in some obscure corner of the city, we come upon a rambling old mansion of quaint, picturesque architecture, once the home of refinement and wealth, where the great ones of the country lived in a state of ease, luxury, and almost feudal splendour. It is occupied now by hosts of coloured folk; swarms of black babies crowd the verandahs or climb and tumble about the steps and passages, while the dilapidated balconies are filled with lines of clothes to dry; the negro smokes his pipe beneath the eaves, and the women folk, with their heads turbanned in gay-coloured handkerchiefs, laugh and chatter from the windows and lounge in the doorways. How long ago is it since the clank of the cavaliers' spurs rang upon the crumbling pavement, and sweet ladies with their pretty patched faces laughed from the verandahs, while merry voices and music and hospitality echoed from the now dingy, time-dishonoured halls, and stately dames in the decorous dress and manners of the old days walked to and fro, adding by their gracious presence to the attraction of the festive scene? But these good old days are over; no imperious dames, in stiff brocades and jewelled slippers, pace the wide corridors, or dance the graceful minuet upon the floor; there is no sound of flute and tabor now, but the many sounding notes of labour, the tramp of busy hives of working men and women, and the plaintive voices of the negroes singing is heard instead of it, and who shall say which makes the better music? (56–57)

Hardy acknowledges that slavery was an "inherited evil" that the South endured, but she still waxes nostalgic at times. See also Kennaway, *On Sherman's Track*, 42–43, 133–37.

32. Cowan served as a captain in the regiment, which saw action in several major engagements of the war, including the First Battle of Bull Run, Chancellorsville, and Gettysburg. The trip to New Orleans twenty years after Bull Run brought them face-to-face with some of the very southern regiments they had fought against on the field.

33. See Blight, *Race and Reunion*, chapters 3 and 4.

34. Cowan, *New Invasion of the South*, 1, hereafter cited parenthetically in text.

35. For a detailed discussion of the "restoration of white supremacy" in the South in the years immediately following Reconstruction and the methodical dismantling of African American rights, see Foner, *Reconstruction*, chapter 12.

36. See, for example, his comments on the "marvelous manifestation of the happy condition of the colored people of the South" (86), as well as his inclusion of numerous documents and conciliatory statements from southerners in the book's appendices. For a very different view from another Union Army veteran, see McElwin, *Travels in the South*. In these observations, originally published in the *Elyria Republican*, McElwin comments on the treatment of strangers and outsiders in the South—at one point minding his manners rather than giving his honest opinion on race issues (11)—and offers very negative summary comments on travel in the South (38–39). He often comments favorably on the progress and contributions of the freedmen and on the resentment of white southerners, especially the former planter class: "Engage one of these chivalry in conversation any length of time and he is sure to commence swearing about the 'lazy niggers,' when they are the only working people a traveler sees on the route" (10).

37. In this sense, it is important to keep in mind Grace Elizabeth Hale's description of the way the emerging national marketplace adopted the cultural logic of segregation, imagining the American consumer as white and routinely adopting negative, patronizing, or demeaning racial stereotypes of African Americans in branding strategies. See *Making Whiteness*, especially chapter 4. The southern hospitality myth was perfectly suited to this cultural moment and its particular habits of reinforcing white transregional identity.

38. *Atlanta Journal*, May 12, 1914, 11, quoted in Newman, *Southern Hospitality*, 8.

39. See Blight, *Race and Reunion*, chapter 7. See also Prince, *Stories of the South*, chapter 4. As the national way of remembering the Civil War shifted away from slavery and emancipation (its political cause and effect) and toward themes of regional reconciliation and mutual sacrifice, authors associated with this growing and popular field of plantation literature—which included fiction, poetry, sketches, memoir, and travel writing—spread positive, sentimental, and highly romanticized views of the Old South. Prince argues that authors such as Thomas Nelson Page and Joel Chandler Harris essentially wrestled narrative control over the South away from more progressive voices, "insisting on the exclusive rights of white southerners to tell the South's story to the nation" (11). Prince argues that the cultural work performed by these authors in the 1880s and 1890s made it easier for Americans to turn their backs on the failed promises of Reconstruction: "The political retreat from Reconstruction could not have occurred without a contemporaneous cultural retreat from Reconstruction" (2). Travel writing about the South, steeped in nostalgia, also helped to soften the effects of this cultural retreat from the Reconstruction. See, for example, Ralph, *Dixie*. Ralph notes that the volume's contents originally appeared in *Harper's* "as a series of papers upon the development of what may well be called 'Our New South'" (v), but the contents are steeped in a nostalgia for the Old South that sees little possibility for the development of the now-free black citizens: "I learned long ago that there are two sorts of colored folks in the South—the rude, dull field hands, and the spruce, polite, and far more

intelligent and ambitious house-servants, both originating in and descending from similar classes in the time of slavery" (381–82).

40. For a discussion of how the emergence of a rising and diverse black middle class—the "New Negro"—was clouded by persistent stereotypes of the "Old Negro," see chapter 1 of G. E. Hale, *Making Whiteness*.

41. Later in this essay in which Page calls for a new generation of historians of the Old South, he idealizes the Old South as "a civilization so pure, so noble, that the world to-day holds nothing equal to it. After less than a generation it has become among friends and enemies the recognized field of romance. Its chief attribute was conservatism. Others were courage, fidelity, purity, hospitality, magnanimity, honesty, and truth" (Page, *Old South*, 5, 43).

42. Page, *Social Life in Old Virginia*, 1, hereafter cited parenthetically in text. Most particularly, Page singles out Harriet Beecher Stowe for creating a false picture of slavery in the Old South, one that no southerner "would willingly have stand as a final portrait of Southern life" (2). He also complains about the way the typical southerner has been caricatured on the contemporary stage as an "underbred little provincial" or a "sloven" (3, 4). In closing, Page asserts that the best remnants of the Old South still exist and persist—and that the South provides one of the "final refuges of old-fashioned gentility and distinguished manners, . . . [and] old-time good breeding and high courtesy"(5).

43. Silber, *Romance of Reunion*, 78, 79.

44. Ibid., 137. See also G. E. Hale, *Making Whiteness*, 21–22.

45. At a time when the so-called New Woman was emerging to challenge traditional gender expectations in America, Page places the woman firmly back in the domestic sphere as "the mistress . . . the most important personage about the home, the presence which pervaded the mansion, the centre of all that life, the queen of that realm" (34).

46. Page goes on, with characteristic hyperbole, to describe the hospitable social interactions among the planter class, with their "perpetual round of dinners, teas, and entertainments" and the "visits of friends and relatives" that lasted "a month or two, or as long a time as they pleased." He presents the southern planter's openhanded manner of hospitality as defying the laws of physics, claiming that it was "a mystery how the house ever held the visitors. . . . The walls seemed to be made of india-rubber, so great was their stretching power. No one who came, whether friend or stranger, was ever turned away. If the beds were full—as when were they not!—pallets were put down on the floor in the parlor or the garret for the younger members of the family, sometimes even the passages being utilized" (77–79).

47. Page makes the same claim in his essay "The Old South": "The tendency to hospitality was not local nor narrow; it was the characteristic of the entire people, and its concomitant was a generosity so general and so common in its application that it created the quality of magnanimity as a race characteristic" (Page, *Old South*, 45).

48. Ibid., 280, 283, 284.

49. For a discussion of how the emergence of a rising and diverse black middle class—the "New Negro"—was clouded by persistent stereotypes of the "Old Negro," see chapter 1 of G. E. Hale, *Making Whiteness*.

50. See Chapter 7 of Du Bois, *Souls of Black Folk*, 123–24; Douglass, *Life and Times*, 67–68, 134–35; and Dunbar, *Folks from Dixie*, 185–204.

51. Among the first successful African American novelists, Charles Chesnutt had to negotiate a literary marketplace dominated by white readers, writers, editors, and assumptions, and this fact informed the "moral" and political agenda of his fictions. As a mixed-race individual whose formative years were spent in the South as it moved through Reconstruction and into segregation, Chesnutt was keenly aware of his own status as a perpetual stranger in the South (and in the nation more broadly). His fictions set out to challenge his white readers—his main readership—to see and acknowledge this pervasive injustice. In an early journal entry where he contemplates pursuing a career as a writer, Chesnutt muses, "The object of my writings would be not so much the elevation of the colored people as the elevation of the whites, —for I consider the unjust spirit of caste which is . . . so powerful as to subject a whole race and all connected with it to scorn and social ostracism—I consider this a barrier to the moral progress of the American people." From a journal entry dated May 29, 1879, in Chesnutt, *Journals of Charles W. Chesnutt*, 139–40.

52. For detailed descriptions and analyses of the novel's relationship to the historical events surrounding the Wilmington coup, see M. Wilson, *Whiteness*; and Sundquist, *To Wake the Nations*.

53. Du Bois, *Souls of Black Folk*, vii. Chesnutt's novel manages to touch on virtually every major topic and form of cultural production associated with what was commonly referred to as "the Negro Question" in the South: the politics of white supremacy, disfranchisement, Lost Cause ideology, lynching and political violence, the Ku Klux Klan, segregation, miscegenation, white emigration and tourism, advertising and media representation of race, minstrelsy and cakewalks, and competing theories of racial uplift.

54. Chesnutt, *Marrow of Tradition*, 269, hereafter cited parenthetically in text. As Sundquist notes, "*The Marrow of Tradition*, one could say, is devoted to the question of 'propagation'—or, to use the novel's more frequent words, to 'generation' and 'degeneration'" (*To Wake the Nations*, 408).

55. See, for example, Sundquist, *To Wake the Nations*, 427–31.

56. Chesnutt, *House behind the Cedars*, 115.

57. As Chesnutt introduces the two men, he pointedly draws on specific language from the recent *Plessy v. Ferguson* decision in describing Miller, explaining how an "American eye" may detect a "visible admixture" of African blood in Miller (49). Chesnutt's description in the passage implicitly contrasts worldly or cosmopolitan perspectives that see humans as essentially the same with narrower, more provincial (i.e., "American") viewpoints that see race first and foremost when considering an individual's worth. Chesnutt's quoting of this particular passage of the Supreme Court ruling is notable, for rather than creating a sense of certitude regarding racial categories of white and black, the passage from which this phrase is drawn underscores the utter ambiguity of the color line. What is a "visible admixture" of African blood? The Supreme Court itself refrained from weighing in on this question, instead leaving it up to the states. And in his 1889 essay "What Is a White Man?" Chesnutt had demonstrated this arbitrary and capricious drawing of the color line by surveying the convoluted and

inconsistent definitions of black and white identity across these and other state laws. Importantly, Chesnutt's description of one of the novel's villains—the young, degraded white aristocrat Tom Delamere—includes similar language to that seen in the description of Miller. Tom is described as "dark almost to swarthiness," with "black eyes" and "curly hair of raven tint" (15–16). The similar descriptions could just be Chesnutt's way of underscoring the arbitrary nature of the color line, or he could be hinting at a mixed racial ancestry for Tom. Later in the novel, we have the briefest mention of an incident that may point to the possibility that Tom is the son of a slave named Black Sally (207), but Chesnutt leaves the question unanswered and utterly ambiguous.

58. Elsewhere in the text, Chesnutt expands this theme of coercion to include the southern hospitality industry itself, offering a detailed critique of the way the developing southern tourism industry reinforced the racial status quo. At the opening of chapter 8, "The Cakewalk," Chesnutt describes in detail how a "party of Northern visitors ... interested in the study of social conditions and especially in the negro problem" are "taken courteously under the wing of prominent citizens and their wives," who carefully plan and stage the visitors every move over the course of a day, all the while "sighing sentimentally over the disappearance of the good old negro of before the war, and gravely deploring the degeneracy of his descendants" (115). They also are careful to be present with the guests when they desire to visit the "colored mission school." The gracious care and attention of the hosts, along with the carefully selected examples of black life and culture, work together to sway the northern visitors:

> The visitors were naturally much impressed by what they learned from their courteous hosts, and felt inclined to sympathize with the Southern people, for the negro is not counted as a Southerner, except to fix the basis of congressional representation. There might of course be things to criticise here and there, certain customs for which they did not exactly see the necessity, and which seemed in conflict with the highest ideals of liberty: but surely these courteous, soft-spoken ladies and gentlemen, entirely familiar with local conditions, who descanted so earnestly and at times pathetically upon the grave problems confronting them, must know more about it than people in the distant North, without their means of information. The negroes who waited on them at the hotel seemed happy enough.... Surely a people who made no complaints could not be very much oppressed. (116–17)

59. Chesnutt's novel shows the inevitable consequences of this eye-for-an-eye form of justice through the conflict between Captain McBane and the heroic though tragic figure of Josh Green. Green fulfills his lifelong plan of revenge against McBane for the murder of his father, but he ends up dead in the process. Miller, in contrast, is alive, but he faces the irrevocable loss of his child.

60. For discussions of this complicated ethical dilemma in modern states, see Rotberg and Thompson, *Truth v. Justice*.

61. M. Wilson, *Whiteness*, xii.

62. Chesnutt inscribes this conflict between romance and realism within the plot of the novel through the love triangle involving Tom Delamere, Clara Pemberton, and Lee Ellis. Matt Wilson suggests that the inclusion of this subplot is a nod to the demands of the marketplace and white readers' expectations, but one can also argue that its in-

clusion is in fact an indictment of romance, particularly when comparing the relative ethics of Ellis's behavior in his wooing of Clara and his decidedly detached stance on racial politics. See M. Wilson, *Whiteness*, 234–235n 14.

Chapter 6. The Modern Proliferation of the Southern Hospitality Myth

1. In *Dreaming of Dixie*, the historian Karen L. Cox surveys a wide range of modern cultural forms—popular song, advertisements, radio, film, literature, and tourism campaigns—to show how a remarkably consistent, stereotyped picture of the American South emerged and proliferated in the United States from the 1890s through the 1950s. Cox correctly underscores the role of nonsouthern consumers and creators of popular culture—from popular songwriters to Hollywood producers to corporate advertisers—in the creation of this image, but southerners were likewise savvy to the potential economic development and profit that could go along with this image of the South. And southerners responded to these growing perceptions of the region by giving consumers "exactly what they had come to expect of the South," including, as Cox describes it, "that ubiquitous feature of life in Dixie known as southern hospitality" (K. L. Cox, *Dreaming of Dixie*, 7).

2. See, for example, Bone, Ward, and Link, *Creating and Consuming the American South*; and Cobb, *Selling of the South*.

3. See Brundage, *Southern Past*, 221.

4. Quoted in Gregory, "David F. Friedman."

5. Production details are drawn from Bankard, "Herschell Gordon Lewis Guide."

6. Rather than the two thousand residents implied by the title, the crowd numbers a few hundred at best. Friedman and Lewis shot the film in Saint Cloud, Florida, and many of the film's outdoor locations were later transformed into Disney World's Magic Kingdom. The first verse and chorus of the film's theme song run as follows: "There's a story you should know from a hundred years ago / And a hundred years we've waited now to tell / Now the Yankees come along and they'll listen to this song / And they'll quake in fear to hear this Rebel yell / Chorus: Yeeeeehaw! Oh, the South's gonna rise again! Yeeeeehaw! Oh, the South's gonna rise again!" (*Two Thousand Maniacs!*). The next three verses focus on Confederate heroes Robert E. Lee, Stonewall Jackson, and J. E. B. Stuart, respectively.

7. Certainly whites were victims of lynching in the South as well, including abolitionists in the antebellum period and white civil rights workers in the film's contemporary moment. With this in mind, the film could be said to conjoin the earlier form of anti-abolitionist intraracial violence with the contemporary political moment in the South that was dominated by the civil rights movement and saw white participation among the freedom riders. Still, the majority of victims of lynching in the South were always African American, and in the twentieth century, consumer culture and mass media transformed the practice of lynching into a modern commodified spectacle. For a discussion of this modern transformation of lynching, see chapter 5 of G. E. Hale, *Making Whiteness*. As Hale points out, even though the number of lynchings decreased in the twentieth century, their message became more powerful, for these modern "spectacle lynchings" were performed "in public, attended by thousands, captured

in papers by reporters who witnessed the tortures, and photographed for spectators who wanted a souvenir" (202).

8. See chapter 6 of K. L. Cox, *Dreaming of Dixie*, for a fairly comprehensive survey of these efforts across several southern states.

9. These phrases are drawn from display ads that routinely appeared in the *New York Times* from 1960 to 1964 for resorts in Hot Springs, Arkansas; Fort Pierce, Florida; and White Sulphur Springs, West Virginia. The use of the modifiers "true," "real," and "warm" suggests the jaded nature of the discourse; other modifiers commonly used include "traditional," "authentic," and "historic."

10. *New York Times*, 15 May, 1966, Ad. 4; *Wall Street Journal*, 13 July 1960, 6.

11. See, for example, Whitelegg, "From Smiles to Miles."

12. *Two Thousand Maniacs!* In the film's opening scenes we learn that Tom White (played by William Kerwin) was on his way to a teacher's convention in Atlanta when his car broke down, and Terry Adams (played by Playboy Playmate Connie Mason) gave him a lift. Their budding romance provides the closest thing to a subplot amid the film's violence.

13. While the killing of the cat could certainly be taken as a veiled reference to the subject of race, it could also be a deferential allusion to the 1962 gothic horror film *Tales of Terror*, which included a loose adaptation of Poe's "The Black Cat," starring Vincent Price and Peter Lorre.

14. McPherson, *Reconstructing Dixie*, 7. In contrast to the original *Two Thousand Maniacs!*, the recent remake of the film titled *2001 Maniacs*, an homage to the cult status of the original, incorporates race in a very direct and offensive manner. The victims in this film include an interracial couple: an African American man and an Asian American woman.

15. Douglas Egerton has described how southern authorities commonly sentenced rebellious or criminal slaves to be dismembered, either after execution or, in the most extreme cases, while still alive. See D. R. Egerton, "Peculiar Mark of Infamy," 149–60. Calling to mind the specific film scene, some historical sources say the slave Gabriel Prosser, who led an unsuccessful revolt in 1800, "was executed by having a horse attached to each of his four limbs, and was thus torn asunder." For example, see "Gabriel's Defeat." Though apocryphal, this particular account of Gabriel's death circulated through some northern papers that, in the wake of Nat Turner's failed revolt of 1831, revisited the story of Gabriel's earlier revolt. The *Liberator* acknowledges the *Albany Evening Journal* as the source of its copy, and it also appeared in The *Free Enquirer*. For an account of Gabriel Prosser's execution by hanging, see D. R. Egerton, *Gabriel's Rebellion*, 108–11. Similarly, several separate sources describe slaves being punished or killed by being placed in a barrel lined with nails and rolled down a hill. See, for example, Roper, *Narrative*, 24; *Slave Narratives*, produced by the Federal Writers' Project, 297; and Rothert, *History of Muhlenberg County*, 341.

16. See Dobbins, "Southern Hospitality"; and Bellocq, "Southern Hospitality."

17. For example, the headline of a May 19, 1963, *New York Times* front-page story on President Kennedy's visit to the South that same year reads "Kennedy, in South, Hails Negro Drive for Civil Rights." In the accompanying photo, the segregationist and white supremacist governor George Wallace steps aside to let Kennedy take the podium to

speak; yet again, the photo caption reads "Southern Hospitality." Likewise, a December 1, 1964, *Chicago Daily Defender* photo carries the caption: "Southern Hospitality—Montgomery Style." The photo shows the results of the bombing in Montgomery, Alabama, of a black resident's home.

18. Berkowitz, "David Duke's Welcome Wagon."

19. Petrie, "Economic Sanctions."

20. Quoted in Burns, "NAACP Plans More Flag Protests." EURO's instructions to its members included the following: "DO NOT DISTRIBUTE ANY LITERATURE.... Do not bring ANY WEAPONS OF ANY KIND.... Do not WEAR ANYTHING OFFENSIVE. If you have a pin or a shirt that is offensive, it will be the only thing the media will look at. That will then be how the entire event is represented." Quoted in Berkowitz, "David Duke's Welcome Wagon," emphasis in original.

21. Certainly not all the flag supporters in these debates are white supremacists or racists, but the episode shows that the flag cannot be entirely separated from racist connotations. For a particularly tragic case involving the complex symbolism of the Confederate flag, see chapter 5 of Horwitz, *Confederates in the Attic*.

22. Iacobelli, "White Pride Group."

23. "Nikki Haley Defends Confederate Flag."

24. King, *Sombreros and Motorcycles*, 21.

25. Starnes, introduction to *Southern Journeys*, 1.

26. Silber, *Romance of Reunion*, 67.

27. *Atlanta Journal*, May 12, 1914, 11. Quoted in Newman, *Southern Hospitality*, 8. Graves, who rose to be a prominent editor for William Randolph Hearst and a vice presidential nominee for Hearst's short-lived political party, was described by the *Saturday Evening Post* in 1908 as the "silvern-toungued [sic] orator from Dixie." Graves here and elsewhere turned his rhetorical talents to promoting tourism in the South, even writing a romantic promotional brochure for the Savannah, Florida and Western Railway Company. In promoting the South, Graves had a particular image in mind that he knew nostalgic Americans in the modern age would appreciate, and one Americans were already very familiar with, a version of the plantation ideal that had been developed through plantation fiction, minstrelsy, and Lost Cause rhetoric. See, for example, "Laurels of Demosthenes." See also Silber, *Romance of Reunion*, 91–93.

28. Quoted in Hughes, "Rich Georgian Strangely Shot," 85. See also pp. 85–87 for a description of Graves's fearmongering and race-baiting editorials. Nonetheless, Graves managed to run for president, and he was a generally accepted spokesperson and advocate for all things southern, including the tourism trade, illustrating the continuing disparity between ethics and politics in the discourse of southern hospitality.

29. Brundage, *Southern Past*, 183–84.

30. See K. L. Cox, *Dreaming of Dixie*, 148. Cox notes that during this period, "the South's urban tourist literature often combined the nostalgia northerners had for the Old South with ideas of progress and innovation that suggested that the region had entered the era of the New South."

31. Brundage, *Southern Past*, 184.

32. Rosewood was a black community that included a rail stop for the Seaboard Airline Railroad, which transported thousands of tourists to southern cities from Vir-

ginia through Florida. Following the lynching of a Rosewood resident by a white mob on spurious charges of rape, the town's residents decided to defend themselves against the growing white mob, but during a week of unrestrained violence, the mob murdered several black citizens and burned the entire town to the ground. Black residents were forced to flee the conflagration, never to return. See Dye, "Rosewood, Florida."

33. Brundage, *Southern Past*, 213. See also Yuhl, *Golden Haze of Memory*, for a comprehensive history of Charleston's creation of a historic tourist destination.

34. As W. Fitzhugh Brundage concisely explains, these markers "taught native Virginians and tourists about what was historically significant and, by implication, what was not. To travel the road to Virginia was literally to enter a system of signs through which the state promoted a certain narrative of history—a narrative that dwelled on the state's vaunted contributions to the nation's development." These signifying systems offered what Brundage describes as "a veneer of encyclopedic objectivity," and they also served to "revalue southern history" in the traveler's imagination. See Brundage, *Southern Past*, 197, 198–99.

35. Quoted in K. L. Cox, *Dreaming of Dixie*, 153.

36. The poem is dedicated to Roscoe C. Lewis, a fellow writer on the project who authored *The Negro in Virginia*. See Sanders, *Afro-modernist Aesthetics*, 115–16.

37. S. A. Brown, *Collected Poems of Sterling A. Brown*, 209–10.

38. Sanders, *Afro-modernist Aesthetics*, 115, 116.

39. J. Jackson, "Bungleton Green."

40. Seiler, *Republic of Drivers*, 114–15, 115.

41. *Negro Motorist Green Book*, 1.

42. McGee, "Open Road."

43. Ramsey, with Strauss, *Ruth and the Green Book*, 9.

44. Ibid., 20.

45. The play premiered at the Balzer Theater in Atlanta in July 2010, and a staged reading featuring former NAACP chairman Julian Bond was also performed at the Lincoln Theater in Washington in September of that year.

46. Ricoeur points out that while narratives of collective memory can include wounds and traumas for some groups, narratives of the past can also provide sites of healing, for "it is always possible to tell in another way. This exercise of memory is here an exercise in *telling otherwise*, and also in letting others tell their own history." For Ricoeur, "telling otherwise" takes us to the "ethico-political level" of collective memory and the "duty to remember," which includes "transmitting the meaning of past events to the next generation. The duty, therefore, is one which concerns the future; it is an imperative directed towards the future, which is exactly the opposite side of the traumatic character of the humiliations and wounds of history. It is a duty, thus, to tell." See Ricoeur, "Memory and Forgetting," 5, 9–10.

47. For a wide range of analyses of both the successes and the recurring conflicts of these endeavors, see Oliver and Horton, *Slavery and Public History*; and part 2 of K. L. Cox, *Destination Dixie*.

48. "Project Update." This is a far cry from the state of affairs described by Tony Horwitz in 1999 when he wrote about the conflicts between black and white residents over the way Nat Turner should be remembered. In Horwitz's *New Yorker* article titled

"Untrue Confessions," he portrays the historical representation of Nat Turner as an essentially unresolvable conflict: "Interpretation of history always reveals as much about the present as it does about the past. But with Nat Turner the contemporary echo is especially loud, raising raw and unresolved questions about race, religious zealotry, and revolutionary violence. Even at a distance of more than a century and a half, the story of a black man who massacred whites in the name of God and freedom remains incendiary." Horwitz is right in noting that historical representations reveal as much about the present as about the past, and the fact that this is taking place now is indicative of change and of a healthier, though perhaps fitful, willingness to engage this complex history.

49. Alderman and Modlin, "Southern Hospitality," 6, 25.

50. See Lassiter and Crespino, *Myth of Southern Exceptionalism*, 6; Wiese, "African-American Suburbanization and Regionalism"; and Odem, "Latin American Immigration."

51. See Romine, *Real South*, 2–3. Griffin and Thompson, "Enough about the Disappearing South," 52–53; and Elias, "Postmodern Southern Vacation," 278.

52. Far too often, this basic and simple historical fact is unacknowledged or even willfully forgotten. A concise illustration of this fact may be found in Pitzer, *Southern Hospitality Cookbook*. Pitzer's cookbook is rather unique in that her preface attempts to provide a detailed explanation of the historical origins of southern hospitality with several quotes and examples from historical sources. She traces southern hospitality from the revolutionary period, up through the Civil War and "the dark days following the war." Throughout her account of this history, however, she makes no mention of the slave labor or domestic workers who made these social habits possible. Instead, she blithely concludes, "A look at the history of southern hospitality suggests that the one true constant is this passion for a party. Bad times or good, the South will have parties"(11). Like Lang, Pitzer identifies the challenges facing southerners today: "In our fast-paced, servantless, trimmed down times, our challenge is to find new ways of continuing the old spirit of southern parties" (11).

53. For a thorough examination of this psychological conflict of white southerners written as the South was moving through the process of integration, see Warren, *Segregation*. For a more recent analysis that considers the South's loss of white supremacy alongside post–World War II Germany's loss of racial superiority, see J. Smith, *Finding Purple America*, 50–64.

54. "Top 25 US Consumer Magazines."

55. See Romine, *Real South*, 15. See also 14–16, 227–29.

56. See Logue and McCalla, *Life at Southern Living*, 30–32, 52–60.

57. Ibid., 31.

58. D. Roberts, "Living Southern in *Southern Living*," 89. Roberts's essay, though brief, offers the best general cultural analysis of *Southern Living* magazine.

59. Quoted in Logue and McCalla, *Life at Southern Living*, 33–34.

60. Jon Smith discusses the broader implications of this process of "imagining oneself as *victim*" in *Finding Purple America*; see especially 55–59.

61. Raines, "Getting to the Heart of Dixie."

62. Logue and McCalla, *Life at Southern Living*, 39.

63. Logue and McCalla describe their own mortification over the first issue, but as they go on to explain, even with the strange opening message and even with the first issue's "dated, random, dreary design," the magazine was instantly popular: "Many readers wrote to express their instant affection for the magazine. They couldn't be sure of what it was, but it was *theirs*." See Logue and McCalla, *Life at Southern Living*, 38–39; 54–56; 56, 59. For a detailed analysis of the "coded language" of the first issue's editorial message, see D. Roberts, "Living Southern in *Southern Living*."

64. Indeed, the very first image of an African American to appear in the magazine seems right out of the nineteenth century. Diane Roberts describes the offensive image from the second issue of March 1966: "The magazine printed its first picture of an African-American, a 'menu boy' of ten or eleven, in a feature on a Smyrna, Georgia restaurant called Aunt Fanny's Cabin. The restaurant purported to be a much enlarged, 'genuine' slave cabin serving genuine old southern food. The menu boys wore chalk sandwich boards and recited the menu. The story says, 'As you eat happily, several Negro boys put on a singing, dancing show of century-old songs'" (D. Roberts, "Living Southern in *Southern Living*," 87).

65. See D. Roberts, "Living Southern in *Southern Living*," 98n27; see also Elias, "Postmodern Southern Vacation," on the continuing coded racial language of travel ads in *Southern Living* in more recent years, especially pp. 265–69.

66. M. N. Jones, "Defining the Southern," 139–40.

67. Ibid., 140.

68. Ibid.

69. D. Roberts, "Living Southern in *Southern Living*," 96. Roberts argues that in more recent years, the typical representations of African Americans in the magazine essentially reassure the predominantly white readership by portraying blacks in the same "comfortable, decorated bourgeois world" and implying they are "just like us" (see pp. 95–96).

70. Ricoeur, "Memory and Forgetting," 6, 7. I choose to draw on Ricoeur here, rather than directly from Freud, due to Ricoeur's explicit emphasis on the ethics of memory. For another discussion of mourning and melancholia as it pertains to the South, see Lisa Hinrichsen's recent book, *Possessing the Past*.

71. See Deen and Cohen, *It Ain't All about the Cookin'*, 169. For Deen's discussion of southern hospitality as both a domestic tradition and a business model, see pp. 215–19, 239–40.

72. "Timeline of Paula Deen's Downfall."

73. Deen and Cohen, *It Ain't All about the Cooking*, 11, 12.

74. Ibid., 10.

75. Ricoeur, *Memory, History, Forgetting*, 95.

76. "Paula Deen on Race." The video includes other awkward moments on the subject of race. For a scathing critique of the video interview in light of the 2013 controversy, see Frank Bruni's editorial, "Paula's Worst Ingredients."

77. *Transcript of the Testimony of Paula Deen*, 125, 127, 129.

78. Ibid., 129–31. For readability, I have modified the typescript of the deposition to more clearly indicate the speakers, and I have also removed objections from Deen's attorney.

79. Moskin, "Culinary Birthright in Dispute."
80. Twitty, "Open Letter to Paula Deen."
81. Southern Foodways Alliance, "About Us."
82. Southern Foodways Alliance, "Southern Food Primer."
83. For example, Sarah Rutledge in *The Carolina Housewife*, in explaining the need for such a cookbook, points to the unique circumstances of slavery: "French or English Cookery Books are to be found in every bookstore; but these are for French or English servants, and almost always require an apparatus either beyond our reach or too complicated for our native cooks" (3). Mary Randolph, in *The Virginia Housewife*, emphasizes the need for establishing methodical routines of preparation for the slaves, noting at one point, for example, that the dinner table should be prepared for service every morning "with the same scrupulous regard to exact neatness and method, as if a grand company was expected. When the servant is expected to do this daily, he soon gets into the habit of doing it well; and his mistress having made arrangements for him in the morning, there is no need for bustle and confusion in running after things that may be called for during the hour of dinner" (v). See also see Bryan, *Kentucky Housewife*, vii. In *Recollections of a Southern Matron*, Caroline Gilman describes these duties and contrasts them with the popular conception of the southern lady: "A planter's lady may seem indolent, because there are so many under her who perform trivial services; but the very circumstance of keeping so many menials in order is an arduous one, and the *keys* of her establishment are a care of which a Northern housekeeper knows nothing, and include a very extensive class of duties. Many fair, and even aristocratic girls, if we may use this phrase in our republican country, who grace a ball-room, or loll in a liveried carriage, may be seen with these steel talismans, presiding over storehouses, and measuring, with the accuracy and conscientiousness of a shopman, the daily allowance of the family" (47). See also Fox-Genovese, *Within the Plantation Household*, especially chapter 2, for detailed analysis of the complex and often fraught relationship that could exist between a mistress and her slaves.
84. For example, see J. Egerton, *Southern Food*, 13–15, 20, 38–39.
85. See Brundage, "From Appalachian Folk to Southern Foodways"; and Romine, "God and the MoonPie."
86. In this regard, it is worth noting that the founder's meeting of the Southern Foodways Alliance was held in Birmingham, Alabama, in 1999 at the headquarters of *Southern Living* magazine, and the *Southern Living* magazine and website have often partnered with the SFA, running stories and profiles on the SFA and its members. At the same time as it is willing to align itself with *Southern Living*, the SFA draws a clear line of demarcation between itself and Paula Deen, even though it is apparent that many consumers move easily among these different entities. After the Paula Deen controversy in 2013, the following was posted on the SFA's "Southern Six-Pack Blog" (note the allusion to southern hospitality):

> Over the years many of you have asked the SFA, "Why don't y'all do something with Paula Deen? She's Southern. You're the Southern Foodways Alliance. Seems like a perfect fit." We were (hopefully) polite in our answer which went something like this, "Yes, she's from

the South but she's not cooking the kind of Southern food we celebrate." Our focus is on the men and women who work, mostly in their own communities, making great food out of often modest ingredients. For SFA, acceptable excesses are in hospitality and graciousness, not in butter, salt, and sour cream. We don't find any joy in what happened to Ms. Deen this week. But it did happen. The commentary churned up by Ms. Deen's very public implosion says much about the Southern larder, the Southern table, and the great Southern cooks who populate our region. (Hall, "Southern Six-Pack")

Epilogue. New Strangers of the Contemporary South

1. Dewell, "It's All about the Experience!"
2. "Your Guests Expect Southern Hospitality."
3. According to the Southern Poverty Law Center, these immigrant laborers are often especially vulnerable in southern states due to the region's generally weaker labor laws. See "Immigrant Justice" and related links.
4. "Guidelines."
5. Drake, "Hospitality Course Covers 'Friendly.'" Other southern locales have developed similar programs. For example, see "Music City's Hospitality Workers"; and the "Five Star Southern Hospitality Training Program."
6. "Sweet Home Alabama."
7. Chandler, "Alabama House Passes Arizona-Style Immigration Law."
8. Valdes, "New Alabama Law."
9. Preston, "In Alabama, a Harsh Bill."
10. Ibid.
11. The law reads, "Every person working for the State of Alabama or a political subdivision thereof, including, but not limited to, a law enforcement agency in the State of Alabama or a political subdivision thereof, shall have a duty to report violations of this act. Failure to report any violation of this act when there is reasonable cause to believe that this act is being violated is guilty of obstructing governmental operations as defined in Section 13A-10-2, Code of Alabama 1975, and shall be punishable pursuant to state law." Alabama HB 56, p. 17.
12. De Lollis, "Hotel."
13. Dewskin, "Alabama's Immigration Law."
14. "Hey Mercedes." Interestingly, the editorial board issued a somewhat apologetic editorial a few months later after Missouri passed a similar law. See "Alas, Poor Alabama."
15. Quoted in "Alabama Nabs Foreign Auto Execs."
16. See Azziz, "Alabama Immigration Law." For an interesting perspective on the law from a Chinese immigrant, see Huang, "Southern Hospitality."
17. Elliot, "Clergy Sues."
18. Fred L. Hammond, "Alabama's Immigration Law."
19. Elliot, "Clergy Sues."
20. Cross's resolution, which did not make it out of committee, read as follows:

RESOLUTION CALLING FOR THE AFFIRMATION OF ALABAMA BAPTIST CHURCHES TO PROVIDE A WELCOMING, HOSPITABLE ENVIRONMENT FOR THE IMMIGRANTS AND ALIENS IN OUR MIDST

WHEREAS, the people of God are always considered aliens and strangers in the land (1 Peter 2:11); and

WHEREAS, God commanded the people of Israel to "not mistreat an alien or oppress him, for you were aliens in Egypt" (Exodus 22:21); and

WHEREAS, We are commanded to be hospitable "to strangers, for by doing so some people have entertained angels without knowing it" (Hebrews 13:2); and

WHEREAS, Many of the immigrants to our state from other nations, both legal and illegal, have many physical, financial, and social needs; and

WHEREAS, Jesus says in Matthew 25:40 that whatever we do for the least of these, we do for Him; and

WHEREAS, Alabama has enacted some of the strongest laws in the nation in response to illegal immigration to our state;

THEREFORE, BE IT RESOLVED, we the messengers to the Alabama Baptist State Convention meeting in Montgomery, Alabama, November 13–14, 2012 affirm the call for Christians to show hospitality, Christian love, and care for immigrants and aliens in our presence; and

BE IT FURTHER RESOLVED, that though we are to submit to the governing authorities and live quiet, peaceful lives (1 Peter 2:13–17; 1 Timothy 2:1–6), we are to first show love and concern for all people according to God's higher law as we love our neighbor as ourselves (Matthew 22:36–40); and

BE IT FURTHER RESOLVED, that we encourage Alabama Baptist churches and individual Christians to care for all of those in need as God places them in our path whether they are here legally or not; and

BE IT FURTHER RESOLVED, that we share the gospel of Jesus Christ with all people in all circumstances praying that all come to salvation in Christ; and

BE IT FURTHER RESOLVED, that we seek to make disciples of all nations, including the immigrants of the nations that God has sovereignly brought to our state through various means according to Matthew 28:18–20; and

BE IT FINALLY RESOLVED, that we seek to be good citizens in our state and nation only because we are first citizens of the Kingdom of God who represent Christ as His ambassadors. (Cross, "Are Alabama Baptists Wrong?")

21. Ibid.
22. Ibid.

The fact that Southern Baptists are divided on the issue may also be seen in a vote on an immigration amendment at a Southern Baptist Convention meeting earlier that year. A blog post on SBC Voices describes an "immigration brouhaha" at the SBC annual meeting over a resolution submitted on the issue. According to the SBC Voices blog, "The amendment was defeated by a razor thin margin of 766–723." In the blog discussion that followed, Cross and others pushed for a more progressive approach to immigration. See Miller, "Immigration Brouhaha at SBC."

23. As discussed in chapter 3, the Epistle to Philemon was continually cited by both sides of the Fugitive Slave Law debate, and Cross's interpretation parallels that of the abolitionists. At one point he quotes a colleague who specifically notes that "in many ways, Onesimus, as a runaway slave, was the counterpart in that day and context to an 'illegal immigrant' today." Through a reading of Philemon, Cross proposes that churches possibly take a more active role in assisting illegals—whether it be to help them on a path to citizenship, to help them return to native countries, to help keep immigrant families in tact during legal processes, or to provide a sanctuary for them against persecution. See Cross, "Could Alabama Baptists Lead the Way?"

24. Indeed, as this book was going to press the issue of immigration was dominating the presidential primary season, while new, inhospitable laws were being passed in southern states (North Carolina HB 2, Mississippi HB 1523) allowing for open discrimination against gays, lesbians, unwed mothers, and bisexual or transgender individuals.

BIBLIOGRAPHY

Aaseng, Nathan. *African American Religious Leaders*. Infobase Publishing, 2003.
"Abolition Hospitality." *Liberator* 7, no. 22 (May 26, 1837): 87.
Adams, Francis Colburn. *Manuel Pereira; or, The Sovereign Rule of South Carolina, with Views of Southern Laws, Life, and Hospitality*. Washington: Buell & Blanchard, 1853.
Alabama HB 56. Legiscan.com. http://legiscan.com/AL/text/HB56/id/321074/Alabama-2011-HB56-Enrolled.pdf. Accessed October 13, 2013.
"Alabama Nabs Foreign Auto Execs in Immigration Crackdowns." *MBJ Business* (blog), *Mississippi Business Journal*, December 5, 2011. http://msbusiness.com/businessblog/2011/12/05/alabama-nabs-foreign-auto-execs-in-immigration-crackdowns/. Accessed February 27, 2014.
"Alas, Poor Alabama, We Might Have Spoken Too Soon." *St. Louis Post-Dispatch*, March 19, 2012. http://www.stltoday.com/news/opinion/columns/the-platform/editorial-alas-poor-alabama-we-might-have-spoken-too-soon/article_bf5dc39a-32e1-599f-a333-f930a7ea99d6.html. Accessed February 15, 2014.
Alderman, Derek H., and E. Arnold Modlin Jr. "Southern Hospitality and the Politics of African American Belonging: An Analysis of North Carolina Tourism Brochure Photographs." *Journal of Cultural Geography* 30, no. 1 (February 2013): 6–31.
The American Anti-Slavery Almanac for 1836. Boston: Webster & Southard, 1835.
The American Anti-Slavery Almanac for 1837. Boston: Southard & Hitchcock, 1836.
The American Anti-Slavery Almanac for 1839. New York & Boston: S. W. Benedict; Isaac Knapp, 1838.
The American Anti-Slavery Almanac for 1840. New York: American Anti-Slavery Society, 1839.
The American Anti-Slavery Almanac for 1841. New York: S. W. Benedict, 1840.
Anderson, Benedict. *Imagined Communities: Reflections on the Origin and Spread of Nationalism*. Rev. ed. New York: Verso, 1991.
Andrews, Sidney. *The South since the War*. Boston: Ticknor & Fields, 1866.
Anecdotes for the Family and Social Circle. New York: American Tract Society, 1832.
Appiah, Kwame Anthony. *Cosmopolitanism: Ethics in a World of Strangers*. New York: W. W. Norton, 2006.
The Art of Good Behaviour; and Letter Writer on Love, Courtship, and Marriage: A Complete Guide for Ladies and Gentlemen, Particularly Those Who Have Not Enjoyed the Advantages of Fashionable Life. New York: Huestis & Cozans, 1850.
The Art of Pleasing; or, The American Lady and Gentleman's Book of Etiquette. Compiled from the latest and best authorities. Cincinnati: H. M. Rulison, Queen City Publishing House, 1855.
Arvine, Rev. Kazlitt. *Our Duty to the Fugitive Slave: A Discourse Delivered on Sunday, Oct. 6, in West Boylston, Mass., and in Worcester, Dec. 15*. Boston: John P. Jewett, 1850.

Atkinson, Charles F., and Francis William Loring. *Cotton Culture and the South with Reference to Emigration.* Boston: A. Williams, 1869.

Atwater, Rev. Cowles H. *Incidents of a Southern Tour; or, The South, as Seen with Northern Eyes.* Boston: J. P. Magee, 1857.

Azziz, Naeesa. "Alabama Immigration Law Unites Blacks, Latinos." BET.com, Black Entertainment Television, LLC, October 23, 2011. http://www.bet.com/news/national/2011/10/23/alabama-immigration-law-unites-blacks-latinos.html. Accessed October 17, 2013.

Bankard, Bob. "The Herschell Gordon Lewis Guide." *phillyBurbs.com.* http://www.phillyburbs.com/hgl/index.shtml. Accessed September 12, 2006.

Barker, Louisa Jane Whiting. *Influence of Slavery upon the White Population, by a Former Resident of Slave States; Anti-Slavery Tracts; no.9.* New York: American Anti-Slavery Society, 1855.

Beecher, Catharine E. *A Treatise on Domestic Economy.* Boston: Marsh, Capen, Lyon & Webb, 1841.

Beecher, Charles. *The Duty of Disobedience to Wicked Laws: A Sermon on the Fugitive Slave Law.* New York: John A. Gray, 1851.

Bellocq, Pierre. "Southern Hospitality." Cartoon. *New York Times*, May 12, 1963, E3.

Benhabib, Seyla. *Another Cosmopolitanism: Hospitality, Sovereignty, and Democratic Iterations.* Edited by Robert Post. Oxford: Oxford University Press, 2006.

Berkowitz, Bill. "David Duke's Welcome Wagon." *Working for Change.* http://workingforchange.com/article.cfm?ItemId=1306. Accessed February 13, 2006.

Bleser, Carol, ed. *Secret and Sacred: The Diaries of James Henry Hammond, a Southern Slaveholder.* Columbia: University of South Carolina Press, 1988.

Blight, David. *Race and Reunion: The Civil War in American Memory.* Cambridge, Mass.: Harvard University Press, 2009.

Bobbitt, Mary Reed. *A Bibliography of Etiquette Books Published in America before 1900.* New York: New York Public Library, 1947.

Bolster, W. Jeffrey. *Black Jacks: African American Seamen in the Age of Sail.* Cambridge, Mass.: Harvard University Press, 1998.

Bone, Martyn. *The Postsouthern Sense of Place in Contemporary Fiction.* Baton Rouge: Louisiana State University Press, 2005.

Bone, Martyn, Brian Ward, and William A. Link, eds. *Creating and Consuming the American South.* Gainesville: University Press of Florida, 2015.

Bourdieu, Pierre. "The Forms of Capital." In *Cultural Theory: An Anthology,* edited by Imre Szeman and Timothy Kaposy, 81–93. Chichester, England: Wiley-Blackwell, 2011.

Bourne, George. *Picture of Slavery in the United States of America.* Middletown, Conn.: E. Hunt, 1834.

Brinton, Daniel G. *A Guide Book of Florida and the South: For Tourists, Invalids and Emigrants.* Philadelphia: George Maclean, 1869.

Brown, David. *The Planter; or, Thirteen Years in the South. By a Northern Man.* Philadelphia: H. Hooker, 1853.

Brown, Sterling Allen. *The Collected Poems of Sterling A. Brown.* Evanston, Ill.: Northwestern University Press, 1996.

Brown, William Wells. *The American Fugitive in Europe: Sketches of Places and People Abroad*. Boston: John P. Jewett, 1855.

———. *The Narrative of William W. Brown, a Fugitive Slave, Written by Himself*. Boston: Anti-Slavery Office, 1847.

———. *Three Years in Europe; or, Places I Have Seen and People I Have Met*. London: Charles Gilpin, 1852.

Brundage, W. Fitzhugh. "From Appalachian Folk to Southern Foodways: Why Americans Look to the South for Authentic Culture." In Bone, Ward, and Link, *Creating and Consuming the American South*, 27–48.

———. *Lynchings in the New South: Georgia and Virginia, 1880–1930s*. Urbana: University of Illinois Press, 1993.

———. *The Southern Past: A Clash of Race and Memory*. Cambridge, Mass.: Harvard University Press, 2009.

———, ed. *Where These Memories Grow: History, Memory, and Southern Identity*. Chapel Hill: University of North Carolina Press, 2000.

Bruni, Frank. "Paula's Worst Ingredients." *New York Times*, June 24, 2013. http://www.nytimes.com/2013/06/25/opinion/bruni-paulas-worst-ingredients.html. Accessed June 1, 2014.

Bryan, Lettice. *The Kentucky Housewife*. Cincinnati: Shepard & Stearns, 1839.

Buinicki, Martin. "Imagining Sites of Memory in the Post–Civil War South: The National Cemetery in Woolson's 'Rodman the Keeper'" In *Witness to Reconstruction: Constance Fenimore Woolson and the Postbellum South, 1873–1894*, edited by Kathleen Diffley, 162–76. Jackson: University Press of Mississippi, 2011.

Bungay, G. W. "A Scene in Boston." *Liberator*, September 13, 1850, 148.

Burns, Jim. "NAACP Plans More Flag Protests, Despite Counter Protests." CNSNews.com. http://www.csnnews.com. Accessed August 14, 2006.

Butt, Martha Haines. *Anti-Fanaticism: A Tale of the South*. Philadelphia: Lippincott, Grambo, 1853.

Calabrella, Baroness E. C. de. *The Ladies' Science of Etiquette, and Hand Book of the Toilet*. New York: Wilson, 1844.

Carey, John. *Learning Is Better than House or Land; as Exemplified in the History of Harry Johnson and Dick Hobson*. Boston: Munroe & Francis, 1824.

Carothers, P. W. B. "Modern Hospitality." *Godey's Lady's Book*, August 1853, 120–28.

C.C.O. "On Hospitality." *The Friend: A Religious and Literary Journal* 7, no. 15 (January 18, 1834): 113.

Chandler, Kim. "Alabama House Passes Arizona-Style Immigration Law." AL.com, April 4, 2011. http://blog.al.com/spotnews/2011/04/alabama_house_passes_arizona-s.html. Accessed February 27, 2014.

Chesnutt, Charles W. *The House behind the Cedars*. Boston: Houghton, Mifflin, 1900.

———. *The Journals of Charles W. Chesnutt*. Edited by Richard H. Brodhead. Durham, N.C.: Duke University Press, 1993.

———. *The Marrow of Tradition*. Boston: Houghton, Mifflin, 1901.

———. "What Is a White Man?" *Independent* 41 (May 30, 1889): 5–6.

"Church Hospitality." *Christian Register*, September 19, 1846, 150.

Cobb, James C. *The Selling of the South: The Southern Crusade for Industrial Development, 1936–1990*. 2nd ed. Urbana: University of Illinois Press, 1993.
Cobb, James C., and William Stueck, eds. *Globalization and the American South*. Athens: University of Georgia Press, 2005.
"Colored Seamen in South Carolina." *Liberator*, September 20, 1850, 150.
Cooper, James Fenimore. *The Spy: A Tale of the Neutral Ground*. 1821. New York: W. A. Townsend, 1859.
Cowan, John F. *A New Invasion of the South. Being a Narrative of the Expedition of the Seventy-First Infantry, National Guard, through the Southern States to New Orleans. February 24–March 7, 1881*. New York: Board of Officers Seventy-First Infantry, 1881.
Cox, John D. *Traveling South: Travel Narratives and the Construction of American Identity*. Athens: University of Georgia Press, 2005.
Cox, Karen L., ed. *Destination Dixie: Tourism and Southern History*. Gainesville: University Press of Florida, 2012.
———. *Dreaming of Dixie: How the South Was Created in American Popular Culture*. Chapel Hill: University of North Carolina Press, 2011.
Crane, Gregg D. *Race, Citizenship, and Law in American Literature*. Cambridge: Cambridge University Press, 2002.
Criswell, Robert. *"Uncle Tom's Cabin" Contrasted with Buckingham Hall*. New York: D. Fanshaw, 1852.
Cross, Alan. "Are Alabama Baptists Wrong to Minister to Illegal Immigrants?" *Downshore Drift* (blog), November 13, 2012. http://www.downshoredrift.com/downshoredrift/2012/11/are-alabama-baptists-wrong-to-minister-to-illegal-immigrants.html. Accessed February 27, 2014.
———. "Could Alabama Baptists Lead the Way in Immigration Reform in America?" *Downshore Drift* (blog), November 15, 2012. http://www.downshoredrift.com/downshoredrift/2012/11/could-alabama-baptists-lead-the-way-in-immigration-reform-in-america.html. Accessed February 27, 2014.
Cuenca, Carme Manuel. "An Angel in the Plantation: The Economics of Slavery and the Politics of Literary Domesticity in Caroline Lee Hentz's *The Planter's Northern Bride*." *Mississippi Quarterly* 51, no.1 (Winter 1997): 87–104.
"Daniel Webster." *Liberator*, March 29, 1850, 52.
"A Day at Summerville." *Southern Literary Journal and Magazine of Arts* 1, no. 3 (May 1837): 227–31.
"Declaration of Sentiments of the Colored Citizens of Boston on the Fugitive Slave Bill." *Liberator*, October 11, 1850, 162.
Deen, Paula, and Sherry Suib Cohen. *It Ain't All about the Cookin'*. New York: Simon & Schuster, 2007.
De Lollis, Barbara. "Hotel: Fallout from Alabama's Controversial Immigration Law." *USA Today Travel*, March 12, 2012. http://travel.usatoday.com/hotels/post/2012/03/mobile-ala-loses-convention-due-to-immigration-law/644713/1. Accessed October 17, 2013.
Derby, James Cephas. *Fifty Years among Authors, Books and Publishers*. New York: G. W. Carleton, 1884.

Derrida, Jacques. "Hostipitality." Translated by Barry Stocker and Forbes Morlock. *Angelaki* 5, no. 3 (December 2000): 3–18.

Derrida, Jacques, and Anne Dufourmantelle. *Of Hospitality: Anne Dufourmantelle Invites Jacques Derrida to Respond*. Translated by Rachel Bowlby. Stanford, Calif.: Stanford University Press, 2000.

Dewell, Debbie. "It's All about the Experience!" *Southern Hospitality Magazine*, Fall 2006, 4. http://www.southernhospitalitymagazine.com/pdfs/SHM_FALL_WEB.pdf. Accessed May 7, 2010.

Dewskin, Elizabeth. "Alabama's Immigration Law Could Cost Billions Annually." *Bloomberg Businessweek*, February 14, 2012. http://www.businessweek.com/articles/2012-02-14/alabamas-immigration-law-could-cost-billions-annually. Accessed October 17, 2013.

Dictionary of North Carolina Biography. Edited by William S. Powell. Vol. 6. Chapel Hill: University of North Carolina Press, 1996.

"Did Willie Do Wrong?" *Liberator*, October 11, 1850, 164.

Dobbins, James. "Southern Hospitality." Cartoon. *New York Times*, December 31, 1961, E6.

Douglass, Frederick. *The Life and Times of Frederick Douglass*. Boston: De Wolfe & Fiske, 1892.

———. *My Bondage and My Freedom*. New York: Miller, Orton & Mulligan, 1855.

Drake, John C. "Hospitality Course Covers 'Friendly.'" *Columbia, SC, State*, July 21, 2004, sec. B.

Drew, Benjamin. *Refugees from Slavery: Autobiographies of Fugitive Slaves in Canada*. Edited by Tilden G. Edelstein. Mineola, N.Y.: Dover, 2004.

Du Bois, W. E. B. *The Souls of Black Folk*. Chicago: A. C. McClurg, 1903.

Duck, Leigh Anne. *The Nation's Region: Southern Modernism, Segregation, and U.S. Nationalism*. Athens: University of Georgia Press, 2006.

Dunbar, Paul Laurence. *Folks from Dixie*. New York: Dodd, Mead, 1899.

Dye, Thomas R. "Rosewood, Florida: The Destruction of an African American Community." *Historian* 58, no. 3 (Spring 1996): 605–22.

Eastman, Mary Henderson. *Aunt Phillis's Cabin; or, Southern Life as It Is*. Philadelphia: Lippincott, Grambo, 1852.

"Editorial Remarks." *Southern Literary Messenger* 1, no. 5 (January 1835): 254.

Egerton, Douglas R. *Gabriel's Rebellion: The Virginia Slave Conspiracies of 1800 and 1802*. Chapel Hill: University of North Carolina Press, 1993.

———. "A Peculiar Mark of Infamy: Dismemberment, Burial, and Rebelliousness in Slave Societies." In *Mortal Remains: Death in Early America*, edited by Nancy Isenberg and Andrew Burstein, Editors, 149–60. Philadelphia: University of Pennsylvania Press, 2003.

Egerton, John. *Southern Food: At Home, on the Road, in History*. Chapel Hill: University of North Carolina Press, 1993.

Elias, Amy J. "Postmodern Southern Vacation: Vacation Advertising, Globalization, and Southern Regionalism." In *South to a New Place: Region, Literature, Culture*, edited by Suzanne Jones and Sharon Monteith, 253–82. Baton Rouge: Louisiana State University Press, 2002.

Elliot, Debbie. "Clergy Sues to Stop Alabama's Immigration Law." Aired on *All Things Considered*, August 23, 2011. National Public Radio. http://www.npr.org/2011/08/23/139887408/clergy-sue-to-stop-alabamas-immigration-law. Accessed February 20, 2014.

Emerson, Ralph Waldo. "The Fugitive Slave Law—Lecture at New York." In *The Complete Works of Ralph Waldo Emerson*, 11:217–44. Boston: Houghton Mifflin, 1904.

"En Avant!" *Southern Literary Messenger* 16, no. 3 (March 1850): 142–44.

Evangelicus. *Onesimus; or, The Apostolic Directions to Christian Masters, in Reference to Their Slaves*. Boston: Gould, Kendall & Lincoln, 1842.

"The Family Circle. Social Intercourse." *New-York Mirror*, June 30, 1838, 3.

Fanuzzi, Robert. *Abolition's Public Sphere*. Minneapolis: University of Minnesota Press, 2003.

Farnham, Christie Anne. *The Education of the Southern Belle: Higher Education and Student Socialization in the Antebellum South*. New York: New York University Press, 1995.

Faust, Drew Gilpin. *This Republic of Suffering: Death and the American Civil War*. New York: Alfred A. Knopf, 2008.

"Five Star Southern Hospitality Training Program." A collaboration between the Alabama Office of Workforce Development at Faulkner State Community College, the Gulf Shores & Orange Beach Tourism, the Foley Convention and Visitors Bureau, the Coastal Alabama Business Chamber, and the South Baldwin Chamber of Commerce. http://www.gulfshores.com/5star/. Accessed August 22, 2016.

Foner, Eric. *Reconstruction: America's Unfinished Revolution, 1863–1877*. New York: Harper & Row, 1988.

Foster, A. "Visit to a Southern Plantation." *Western Recorder*, October 10, 1826, 164.

Foucault, Michel. *The Archaeology of Knowledge*. New York: Pantheon, 1972.

Fox, William. "Mental Hospitality (from *Fox's Sermons*)." *Christian Register*, January 11, 1834, 5–6.

Fox-Genovese, Elizabeth. *Within the Plantation Household: Black and White Women of the Old South*. Chapel Hill: University of North Carolina Press, 1988.

Fox-Genovese, Elizabeth, and Eugene D. Genovese. *The Mind of the Master Class: History and Faith in the Southern Slaveholders' Worldview*. Cambridge: Cambridge University Press, 2005.

Franchot, Jenny. *Roads to Rome: The Antebellum Protestant Encounter with Catholicism*. Berkeley: University of California Press, 1994.

Frost, Sarah Annie [S. A. Shields]. "Sambo: A Man and a Brother." *Lippincott's Magazine of Popular Literature and Science*, August 1878, 242–46.

Frothingham, Octavius Brooks. "Christian Hospitality." *Christian Inquirer*, October 1, 1859, 1.

"The Fugitive Slave to the Christian." *Liberator*, April 5, 1850, 20.

"Gabriel's Defeat." *Liberator*, September 17, 1831, 1.

Genovese, Eugene. *The Political Economy of Slavery*. New York: Random House, 1965.

Gilman, Caroline. *Recollections of a Southern Matron*. New York: Harper & Brothers, 1838.

Goddard, Frederick B. *Where to Emigrate and Why*. New York: Frederick B. Goddard, 1869.

Gray, Richard. "Foreword: Inventing Communities, Imagining Places; Some Thoughts on Southern Self-Fashioning." In *South to a New Place: Region, Literature, Culture*, edited by Suzanne Whitmore Jones and Sharon Monteith, xiii–xxiii. Baton Rouge: Louisiana State University Press, 2002.

Greenberg, Kenneth S. *Honor and Slavery: Lies, Duels, Noses, Masks, Dressing as a Woman, Gifts, Strangers, Humanitarianism, Death, Slave Rebellions, the Proslavery Argument, Baseball, Hunting, and Gambling in the Old South*. Princeton, N.J.: Princeton University Press, 1997.

Greene, Harlan, and Stephen Hoffius. "The Charleston 100." *Charleston Magazine*, November 2007. http://charlestonmag.com/100most/60–80.html. Accessed March 20, 2009.

Greenspan, Ezra, ed. *The William Wells Brown Reader*. Athens: University of Georgia Press, 2008.

Greeson, Jennifer. *Our South: Geographic Fantasy and the Rise of National Literature*. Cambridge, Mass.: Harvard University Press, 2010.

Gregory, Mike. "David F. Friedman: Wage Earner of Sin." An Interview with David F. Friedman. reel.com, 2007. http://www.reel.com/reel.asp?node=features/interviews/friedman. Accessed January 12, 2009.

Griffin, Larry J., and Ashley B. Thompson. "Enough about the Disappearing South: What about the Disappearing Southerner?" *Southern Cultures* 9, no. 3 (2003): 51–65.

Grimke, Sarah M. "Narrative and Testimony of Sarah M. Grimke." *Christian Reflector*, May 22, 1839, 81.

"Guidelines: Lodgings." *Southern Hospitality Magazine*. http://www.southernhospitalitymagazine.com/pdfs/SHM%20EXPERIENCE%20GUIDELINES.pdf. Accessed May 7, 2010.

Hale, Edward E. *Christian Duty to Emigrants: A Sermon Delivered before the Boston Society for the Prevention of Pauperism*. Boston: John Wilson & Son, 1852.

Hale, Grace Elizabeth. *Making Whiteness: The Culture of Segregation in the South, 1890–1940*. New York: Random House, 1998.

Hale, Sarah Josepha. *Liberia; or, Mr. Peyton's Experiments*. New York: Harper & Brothers, 1853.

———. *Manners; or, Happy Homes and Good Society All the Year Round*. Boston: J. E. Tilton, 1868.

———. *Northwood; or, Life North and South*. 5th ed. New York: H. Long & Brother, 1852.

Hall, Melissa Booth. "Southern Six-Pack." June 28, 2013. Southern Foodways Alliance. https://www.southernfoodways.org/southern-six-pack-71/. Accessed February 23, 2016.

Hamer, Philip M. "British Consuls and the Negro Seamen Acts, 1850–1860." *Journal of Southern History* 1, no. 2 (May 1935): 138–68.

———. "Great Britain, the United States, and the Negro Seamen Acts, 1822–1848." *Journal of Southern History* 1, no. 1 (February 1935): 3–28.

Hamilton, Holman. *Prologue to Conflict: The Crisis and Compromise of 1850.* Lexington: University Press of Kentucky, 1964.

Hammond, Fred L. "Why Alabama's Immigration Law Is an Assault on Religious Values." *Tikkun.* http://www.tikkun.org/nextgen/why-alabamas-immigration-law-is-an-assault-on-religious-values. Accessed February 27, 2014.

Hammond, James Henry. "Hammond's Letters on Slavery." In *The Pro-Slavery Argument,* 99–174. Charleston: Walker, Richards, 1852.

Hardy, Lady Duffus. *Down South.* London: Chapman & Hall, 1883.

Harness, A. C. *The Great Trial; or, The Genius of Civilization Brought to Judgement.* Philadelphia: Barclay, 1873.

Hartley, Florence. *The Ladies' Book of Etiquette, and Manual of Politeness.* Philadelphia: G. G. Evans, 1860.

Hedrick, Joan D. *Harriet Beecher Stowe: A Life.* Oxford: Oxford University Press, 1994.

Hemphill, C. Dallett. *Bowing to Necessities: A History of Manners in America, 1620–1860.* Oxford: Oxford University Press, 2002.

Hentz, Caroline Lee. *The Planter's Northern Bride.* Philadelphia: T. B. Peterson, 1854.

Hermes. "The Science of Hospitality." *New-York Mirror,* July 6, 1833, 5.

"Hey Mercedes, Time to Move to a More Welcoming State." *St. Louis Post-Dispatch,* November 22, 2011. http://www.stltoday.com/news/opinion/columns/the-platform/editorial-hey-mercedes-time-to-move-to-a-more-welcoming/article_b5cc5237-d199-570c-8735-caa81e247249.html. Accessed February 15, 2014.

Hinrichsen, Lisa. *Possessing the Past: Trauma, Imagination, and Memory in Post-Plantation Literature.* Baton Rouge: Louisiana State University Press, 2015.

"Hints for Our Native Southerners: What They Should Do Before the Winter Tourist Comes." *Life,* December 13, 1923, 5.

"A Hint to Southern Plantation Owners." *Forest and Stream: A Journal of Outdoor Life, Travel, Nature Study, Shooting, Fishing, Yachting,* September 4, 1879, 610.

Hodgson, Telfair. *A Sermon in Behalf of the Southern Sufferers, Preached by the Rev. Telfair Hodgson, at St. Mary's Church, Keyport, N.J., January 27, 1867.* Princeton, N.J.: Printed at the Standard Office, 1867.

Honig, Bonnie. *Democracy and the Foreigner.* Princeton, N.J.: Princeton University Press, 2001.

Horwitz, Tony. *Confederates in the Attic: Dispatches from the Unfinished Civil War.* New York: Knopf, Doubleday, 2002.

———. "Untrue Confessions." *New Yorker,* December 13, 1999, 80.

"Hospitality." *Christian Register,* August 29, 1846, 138.

"Hospitality." *Liberator,* November 26, 1847, 190.

"Hospitality of 'The Church.'" *Christian Register,* February 1, 1845, 18.

"Hospitality of the Olden Time." *Godey's Magazine and Lady's Book,* March 1847, 127.

Huang, Yunte. "Southern Hospitality, but Not for Newcomers." *New York Times,* November 20, 2011, SR5.

Hughes, Tom. *"Rich Georgian Strangely Shot": Eugene Grace, "Daisy of the Leopard Spots" and the Great Atlanta Shooting of 1912.* Jefferson, N.C.: McFarland, 2012.

Hundley, Daniel R. *Social Relations in Our Southern States.* New York: Henry B. Price, 1860.

Hutchinson, Susan D. Nye. "Mrs. Hutchinson's Letter" (to the Ladies of the Abolition Society of Massachusetts). *African Repository and Colonial Journal* 12, no. 5 (May 1836): 154–57.

Iacobelli, Pete. "White Pride Group, Confederate Flags Welcome Motorists to S.C." *Savannah Morning News on the Web*. http://savannahnow.com. Accessed August 14, 2006.

"Immigrant Justice." Southern Poverty Law Center. http://www.splcenter.org/what-we-do/immigrant-justice. Accessed April 4, 2014.

"Imprisonment of Colored Seamen." *Liberator*, October 4, 1850, 157.

Isaac, Rhys. *The Transformation of Virginia, 1740–1790*. Chapel Hill: University of North Carolina Press, 1982.

Jackson, Jay. "Bungleton Green: Southern Hospitality." Comic Strip. *Chicago Defender*, June 21, 1941, 15.

Jackson, Leon. *The Business of Letters: Authorial Economies in Antebellum America*. Stanford, Calif.: Stanford University Press, 2008.

Jarrett, Calvin D. "Calvin H. Wiley: Southern Education Leader." *Peabody Journal of Education* 41, no. 5 (March 1964): 276–88.

Jeffrey, Julie Roy. *The Great Silent Army of Abolitionism: Ordinary Women in the Antislavery Movement*. Chapel Hill: University of North Carolina Press, 1998.

Johnson, James Gibson. "Southern Fiction Prior to 1860: An Attempt at a First-Hand Bibliography." PhD diss., University of Virginia, 1968.

Jones, Charles H., ed. *Appleton's Handbook of American Travel: Southern Tour*. New York: D. Appleton, 1873.

Jones, Megan Norris. "Defining the Southern in *Southern Living*." MA thesis, University of Missouri, December 2009. https://mospace.umsystem.edu/xmlui/bitstream/handle/10355/5339/research.pdf?sequence=3. Accessed November 11, 2015.

Julian, L. H. "America's Welcome to Kossuth." *National Era*, December 11, 1851, 197.

Kant, Immanuel. *Perpetual Peace: A Philosophical Sketch*. 1795. Minneapolis: Filiquarian, 2007.

Kaplan, Amy. "Manifest Domesticity." In *No More Separate Spheres! A New Wave American Studies Reader*, edited by Cathy N. Davidson and Jessamyn Hatcher, 183–207. Durham, N.C.: Duke University Press, 2002.

Kasson, John F. *Rudeness and Civility: Manners in Nineteenth-Century Urban America*. New York: Hill & Wang, 1990.

Kaufman, Theodor. *Effects of the Fugitive Slave Law*. Broadside. New York: Hoff & Bloede, 1850.

Keller, Ralph A. "Methodist Newspapers and the Fugitive Slave Law: A New Perspective for the Slavery Crisis in the North." *Church History* 43, no. 3 (September 1974): 319–39.

Kennaway, John H. *On Sherman's Track; or, The South after the War*. London: Seeley, Jackson, & Halliday, 1867.

King, P. Nicole. *Sombreros and Motorcycles in a Newer South: The Politics of Aesthetics in South Carolina's Tourism Industry*. Jackson: University Press of Mississippi, 2012.

Kirkland, Mrs. C. M. "A Chapter on Hospitality." *Godey's Magazine and Lady's Book*, May 1846, 222–25.

Koger, Larry. *Black Slaveowners: Free Black Slave Masters in South Carolina, 1790–1860.* Jefferson, N.C.: McFarland, 1985.

Komlos, John. *Louis Kossuth in America, 1851–1852.* Buffalo, N.Y.: East European Institute, 1973.

"Kossuth." *Gleason's Pictorial Drawing-Room Companion,* November 29, 1851, 492.

"Kossuth and Congress." *New York Daily Times,* December 8, 1851, 2.

"Kossuth and Intervention." *Southern Quarterly Review* 6, no. 11 (July 1852): 221–35.

Kreyling, Michael. *Inventing Southern Literature.* Jackson: University Press of Mississippi, 1998.

———. *The South That Wasn't There: Postsouthern Memory and History.* Baton Rouge: Louisiana State University Press, 2010.

Ladd, Dr. "Sketch of the Character of the S. Carolinians—Their Luxury and Dissipations—Fatal Effects of Luxury—Hospitality of South Carolina." *American Museum, or, Universal Magazine,* February 1789, 130–31.

Lang, Rebecca D. *Rebecca Lang's Southern Entertaining for a New Generation.* Nashville: Cumberland House, 2004.

Lassiter, Matthew D., and Joseph Crespino, eds. *The Myth of Southern Exceptionalism.* Oxford: Oxford University Press, 2010.

"The Laurels of Demosthenes." *Saturday Evening Post,* September 19, 1908, 17.

Le, Van. "Lake Research Poll: 66% of African American Voters Support Immigration Reform with Citizenship," May 1, 2013. America's Voice. http://americasvoice.org/blog/lake-research-poll-66-of-african-american-voters-support-immigration-reform-with-citizenship/. Accessed October 17, 2013.

Leavitt, Sarah A. *From Catherine Beecher to Martha Stewart: A Cultural History of Domestic Advice.* Chapel Hill: University of North Carolina Press, 2002.

Ledyard, Catherine. "Kossuth." *National Era,* December 11, 1851, 198.

Lehuu, Isabelle. "Sentimental Figures: Reading *Godey's Lady's Book* in Antebellum America." In *The Culture of Sentiment: Race, Gender, and Sentimentality in Nineteenth-Century America,* edited by Shirley Samuels, 73–91. Oxford: Oxford University Press, 1992.

"Letter to Henry Clay." *Liberator,* April 19, 1850, 64.

Levine, Robert S. *Martin Delany, Frederick Douglass, and the Politics of Representative Identity.* Chapel Hill: University of North Carolina Press, 1997.

"Liberation of Kossuth." *National Era,* October 9, 1851, 162.

The Liberty Almanac for 1850. New York: American Anti-Slavery Society, 1849.

The Liberty Almanac for 1852. New York: American Anti-Slavery Society, 1851.

Lichtenstein, Alex. "Right Church, Wrong Pew: Eugene Genovese & Southern Conservatism." *New Politics* 6, no. 3 (Summer 1997): 59–68.

Lincoln, Abraham. "A House Divided: Speech Delivered at Springfield, Illinois, at the Close of the Republican State Convention, June 15, 1868." In *Abraham Lincoln: His Speeches and Writings,* 372–81. Cambridge, Mass.: Da Capo Press, 2001.

Logue, John, and Gary McCalla. *Life at Southern Living: A Sort of Memoir.* Baton Rouge: Louisiana State University Press, 2000.

Lord, John C. *"The Higher Law," in its Application to the Fugitive Slave Bill: A Sermon on* the Duties Men Owe to God and to Governments. New York: Union Safety Committee, 1851.

Loughran, Trish. *The Republic in Print: Print Culture in the Age of U.S. Nation Building, 1770–1870.* New York: Columbia University Press, 2007.

Luraghi, Raimondo. *The Rise and Fall of the Plantation South.* New York: Franklin Watts, 1978.

Maddex, Jack P., Jr. *The Reconstruction of Edward A. Pollard: A Rebel's Conversion to Postbellum Unionism.* Chapel Hill: University of North Carolina Press, 1974.

Mauss, Marcel. *The Gift: The Form and Reason for Exchange in Archaic Societies.* Translated by W. D. Halls. Foreword by Mary Douglas. New York: W. W. Norton, 1990.

McElwin, Henry. *Travels in the South: A Series of Letters.* Elyria, Ohio, 1882.

McGee, Celia. "The Open Road Wasn't Quite Open to All." *New York Times*, August 22, 2010, C1.

McKivigan, John R. *Forgotten Firebrand: James Redpath and the Making of Nineteenth-Century America.* Ithaca, N.Y.: Cornell University Press, 2008.

McNulty, Tracy. *The Hostess: Hospitality, Femininity, and the Expropriation of Identity.* Minneapolis: University of Minnesota Press, 2007.

McPherson, Tara. *Reconstructing Dixie: Race, Gender, and Nostalgia in the Imagined South.* Durham, N.C.: Duke University Press, 2003.

"Mental Hospitality." *Christian Inquirer*, December 20, 1856, 2.

Michel, Jean-Baptiste. "Quantitative Analysis of Culture Using Millions of Digitized Books." *Science* 331, No. 6014 (January 14, 2011): 176–82.

Miller, Dave. "Immigration Brouhaha at SBC." *SBC Voices*, June 15, 2011. http://sbcvoices.com/immigration-brouhaha-at-sbc/. Accessed March 10, 2014.

Minor, Lucian. "Letters from New England—No. 1," *Southern Literary Messenger* 1, no. 3 (November 1834): 84–88.

———. "Letters from New England—No. 2." *Southern Literary Messenger* 1, no. 4 (December 1834): 166–69.

———. "Letters from New England—No. 5." *Southern Literary Messenger* 1, no. 8 (April 1835): 421–27.

Mitchell, Laura L. "'Matters of Justice between Man and Man': Northern Divines, the Bible, and the Fugitive Slave Act of 1850." In *Religion and the Antebellum Debate over Slavery*, edited by John R. McKivigan and Mitchell Snay, 134–65. Athens: University of Georgia Press, 1998.

M.L.C. "Women at the South and at the West." *Phrenological Journal and Science of Health* 58, no. 3 (March 1874): 174–76.

Moskin, Julia. "A Culinary Birthright in Dispute," *New York Times*, June 26, 2013. NYTimes.com. http://www.nytimes.com/2013/06/26/dining/paula-deens-words-ripple-among-southern-chefs.html. Accessed July 7, 2015.

Moss, Elizabeth. *Domestic Novelists of the Old South: Defenders of Southern Culture.* Baton Rouge: Louisiana State University Press, 1992.

Mott, Frank Luther. *A History of American Magazines, 1865–1885.* Cambridge, Mass.: Harvard University Press, 1957.

"Mr. Webster's Speech on Slavery." *Liberator*, April 12, 1850, 57.

"Music City's Hospitality Workers Get a Crash Course in Southern Hospitality." *Nashville Business Journal*, September 6, 2009 http://www.bizjournals.com/nashville/stories/2009/09/07/focus1.html. Accessed February 1, 2014.

The Negro Motorist Green Book. 1949 ed. New York: Victor H. Green, 1949.

Newman, Harvey K. *Southern Hospitality: Tourism and the Growth of Atlanta*. Tuscaloosa: University of Alabama Press, 1999.

"Nikki Haley Defends Confederate Flag: CEOs Haven't Complained." *TPM: Talking Points Memo*. http://talkingpointsmemo.com/livewire/nikki-haley-confederate-flag-ceos. Accessed July 10, 2015.

Nunberg, Geoffrey. "Google's Book Search: A Disaster for Scholars." *Chronicle of Higher Education*, August 31, 2009. http://chronicle.com/article/Googles-Book-Search-A/48245/. Accessed July 5, 2016.

O'Brien, Michael. *Conjectures of Order: Intellectual Life and the American South, 1810–1860*. Vol. 1. Chapel Hill: University of North Carolina Press, 2004.

Odem, Mary E. "Latin American Immigration and the New Multiethnic South." In Lassiter and Crespino, *Myth of Southern Exceptionalism*, 234–60.

Ogle, Oliver. "The Wedding," *Lady's Book*, November 1835, 204–7.

Oliver, James, and Lois E. Horton, eds. *Slavery and Public History: The Tough Stuff of American Memory*. Chapel Hill: University of North Carolina Press, 2009.

"The 'Organ' upon Kossuth." *New York Daily Times*, December 13, 1851, 2.

"Outlines of English Literature." *Southern Literary Messenger* 18, no. 8 (August 1852): 511–12.

Page, Thomas Nelson. *The Old South: Essays Social and Political*. New York: Charles Scribner's Sons, 1892.

———. *Social Life in Old Virginia before the War*. New York: Charles Scribner's Sons, 1897.

"Paula Deen on Race in 2012 TimesTalk." NYTimes.com. http://www.nytimes.com/video/us/100000002296089/paula-deen-on-race-in-2012-timestalk.html. Accessed June 1, 2014.

Peacock, James L. *Grounded Globalism: How the U.S. South Embraces the World*. Athens: University of Georgia Press, 2007.

Peacock, James L., Harry L. Watson, and Carrie R. Matthews, eds. *The American South in a Global World*. Chapel Hill: University of North Carolina Press, 2005.

Petrie, Phil W. "Economic Sanctions Still On in South Carolina." *Crisis* 109, no. 2 (March–April 2002): 54.

"Philemon and Onesimus." *Liberator*, May 6, 1853, 1.

Phillipson, Coleman. *The International Law and Custom of Ancient Greece and Rome*. New York: Macmillan, 1911.

Pitzer, Amy. *Southern Hospitality Cookbook: Menus and Recipes for Entertaining Simply & Graciously*. Atlanta: August House, 1994.

Pollard, Edward A. *The Lost Cause Regained*. New York: G. W. Carleton.

———. *The Virginia Tourist: Sketches of the Springs and Mountains of Virginia*. Philadelphia: J. B. Lippincott, 1870.

The Poor Organ Grinder from Hungary. Broadside. New York: T. W. Strong, ca. 1852.

Preston, Julia. "In Alabama, a Harsh Bill for Residents Here Illegally." *New York Times*, June 4, 2011, A10.

Prince, K. Stephen. *Stories of the South: Race and the Reconstruction of Southern Identity*. Chapel Hill: University of North Carolina Press, 2014.

"Project Update: Nat Turner/1831 Southampton Insurrection Train & Restoration of the Rebecca Vaughan House." Southampton County Board of Supervisors, Regular Session, February 25, 2013. http://southamptoncounty.org/MediaArchive/. Accessed March 2, 2014.

"Pro-Slavery as It Is." *Liberator*, January 17, 1840, 10.

"A Puzzle for Philemon." *Liberator*, July 5, 1850, 107.

Raines, Howell. "Getting to the Heart of Dixie." Review of *Encyclopedia of Southern Culture*. *New York Times*, September 17, 1989. NYTimes.com. http://www.nytimes.com/1989/09/17/books/getting-to-the-heart-of-dixie.html. Accessed July 10, 2015.

Ralph, Julian. *Dixie; or, Southern Scenes and Sketches*. New York: Harper & Brothers, 1896.

Ramsey, Calvin Alexander, with Gwen Strauss. *Ruth and the Green Book*. Illustrations by Floyd Cooper. Minneapolis: Carolrhoda Books, 2010.

Randolph, J. Thornton [Charles Jacob Peterson]. *The Cabin and the Parlor; or, Slaves and Masters*. Philadelphia: T. B. Peterson, 1852.

Randolph, Mary. *The Virginia Housewife; or, Methodical Cook*. Philadelphia: E. H. Butler, 1860.

Redpath, James. *The Roving Editor; or, Talks with Slaves in the Southern States*. New York: A. B. Burdick, 1859.

Reid, Whitelaw. *After the War: A Southern Tour*. London: Sampson Low, Son, & Marston, 1866.

"Report of the Committee on Slavery, Adopted by the Methodist Anti-Slavery Convention, held at Lynn, Mass., Oct. 25th and 26th, 1837—and Ordered to Be Published in *Zion's Herald*." *Zion's Herald*, November 29, 1837, 1.

Reynolds, David S. *Walt Whitman's America: A Cultural Biography*. New York: Random House, 2011.

Ricoeur, Paul. "Memory and Forgetting." In *Questioning Ethics: Contemporary Debates in Philosophy*, edited by Richard Kearney and Mark Dooley, 5–11. New York: Routledge, 2002.

———. *Memory, History, Forgetting*. Chicago: University of Chicago Press, 2004.

Roberts, Diane. "Living Southern in *Southern Living*." In *Dixie Debates: Perspectives on Southern Culture*, edited by Richard H. King and Helen Taylor, 85–93. New York: New York University Press, 1996.

Roberts, Timothy Mason. *Distant Revolutions: 1848 and the Challenge to American Exceptionalism*. Charlottesville: University of Virginia Press, 2009.

Robinson, Zandria F. *This Ain't Chicago: Race, Class, and Regional Identity in the Post-Soul South*. Chapel Hill: University of North Carolina Press, 2014.

Romine, Scott. "God and the MoonPie: Consumption, Disenchantment, and the Reliably Lost Cause." In Bone, Ward, and Link, *Creating and Consuming the American South*, 49–71.

———. *The Narrative Forms of Southern Community*. Baton Rouge: Louisiana State University Press, 1999.

———. *The Real South: Southern Narrative in the Age of Cultural Reproduction*. Baton Rouge: Louisiana State University Press, 2008.

Roper, Moses. *A Narrative of the Adventures and Escape of Moses Roper, from American Slavery*. Philadelphia: Merrihew & Gunn, 1838.

Rosello, Mireille. *Postcolonial Hospitality: The Immigrant as Guest*. Stanford, Calif.: Stanford University Press, 2001.

Rotberg, Robert I., and Dennis Thompson, eds. *Truth v. Justice: The Morality of Truth Commissions*. Princeton, N.J.: Princeton University Press, 2000.

Rothert, Otto Arthur. *A History of Muhlenberg County*. Louisville, Ky.: John P. Morton, 1913.

Rowe, O. M. E. "The Quaker Poet." *Friends' Intelligencer*, January 7, 1883, 11–13.

Rutledge, Sarah. *House and Home; or, The Carolina Housewife*. Charleston, S.C.: John Russell, 1855.

Ryan, Susan M. *The Grammar of Good Intentions: Race and the Antebellum Culture of Benevolence*. Ithaca, N.Y.: Cornell University Press, 2003.

Sanders, Mark A. *Afro-Modernist Aesthetics & the Poetry of Sterling A. Brown*. Athens: University of Georgia Press, 1999.

"Scenes from Louisiana." *Christian Watchman*, April 18, 1828, 1.

Schweninger, Loren, ed. *The Southern Debate over Slavery: Petitions to Southern Legislatures, 1778–1864*. Vol. 1. Champaign: University of Illinois Press, 2001.

Scott, Frank William. *Newspapers and Periodicals of Illinois, 1814–1879*. Vol. 6. Springfield: Illinois State Historical Society, 1910.

Seidel, Kathryn Lee. *The Southern Belle in the American Novel*. Gainesville: University Press of Florida, 1985.

Seiler, Cotton. *Republic of Drivers: A Cultural History of Automobility in America*. Chicago: University of Chicago Press, 2009.

Seward, William H. *The Works of William H. Seward*. Edited by George E. Baker. Vol. 1. New York: Redfield, 1853.

"Signs of Character: Physiognomy. Effects of Climate." *American Phrenological Journal* 37, no. 3 (March 1863): 59–60.

Silber, Nina. *The Romance of Reunion: Northerners and the South, 1865–1900*. Chapel Hill: University of North Carolina Press, 1993.

Slave Narratives: A Folk History of Slavery in the United States. Vol. 4: *Georgia Narratives*. Washington, D.C.: Federal Writers' Project, 1941.

Smith, Andrew F., ed. *The Oxford Encyclopedia of Food and Drink in America*. Oxford: Oxford University Press, 2004.

Smith, Daniel Blake. *Inside the Great House*. Ithaca, N.Y.: Cornell University Press, 1986.

Smith, Jon. *Finding Purple America: The South and the Future of American Cultural Studies*. Athens: University of Georgia Press, 2013.

"The South and Intervention." *New York Daily Times*, February 5, 1852, 2.

Southern Foodways Alliance. "About Us: Mission." https://www.southernfoodways.org/about-us/. Accessed February 21, 2016.

———. "Southern Food Primer: Community." https://www.southernfoodways.org/scholarship/southern-food-primer/. Accessed February 21, 2016.

"Southern Hospitality." *New York Times*, May 19, 1963, 1.

"Southern Hospitality—Montgomery Style." *Chicago Daily Defender*, December 1, 1964, 1.

"Southern Literature." *Putnam's Monthly Magazine of Literature, Science, and Art*, February 1857, 207–14.

Southern Living 2013 Media Kit: Audience. http://www.southernliving.com/static/pdf/2013_audience.pdf. Accessed July 7, 2015.

Spencer, Donald S. *Louis Kossuth and Young America: A Study of Sectionalism and Foreign Policy, 1848–1852*. Columbia: University of Missouri Press, 1977.

Starnes, Richard, ed. *Southern Journeys: Tourism, History, and Culture in the Modern South*. Tuscaloosa: University of Alabama Press, 2003.

Stowe, Harriet Beecher. "The Freeman's Dream: A Parable." *National Era*, August 1, 1850, 121.

———. *Uncle Tom's Cabin*. Boston: John P. Jewett, 1852.

Stowe, Steven M. *Intimacy and Power in the Old South: Ritual in the Lives of the Planters*. Baltimore: Johns Hopkins University Press, 1987.

Sundquist, Eric J. *To Wake the Nations: Race in the Making of American Literature*. Cambridge, Mass.: Harvard University Press, 1994.

"Sweet Home Alabama." Official Travel Site of Alabama: Alabama Tourism Department. http://alabama.travel/experience-alabama/hospitality. Accessed February 20, 2014.

Thoreau, Henry David. *The Essays of Henry D. Thoreau*. Edited by Lewis Hyde. New York: Macmillan, 2002.

"A Timeline of Paula Deen's Downfall." TVGuide.com. http://www.tvguide.com/news/paula-deen-scandal-timeline-1067274/. Accessed July 17, 2015.

"To Kossuth." *Southern Literary Messenger* 17, no. 5 (May 1851): 318.

"Top 25 US Consumer Magazines for December 2013," *Alliance for Audited Media*. http://auditedmedia.com/news/research-and-data/top-25-us-consumer-magazines-for-december-2013/. Accessed July 7, 2015.

Tower, Philo. *Slavery Unmasked: Being a Truthful Narrative of a Three Years' Residence and Journeying in Eleven Southern States; To Which Is Added the Invasion of Kansas, including the Last Chapter of Her Wrongs*. Rochester, N.Y.: E. Darrow & Brother, 1856.

"Transcript of Plessy v. Ferguson (1896)." *Our Documents*. http://www.ourdocuments.gov/doc.php?flash=true&doc=52&page=transcript. Accessed June 10, 2015.

Transcript of the Testimony of Paula Deen; Lisa Jackson v. Paula Deen, et al. 4:12-CV-0139. Savannah: Tom Crites & Associates International, 2013.

Twitty, Michael W. "An Open Letter to Paula Deen." *Afroculinaria*. http://afroculinaria.com/2013/06/25/an-open-letter-to-paula-deen/. Accessed June 15, 2015.

Two Thousand Maniacs! Directed by Herschell Gordon Lewis. Friedman-Lewis Productions, 1964.

Valdes, Gustavo. "New Alabama Law Unsettling for Some Undocumented Immigrants." CNN.Com. October 3, 2011. http://www.cnn.com/2011/10/03/justice/alabama-immigration-law-reaction/. Accessed February 27, 2014.

Vidi. *Mr. Frank, the Underground Mail-Agent.* Philadelphia: Lippincott, Grambo, 1853.

Wallerstein, Immanuel. "What Can One Mean by Southern Culture?" In *The Evolution of Southern Culture*, edited by Numan V. Bartley, 1–13. Athens: University of Georgia Press, 1988.

Warren, Robert Penn. *Segregation: The Inner Conflict of the South.* New York: Random House, 1956.

Weiner, Marli F. *Mistresses and Slaves: Plantation Women in South Carolina, 1830–1880.* Champaign: University of Illinois Press, 1997.

Weld, Theodore Dwight. *American Slavery as It Is: Testimony of a Thousand Witnesses.* New York: American Anti-Slavery Society, 1839.

Whalen, Terence. *Edgar Allan Poe and the Masses.* Princeton, N.J.: Princeton University Press, 1999.

"Whimsicalities." *Southern Literary Messenger* 18, no. 4 (April 1852): 256.

Whitelegg, Drew. "From Smiles to Miles: Delta Air Lines Flight Attendants and Southern Hospitality." *Southern Cultures* 11, no. 4 (Winter 2005): 7–27.

Whitman, Walt. *Leaves of Grass.* Brooklyn, N.Y.: [Rome Brothers], 1855.

Whittier, John Greenleaf. "Kossuth." *National Era*, December 1851, 194.

———. "A Sabbath Scene." *Liberator*, July 5, 1850, 108.

———. *The Stranger in Lowell.* Boston: Waite, Peirce, 1845.

Wiencek, Henry. "The Dark Side of Thomas Jefferson," *Smithsonian Magazine*, October 2012. http://www.smithsonianmag.com/history/the-dark-side-of-thomas-jefferson-35976004/#5AMKyXHGEsxBjXrg.99. Accessed June 12, 2014.

Wiese, Andrew. "African-American Suburbanization and Regionalism." In Lassiter and Crespino, *Myth of Southern Exceptionalism*, 210–33.

Wiley, Calvin Henderson. *Roanoke, or, Where Is Utopia?* Philadelphia: T. B. Peterson, 1852.

Wilson, Charles Reagan, ed. *The New Encyclopedia of Southern Culture.* 24 vols. Chapel Hill: University of North Carolina Press, 2006–13.

Wilson, Charles Reagan, and William Ferris, eds. *Encyclopedia of Southern Culture.* Chapel Hill: University of North Carolina Press, 1989.

Wilson, Matthew. *Whiteness in the Novels of Charles W. Chesnutt.* Jackson: University Press of Mississippi, 2009.

Wong, Edlie L. *Neither Fugitive nor Free: Atlantic Slavery, Freedom Suits, and the Legal Culture of Travel.* New York: New York University Press, 2009.

Woodell, Harold. "Justice Denied in the Old South: Three Novels by F. Colburn Adams." *Southern Literary Journal* 11, no. 1 (Fall 1978): 54–63.

Woolson, Constance Fenimore. *Rodman the Keeper: Southern Sketches.* New York: Appleton, 1880.

———. "Up the Ashley and Cooper." *Harper's Monthly*, December 1875, 1–24.

Wright, Julia McNair. *The Cabin in the Brush.* Philadelphia: J. P. Skelly, 1870.

———. *The Complete Home: An Encyclopædia of Domestic Life and Affairs.* Philadelphia: J. C. McCurdy, 1879.

Wyatt-Brown, Bertram. *Southern Honor: Ethics and Behavior in the Old South*. Oxford: Oxford University Press, 1982.

X Y Z. "Letters from the South West to Mr. A. Tappan: Letter II." *American Anti-Slavery Reporter*, March 1834, 42.

"Your Guests Expect Southern Hospitality." *Southern Hospitality Magazine*, Fall 2006, 28. http://www.southernhospitalitymagazine.com/pdfs/SHM_FALL_WEB.pdf. Accessed May 7, 2010.

Yuhl, Stephanie E. *A Golden Haze of Memory: The Making of Historic Charleston*. Chapel Hill: University of North Carolina Press, 2005.

Zenneck, A. *Murder of Louisiana Sacrificed on the Altar of Radicalism*. Broadside. N.p., 1871.

Zinn, Howard. *The Southern Mystique*. New York: Alfred A. Knopf, 1964.

Zylinska, Joanna. *The Ethics of Cultural Studies*. London: Continuum, 2005.

Index

abolition hospitality, 25, 49, 70–76, 98–100, 216–18

abolitionism: antebellum critiques of, 41–44, 131–32, 232n55; and the Fugitive Slave Law, 80–84, 190, 217, 234n9; Garrisonian, 38; Greeson on, 226n28, 232n51; and Kossuth, 127–28; and mental hospitality, 67–76; and the Negro Seamen Acts, 111, 190; and northerners, 90–95; and progressive ideologies, 10; white, 100

Act for Better Regulation and Government of Free Negroes and Persons of Color, 107

active forgetting, 167

Adams, Francis Colburn, 240n22; *Justice in the By-Ways*, 112; *Manuel Pereira*, 111–16, 163, 240nn23–24; *Our World; or, The Slaveholder's Daughter*, 112; *Uncle Tom at Home*, 112

Adams, John Quincy, 123

Adams, Nehemiah, *South-Side View of Slavery*, 91

Addy, Samuel, 215

advertising, 168, 172, 197–98, 200

advice literature. *See* etiquette

African Americans: as alien presence, 7, 79, 104–5, 118, 131–33, 148; and "culinary injustice," 207–8; narratives of, 97–103, 159–61, 251n51; political power of, 173; portrayal of, 8–10, 142–43, 156; post–civil rights, 7, 193, 220n11; post-Reconstruction, 150–51; as service laborers, 8–10, 82, 194, 198, 204–7; and tourism, 178–91; Zinn on, 104. *See also* race and racism; racial politics; segregation; slavery

Afroculinaria (website), 207

Alabama, 27, 107, 176, 184, 195–97, 213–18

Alabama Baptist Convention, 217–18

Alderman, Derek H., 191

alien populations. *See* immigration; strangers and foreigners

almanacs, 25, 41–44, 81–83, 232n55

Althusser, Louis, 45

American Anti-Slavery Almanac, The, 41–43

American Anti-Slavery Reporter, 40

American Anti-Slavery Society, 43

American Tract Society, 134

Anderson, Benedict, 220n13

Andersonville National Cemetery, 141, 245n14

Anecdotes for the Family and Social Circle, 229n24

antebellum hospitality: and abolition hospitality, 25, 49, 70–76, 98–100, 216–18; and benevolence, 32; and class, 29; and etiquette, 56–60, 95; and exclusionary politics, 56; and mental hospitality, 67–76; Minor on, 28–35; and modern racial dynamics, 181, 185; and origins of southern hospitality, 2–4, 11–13, 23–24, 219n3; and pro-southern texts, 44–47, 49–51; sacred and secular models of, 51–56; and sectionalism, 37–38, 48–51, 151–52; and slavery, 8–10, 39–44, 48–51; and social capital, 36–37, 41–42, 91, 169–70; and sovereignty, 35–39, 106, 111; and Wiley's *Roanoke*, 61–65. *See also* postbellum hospitality

antirendition literature, 84–88, 97

antislavery texts: and abolition hospitality, 70–76, 98–100; almanacs, 25, 41–44, 81–83, 232n55; and ethics of hospitality, 39–47, 79–88, 159–60; and the Fugitive Slave Law, 79–88, 97–103, 190; and mental hospitality, 67–76. *See also* abolitionism

Appiah, Kwame Anthony, 27

aristocratic hospitality: and etiquette, 57; and forgetting, 76; vs. liberal hospitality, 46, 72; and nostalgia, 65, 139, 152; Page on, 156; of the planter class, 23, 62–65, 105; Pollard on, 147–48; in pro-southern texts, 49–51; vs. republican hospitality, 24–25, 53–54, 60–61, 65; and Wiley's *Roanoke*, 61–65; and Woolson's "Southern Sketches," 139. *See also* class

Arizona, 17, 214

281

Art of Good Behavior, The, 57–58
Art of Pleasing, The, 58–59, 228–29n23
Arvine, Kazlitt, 234n19; "Our Duty to the Fugitive Slave," 86
asylum, 52, 81–82, 119
Atwater, Cowles H., 224n3

Barker, Louisa Jane Whiting, "Influence of Slavery upon the White Population, by a Former Resident of Slave States," 43–44
Beason, Scott, 213–14
Beecher, Catherine, 87; *Treatise on Domestic Economy*, 59–60
Beecher, Charles, "The Duty of Disobedience to Wicked Laws," 85–86
Bellocq, Pierre, 176–77
benevolence: and antebellum hospitality, 32; and consumerism, 58–59; toward fugitive slaves, 99–100, 103; and honor, 33; and mental hospitality, 68; between North and South, 31, 37–39; and pro-southern texts, 49–51, 90; strangers and foreigners, 54–56; in Whittier's *Stranger in Lowell*, 73–75
Benhabib, Seyla, 25–27, 116–17, 222n26; *Another Cosmopolitanism*, 110
Benton, Thomas Hart, 124
Beverly, Robert, *History of Virginia*, 30
biblical hospitality. *See* Christianity
Birmingham Campaign, 202
black identity. *See* racial identity
Blight, David, *Race and Reunion*, 146, 148, 243n4, 245n15
Bone, Martyn, 13; *Creating and Consuming the American South*, 3
Boston Traveler, 176
Bourdieu, Pierre, 36–37, 41, 169
Bourne, George, 43; *Picture of Slavery in the United States of America*, 39–40
boycott, of South Carolina tourism, 27, 178–80, 185
Breeding, Vincent, 179
Brigadoon (musical), 171
Brown, David, *The Planter*, 237n46
Brown, Sterling A., "Remembering Nat Turner," 184–85
Brown, Wells, 98–99, 238n51
Brown, William Wells: *American Fugitive in Europe*, 97–103, 237n48; *Three Years in Europe*, 97, 238n51

Brown v. Board of Education, 104, 169
Brundage, W. Fitzhugh, 209–10, 256n34; *Lynchings in the New South*, 244n5; *The Southern Past*, 181–82
Butt, Martha Haines, *Anti-Fanaticism*, 90–93

Calabrella, Baroness de, *Ladies' Science of Etiquette*, 23, 58, 228–29n23
Carey, John, *Learning Is Better Than House or Land*, 226n25
Carothers, P. W. B., "Modern Hospitality," 49–51, 65
C. C. O., "On Hospitality," 54–56, 60
Center for American Progress, 215
Center for Business & Economic Research, 214
Center for Sustainable Tourism, 191
Center for the Study of Southern Culture, 208
Chaney, James, 175
Channing, William Ellery, 69, 231n44
charity, 73–75, 85, 95, 99–100, 103, 105. *See also* benevolence
Charleston (S.C.), 22, 107–8, 111–16, 179, 181–84, 188
Charleston Magazine, 114–15
Chesnutt, Charles W., 26, 251n51; *The House behind the Cedars*, 162–63; *The Marrow of Tradition*, 161–67, 251n57, 252–53n62, 252nn58–59; "What Is a White Man?," 251–52n57
Chicago Defender, 185–87
Christian Inquirer, 68, 231n40
Christianity: and antirendition literature, 84–88; and consumerism, 53–55, 135; and domesticity, 88; and ethics of hospitality, 55–60; and etiquette, 57, 229n24; and the Fugitive Slave Law, 78–79, 80–82; and immigration, 216–18; Lot's "sacred guests," 56; and mental hospitality, 67–76; Paul's letter to Philemon, 55, 78–79, 218, 262n23; Paul's letter to the Hebrews, 67–71; in pro-southern texts, 49–51; and Reconstruction, 133–39; and republican idealism, 60–61, 65; vs. secular hospitality, 52–55; and slavery, 39–40; and the stranger, 54–56, 59–60, 128, 130, 231n44, 231n46; in Wright's *Cabin in the Brush*, 136–38

Christian Register, 67, 231n46
citizenship: and cosmopolitanism, 71, 103, 110, 112–13, 119; of freed slaves, 131; and Kant, 120, 222n26; and Reconstruction, 143; restrictions of, 188; rights of, 108, 237n49; and strangers and foreigners, 118
civil disobedience, 86–87, 106, 108–9
Civil Rights Act of 1964, 169, 187–88
civil rights movement: and African American return to the South, 7, 93; and collective memory, 23; and immigration, 216; southern hospitality post–civil rights, 26–27, 201; and *Southern Living*, 196–99; and *Two Thousand Maniacs!*, 175–77; and usage of term "southern hospitality," 13; white involvement in, 175, 253n7. *See also* race and racism; racial politics
Civil War, 143, 148–52
class: and antebellum hospitality, 29; and Christianity, 131; and etiquette, 55–56; fluidity, 52–54, 95–96, 146, 228n21; and the Fugitive Slave Law, 78; identity, 96, 135, 163; and mental hospitality, 75; nouveau riche, 147; prejudices, 128; and Reconstruction, 143; and *Southern Living*, 198; upward mobility, 59, 96, 187. *See also* planter class
Clay, Henry, 77
Coleman-Singleton, Sharonda, 22
collective memory: abuses of, 23, 223n38; and ethics of hospitality, 191; and heritage tourism, 181–82; and identity, 23, 202–4; and melancholia, 200, 223n37; vs. personal memory, 203–4; politics of, 8; race and racism within, 8, 23, 116; and Reconstruction, 23; Ricoeur on, 23–24, 222n37, 223n38, 256n46; and sectionalism, 23–24; and trauma, 23–24, 161, 220n13, 256n46. *See also* cultural memory; forgetting
Columbia Metropolitan Convention and Visitors Bureau, 212
Compromise of 1850, 77–80, 89, 102, 123–26, 233n4
Condon, Charlie, 179
conduct-of-life literature, 229n24. *See also* Wright, Julia McNair
Confederate flag boycott, 27, 178–80, 255nn20–21

Confederate Memorial, 178
Connor, Bull, 196
conspicuous consumption, 2, 33, 46, 49–50, 53–54, 157, 193
consumerism: and Christianity, 53–55, 135; and etiquette, 58–59; exclusionary history of, 180–83; and identity, 3, 193, 195; and immigrants, 215; and nostalgia, 26; and segregation, 132, 249n37; vs. traditional hospitality, 52
cookbooks, 192, 201, 209–10, 257n52, 259n83
Cooper, Floyd, 189
Cooper, James Fenimore, *The Spy*, 235n35
cosmopolitanism: and abolition hospitality, 71; Benhabib on, 27, 110–12; and citizenship, 71–72, 103, 110, 112–13, 119; and globalization, 27; and identity, 102–3, 112, 125; and Kant, 71–72, 108, 110, 222n26; and mental hospitality, 71–72, 75; norms of justice, 110–11; and strangers and foreigners, 118, 125; Thoreau on, 110, 240n18. *See also ethnos* and *demos* concepts; immigration; sovereignty; universal hospitality
"country cosmopolitanism" (Robinson), 220n11
Cowan, John Franklin, 248n32; *A New Invasion of the South*, 148–51
Cowles, Genevieve and Maude, 153–54
Cox, John D., *Traveling South*, 237n49
Cox, Karen L., *Dreaming of Dixie*, 253n1, 255n30
Crane, Gregg D., 82–84, 87
Crespino, Joseph, *The Myth of Southern Exceptionalism*, 3–4
Criswell, Robert, *"Uncle Tom's Cabin" Contrasted with Buckingham Hall*, 236n44
Cross, Alan, 217–18, 260–61n20
Cuenca, Carme Manual, 236–37n45
"culinary injustice" (Twitty), 207–8
cultural capital, 36–37, 41, 91
cultural identity, 23, 112, 151, 185
cultural memory: and the Confederate flag debate, 179–80, 185; and Deen, 202–6; and ethics of hospitality, 4, 17–18, 22–23, 180; and forgetting, 17–18; and historical narratives, 44–47, 219n8; and melancholia, 200; politics of, 8; and racial identity, 116; and slavery, 17–18, 75–76, 148, 170;

INDEX 283

cultural memory (*continued*)
  and tradition, 6, 22. *See also* collective memory; forgetting
Cunningham, Emory, 196–97

Dawson, William, 123–25
Decatur (AL) Daily News, 215
Decoration Day, 245n15
Deen, Paula, 27, 192, 200–208; *It Ain't All about the Cooking*, 202–3
demos and *ethnos* concepts (Benhabib), 116–17
Derrida, Jacques: and ethics of hospitality, 20–22, 53; and hospitality as risk, 21, 69; and hospitality of invitation and visitation, 21, 69–70, 231n45; and the paradoxes of hospitality, 20, 110, 222n31; and politics of hospitality, 20–22, 53, 55–56, 104; and the right of the guest, 20–21; and universal hospitality, 20–21, 110; on the unknown nature of hospitality, 20, 22, 27, 210
desegregation, 169, 177, 194
DiGiacomo, Fran, "Southern Hospitality," 13–14
discrimination, 22, 101, 132, 187–88, 196, 262n24
Dixie Highway, 182
Dobbins, James, 176
domesticity: and Christianity, 88; domestic social space, 24–25, 77–84, 91–92, 109, 111, 131, 143; and etiquette, 56–60; and the Fugitive Slave Law, 77–84; and Hale, 105, 239n5; Kaplan on, 244n7; Page on, 154–59, 250n45; and postbellum hospitality, 134–39. *See also* etiquette
Douglass, Frederick, 159, 210, 237n47; *My Bondage and My Freedom*, 97–98, 102–3, 237–38n50; *Narrative of the Life of Frederick Douglass, an American Slave*, 97
Douglass, Stephen, 77
Dred Scott decision, 237n49
Drew, Benjamin, *A North Side View of Slavery*, 235n33
Du Bois, W. E. B., *The Souls of Black Folk*, 159
Duck, Leigh Anne, 3
Duke, David, 178
Dunbar, Paul Laurence: *Folks from Dixie*, 161; "Nelse Hatton's Vengeance," 161, 167
Dupre, Karen, "Southern Hospitality," 16–17

Dyer Anti-Lynching Bill, 183
Dyke, Larry, "Southern Hospitality," 16–17

Eastman, Mary Henderson, *Aunt Phyllis's Cabin*, 92–93, 235n35
Edelstein, Tilden G., 235n33
Egerton, Douglas, 254n15
Egerton, John, 17; *Southern Food*, 209–10
Ehringer, Britt, "Southern Hospitality," 18–20
Elias, Amy, 193
Emanuel African Methodist Episcopal (AME) Church, 22, 179
Emerson, Ralph Waldo, 82
emigration, 26, 145
"En Avant" (article), 119, 122
Encyclopedia of Southern Culture, 4, 6
Esso Standard Oil Company, 188
ethics of hospitality: in antislavery texts, 39–47, 79–88, 159–61; and Chesnutt's *Marrow of Tradition*, 161–67; and Christianity, 55–56; Derrida on, 20–22, 53; and globalization, 27; and immigration, 213–18; and Kant, 71–72, 222n31; and memory, 4, 17–18, 22–23, 180, 191; and mental hospitality, 67–76; modern dilemmas in, 218; and the Negro Seamen Acts, 111; and pro-slavery texts, 89–90; and segregation, 8, 177, 210; and slavery, 8, 24, 177; in Stowe's *Uncle Tom's Cabin*, 93; Woolson on, 139. *See also* politics of hospitality
ethics of memory, 17–18, 22–23, 180, 191. *See also* collective memory; cultural memory
ethnos and *demos* concepts (Benhabib), 116–17
etiquette: books on, 23, 52–53, 56–60, 73, 134, 228–29n23, 228n19; and Christianity, 57, 229n24; and consumerism, 58–59; and education, 228n17; and Jim Crow, 183; and politics of hospitality, 57
European-American Unity and Rights Organization (EURO), 178–79
European revolutions, 119
exceptionalism, southern: background of, 2–4, 8; defense of, 48; Greeson on, 221n20; and integration, 206; and northerners, 39; race and racism within, 194; and regional reconciliation, 132–33; and Wiley's *Roanoke*, 61

exclusionary politics, 7, 21, 56, 62, 79, 218.
See also politics of hospitality

Farnham, Christie Anne, 228n17
Faulkner, William, *Absalom, Absalom!*, 63
Federal Writers' Project (WPA), 184
Fitzhugh, George, *Sociology for the South*, 235n33
Food Network, 201
foodways, 207–10
Foote, Henry, 123–27
foreigners. See strangers and foreigners
Forest and Stream (journal), 145
forgetting: active forgetting, 167; and Adams's treatment of Jehu Jones Sr., 114; and aristocratic hospitality, 76; and collective identity, 23–24; and cultural memory, 17–18; and remembering, 148, 151, 161; Ricoeur on, 23, 46–47; and segregation, 23; and slavery, 204–6; and trauma, 220n13. See also collective memory; cultural memory
Forsyth, Pauline, "Sketches of Southern Life," 227n3
Foster, A., 40–41; "Visit to a Southern Plantation," 35–37
Fourteenth Amendment, 237n49
Fox, William, *Christian Morality*, 67–68; "Mental Hospitality," 67–68
Fox-Genovese, Elizabeth, *The Mind of the Master Class*, 44–47
freed slaves, 38, 131, 134–43, 151–52. See also slavery
Freud, Sigmund, 200, 223n38, 223n40
Friedman, David, 170
Friend, 54
Frost, Sarah Annie (S. A. Shields), *Frost's Laws and By-Laws of American Society*, 246n16
Frothingham, Octavius Brooks, "Christian Hospitality," 68–70, 231n44
Fugitive Slave Law of 1793, 77, 233n1
Fugitive Slave Law of 1850: and abolitionism, 80–84, 190, 217, 234n9; and antislavery texts, 79–88, 97–103, 190; Brown and Douglass on, 97–103; debate about, compared to immigration debate, 215, 217–18; defined, 25, 51; and domestic social space, 77–84; and Hale's *Liberia*, 104–6; Keller on, 233n4; and Kossuth, 122–23, 128;
and northerners, 82–84, 88–97; politics of, 77–79, 233nn6-7; and pro-slavery texts, 88–97
fugitive slaves, 67, 71, 106, 109, 127–29. See also slavery
"Fugitive Slave to the Christian, The" (poem), 80
Fulton County Commission, 172

Garibaldi, Giuseppe, 119–20
Garrison, William Lloyd, 37–38, 70, 231n44; *Letter to Kossuth concerning Freedom and Slavery in the United States*, 127
Garrisonian abolitionism, 38
gender: and feminine identity, 81–82, 93–94, 96–97; hierarchies of, 8, 90; and honor, 56; pictorial representations of, 18–19, 66–67; politics of, 56; and racial identity, 193–94; and southern womanhood, 173, 247–48n28
Genovese, Eugene, *The Mind of the Master Class*, 44–47
gift exchanges, 32–33, 35–37, 161. See also planter class
Gilded Age, 157
Glass, Eddie, "Southern Hospitality," 14
Gleason's Pictorial Drawing Room Companion, "Kossuth," 242n37
globalization, 13, 27, 192–94, 222n26, 223n43
Goddard, Frederick B., *Where to Emigrate and Why*, 145
Godey's Magazine and Lady's Book, 49–51, 59, 65–67, 105, 224n2, 246n16
Gone with the Wind (novel and film), 13, 221n21
Goodman, Andrew, 175
goodwill. See benevolence
Graves, John Temple, 181, 255nn27-28
Gray, Richard, 16; *South to a New Place*, 10–11
Great Britain, 108
Great Migration, 187
Green, Victor H., *The Negro Motorist Green Book*, 187–90
Greenburg, Kenneth, 32–34
Greenspan, Ezra, 100
Greeson, Jennifer, 3, 221n20, 226n28, 232n51
Griffin, Larry J., 193
group identities, 6
guests and hosts: and abolition hospitality, 71, 98–100; and complicity with slavery,

guests and hosts (*continued*)
43–44, 165–67; Derrida on, 20–21; in
Eastman's *Aunt Phyllis's Cabin*, 92–93;
and ethics of hospitality, 211–18; and
etiquette, 52–60; and Kant, 71–72; Kossuth
as "guest of the nation," 25, 117, 123–27; and
leisure, 23, 193–94; Lot's "sacred guests,"
56; and regional reconciliation, 137; right
of the host, 82, 88; and social capital,
36–37, 41–42; Thoreau on, 109. *See also*
Christianity

Hale, Edward Everett, "Christian Duty to
Emigrants," 128–29
Hale, Grace Elizabeth, 3, 174, 249n37; *Making
Whiteness*, 243n4, 244n5
Hale, John Parker, 123–26
Hale, Sarah Josepha: *Liberia, or Mr. Peyton's
Experiment*, 104–6, 239n3; *Manners*, 239n5;
Northwood, 239n3
Haley, Nikki, 179
Hamer, Philip M., 241n28
Hammon, Micky, 213
Hammond, Fred L., 216
Hammond, James Henry, 33–34, 108; "Letters
on Slavery," 225n20
Hampton, Wade, 33
Hardy, Duffus, *Down South*, 248n31
Harness, A. C., *The Great Trial*, 244n9
Harper's, 249n39
Harris, Joel Chandler, 249n39
Hartley, Florence, *The Ladies Book of Etiquette
and Manual of Politeness*, 57
Hemphill, C. Dallett, 228n21
Hentz, Caroline Lee, 235n40; *The Planter's
Northern Bride*, 93–97, 236n42,
236nn44–45
heritage tourism, 3, 13, 171, 178–85, 191, 256n34.
See also race and racism; tourism
Hermes [pseud.], 227n8; "Science of
Hospitality," 53–54, 55, 58
Higgs, Lawton, 216
Hinrichsen, Lisa, *Possessing the Past*, 223n40
"Hints for Our Native Southerners: What
They Should Do before the Winter Tourist
Comes," 182–83
Hoar, Samuel, 107–9, 240n22
Hodgson, Telfair, 148; "A Sermon in Behalf of
Southern Sufferers," 130–31

Honig, Bonnie, 121; *Democracy and the
Foreigner*, 118
honor, 7, 31–35, 44, 56, 61–63, 109–12, 225n20
Horowitz, Tony, "Untrue Confessions," 256–
57n48
hospitality. *See* Derrida, Jacques; ethics
of hospitality; politics of hospitality;
southern hospitality; *specific types of
hospitality*
Hospitality Association of South Carolina, 212
hospitality industries. *See* tourism
hostility: and Adams' *Manuel Pereira*, 113;
Derrida on, 20; ironic resignification
of, 174–75; toward Kossuth, 25; between
North and South, 141; race and racism, 97,
100–101, 166–67, 187–88; and violence, 104
hosts. *See* guests and hosts
Howells, William Dean, 167
Hundley, Daniel R., *Social Relations in Our
Southern States*, 224–25n9
Hungary, 117–23, 242n51
Hurd, Cynthia Marie Graham, 22

identity: class, 96, 135, 163; collective, 23;
constructed, 201; and consumerism,
3, 193, 195; continuity of, 192–94; and
cosmopolitanism, 102–3, 112, 125;
cultural, 23, 112, 151, 185; Derrida on,
20–21; Lang on, 192–94; marketable,
169, 177, 195; and memory, 23, 116, 170,
193, 202–6; performed, 19, 198, 220n11;
personal, 70, 73; politics of, 135, 251–
52n57; race and racism, 101–3, 163–64; and
Reconstruction, 143; regional, 1, 7, 12–13,
60–61, 131–35, 182, 192–93; transregional,
88–96; and Wiley's *Roanoke*, 61–62.
See also national identity; racial identity;
southern identity
imaginary communities, 193–95, 219n9.
See also southern identity
Imboden, J. D., 145
immigration, 145, 151, 193, 213–18, 260n11,
261n22, 262nn23–24
individual memory, 23, 202–4, 222n37. *See also*
collective memory; cultural memory
inequality. *See* race and racism
institutionalized racism, 199, 204–7
Isaac, Rhys, *The Transformation of Virginia*,
2, 30, 33

Jackson, Jay, *Bungleton Green* (comic strip), 185–87
Jackson, Susie, 22
Jefferson, Thomas, 10, 220–21n15
Jeffrey, Julie Roy, 233n6, 234n9
Jim Crow laws, 2, 23, 132, 151, 182–90, 197, 216
Jones, Charles H., *Appleton's Handbook of American Travel*, 247n19
Jones, Dwight C., 178
Jones, Jehu, Jr. and Sr., 114–15, 241n27
justice, norms of, 110–11

Kansas-Nebraska Act, 235n33
Kant, Immanuel, 20, 108, 120, 222n26; *Perpetual Peace*, 71–72, 110, 222n31
Kaplan, Amy, 244n7
Kasson, John F., 228n21
Kaufman, Theodor, "Effects of the Fugitive Slave Law," 80–81
Keller, Ralph A., 233n4
King, Martin Luther, Jr., 196, 198, 208, 216
King, Nicole, 180
Kirkland, C. M., "A Chapter on Hospitality," 59
Komlos, John, *Louis Kossuth in America*, 242n51
Kossuth, Louis, 25, 106, 117–29, 241nn30–32, 242nn37–38, 242nn51–52, 243n54
Kreyling, Michael, 3
Ku Klux Klan, 139, 175, 178, 251n53

Ladd, Dr., "Sketch of the Character," 225–26n22
Lafayette, Marquis de, 118–19
Lance, Ethel Lee, 22
Lang, Rebecca, *Southern Entertaining for a New Generation*, 192–94
Lassiter, Matthew D., *The Myth of Southern Exceptionalism*, 3–4
Ledyard, Catherine, "Kossuth" (poem), 122
Lehuu, Isabelle, 227n6
"lenticular logic" (McPherson), 173. *See also* race and racism
Levinas, Emmanuel, 20
Lewis, Herschell Gordon, *Blood Feast* (film), 170
Liang, Kevin, 221n24; "Southern Hospitality," 14–16
Liberator, The, 37, 42, 70–71, 80, 233n7. *See also* antislavery texts

Liberia, 30, 104–6, 224n7, 239n3, 241n27
Liberty Almanac for 1852, 81–83
Life, 8–9, 182–83
lifestyle industries, 26, 169, 177, 192–93. *See also* tourism
Lincoln, Abraham, 133–34
Lippincott, Grambo & Co., 92, 235n34, 247n18
Lippincott's Magazine of Literature, Science, and Education, 247n18
local color writing, 149–50, 152, 246–47n18
Logue, John, 258n63; *Life at Southern Living*, 197–98
Lord, John C., 89
Lost Cause ideology, 26, 144–46, 149–52, 159, 162, 181
Lot's "sacred guests," 56
Loughran, Trish, *The Republic in Print*, 12–13
Lowell (Mass.), 72–76, 232n50
lynchings, 133, 171, 174, 183, 224n7, 243–44n5, 253n7

Maddex, Jack P., Jr., *Reconstruction of Edward A. Pollard*, 247n26
Mallard, Robert, 187
manners. *See* etiquette
Mardi Gras, 148–51
Massachusetts Magazine, 226n22
Mauss, Marcel, *The Gift*, 32–33
McCalla, Gary, 258n63; *Life at Southern Living*, 197–98
McElwin, Henry, *Travels in the South*, 249n36
McKivigan, John R., 246n17
McNulty, Tracy, 51–52, 221–22n26
McPherson, Tara, 3, 173; *Reconstructing Dixie*, 19
melancholia, 200, 201, 206, 208, 223n38. *See also* mourning; nostalgia
Memorial Day, 142, 245n15
memorialization groups, 181
mental hospitality, 67–76, 109–10, 167
Methodist Anti-Slavery Convention, 42; "Report of the Committee on Slavery," 227n38
Middleton-Doctor, Depayne, 22
Minor, Lucian, 43–44, 157–58, 192; "Letters from New England," 28–35, 37–41, 53, 224n7
"Mississippi Burning" code, 175
Mississippi Free Trader, 127

Mitchell, Laura I., 234n27
Modlin, E. Arnold, Jr., 191
Molière, *Amphytrion*, 53
Montgomery White Sulphur Springs, 146, 248n30
Monticello, 10, 220–21n15
moral fiction. *See* Wright, Julia McNair
"Mother Emmanuel" AME church, 22, 179
mourning, 154, 200, 201, 208, 223n38. *See also* melancholia; nostalgia

NAACP, 27, 178–80, 183, 185, 215–16
National Enquirer, 201
National Era, 86, 122, 242n37
national identity, 12–13, 57, 78, 80, 105–6, 118–19, 130–33
national reconciliation, 26, 28–29, 132–33, 139–41, 144, 148–52. *See also* sectionalism
National Temperance Society, 134
Nat Turner/1831 Southampton Insurrection Trail, 191
Negro Affairs Project (WPA), 184
"Negro question," debates about, 152–153, 251n53
Negro Seamen Acts, 25, 106–17, 190, 239n9, 240n22
New England Anti-Slavery Society, 37, 70
New Jersey, 131
New South, 152–53, 171, 182–84
New York Daily Times, 117, 242n38
New Yorker, 256–57n48
New York Independent, 246n17
New-York Mirror, 53, 228n14
New York Times, 172, 202, 204, 207, 254n9, 254n17
Norfolk Industrial Park, 172
North Carolina, 4, 61–65, 107, 161, 191, 208, 230nn32–33
northerners: and emigration and immigration, 145; and the Fugitive Slave Law, 82–84, 88–97; hospitality of, 28–29, 34; idea of southern hospitality, 8, 26, 45; and industrialization, 72, 132, 232nn50–51; and Kossuth, 25, 118–19, 242n51; postbellum attitudes, 130–43; and Redpath, 44–46, 246n17; and the right to hospitality, 88; and slavery, 41–43, 72; and southern exceptionalism, 39; stereotypes of, 31; and *Two Thousand Maniacs!*, 168–76;
as visitors to the South, 36–37, 90–93, 144, 180–83, 247n23. *See also* southern identity
nostalgia: and aristocratic hospitality, 65, 139, 152; and heritage tourism, 3, 178–85, 191, 256n34; industry of, 13; and Lost Cause ideology, 152, 159; and melancholia, 200; for the "Old South," 50–51; and plantation literature, 132, 152–60; and race, 139, 152–53, 182–83; and romance, 161, 167; and slavery, 151–56. *See also* collective memory; cultural memory
nullification crisis, 37
Nunn, Alexander, 198
Nute, Cherrie, "Southern Hospitality," 14

O'Brien, Michael, 65, 221n19; *Conjectures of Order*, 60–61
Odum Institute for Research in Social Science, 1
Old South. *See* antebellum hospitality
Onesimus, 78–79, 262n23. *See also* slavery

Page, Thomas Nelson, 192, 209, 249n39, 250nn41–42, 250nn45–46; "The Negro Question" (polemic), 159; *The Old South*, 153; "The Old South," 250n47; *Social Life in Old Virginia before the War*, 153–60
Patrick, Melissa Self, 216
Paul (apostle): letter to Philemon, 55, 78–79, 218, 262n23; letter to the Hebrews, 67–71, 231n40
performed identity, 19, 198, 220n11
Philemon, 55, 78–79, 218, 262n23. *See also* slavery
pineapple symbol, 14, 16, 18, 211, 221n23
Pinkney, Clementa C., 22
Pitzer, Amy, *Southern Hospitality Cookbook*, 257n52
plantation homes: economic development of, 145–46; and exclusionary politics, 56; as extension of self, 33; and the origins of hospitality, 2, 31; representations of, 16–18, 24, 40, 237–38n50
plantation literature, 132–33, 134–48, 149–60, 181, 249n39
planter class: aristocratic hospitality of, 23, 54, 62–65, 105; in Butt's *Anti-Fanaticism*, 90–91; and conspicuous consumption, 2, 157; in Fox-Genovese and Genovese's

Mind of the Master Class, 44–46; in Hentz's *Planter's Northern Bride*, 93–97; Page on, 250n46; postbellum, 141–48, 249n36; and slavery, 185, 246n16; and social capital, 36–37, 41–42, 91, 169–70; social practices of, 2, 11, 30–33, 35–37, 40–41

Plessy v. Ferguson, 132, 251n57

Poe, Edgar Allan, 30, 224n7

politeness, 24, 36, 57, 213. *See also* etiquette

political broadsides and cartoons, 80–81, 121, 174–77

politics: avoidance of, 51, 151, 196–97; cultural, 118; of disruption (Hale), 124; vs. ethics, 4, 56, 213–18; exclusionary, 7, 21, 56, 62, 79, 218; and the Fugitive Slave Law, 77–79; of gender, 56; of identity, 135; national, 111–16, 143; and the Negro Seamen Acts, 111–16; and sectionalism, 126–27. *See also* racial politics

politics of hospitality: and Chesnutt's *Marrow of Tradition*, 161–67; definition and treatment of strangers and foreigners, 38, 56; Derrida on, 20–22, 53, 55–56, 104; and etiquette, 57; and Hentz's *Planter's Northern Bride*, 93–97; and immigration, 213–18; and the Negro Seamen Acts, 111–16; post–civil rights, 27; and sovereignty, 70; and Wiley's *Roanoke*, 63–64; and Woolson's "Southern Sketches," 139–43. *See also* ethics of hospitality

Polk, Leonidas L., 195

Pollard, Edward A., 149–50, 153, 181, 247n23, 247n26, 247nn19–20; *The Lost Cause*, 144; *The Lost Cause Regained*, 144–46; *The Virginia Tourist*, 143–48, 246–47n18

postbellum hospitality: and Chesnutt's *Marrow of Tradition*, 161–67; and Cowan's *New Invasion of the South*, 148–52; and domesticity, 131–36; and emancipation, 133–34; and northerners, 130–43; and plantation literature, 152–60; and Pollard's *Virginia Tourist*, 143–48; and Reconstruction, 131–33; and Woolson's "Southern Sketches," 139–43; and Wright's *Cabin in the Brush*, 134–39. *See also* antebellum hospitality

Presbyterian Board of Publications, 134

Prince, K. Stephen, 249n39; *Stories of the South*, 243n4

print culture, 12–13

Procrustes, 163–64

Progressive Farmer (magazine), 195–98

propaganda, 42–43, 80, 98, 233n6

pro-slavery texts, 48–51, 88–97, 104–6, 120, 143–48, 230n34, 236nn43–44

Prosser, Gabriel, 254n15

public memory, 151, 179–80. *See also* collective memory; cultural memory

race and racism: and the absolute stranger, 104; and antirendition literature, 84–85; Brown and Douglass on, 97–103; and cosmopolitanism, 112–13; and Green's *The Negro Motorist Green Book*, 187–89; and Hale's *Liberia*, 104–6; and Hentz's *Planter's Northern Bride*, 95–96; hierarchies of, 8, 12, 90, 96; history of, 3–4; and hostility, 97, 100–101, 166–67, 187–88; and identity, 101–3, 163–64; and immigration, 193, 214–16; institutionalized racism, 199, 204–7; and "lenticular logic" (McPherson), 173; and memory, 8, 23, 116; and mental hospitality, 75; modern struggles, 181, 185, 198–99, 204; and the Negro Seamen Acts, 111–16; and nostalgia, 139, 152–53, 182–83; persistence of, within southern hospitality myth, 97, 201; and postbellum narratives, 131, 144–45, 149–50, 161–67, 245–46n15; regressive and progressive ideologies of, 7–8, 133; and shared heritage, 89; and southern exceptionalism, 194; and southern foodways, 208–10; and sovereignty, 111; and tourism, 178–91, 252n58; and *Two Thousand Maniacs!*, 172–74; and violence, 22–23, 132–33, 138–39, 161, 167, 171–76, 181; and whiteness, 101–3. *See also* racial politics; segregation

racial identity: affirmation of, 148; and the color line, 161, 163–64, 251–52n57; and "country cosmopolitanism" (Robinson), 220n11; and cultural memory, 116; and gender, 193–94; and immigration, 193; loss of, 184, 206; and sectionalism, 7; and segregation, 3, 185; and slavery, 10; and *Southern Living*, 195, 198; in Wright's *Cabin in the Brush*, 135

racial politics: avoidance of, 151; grassroots efforts, 215–18; and Lost Cause ideology,

racial politics (*continued*)
    162; and memory, 8, 23, 116; Page on, 152–59; Pollard on, 181; and Reconstruction, 131–38, 143, 148–52; and *Southern Living*, 196–97, 199; and Wiley's *Roanoke*, 64. *See also* politics
Raines, Howell, 197
Ramsey, Calvin Alexander: *The Green Book* (play), 190–91; *Ruth and the Green Book*, 189–91, 209
Randolph, Mary, *The Virginia Housewife*, 259n83
Reconstruction: and Christianity, 133–39; and collective memory, 23; and national domestic space, 143; and persistence of southern hospitality myth, 2, 7; and Pollard's *Virginia Tourist*, 143–48; and postbellum hospitality, 131–33; and racial politics, 131–38, 143, 148–52; and segregation post-Reconstruction, 132, 150–51; and usage of term "southern hospitality," 13; women writers during, 133–43. *See also* sectionalism
Redpath, James, 44–46, 246n17; *Roving Editor*, 44; *Southern Notes*, 227n45
Reed, John Shelton, 1
refuge/refugee, 79, 119, 122, 135–39, 148
regional identity, 7, 12–13, 60–61, 131–35, 182, 192–93. *See also* identity; northerners; southern identity
regional reconciliation, 8, 29, 132–33, 137–41, 146–48, 152, 249n39. *See also* sectionalism
religion. *See* Christianity
repetition: in Beecher's sermon, 85; and collective memory (Ricoeur), 223n38; through discourse, 7, 13, 211; and identity, 201; of melancholia, 208; naturalizing southern hospitality, 168–70; patterns of, 177, 194, 201; in pictorial images, 18, 24; and southern hospitality, 13, 168–70
Repository & Observer, 35
repression: and active forgetting, 167; and collective memory, 23–24; of melancholia, 208; patterns of, 169, 177, 201, 208, 210; and segregation, 185; and *Southern Living*, 197; and violence, 162
republican hospitality, 24–25, 53–54, 60–61, 65. *See also* aristocratic hospitality; class

Rich, Kerry, 213
Ricoeur, Paul: and ethics of memory, 23, 256n46; and forgetting, 46–47; on melancholia and mourning, 200, 223n38; *Memory, History, Forgetting*, 222–23n37, 223n38; and personal memory, 203; "telling otherwise" concept of, 24, 191, 256n46. *See also* collective memory; cultural memory
Roberts, Diane, 196, 258n64, 258n69
Roberts, Timothy Mason, 127–28, 242–43n52
Robinson, Zandria F., 220n11
Romine, Scott, 13, 193, 209–10
Rosello, Mireille, 56, 228n13
Rosewood massacre, 183, 255–56n32
Rutledge, Sarah, *House and Home*, 259n83
Ryan, Susan M., 232n54

Sanders, Mark, 185
Sanders, Tywanza, 22
Saturday Evening Post, 255n27
Schwerner, Michael, 175
Scott, Sir Walter, *Rob Roy*, 12
secession, 7, 116
sectionalism: and antebellum hospitality, 37–38, 48–51, 151–52; and antislavery texts, 43; background, 48–49; and collective memory, 23–24; and the Compromise of 1850, 89; and Kossuth, 118, 126–27, 242n38; Lincoln on, 133–34; and mental hospitality, 67; and persistence of southern hospitality myth, 2, 7–8; and prejudices, 141–42; and racial identity, 3; and racial politics, 133, 148; and regional identity, 131–35; and regional reconciliation, 8, 29; and slavery, 12, 77–79, 80, 98; and sovereignty, 108. *See also* Reconstruction
segregation: and African American travelers, 180–91; and Chesnutt's *Marrow of Tradition*, 161–67; and collective memory, 23; and consumerism, 132, 249n37; Deen's experiences of, 202–5; elimination of, 169, 177, 194; and ethics of hospitality, 8, 177, 210; and Lost Cause ideology, 162; naturalizing of, 7, 133; and persistence of southern hospitality myth, 2, 180; and plantation literature, 152; post-Reconstruction, 26, 132, 150; progressive critiques of, 10; and racial identity, 3; and

racial violence, 173, 177; and *Southern Living*, 195–98; and white supremacy, 194
Seidel, Kathryn, 237n45
Seiler, Cotten, *Republic of Drivers*, 187
Seventy-First New York National Guard, 148–49
Severnsen, Kim, 204
Seward, William, 79–80, 88, 126
shock films, 168–76
shoddyism (Pollard), 146–47
Silber, Nina, 147, 156, 243n4, 245n10, 247n20
Simmons, Daniel, 22
Sixteenth Street Baptist Church (Birmingham, Ala.), 196
slavery: and antebellum hospitality, 8–10, 39–44, 48–51; and Brown's *American Fugitive in Europe*, 98–100; and Chesnutt's *Marrow of Tradition*, 161–67; and citizenship, 131; complicity with, 41–44, 165–67; debate over, 72, 77–79, 108, 123–29; and ethics of hospitality, 8, 24, 177; and exclusionary politics, 79; and foodways, 209–10; and forgetting, 204–6; fugitive slaves, 71, 103, 106, 109, 127–29; and heritage tourism, 191; and honor, 31–35; and Kossuth, 118; and memory, 17–18, 23, 75–76, 148, 170; and mental hospitality, 67–76; Minor on, 29–30, 37–39, 157–58; and the Negro Seamen Acts, 106–17; and northerners, 41–44, 72; and persistence of southern hospitality myth, 2, 7; and plantation literature, 152–58; and the planter class, 185, 246n16; and sectionalism, 12, 77–79, 80, 98; and service laborers, 212–13; and *Two Thousand Maniacs!*, 174; and Wiley's *Roanoke*, 61–65. *See also* antislavery texts; Fugitive Slave Law of 1850; race and racism
social capital, 36–37, 41–42, 91, 169–70. *See also* tourism
"social reconstruction" (Pollard), 143–48
Sodom, 55–56, 166
Sons of Confederate Veterans, 18
Southampton County (Va.) Historical Society, 191
South Carolina, 27, 37, 106–17, 175–85, 212–13
Southern Baptist Convention, 217, 261n22
Southern Focus Poll, 1, 13, 193
Southern Foodways Alliance, 208–10, 259–60n86

southern honor. *See* honor
southern hospitality: African American critiques of, 159–63; and the African American traveler, 185–91; alternative narratives of, 18–19, 190–91; Brown and Douglass on, 97–103; and Chesnutt's *Marrow of Tradition*, 161–67; and Christianity, 216–18; commercialization of, 211–12; commodification of, 59; and Cowan's *New Invasion of the South*, 148–52; and Deen, 200–208; defining identity, 1–8; and Derrida, 20–22; historical view of, 23–28; and Hodgson's sermon, 130–31; and immigration, 213–18; ironic resignification of, 174–78; and lifestyle industries, 192–200; modern proliferation of, 168–78; and modern tourism, 178–85; and the Negro Seamen Acts, 111–17; persuasive powers of, 6, 12, 42, 51, 79, 227n38; pictorial representations of, 13–20; pineapple as symbol of, 14–18, 211; and plantation literature, 152–60; Pollard on, 143–48; in a postbellum world, 132–33; and southern foodways, 208–10; Thoreau on, 108–9; and transregional identity, 88–97; and *Two Thousand Maniacs!*, 168–78; usage of term, 11–13, 221n19; and Woolson's "Southern Sketches," 139–40; Zinn on, 104. *See also* antebellum hospitality; postbellum hospitality
"Southern Hospitality Experience" program, 211
southern identity: branding of, 26, 168–71, 177, 180; constructed identity, 201, 204; continuity of, 192–94; contradictions in, 61–62, 65; and cultural memory, 116, 170, 193, 206; exclusionary, 116; and food, 207–10; and Gray's "southern self-fashioning," 10–11; pictorial representations of, 13–20; process of defining, 1–8, 12–13, 192–94; and *Southern Living*, 194–200; "symbolic southernness" (Griffin and Thomas), 193; and whiteness, 157, 162–63. *See also* northerners
Southern Lady archetype, 156–57, 259n83. *See also* domesticity
Southern Literary Journal, 226n22
Southern Literary Messenger, 28–30, 39, 119–20, 127, 224n7

INDEX 291

Southern Living, 6, 26, 169, 192, 194–200, 258nn63–64, 259n86
Southern Poverty Law Center, 212, 215, 260n3
Southern Quarterly Review, 243n54
sovereignty, 35–39, 69–70, 106, 108, 110–16
"spectacle lynching" (Hale), 174, 244n5, 253–54n7
Spencer, Donald S., 124, 241n30
Stearns, Jonathan, 89
stereotypes: of African Americans, 151, 181–83, 249n37; antebellum, 48–51; of Kossuth, 121; of northerners, 31; of slaves, 131; of the South, 50, 173, 253n1
St. Louis Post-Dispatch, 215
Stowe, Harriet Beecher, 112, 235n40, 250n42; *The American Woman's Home*, 59–60; "The Freeman's Dream," 86–87; *Uncle Tom's Cabin*, 51, 86–88, 92, 93, 237n46, 243n56
Stowe, Steven M., 32
strangers and foreigners: and abolition hospitality, 70–76, 98–100; absolute, 104–5; African Americans as, 79, 104–5, 118, 131–33, 148; and Butt's *Anti-Fanaticism*, 90–91; and Chesnutt's *House behind the Cedars*, 162–63; and Christianity, 54–56, 59–60, 130, 216–18; and citizenship, 118; and cosmopolitanism, 118, 125; Derrida on, 20–21; emigration and immigration, 145; ethical response to, 25–27, 210; fear of, 128; and the Fugitive Slave Law, 88, 97, 122; in Hale's *Liberia*, 104–6; and Kossuth, 117–22, 125; and mental hospitality, 67–70; on native land, 100–101, 118, 131; and the Negro Seamen Acts, 111; and politics of hospitality, 38, 56; rights of, 20–21; social practices involving, 29–32; and Thoreau, 110; and Wiley's *Roanoke*, 62; and Wright's *Cabin in the Brush*, 135–37
Strong, T. W., "The Poor Organ Grinder from Hungary," 121
Student Nonviolent Coordinating Committee's Summer Project of 1964, 175. *See also* civil rights movement

Tarpley, Frank H., "Southern Hospitality," 14–15
Taylor, Zachary, 123–24

Thackeray, William Makepeace, 60
Thompson, Ashley B., 193
Thompson, Myra, 22
Thoreau, Henry David: "Civil Disobedience," 106–10; *Walden*, 240n18
tourism: and African American travelers, 178–91; and Alabama's immigration law, 213; boycott of, 27, 178–80, 185; and branding of identity, 26, 168–71, 177, 180; heritage, 3, 13, 171, 178–85, 191, 256n34; and Pollard's *Virginia Tourist*, 143–48; postbellum, 132; race and racism, 178–91, 252n58; and segregation, 180–85, 191; and service laborers, 211–13; Silber on, 147; study of brochures, 191; in *Two Thousand Maniacs!*, 168–72. *See also* consumerism; heritage tourism
"tourist homes," 188–90
Tower, Philo, *Slavery Unmasked*, 91
tradition: affirmation of, 192, 194; of the antebellum planter class, 32, 46–47; and aristocratic hospitality, 61; and cultural memory, 6, 22; defining culture, 5–6; and foodways, 207–10; and foreignness, 118; hospitality as, 93, 115, 171; secular vs. Christian, 52–53; and *Southern Living*, 194–97; values of, 153–54
transregional identity, 7, 88–96
traumatic memory, 23–24, 161, 220n13. *See also* collective memory; cultural memory; forgetting
travel writing: A. Foster's travel sketches, 35–37, 40–41; Brown and Douglass, 97–103, 238n51; and the Fugitive Slave Law, 88–97; and Fox-Genovese and Genovese's *Mind of the Master Class*, 44–47; and Green's *Negro Motorist Green Book*, 187–90; and Minor's "Letters from New England," 34–35, 37–41; and nostalgia, 151–52, 249n39; reinforcing the myth of southern hospitality, 26; X Y Z's *Letters from the Southwest*, 40
Turner, Nat, 37–38, 184–85, 191, 224n7, 254n15, 256–57n48
Twitty, Michael W., "Open Letter to Paula Deen," 207–8

2001 Maniacs! (film), 178, 254n14
Two Thousand Maniacs! (film), 26, 168–76, 253nn6–7, 254n12

underground hospitality networks, 185–91
Underwood, Joseph, 123, 126
United Daughters of the Confederacy, 18, 181
United Nations Declaration of Human Rights, 110
universal hospitality, 20–21, 46, 71–72, 109–10, 120, 222n26, 222n31
Upham, Thomas, 87–88

Vesey, Denmark, 107
Vidi, *Mr. Frank, the Underground Mail-Agent*, 236n43
violence: in Chesnutt's *Marrow of Tradition*, 165; and the civil rights movement, 175–77, 196; and collective memory, 23; and exclusion, 21; and hostility, 104; and lynchings, 133, 171, 174, 183, 224n7, 243–44n5, 253n7; "Mother Emmanuel" AME church tragedy, 22; and Nat Turner, 37–38, 184–85, 191, 224n7, 254n15, 256–57n48; political, 246n17, 251n53; racial, 22–23, 132–33, 138–39, 161–67, 171–76, 181; Rosewood massacre, 255–56n32; in *Two Thousand Maniacs!*, 168–73
Virginia, 2, 12, 30, 143–48, 153–60, 184, 191

Walker, David, "An Appeal to the Coloured Citizens of the World," 240n23
Wallace, George, 196, 198, 254n17
Wallace, Lurleen, 198
Wallerstein, Immanuel, 11, 219n4
Washington, George, 119, 125, 233n1
Washington Republic, 242n38
Webster, Daniel, 77, 81–82, 109–10, 121, 123
Weld, Theodore Dwight, *American Slavery as It Is*, 93
Wells, Ida B., 181
Western Recorder, 35
White, Thomas Willis, 29–30, 224n7
white exclusionary myth, 7, 26, 97, 113, 133, 143, 180. *See also* exclusionary politics
whiteness: and antirendition literature, 84–85; and benevolence, 99–100; and Chesnutt's fiction, 167; and conspicuous consumption, 157; and cultural solidarity, 79; and "lenticular logic" (McPherson), 173; race and racism, 101–3; and Reconstruction, 131–33; Wright on, 135. *See also* racial identity
white supremacy: and Hammond, 33; and Lost Cause ideology, 153, 159, 162; "Mother Emmanuel" AME church tragedy, 22, 179; myth of, 202–6; Page on, 152–60; Pollard on, 144–48; in postbellum narratives, 133; and segregation, 194; and social capital, 170; and *Southern Living*, 197–98
Whitman, Walt: *Leaves of Grass*, 84; "Song of Myself," 84, 99
Whittier, John Greenleaf: "Kossuth" (poem), 122–23; *The Stranger in Lowell*, 72–76, 232n50
Wiencek, Henry, 220n15
Wiley, Calvin Henderson, 230nn32–34; *Roanoke, or, Where Is Utopia?*, 61–65, 72, 229–30n31
Wilson, Charles Reagan, *New Encyclopedia of Southern Culture*, 219n3
Wilson, John L., 107, 241n27
Wilson, Matt, *Whiteness in the Novels of Charles W. Chesnutt*, 167
womanhood, 96–97, 173, 247–48n28
Wong, Edlie, 239n9; *Neither Fugitive nor Free*, 240nn21–23
Woodell, Harold, 240n22
Woolson, Constance Fenimore, 134; *Rodman the Keeper*, 139–43, 245–46n15, 245n12; "Up the Ashley and Cooper," 244–45n10
Wright, Julia McNair, 143; *The Cabin in the Brush*, 135–39, 244n8; *The Complete Home*, 52–53; *Complete Woman's Home*, 134–35
Wright, Richard, 210
Wyatt-Brown, Bertram, 31–33, 225n20, 247n25

xenophobia, 106, 239n1. *See also* race and racism; segregation
X Y Z, "Letters from the Southwest," 40–41

Zenneck, A., *Murder of Louisiana Sacrificed on the Altar of Radicalism*, 174
Zinn, Howard, 104, 238–39n1

The New Southern Studies

The Nation's Region: Southern Modernism, Segregation, and U.S. Nationalism
    by Leigh Anne Duck
Black Masculinity and the U.S. South: From Uncle Tom to Gangsta
    by Riché Richardson
Grounded Globalism: How the U.S. South Embraces the World
    by James L. Peacock
Disturbing Calculations: The Economics of Identity in Postcolonial Southern Literature, 1912–2002
    by Melanie R. Benson
American Cinema and the Southern Imaginary
    edited by Deborah E. Barker and Kathryn McKee
Southern Civil Religions: Imagining the Good Society in the Post-Reconstruction Era
    by Arthur Remillard
Reconstructing the Native South: American Indian Literature and the Lost Cause
    by Melanie Benson Taylor
Apples and Ashes: Literature, Nationalism, and the Confederate States of America
    by Coleman Hutchison
Reading for the Body: The Recalcitrant Materiality of Southern Fiction, 1893–1985
    by Jay Watson
Latining America: Black-Brown Passages and the Coloring of Latino/a Studies
    by Claudia Milian
Finding Purple America: The South and the Future of American Cultural Studies
    by Jon Smith
The Signifying Eye: Seeing Faulkner's Art
    by Candace Waid
Sacral Grooves, Limbo Gateways: Travels in Deep Southern Time, Circum-Caribbean Space, Afro-creole Authority
    by Keith Cartwright
Jim Crow, Literature, and the Legacy of Sutton E. Griggs
    edited by Tess Chakkalakal and Kenneth W. Warren
Sounding the Color Line: Music and Race in the Southern Imagination
    by Erich Nunn
Borges's Poe: The Influence and Reinvention of Edgar Allan Poe in Spanish America
    by Emron Esplin
Eudora Welty's Fiction and Photography: The Body of the Other Woman
    by Harriet Pollack
Keywords for Southern Studies
    edited by Scott Romine and Jennifer Rae Greeson
The Southern Hospitality Myth: Ethics, Politics, Race, and American Memory
    by Anthony Szczesiul

Navigating Souths: Transdisciplinary Explorations of a U.S. Region
   edited by Michele Grigsby Coffey and Jodi Skipper
Where the New World Is: Literature about the U.S. South at Global Scales
   by Martyn Bone
Red States: Indigeneity, Settler Colonialism, and Southern Studies
   by Gina Caison

www.ingramcontent.com/pod-product-compliance
Lightning Source LLC
Chambersburg PA
CBHW011749220426
43669CB00022B/2953